Les convergences entre passé et futur dans les collections des arts du spectacle

**Société internationale des bibliothèques
et musées des arts du spectacle**

(28ᵉ Congrès : Munich, 26-30 juillet 2010)

Connecting Points: Performing Arts Collections Uniting Past and Future

**International Association of Libraries
and Museums of the Performing Arts**

(28th Congress: Munich, 26-30 July 2010)

P.I.E. Peter Lang

Bruxelles · Bern · Berlin · Frankfurt am Main · New York · Oxford · Wien

Les convergences entre passé et futur dans les collections des arts du spectacle

**Société internationale des bibliothèques
et musées des arts du spectacle**

(28ᵉ Congrès : Munich, 26-30 juillet 2010)

Connecting Points: Performing Arts Collections Uniting Past and Future

**International Association of Libraries
and Museums of the Performing Arts**

(28th Congress: Munich, 26-30 July 2010)

Actes édités par / Proceedings edited by
Helen Baer, Claudia Blank, Kristy Davis, Andrea Hauer
& Nicole Leclercq

sous la direction de / directed by
Nicole Leclercq

Ce volume est publié par / This volume has been published by
la Société internationale des bibliothèques et musées
des arts du spectacle (SIBMAS)

Avec le soutien de / with the support of
Deutsches Theatermuseum (Munich)
& les Archives et Musée de la Littérature (Brussels).

Nous souhaitons remercier pour leur aide à la réalisation des présents actes
/ We would like to thank the following for their help in making this publica-
tion possible: Sarah Bélanger, Claire Hudson, Véronique Meunier, Chloé
Money, Marc Quaghebeur, Laurent Tock, Jan Van Goethem & Rodrigue
Narbone.

© P.I.E. PETER LANG S.A.
Éditions scientifiques internationales
Bruxelles / Brussels, 2014
1 avenue Maurice, B-1050 Bruxelles, Belgique
www.peterlang.com ; info@peterlang.com

Imprimé en Allemagne / Printed in Germany

ISBN 978-2-87574-144-8
D/2014/5678/26

« Die Deutsche Nationalbibliothek » répertorie cette publication dans la « Deutsche Nationalbibliografie » ; les données bibliographiques détaillées sont disponibles sur le site <http://dnb.d-nb.de>.

"Die Deutsche Nationalbibliothek" lists this publication in the "Deutsche Nationalbibliografie";
detailed bibliographic data is available on the Internet at <http://dnb.d-nb.de>.

Table of Contents/Table des matières

4. THIRD SESSION
4. TROISIÈME SESSION

OPENING SESSION

SÉANCE INAUGURALE

Foreword

Claudia BLANK

The 28th SIBMAS conference was an exceptional one, which brought about a closer relationship between our association of theatre collections and theatre researchers. For the first time in the history of SIBMAS and IFTR, spanning over 50 years, the conferences of these two associations took place in the same city at the same time and thereby offered opportunities to present joint events.

The second special feature was the German Theatre Museum's 100th anniversary, and the Museum was able to invite its colleagues from all over the world to this conference. It was an opportune time to reflect and look back at the past as well as look into the future. We did this jointly, under the theme of "Connecting Points: Performing Arts Collections Uniting Past and Future".

We are grateful for the many suggestions received, the exchange of ideas, and the strengthening of our personal contacts with our international colleagues which this opportunity provided.

I'm pleased that this publication bears witness to this and I should like to give my warm thanks to Nicole Leclercq, Helen Baer, Susan Cole, Kristy Davis and Andrea Hauer for their work.

Avant-propos

Claudia BLANK

Le 28ᵉ congrès de la SIBMAS a été exceptionnel en ce sens qu'il a permis une relation plus étroite entre notre association et les chercheurs. Pour la première fois dans l'histoire de la SIBMAS et de la FIRT, dont les origines remontent à plus de 50 ans, les congrès de ces deux associations se sont déroulés dans la même ville au même moment, ce qui a permis de proposer des manifestations communes.

Une deuxième particularité est que le Musée du théâtre allemand a pu inviter ses collègues du monde entier à ce congrès, à l'occasion de son centième anniversaire : un moment opportun pour réfléchir et pour regarder vers le passé tout autant que vers le futur. Nous l'avons fait de manière conjointe, sous le titre « Les Convergences entre passé et futur dans les collections des arts du spectacle ».

À cette occasion, nous avons pu recevoir des suggestions, échanger des idées et renforcer nos contacts personnels avec les collègues internationaux et nous en sommes reconnaissants.

Je suis heureuse que cette publication rende compte de tout cela et je remercie chaleureusement Nicole Leclercq, Helen Baer, Susan Cole, Kristy Davis et Andrea Hauer pour leur travail.

Opening Speech

Claire HUDSON

President SIBMAS (London – United Kingdom)

Ladies and gentlemen,

Mesdames et messieurs,

I am delighted to be welcoming you here to the Munich Museum of Ethnology, the venue for this, the 28th SIBMAS conference.

For an organisation whose main *raison d'être* is to create an international network for sharing knowledge and expertise, the biennial conference is one of our most important activities. I know how hard the organisers work to plan these events and to deliver a first-rate conference. I would therefore like to begin by thanking the City of Munich, the Museum of Ethnology, and of course Dr Claudia Blank and her colleagues at the German Theatre Museum for all the work they have already done on our behalf. I would also like to congratulate the German Theatre Museum on the occasion of its 100th birthday this year – quite an achievement and one to be celebrated.

This is actually the second time that this fine city has hosted a SIBMAS conference – our sixth was held here in Munich in 1963. Despite the advances made in communication technology since then, personal contact, the ability to meet and converse in person with our fellow professionals, and the opportunity for us to see the host institution, its collections and understand the culture within which it operates, are still invaluable to us.

The management of Performing Arts collections demands a very broad set of skills. Our collections tend to be extremely diverse in their physical make-up, ranging from costumes, works of art, photographs, archives and time-based media such as film. As well as knowledge of performance history and practice itself, we need to know about developing, documenting and conserving these diverse collections, and about how to connect with our audiences through exhibitions, displays and publications. The arrival of new technology for creating content, organising and accessing it has added further skills to what was already a very demanding list. In my own career I have found my involvement with SIBMAS and attendance of its conferences to be of enormous benefit. It provides an opportunity to learn from the people with whom, professionally, we have the most in common. In times of financial stringency there is, if anything, even more of a need to optimise the resources we have, to collaborate and share, and to avoid duplicating what has already been done elsewhere. All this depends on nurturing an active professional network.

I greatly look forward to further expanding my own knowledge over the course of the next five days, and at the same time enjoying your company and all that this admirable city has to offer.

Discours inaugural

Claire HUDSON

Présidente SIBMAS *(Londres – Royaume-Uni)*

Ladies and gentlemen,

Mesdames et messieurs,

J'ai le plaisir de vous accueillir ici, au Musée d'ethnologie de Munich, où se déroule le 28ᵉ congrès de la SIBMAS.

Pour une organisation dont la principale raison d'être est de créer un réseau international de partage d'expertises et de connaissances, le congrès bisannuel est l'une des manifestations les plus importantes. Je sais combien les organisateurs ont travaillé dur pour préparer cet événement et proposer un congrès de grande qualité. Je voudrais donc commencer par remercier, en notre nom à tous, la Ville de Munich, le Musée d'ethnologie et, bien sûr, le Dr Claudia Blank et ses collègues du Musée allemand du théâtre, pour tout le travail déjà réalisé. Je tiens aussi à féliciter le Musée allemand du théâtre qui fête cette année son centième anniversaire : une belle réussite qui mérite d'être célébrée.

C'est en réalité la deuxième fois que cette belle ville accueille un congrès de la SIBMAS : en 1963 s'est tenu ici à Munich notre sixième congrès. Malgré les progrès qui ont été réalisés depuis lors en matière de technologie de la communication, la possibilité de rencontrer et de discuter en personne avec nos collègues de la profession, l'occasion de visiter l'institution hôte et ses collections tout en comprenant la culture dans laquelle celle-ci s'insère, tout cela demeure inestimable pour nous.

La gestion des collections des arts du spectacle requiert un grand éventail de compétences. Nos collections sont d'une grande diversité d'apparence matérielle, allant des costumes, œuvres d'art, photographies, archives jusqu'aux médias en évolution permanente, tel que le film par exemple. Tout autant que la connaissance de l'histoire du spectacle et de sa pratique, nous devons savoir comment développer, documenter et conserver ces collections diverses et comment atteindre nos publics grâce à des expositions, présentations et publications. L'arrivée de nouvelles technologies pour la création de contenus, leur organisation et leur accès a ajouté de nouvelles compétences à cette liste déjà très exigeante. Dans ma propre carrière, j'ai trouvé que mon implication dans la SIBMAS et ma participation à ses congrès m'avaient été extrêmement profitables. C'est en effet une occasion d'apprendre de ceux dont, professionnellement, nous sommes les plus proches. En ces temps de restrictions budgétaires, il est peut-être encore plus nécessaire d'optimiser nos ressources, de collaborer, de partager et d'éviter de refaire ce qui a déjà été fait ailleurs. Tout cela repose sur l'appartenance à un réseau professionnel actif.

Je me réjouis déjà d'approfondir mes connaissances au cours des cinq prochaines journées, tout en ayant le plaisir d'être en votre compagnie, avec tout ce que cette admirable ville a à nous offrir.

Introduction

Claudia BLANK

German Theatre Museum (Munich – Germany)

Dear Colleagues, a very warm welcome to you all!

For me personally, it's a great pleasure to be able to welcome all of you to a SIBMAS Conference here today, as so often in the past I've been your guest at many other venues: in Mannheim, Stockholm, Helsinki, London, Paris, Rome, Barcelona, Vienna, Glasgow – and now we're here. Our colleagues have staged impressive events and we shall now try to match them: I hope that our efforts can go half-way towards this, because we can't possibly fulfill all expectations. For example, it was an express wish by the previous organiser, Alan Jones, in Glasgow, to whom I'd like to extend a warm welcome, that his concept of an interactive structure be continued in the form of so-called "Expo-Papers". I've attempted to do this, because it worked so wonderfully in Glasgow. And, with some difficulty, I managed to find a venue for this, and made an offer in the invitation to the Conference – only the response was much too low. So the traditional form of presentations will remain. However, these presentations will surely become interactive, since well over half of the participants have asked to deliver spoken presentations, and regular discussion sessions are a feature of the programme structure. And we'll probably be able to take real advantage of these sessions, because after checking through the papers the presentations don't appear to be excessively long. Despite the platform and audience floor set-up, I think we should still be able to see ourselves as a community, coming together here to discuss subjects which unite us all.

For me, this is the really fascinating thing about every SIBMAS Conference: we come together for a few days from many different countries and cities, and all of us sitting together in the same hall ultimately share the same areas of activity, subjects of interest, thoughts and problems.

But despite all these pleasures, today I can't avoid addressing problems as well. It won't have escaped your notice this morning that there are not too many participants at this Conference. We've seen how our Greek colleague had to cancel when the European Union crisis intensified, and shortly before the start of the Conference nearly all our Spanish colleagues had to cancel. We very much regret all these cancellations. So I should like to thank you all the more for making today possible.

These are not easy times: the global financial crisis is causing problems for us all. We must assert and try to strengthen the existence of our institutions. The rapid progress of technical media is constantly presenting us with new challenges. And at a time of increasing globalization, it is necessary on the one hand to develop contacts and on the other hand to highlight our own individuality.

With theatre collections we have reached a crossroads at which on a political level restructurings are occurring or are imminent. For example, there have been changes in London and Stockholm, as well as in Amsterdam, about which we shall hear tomorrow. At such a crossroads it may be a form of counter-strategy to establish connections and mutual support. For me, and I hope for us all, finding connecting points is an essential aspect of this Conference. *Connecting points versus crossroads.*

Theatre collections are often treated as small exotic items compared to the large Fine Art museums of the world, so for this reason we don't need to hide away, but must show our qualities to the public. Ulrike Dembski, who I would like to warmly welcome, called her 2006 SIBMAS Conference in Vienna *Performing Arts Collections on the Offensive*. This appeal has not lost its topicality – indeed, it's more necessary and urgent than ever.

I'd like to thank Ulrike Dembski and Alan Jones very much indeed for their support in the preparation of this Conference. Futhermore I'd like to give my warmest thanks to our host, the Director of the Museum of Ethnology, Claudius Müller for staying here this week. And I'd like to thank cordially the Theatre Museum's small team, which has for months provided its support in the staging of this Conference: especially Monika Haberl and Marion Weltmaier, and very particularly Andrea Hauer for her very impressive commitment. All three will always be available during the Conference, and like all the Theatre Museum personnel will be wearing a name tag showing our logo. Please don't hesitate to approach my colleagues or me if you have any questions, or if you should unfortunately have any problems. We'll all be very pleased to help you.

Furthermore, I've taken up Alan Jones's idea of a special identification on the SIBMAS name tags: small green stars mean that this colleague is attending a SIBMAS Conference for the first time. The small red stars indicate SIBMAS Excom members, all of whom will be very willing to give advice if you have any questions.

The focal point of the Conference is the programme of talks, which I'm looking forward to very much, and the discussions on them. However,

I think that the shared intervals and framework programme are almost just as important as well. These have offered me a very valuable opportunity to establish friendly contacts and make co-operation possible.

Here I take communication to be rather like subtitles, and communication with the theatre researchers is also close to my heart. And so I'm very pleased that for the first time it has been possible to hold our Conference at the same time and in the same city as the world congress of IFTR. Yesterday evening both Excoms met up to have an evening meal together. This evening around a hundred participants at the IFTR Conference, at which only the working groups are initially meeting today, are expected to join us. Tomorrow evening all participants are to meet at a joint session, where we will be able to have discussions amongst ourselves, and some of the IFTR members are then expected at the State reception. You can see that we'll have a large number of personal connecting points.

I hope you find this week stimulating and enjoyable.

Introduction

Claudia BLANK

Musée allemand du théâtre (Munich – Allemagne)

Chers collègues, je vous souhaite chaleureusement la bienvenue à tous !

C'est pour moi un grand plaisir de pouvoir vous accueillir ici aujourd'hui à un congrès de la SIBMAS, tout comme j'ai moi-même si souvent été accueillie en bien d'autres lieux : Mannheim, Stockholm, Helsinki, Londres, Paris, Rome, Barcelone, Vienne et Glasgow. Et nous voilà ici, aujourd'hui. D'impressionnantes manifestations ont été organisées par nos collègues et nous allons essayer d'être à leur hauteur : j'espère que nous pourrons compter sur votre compréhension, car il nous est impossible de répondre à toutes les attentes. Par exemple, l'organisateur du précédent congrès (Glasgow, 2008), Alan Jones que je voudrais saluer chaleureusement, a expressément souhaité que nous prolongions sa conception de structure interactive, sous la forme des « séances d'affiches ». J'ai essayé de le faire, car cela avait merveilleusement fonctionné à Glasgow. Avec quelques difficultés, j'ai pu trouver une salle pour cela et j'en ai fait la proposition dans l'invitation au congrès. Mais les réponses ont beaucoup trop tardé. Nous garderons donc les présentations sous leur forme traditionnelle. Toutefois, ces présentations deviendront sûrement interactives, car plus de la moitié des participants ont demandé à faire une communication orale et les séances habituelles de discussion sont une caractéristique de la structure du programme. Et nous allons probablement pouvoir profiter réellement de ces séances car j'ai pu lire les communications et elles ne me paraissent pas exagérément longues. Malgré l'estrade qui sépare l'orateur du public, je crois que nous devrions être capables de nous voir comme une communauté, réunie ici pour discuter de sujets qui nous concernent tous.

Chaque congrès de la SIBMAS est pour moi une chose fascinante : nous sommes ensemble pendant quelques jours, venant de toutes sortes de pays et de villes, et nous sommes tous assis dans la même salle pour partager finalement les mêmes domaines d'activités, les mêmes centres d'intérêt, idées et problèmes.

Malgré tous ces sujets de satisfaction, aujourd'hui, je ne peux éviter de parler également des problèmes. À votre arrivée ce matin, il ne vous aura pas échappé que le nombre de participants à ce congrès est assez faible. Nous avons vu que nos collègues grecs ont dû annuler leur venue, en raison de l'intensification de la crise de l'Union européenne ; peu avant le congrès, ce sont presque tous nos collègues espagnols qui ont dû renoncer. Nous regrettons vivement ces annulations. Je voudrais donc vous remercier d'autant plus d'avoir rendu possible la rencontre d'aujourd'hui.

Les temps sont difficiles : la crise financière mondiale nous cause à tous des difficultés. Nous devons imposer et essayer de renforcer l'existence de nos institutions. Les progrès rapides des médias techniques nous posent sans cesse de nouveaux défis. Et en cette période de mondialisation croissante, il est nécessaire, d'une part, de développer les contacts, d'autre part de faire apparaître notre individualité.

Avec les collections de théâtre, nous sommes arrivés à un carrefour où des restructurations sur le plan politique se produisent ou sont imminentes. Par exemple, des changements ont eu lieu à Londres et à Stockholm aussi bien qu'à Amsterdam – nous en entendrons parler demain. À un tel carrefour, nouer des contacts et se soutenir mutuellement peuvent constituer une stratégie de défense. Pour moi, comme j'espère pour nous tous, la recherche de liens est un aspect essentiel de ce congrès. Points de connexion *versus* points de croisement.

Comparées aux grands musées des Beaux-Arts dans le monde, les collections théâtrales sont souvent considérées comme de petites choses exotiques et c'est pourquoi nous ne devons pas nous cacher mais montrer nos qualités au public. Ulrike Dembski, à qui je souhaite chaleureusement la bienvenue, a donné à son congrès de 2006 à Vienne le titre : *Les collections d'arts du spectacle passent à l'offensive*. Cet appel n'a rien perdu de son actualité : il est en réalité plus impératif et urgent que jamais.

Je tiens à remercier vivement Ulrike Dembski et Alan Jones pour leur aide dans la préparation de ce congrès. Je tiens aussi à remercier chaleureusement notre hôte, Claudius Müller, directeur du Musée d'ethnologie qui nous accueille ici cette semaine. Nos remerciements vont aussi à la petite équipe du Musée du Théâtre qui a œuvré pendant des mois à la réalisation de ce congrès, spécialement Monika Haberl et Marion Weltmaier, ainsi que, tout particulièrement, Andrea Hauer, pour son engagement impressionnant. Toutes trois seront toujours disponibles pendant ce congrès et, comme tout le personnel du Musée du Théâtre, elles porteront un badge nominatif au logo du musée. N'hésitez pas à contacter mes collègues ou moi-même si vous avez la moindre question ou si vous deviez malheureusement rencontrer un problème. Nous serons très heureux de vous aider.

J'ai en outre repris l'idée d'Alan Jones d'une identification personnalisée sur les badges SIBMAS : les petites étoiles vertes indiquent que cette personne assiste pour la première fois à un congrès de la SIBMAS. Les petites étoiles rouges désignent les membres du Comité exécutif de la SIBMAS, qui seront tout à fait disposés à répondre à vos questions.

Le point central de ce congrès est le programme des communications, que je me réjouis d'entendre, et les discussions qui en découleront. Je pense néanmoins que les pauses et moments partagés en dehors des sessions officielles revêtent pratiquement la même importance. Elles fournissent d'appréciables occasions de nouer des contacts amicaux et des possibilités de coopération.

Ici, je considère la communication plutôt comme un sous-titre et je tiens particulièrement à la communication avec les chercheurs en théâtre. C'est pourquoi je suis très heureuse que pour la première fois, notre congrès se tienne en même temps et dans la même ville que le congrès mondial de la FIRT. Hier soir, les deux comités exécutifs ont pu dîner ensemble et ce soir, nous serons rejoints par quelque cent participants au congrès de la FIRT, qui débute aujourd'hui avec les rencontres des groupes. Demain soir, une session conjointe réunira tous les participants et nous pourrons discuter entre nous ; nous attendons par ailleurs des membres de la FIRT lors de la réception officielle de l'État de Bavière. Comme vous le voyez, nous aurons plusieurs occasions de rencontres personnelles.

J'espère que cette semaine vous paraîtra stimulante et agréable.

Greeting

Klaus WESCHENFELDER

Chair of ICOM Germany

Distinguished audience, dear colleagues and members of SIBMAS!

Thank you very much indeed for the invitation to speak a word of greeting to you on behalf of ICOM Germany. It is a great pleasure and an honour for me to attend the opening of such a promising conference and to address such a respected audience of professionals of museums and libraries from all over the world.

Within the family of museums – and of libraries as well – institutions with collections of performing arts, often called "theatre museums", are maybe a smaller group, but they represent one of the most important facets of cultural activities of mankind. Theatre and all sorts of performing arts pervade our culture at all levels.

To deal with theatre museums reveals in a special way an intriguing relationship between the content – the collection – and the medium of representation.

In the history of the origins of the museum the terms "museum" and "theatre" seemed to be very close, nearly coincident.

To pay tribute to the spirit of Munich, the place where you decided to have your conference, I would like to refer to some local examples while presenting some very brief remarks on this peculiar relationship between museum and performing arts or museums and theatre.

Some of you might know that only a stone's throw away from the Munich State Museum of Ethnology, were we convene, a building called "Alte Münze" (old mint) is situated, which originally housed not only the stables but also the cabinet of curiosities of the Bavarian Court, when it was built in the middle of the 16th century (1563-1567).

The draft for this cabinet – not the design of the architecture but the concept of collecting and presentation – was provided by the Flemish scholar Samuel Quiccheberg.

Quiccheberg was at that time in the heyday of his career, coming from Augsburg where he worked as a librarian in the service of the Fugger family and then acting as an influential advisor at the court of Duke Albrecht V in Munich.

Quiccheberg's draft is considered to be the founding text of the theory of collecting. The text, which lays out the future cabinet of curiosities at the Bavarian court, marks the beginning of the erudite discussion about the museum as a major topic in pre-modern scholarship.

The treatise deals with the principles of collecting and displaying, and it describes the idea of a comprehensive and encyclopaedic knowledge. Interestingly the title of his treatise does not use the term "museum", which was not common at that time, but the term "theatre". It reads as follows:

Inscriptiones vel tituli Theatri Amplissimi, complectentis rerum universitati singulas materias et imagines eximias ut idem recte quos dici posit: promptuarium artificiosarum miraculosarumque rerum, ac omnis rari thesauri et pretiosae supellectilis, structurae atque picturas, quae hic simul in theatro conquiri consuluntur, ut eorum frequenti inspectione tractationeque singularis aliqua rerum cognitio et prudential admirande, cito, facile ac tuto comparari possit.[1]

Quicchelberg calls his idea of the museum a *theatrum amplissimum*, and the term "theatrum" denotes the book as the space of the description as well as the premises of the cabinet as the space of representation.

Quicchelberg evokes the idea of a museum as a rich, lavishly stocked stage with showcases and prestigious cupboards as a scenery and with precious works of art as actors. About one hundred years later the encyclopaedist Athanasius Kircher installed his museum in Rome as a place for performing experiments to demonstrate the knowledge of his period.

Actually the theatre metaphor played a major role in the context of collecting from the 16th century onwards, with changing meanings until today.

Scenography as a part of performing collections is a crucial issue of the museum and it has become an increasing influence on museum work during the last decades. Proper fairs and conferences are provided, such as the forthcoming exhibition "Scenography and Exhibition Design" organised by the Design Department of University of Applied Science in Basel later this year.

---

[1] Samuele a Quicchelberg, *Inscriptiones, vel, Titvli theatri amplissimi, complectentis rerum vniuersitatis singulas materias et imagines eximias*, Monachii, Ex officina Adami Berg, 1565.

Furthermore, a strong emphasis on the symbiotic relationship between museum and theatre is expressed by the occasional collaboration of set designers or directors and museums. Some of you may remember the exhibition on the occasion of the reopening of Villa Stuck, the studio and mansion of the Munich based art nouveau artist Franz von Stuck in 1997, when Stuck's paintings and sculptures were staged by the highly renowned director Robert Wilson.

Speaking about the tight relations between museum and theatre sheds light also to another dimension of museum work.

By this I mean the interdependency of the tangible and the intangible heritage. Whereas museums were for a long time supposed to preserve the tangible cultural heritage, we have learned during the last two or three decades that museums have to be aware of the intangible heritage as well, to be able to contextualise the artefacts and to make them understandable.

It was only in 2003 that UNESCO approved a Convention for Safeguarding of the Intangible Heritage; ICOM adopted the aims of this convention one year later. A couple of countries have ratified the Convention, Germany not being among them.

There is probably no type of collection which demands more strongly that the gap between the tangible and the intangible be bridged, than a collection of performing arts.

The big scope and the broad variety of topics, the galaxy of papers to be given during the next days make clear that you are facing the challenges and you have a lot of ideas about how to tackle it.

In view of such a concentrated expertise and in view of such a vivid and proactive organisation as SIBMAS, I would like to say that I am very happy that you have chosen ICOM as a partner.

The big family of the International Council of Museums (ICOM), founded in 1946, today unites about 30,000 members in about 130 National Committees and about 30 International Committees, of which the German National Committee with more than 4,000 members is the biggest one. The International Committees of ICOM are focussed on special issues of museum work such as documentation and conservation, and on special types of collections. Museums and libraries with collections of performing arts would fit in very well in this scheme by the way.

On behalf of ICOM and ICOM Germany I would like to express my best wishes for your conference. I wish you fruitful discussions and good results and I hope you enjoy your stay in Munich.

Mot de bienvenue

Klaus WESCHENFELDER

Président de l'ICOM Allemagne

Distingué public, chers collègues et membres de la SIBMAS.

Je vous remercie vivement pour cette invitation à prendre la parole pour vous souhaiter la bienvenue, au nom de l'ICOM Allemagne. C'est pour moi un grand plaisir et un honneur d'assister à l'ouverture d'un congrès si prometteur et de m'adresser à un public respectable de professionnels des musées et bibliothèques du monde entier.

À l'intérieur de la grande famille des musées – et des bibliothèques – les institutions qui conservent des collections d'arts du spectacle, souvent appelées « musées du théâtre » sont peut-être minoritaires, mais elles représentent l'une des plus importantes facettes des activités culturelles de l'humanité. Le théâtre et l'ensemble des arts du spectacle imprègnent notre culture à tous les niveaux.

Traiter des musées du théâtre, c'est révéler d'une certaine façon la relation fascinante entre le contenu – la collection – et le moyen de la représenter.

Dans l'histoire de l'origine des musées, les termes « musée » et « théâtre » apparaissent comme très proches, presque concomitants.

Pour rendre hommage à l'esprit munichois, la ville où vous avez décidé de tenir ce congrès, permettez-moi de me référer à des exemples locaux, tout en vous proposant quelques brèves réflexions sur cette relation particulière entre le musée et les arts du spectacle ou entre les musées et le théâtre.

Certains d'entre vous savent peut-être qu'à seulement un jet de pierre du Musée d'ethnologie de Munich où nous sommes réunis, se trouve un bâtiment appelé *Alte Münze* (Ancienne monnaie) qui, à l'origine, abritait non seulement des écuries, mais aussi le Cabinet des curiosités de la cour de Bavière, au moment de son édification au milieu du XVIᵉ siècle (1563-1567).

Le projet de ce cabinet – non pas du point de vue de sa conception architecturale mais de celui de la collection et de la présentation – a été élaboré par l'érudit flamand, Samuel Quiccheberg.

Quiccheberg était à cette époque au sommet de sa carrière. Il venait d'Augsbourg où il avait travaillé comme bibliothécaire au service de la famille Fugger, avant d'œuvrer en tant que conseiller influent, à la cour du Duc Albrecht v à Munich.

Le projet de Quiccheberg est considéré comme le texte fondateur de la théorie de la collection. Le texte à partir duquel sera conçu le futur cabinet de curiosités de la Cour de Bavière marque le début de la discussion savante à propos du musée, en tant que sujet majeur de l'érudition prémoderne.

Le traité porte sur les principes de la collecte et de la présentation, et il décrit l'idée d'un savoir exhaustif et encyclopédique. Il est intéressant de noter que le titre de ce traité n'utilise pas le terme « musée », peu courant à l'époque, mais bien le mot « théâtre » :

> *Inscriptiones vel tituli Theatri Amplissimi, complectentis rerum universitati singulas materias et imagines eximias ut idem recte quos dici posit : promptuarium artificiosarum miraculosarumque rerum, ac omnis rari thesauri et pretiosae supellectilis, structurae atque picturas, quae hic simul in theatro conquiri consuluntur, ut eorum frequenti inspectione tractationeque singularis aliqua rerum cognitio et prudential admirande, cito, facile ac tuto comparari possit.*[1]

Quiccheberg nomme son idée *theatrum amplissimum*, le mot *theatrum* désignant le livre en tant que lieu de description, tout autant que les espaces du cabinet, en tant que lieu de présentation.

Quiccheberg parle des musées comme d'une scène richement et abondamment garnie de vitrines et armoires prestigieuses en guise de décor et de précieuses œuvres d'art comme acteurs. Quelque cent ans plus tard, l'encyclopédiste Athanasius Kircher installera son musée à Rome comme un lieu d'expérimentation visant à manifester les connaissances de son temps.

En réalité, à partir du XVIe siècle, la métaphore théâtrale a joué un rôle majeur dans le contexte de la collecte, avec des changements de signification jusqu'à nos jours.

La scénographie comme élément de présentation des collections est une question fondamentale pour les musées ; elle occupe, depuis ces dernières décennies, une place croissante dans le travail muséal. Des foires spécifiques et des congrès sont organisés, telle l'exposition à venir

---

[1] Samuele a Quiccheberg, *Inscriptiones, vel, Titvli theatri amplissimi, complectentis rerum vniuersitatis singulas materias et imagines eximias*, Monachii, Ex officina Adami Berg, 1565.

« Scenography and Exhibition Design » conçue par le département du design graphique de l'Université des sciences appliquées de Bâle.

Qui plus est, l'accent mis sur la relation symbiotique entre musée et théâtre s'exprime par la collaboration occasionnelle entre les décorateurs ou metteurs en scène et les musées. Certains d'entre vous se souviennent peut-être de l'exposition organisée en 1987 à l'occasion de la réouverture de la Villa Stuck, hôtel particulier et atelier de Franz von Stuck, artiste de l'art nouveau installé à Munich. Les peintures et sculptures de Stuck y avaient été mises en scène par le très célèbre metteur en scène Robert Wilson.

Parler des relations étroites entre musée et théâtre éclaire en outre une autre dimension du travail muséal.

Je veux parler de l'interdépendance entre le patrimoine tangible et l'intangible. Alors que pendant une longue période, les musées étaient censés préserver le patrimoine culturel matériel, depuis deux à trois décennies, nous avons appris à porter attention au patrimoine intangible et contextualiser les objets, afin de les rendre compréhensibles.

C'est en 2003 seulement que l'UNESCO a approuvé la Convention pour la sauvegarde du patrimoine culturel immatériel ; un an plus tard, l'ICOM en a adopté les objectifs. Quelques pays ont ratifié la Convention ; l'Allemagne n'en faisait pas partie.

Plus qu'aucune autre sans doute, les collections des arts du spectacle, exigent que l'écart entre tangible et intangible soit comblé.

L'étendue et la grande variété des sujets, la galaxie des communications qui seront données pendant les prochains jours, montrent clairement que vous affrontez ces défis et que vous avez toutes sortes d'idées sur la manière de les aborder.

Au vu d'un tel rassemblement d'expertises et d'une organisation aussi vivante et dynamique que l'est la SIBMAS, je voudrais vous dire combien je suis heureux que vous ayez choisi l'ICOM comme partenaire.

La grande famille du Conseil international des musées (ICOM), fondée en 1946, réunit aujourd'hui quelque 30 000 membres dans environ 130 comités nationaux et 30 comités internationaux, parmi lesquels le Comité national allemand qui, avec plus de 4 000 membres, est le plus important. Les comités internationaux de l'ICOM se concentrent sur des problèmes particuliers relatifs au travail muséal, tels que la documentation et la conservation, et sur des types de collections spécifiques. Soit dit en passant, les bibliothèques et musées des arts du spectacle s'intègrent très bien dans ce programme.

De la part de l'ICOM et de l'ICOM Allemagne, je tiens à vous exprimer tous mes vœux pour votre congrès. Je vous souhaite des discussions fructueuses et espère que vous apprécierez votre séjour à Munich.

FIRST SESSION

PREMIÈRE SESSION

A Modern Baroque Opera House

Building a Historically Informed Performance Space

Susan M. COLE

ConstellationCenter (United States)

Introduction

ConstellationCenter will be a four-hall performing arts centre in Cambridge, Massachusetts. One of these halls, the Odeon, will be the first hall built in over a hundred years that integrates the stage machinery, sets, and ambience of a baroque opera house into a technologically-advanced modern hall.

In this paper, I will discuss how historical research and the ConstellationCenter Library and Archives have deeply informed the design of our opera house. Beginning with interviews with modern practitioners of baroque opera, the ConstellationCenter design team then built on that research by travelling extensively in Europe to study the architecture and acoustics of extant baroque opera houses. The original research generated from these studies enriched our growing library of books covering the staging, the theatres, the composers, the set designers, and the patrons of 17th and 18th century opera. In addition to using these resources to inform the acoustics and architecture of our opera house, we are working with consultants to build a modern version of shutter and groove scenery and to replicate the experience of candlelight with modern lighting technology. The rich resources of the ConstellationCenter Library and Archives have informed not a reconstruction of a single opera house but instead allowed a filtering of key characteristics of these historic structures into the design of a modern opera house. This process of utilising a variety of resources to understand the theatres of the past has resulted in a design that will allow baroque opera to come alive for contemporary audiences and for generations to come.

What Is ConstellationCenter?

ConstellationCenter will be one of the world's finest performing arts centres. This Center will enable optimal presentation of a wide range of performance events and will be home for more than 500 small to mid-sized cultural organisations in the Cambridge area currently in need of exceptional performance spaces.

The facility will contain four halls within one building, each hall designed to serve several different kinds of performances in a compatible way. The hall called the Odeon will be Boston's only purpose-built opera house, and will be capable of transforming into a concert hall, folk or jazz space, and wide screen movie house. The Great Hall, supporting over 50 different performance layouts, will house a Bach-style pipe organ and a Wurlitzer theatre organ. The third hall, the Jewel Box, offers the intimacy of a small screening room, perfect for independent film screening and small ensemble music. And the fourth hall, the Music Salon, provides an intimate space suited to chamber music, small ensemble music, and experimental films.

Research is at the core of the project; accordingly, ConstellationCenter has conducted an extraordinary amount of research to date through both on-site studies and historical research. Since 2000, the ConstellationCenter team has travelled around the globe to study the acoustics and architecture of historically significant sites. Recognising the importance of creating a more intimate performance experience, we focused our studies on 100 of the world's best performance spaces. These exquisite rooms saw performances by masters such as Beethoven, Haydn, Palestrina, Schönberg, Stravinsky, and Bach.

Our methodical research of these spaces has led to numerous discoveries about the acoustical effects of materials, room shapes, finishes, decorations, and other building elements. These findings led to an optimal acoustic design for each of our four halls. The primary purpose of this research is to create a flexible facility with superb features that will inspire performers and give audiences experiences of unsurpassed power and immediacy.

Through the work of our researchers and consultants a reference collection grew organically until I was hired and brought order to the collection and developed a more guided collection policy. I have also worked to create archives of our research and design process, which will be of use to future researchers.

The Odeon

This paper focuses on one of our halls, the Odeon, and how our research and our reference collection have shaped its design and construction. The Odeon is the only hall in our performing arts centre that will be a traditional theatre with a fixed stage and seating. However, it will be unique from other halls being constructed today because it is modeled on baroque opera houses from the 17th and 18th centuries.

The chief feature of baroque opera was the element of surprise: unexpected visual delights, whether they were a sea monster rising out of the stage spouting mist, a full-size mountain with streams and fountains, or a god descending from the heavens on a cloud illuminated by a heavenly light. Accordingly, the theatres were designed to showcase these magical illusions in the best possible way. A number of inventions and discoveries were necessary for these spectacles to take place: perspective, moving sets, machines, and lighting.

There was a long history in Western drama of scenery since its development in ancient Greek drama but it was traditionally a stationary backdrop to events on the stage. Starting in the Renaissance, however, changing scenery became a key element of the stage. A major milestone in the development of moving scenery was in the 1640s in Venice when Giacomo Torelli invented the shutter and groove system for the Teatro Novissimo. Torelli's system included:

> eight sets of carriages rolling in tracks below the stage. These carriages supported frames in slots of the stage floor, and painted wings were attached to the frames. All the carriages were controlled below stage by a single drum so counterweighted that one stagehand turning a windlass could shift all sixteen wings in orderly unison.[1]

This allowed the scene to change very quickly so that, in what seemed like an instant, the audience was transported from a castle dungeon to a beautiful garden. All of this happened without the curtain ever closing. The scenery was also designed with a perspectival viewpoint creating the illusion of three-dimensional space on a flat backdrop and a sense of great depth. The stages were raked to add to the illusion. This was typically arranged so that the patron of the theatre, usually the local king or prince, was seated at the centre of the focal point. Another key aspect of the baroque opera experience was elaborate trapdoors and machinery so that actors rose out of the stage for great effect, sometimes to evoke a demon rising out of hell or a sinner falling to hell. There were also carriages suspended so that gods or other heavenly creatures could come from above and seem to float or fly to the stage and elaborate machines to create thunder or rolling seas. Throughout the 17th and 18th century stage designers worked to outdo one another with ever more elaborate effects. As Baur-Heinhold describes it:

---

[1] Donald Oenslager, *Stage Design: Four Centuries of Scenic Invention*, New York, Viking Press, 1975, p. 44.

On every stage in Europe *periaktoi* were turning, wings sliding in and out, divine apparitions ascending and descending on flying machines; the earth was opening, spewing forth devils and demons, and swallowing the damned; the sea raged and the heavens stormed. Space had broken its bounds and become indeterminate.[2]

Time and the theatre, however, moved on, and the emphasis in theatre moved from spectacle to realism. By the mid-1800s no one was building these beautiful opera houses anymore. However, there are a number of practitioners around the world who are still committed to researching and staging baroque operas. The Cambridge-Boston area is home to a vibrant early music community, including among others the Boston Early Music Festival, which stages a full historically-informed baroque opera every two years and smaller chamber operas every year. Given Boston's place in the world of early music performance we saw that there was a need and an opportunity to build the first baroque style opera house in over one hundred years.

As I discussed earlier, research is at the core of our design process. Though there are many baroque opera houses described in books and art, we encountered difficulties as so few opera houses of that era exist in good condition. Additionally those in good condition have many times been renovated so extensively that it's hard to tell what is original. However some exceptions exist, such as Drottningholm in Sweden. In cases such as Drottningholm, the theatres were shut up soon after they were built and only rediscovered in the 20th century, so they have been completely free from changes. For our size and needs, we decided to focus our research on the smaller more intimate theatres built for noble courts. Thus we started researching baroque opera by travelling to Europe to study extant baroque opera houses in Sweden, Germany, the Czech Republic, France, Russia, and Italy. We travelled with acousticians, architects, a photographer, a theatre consultant, a lighting designer, and a soprano. In our visits we acoustically measured these spaces, recording the acoustic signature of each space. Extensive photographs were taken, and our architects drew to understand the spaces and how they work. The theatre consultant explored the backstage and under-stage to understand the mechanisms of the stage machinery.

Before, during, and after our research trips we have collected books covering the staging, the theatres, the composers, the set designers, and the patrons of the baroque era, and supplemented these with a number of recordings of modern productions of baroque operas. These materials have been useful first in informing us of which theatres

---

2 Margarete Baur-Heinhold, *The Baroque Theatre*, London, Thames and Hudson, 1967, p. 122-123.

still exist and the history of the development of these theatres. The collection has been and will continue to be useful in further in-depth research done on stage machines, lighting, and other details of the design. Every stage of the design process is documented through reports by historical researchers, acousticians, architects, and lighting and theatre designers.

One example of historical research that I would like to highlight is that of one of our researchers, who performed an in-depth study of performance requirements of the sets during a baroque opera of the period we are interested in. Since there are almost no performance guides or notes existing from this period, she accomplished this by studying the extant librettos of thirty-eight baroque operas to estimate the number of scene changes in these operas. She also studied these librettos to find the typical requirements for lifts, traps, and flying machines. Through all this research she found that performance needs varied widely depending on date and location, but that the most frequent number of stage settings was between six and seven. The researcher also discovered that only rarely are sets re-used in any given opera. She found that out of twenty-five operas that are "set intensive" only five reused sets. The findings of this research are being used by our theatre consultant to design, for example, how our shutter and groove system will function or how many sets need to be loaded into a cartridge.

Determining the ideal acoustics has been of paramount importance to the design of the Odeon. When our acousticians travelled to these baroque opera houses they took extremely advanced acoustic measurements of the spaces that allowed them to create detailed computer models of each opera house. Through their research and ours we identified four precedent spaces: the Markgraefliches Opernhaus in Bayreuth, the Rokokotheater in Schwetzingen, the Royal Opéra at Versailles, and the Drottningholms Slottsteater in Drottningholm. These are all exquisitely preserved examples of the kind of baroque court opera house that we are interested in. Of these four, Schwetzingen and Bayreuth especially influenced our acoustic design:

> These houses are loud as shown by the loudness calculation, and therefore very easy to sing in. They are smaller and louder than modern ones and therefore require less vocal energy from singers, which might have allowed a wider variety of singing techniques as voice would not have to be forced. This also shows the influence of the deep proscenium arch around the stage which creates strong sound reflections [adding to] the singer support. The high loudness of these houses would have also helped to compensate for the musical instruments of the 18th century, which were quieter than modern ones. The orchestra is located on the floor in front of the stage instead of a deep pit, and this also results in a clearer orchestra

sound. Higher musical clarity would have supported music performances integrating compositions.[3]

Using advanced computer modelling programs, our acousticians are able to meld the key acoustic aspects of Schwetzingen, Bayreuth, Versailles, and Drottningholm along with our own original designs to create an exceptional performance space. In exploring the ideal materials for the Odeon, they discovered that though the theatre interiors are illusionistically painted to resemble marble they are all made of wood, stucco, and *papier mâché*. The acoustic effect of these chiefly wood spaces has been likened to that of being inside a violin, creating an extremely resonant sound.

Our theatre and lighting consultants were given a similar task: to update the stage machinery and lighting of the baroque period in order to create the same effects but using modern technology. Our theatre consultant was tasked to create a modern version of the shutter and groove scenery system. The goal was to create a modernised version of this system that could be pre-loaded with shutters and then, ideally, operated by the touch of a button during performances. The theatre consultant studied treatises dating back to the 1500s, historical works including the illustrations of working systems in Diderot's encyclopaedia, and visited extant systems at Český Krumlov in the Czech Republic and Drottningholm. He formulated design requirements from all this research. For instance, he determined that our system will not be made of wood and must be almost completely silent. He is also determining how best to engineer the chariot system that will carry the canvas flats on and off stage. Our lighting consultant has also done extensive research on the history of stage lighting. Through his research we came to understand that both the colour and the movement of the candle flame are essential for the spectacular illusions that the sets and stage machinery aim to create. However, in modern theatres, it is unfeasible to use open flames to light an entire theatre. Therefore he has been researching modern ways to recreate the colour and movement of candle flame by experimenting with different sorts of light sources including tungsten filaments, LEDS, and optic fiber[4].

---

[3] Alban Bassuet, "Acoustics of a Selection of Famous 18th Century Opera Houses: Versailles, Markgräfliches, Drottningholm, Schwetzingen" paper presented at Acoustics'08 Paris: 155th Meeting of the Acoustical Society of America, 5th Forum Acusticum (EAA), 9th Congrès français d'acoustique (SFA). For a published abstract see *Journal of the Acoustical Society of America*, Vol. 123, No. 5, 2008, p. 3192.

[4] For further information on our research into historical stage lighting, please see Susan M. Cole, "Documenting the Ephemerality of Place: The Work of the ConstallationCenter Library and Archives" in Nicole Leclercq, Laurent Rossion, and Alan R. Jones (eds.), *Capturing the Essence of Performance: The Challenges of Intangible Heritage* (proceedings of the 27th Congress of SIBMAS in Glasgow, 2008), Brussels, P.I.E. Peter Lang, 2010.

Conclusion

The findings that I have described above are the product of years of research and dedication by the researchers and consultants at ConstellationCenter. Through this research we are well on our way to constructing a type of theatre that has not been built in over one hundred years. We have more work to do, for instance in determining the decoration and colour schemes and the seating arrangements of the theatre, along with numerous other elements that make up a superb performance space. However, we have applied all the lessons learned from our historical precedents in order to create a modern technologically-advanced baroque opera house. Once the building is completed, our theatre, as well as the ConstellationCenter Library and Archives, will be a resource for practitioners, scholars, and opera enthusiasts.

Abstract

Le ConstellationCenter, centre d'arts du spectacle, comptera quatre salles, à Cambridge, dans le Massachusetts. L'une de ces salles, l'Odéon, sera la première, depuis un siècle, à être construite en intégrant la machinerie de scène et les décors d'un opéra baroque dans une salle moderne dotée d'une technologie de pointe.

Cette communication rend compte de la manière dont les recherches historiques effectuées par le ConstellationCenter ont profondément influencé la conception de notre opéra. Après des entretiens avec des spécialistes locaux de l'opéra baroque, nous avons approfondi nos recherches grâce à de nombreux voyages en Europe pour y étudier l'architecture et l'acoustique des maisons d'opéra baroques existantes.

À partir de ces études, la recherche initiale a enrichi notre bibliothèque de livres sur la mise en scène, les théâtres, les compositeurs, les décorateurs et les mécènes producteurs d'opéras des xviie et xviiie siècles.

En plus de ces ressources destinées à documenter l'acoustique et l'architecture de tels édifices, l'équipe a travaillé avec des consultants sur une version moderne de rideaux et rainures de scène et sur la reproduction de l'effet de l'éclairage à la bougie grâce à des technologies modernes.

La richesse des ressources a permis, non pas la reconstruction d'un simple opéra, mais un filtrage des caractéristiques clé dans la conception d'un opéra moderne.

Cette méthode, qui consiste à utiliser une variété de ressources pour comprendre les théâtres anciens, a débouché sur une conception qui permettra à l'opéra baroque de prendre vie devant le public contemporain et les générations à venir.

Les acteurs des archives

Vincent Radermecker

Archives & Musée de la Littérature (Bruxelles – Belgique)

Il existe trois visions du temps qui engendrent, plus ou moins radicalement, trois manières de voir la vie. Nous voudrions brièvement définir ces visions, les dissocier et y associer trois manières de traiter, dans sa continuité temporelle, un fonds d'archives.

Le critère temporel imprègne le travail de l'archiviste. Loin de toujours classer, encoder et mettre à disposition, ce dernier, lorsqu'il accède à certaines responsabilités, acquiert aussi en amont et valorise en aval. Recevoir, échanger ou acheter un fonds requiert des qualités spécifiques. La valeur mercantile et le sceau d'unicité des documents – et, derrière celle-ci, la mémoire qui les imprègne – impliquent de nouer des contacts prudents, respectueux et fermes quant à l'objectif à atteindre. Il faut parfois savoir jumeler le flair de l'usurier, sa ténacité, avec l'empathie du pasteur ou du prêtre. Dépositaire, héritier ou même marchand, la personne hésite à céder son « trésor ». Il m'est ainsi arrivé d'écouter longuement une veuve, me demandant si je ne m'étais pas mué en psychanalyste. Le fil du temps et les usages imposent heureusement une limite à ces contacts préliminaires. Vient le moment où les caisses s'emballent et se transportent au « -4 », lieu de dépôt de nos fonds.

L'aval du travail, lui aussi, est délicat. Car, lors du don, l'on s'est parfois engagé avec témérité à soumettre un manuscrit à lecture, à réaliser une publication ou encore un hommage sous forme d'exposition. Outre, bien sûr, à ce que le fonds soit dépouillé dans « un délai raisonnable » ou « dans les meilleurs délais ». C'est souvent parce que l'engagement est resté flou et que les contraintes d'une institution sont multiples que cela fragilise le travail de l'attaché scientifique. Il faut du doigté pour expliquer que le « temps » d'une archive n'équivaut pas au temps de la vie mondaine.

Le cœur de l'archivage ne consiste donc pas dans la seule prise de connaissance des documents, suivie d'une mise à disposition aussi rapide et respectueuse que possible. Gérer les contacts avec l'artiste, les héritiers, les chercheurs fait aussi partie du quotidien.

Venons-en maintenant à nos « visions du temps ». La plus connue et la plus familière est celle qu'a formulée saint Augustin. Une division « ontologique » entre passé, présent et futur y préside. Le temps, selon saint Augustin, est une durée. En son sein – et sans qu'aucun des temps ne l'emporte sur les autres – souvenir, attention et prévision/attente se succèdent et se côtoient. Cette vision rejoint l'hymne à Dieu en tant que créateur du monde « visible et invisible ». En effet – et selon la dichotomie fondamentale du platonicisme –, le passé s'assimile à de la « matière » et le futur à des « idées ». L'articulation des trois se vit donc et s'harmonise en tant que la figure divine a créé un homme à la fois corps et esprit.

Pour expliquer sa pensée, saint Augustin use d'une image qui s'impose à lui, la récitation d'un psaume. S'y équilibrent, quand la foi soulève les lèvres, les trois temps – passé, présent, futur – et ce, de sorte que le présent puisse être « d'or ».

Voilà comment les livres XI et XII des *Confessions* de saint Augustin – traduits par Arnaud d'Andilly – expriment cela :

> Par exemple, je veux réciter un psaume que je sais par cœur. Avant que de le commencer mon attention s'étend à tout ce psaume ; mais lorsque je l'ai commencé, autant de versets que j'en ai dits et qui sont passés deviennent l'objet de ma mémoire, et cette action dont mon âme se sépare comme en deux parties, dont l'une est mémoire au regard de ce que j'en ai dit, et l'autre comme une préparation et une attente au regard de ce que j'ai encore à dire. [...] Or ce qui arrive dans le récit de tout ce psaume, arrive aussi dans chacune de ses parties et dans chacune de ses syllabes : il arrive aussi dans un récit de plus longue haleine dont ce psaume pourrait n'être qu'une partie ; il arrive dans toute la vie de l'homme [...].[1]

À cette vision s'oppose le temps chinois, soit une vision plus terre à terre, que François Jullien a décrite dans *Du « temps ». Éléments d'une philosophie du vivre*[2]. Voici ce que dit un quatrain tiré du *Grand commentaire* :

> Le Ciel est élevé, la Terre est en bas
> Ainsi sont déterminés l'initiateur et le réceptif
> À travers cette disposition du bas en haut
> Le plus et le moins de valeur sont en place.[3]

---

[1] Saint Augustin, *La création du monde et le Temps*, Paris, Gallimard (Folio ; 4322), 1993, p. 66-67.

[2] François Jullien, *Du « temps ». Éléments d'une philosophie du vivre*, Paris, Grasset, 2001.

[3] François Jullien, *La pensée chinoise dans le miroir de la philosophie*, Paris, Seuil, 2007, p. 1313.

Pas de flèche du temps, ici. Pas de découpes du tout en parties. Le Yang déploie l'énergie là où le Yin la condense. Le ciel suit son cours là où la terre rassemble et reçoit. Les polarités s'aimantent et se repoussent sans fin, sans qu'aucune ne soit supérieure, subordonnée ou première. Nos cycles du jour et de la nuit, de l'hiver et de l'été… épousent ce schéma. Importe ici la transition, non les éléments.

Qu'en est-il de l'ultime vision du temps à analyser ? Le « Big Bang » a été l'une des plus grandes découvertes du siècle dernier. L'univers dense, homogène, lumineux et torride était, il y a environ 14 milliards d'années, concentré en un point minuscule. Il a explosé, s'est dilaté et s'étend toujours. Avec, à la clé, refroidissement, obscurité et vide sidéral. La vie sur terre, inimaginable aux premiers temps de l'univers, est apparue lors d'un point d'équilibre de ce jaillissement. De même, la maturité d'un être vivant est nécessaire pour qu'une reproduction puisse avoir lieu. Espace et temps sont liés et indissolubles. Plutôt que de « durée » ou d'« alternances », il convient de parler ici du point d'équilibre d'un processus.

C'est cette dernière notion que nous appliquerons en premier au labeur de l'archiviste de théâtre. Venant de clore un fonds, l'employé sent un rayon de soleil sur son visage. Il songe au travail achevé. Entre un collègue qui apporte des caisses et un mot du directeur. Le travailleur enfile ses gants, chausse ses lunettes et se remet au travail. Tout à l'attention de ce qu'il voit, il ordonne, rappareille, scinde, titre, encode… Les documents doivent être protégés et classés pour une mise à disposition optimale. La tâche est répétitive mais sereine. On atteint ici un point d'équilibre. Sortis de leur contexte initial (le propriétaire, et, derrière lui, le créateur du fonds), les documents accèdent à une seconde vie. Les voilà prêts pour d'éventuels chercheurs, des artistes, des curieux ou passionnés… Ce point d'équilibre, un spécialiste l'assure grâce à son expérience, sa sensibilité, son intelligence, mais aussi grâce à des conditions de travail adéquates (espace de stockage, de classification, de rangement ; crayons et assimilés, bases de données et ordinateurs, dossiers ou chemises…).

Deux mots résumeront les avantages et dangers de ce type de travail : « attention » et « sélection ».

Opérer des sélections favorise une intrusion et il y a danger à dépareiller : ceci à la photothèque, cela aux revues, cet autre document aux soins de l'ingénieur du son… Classer prend parfois implicitement comme critère de réussite la rapidité d'accès ! D'où le souci implicite de travailler plus pour le journaliste que pour le scientifique. Des tessons de pots récemment retrouvés dans des puits à ordure de l'époque égyptienne ont fait le bonheur des archéologues. Mais, déterrés voici cent ans, qui s'en serait soucié…

L'avantage de ce travail réside, lui, dans l'humble attention portée à chaque pièce. Nettoyée et identifiée, elle sera conservée et prête pour une « autre vie » ; le fatras s'est mué en collection. Ce type d'attention rejoint le conseil de Louis Jouvet à ses étudiants comédiens :

> Le phénomène de l'attention, c'est d'arriver à être dans cet état de réceptivité parfaite, où rien ne vous occupe que ce qui est devant vous, soit que vous le voyez, soit que vous l'entendiez ; où n'interfère à aucun degré votre personnalité.[4]

Venons-en à notre deuxième vision du temps : l'alternance d'opposés. En quoi cette temporalité rencontre-t-elle une manière d'archiver ? Contrairement à la méthode cartésienne qui divise en parties pour peu à peu résoudre le problème – résolution par traitements successifs – la pensée asiatique privilégie la transition, le passage.

Cette vision duale et dynamique trouve un écho dans la dualité inhérente aux archives, à savoir permettre l'accès à *un* individu, mais aussi sensibiliser à l'humain et à sa fragilité au sens large.

Lors du Congrès à Barcelone en 2004, j'ai évoqué brièvement le phénoménologue tchèque Jan Patočka, signataire de la Chartre 77, et décédé dans sa geôle après un interrogatoire musclé par les forces communistes. Il écrit dans « Phénoménologie de la vie après la mort » :

> Ingarden parle, à propos de l'art, de la « qualité métaphysique » ou « idée » de l'œuvre : au terme de toutes les analyses des différentes « couches », il reste au bout du compte le quelque chose d'unitaire en vertu de quoi l'œuvre agit et dans quoi sa multiplicité prend sa source. Dans l'expérience d'autrui, il y a quelque chose d'analogue, quelque chose d'indépendant de l'existence actuelle de l'autre, de la question de savoir s'il se trouve en nous dans un rapport de réciprocité synchrone. La « qualité métaphysique » de l'autre, nous la percevons alors même qu'il n'est plus, à partir de quoi il demeure présent auprès de nous : des souvenirs, photographies et portraits, de ses paroles, de ses actes et de ses œuvres.[5]

L'archiviste opère un va-et-vient, tantôt identifiant les documents, sa provenance, sa destination, tantôt résumant l'écrit pour le remettre au sein d'une constellation, va-et-vient qui épouse l'« alternance dynamique » évoquée.

Un sixième sens lui fait, mieux qu'au chercheur parfois, sentir ce « quelque chose » qui particularise une personnalité. Avoir travaillé

---

[4] Extrait d'un de ses cours, du 21 novembre 1950. Walter Benjamin, dans son essai sur Kafka, cite un mot de Malebranche : « L'attention est la prière naturelle de l'âme ».

[5] Jan Patočka, « Phénoménologie de la vie après la mort » dans *Papiers phénoménologiques*, Grenoble, Jérôme Million, 1995, p. 149.

plusieurs fonds, et en voir d'autres se traiter autour de soi, rend aussi l'archiviste attentif à la précarité des « neiges d'antan », aux brumes qui entourent ces traces « restes et pertes ».

D'où une réflexion sur cette « identité *post-mortem* ». Patočka note au début de sa contribution :

> Il est pourtant à noter que personne n'a approfondi de manière philosophique la question de savoir comment l'autre vit en nous. Qui est cet autre qui survit ? Quel mode d'être a-t-il ? À quel point il est identique au vivant qu'il fut et comment cette identité se modifie-t-elle ?[6]

Filtrage ? Décantation ? Lente oblitération qui finit par l'oubli ? La spécificité des liens qui unissaient telle personne à telle autre (fils, ami, confrère, époux…) devient sensible lorsqu'on manipule originaux de tout type. Avec, pour l'archiviste, ce constat qu'existe une perméabilité entre intériorité et extériorité au sein de tout être. Nous nous « faisons » au contact et en interaction avec les autres. Ce qui a fait dire à Gombrowicz que, si l'on ne peut choisir qui on est, on peut sélectionner avec qui on vit, dans quel secteur l'on travaille…

L'accès à des documents diversifiés et intimes (correspondance, notes et ébauches, journaux de bord…) favorise cette perception duale : unicité/collectivité. L'écriture autographe, les ratures, les ébauches dans le cas de manuscrits laissent à penser qu'il y a UNE singularité. Que les documents sont porteurs d'une « irréductibilité ». Toutefois, la multiplicité des lettres, les notes de lectures éventuelles, les articles laudateurs ou désapprobateurs, des interviews… témoignent eux, de l'intersubjectivité qui est au cœur de toute personne.

Parallèlement, si on identifie et valorise généralement les pièces en fonction du contenu, de la matérialité, de l'aura de la source en cours d'archivages, se tisse aussi une « toile d'archives » au sein de l'institution. Les lettres s'appellent et se répondent au gré des sorties de livres, des courants littéraires, des événements sociaux ou politiques, des modes de communication… Tout fonds quitte son milieu naturel pour entrer dans une collection plus vaste.

Pour illustrer cette perception duale de l'archive, voici un exemple personnel : le travail que j'effectue sur Jean Louvet et dont j'ai parlé en

---

[6] *Ibid.*, p. 145. Jan Patočka insiste fortement sur ce qu'apportent la présence effective et la réciprocité dans toute relation humaine constructive. Ce n'est qu'ensuite – et comme incidemment – qu'il ajoute que l'être absent peut *aussi* accompagner. Il termine son article : « Il se peut en effet que beaucoup de ce que fut le disparu ne soit actualité que *par moi*, ultérieurement. Il se peut que son être devienne pour moi une impulsion vers du toujours nouveau en me faisant réaliser plus profondément ce que son existence signifiait et signifie encore, en me faisant m'exposer encore et toujours à la mise en question qu'est cet être pour moi. » *Ibid.*, p. 156.

2004 au Congrès de Barcelone[7]. Ce dramaturge vivant, né en 1934, est un auteur politique, porte-parole du désespoir visible et invisible d'une région déshéritée depuis la Deuxième Guerre mondiale, la Wallonie. Certaines de ses pièces mettent en valeur les causes de la débâcle (manque de structuration et de détermination de la classe ouvrière, perte de contact avec le passé, individualisme induit par la société de consommation…) ; d'autres, les symptômes du malaise (agressivité, suicide, folie, marginalité…). La nécessité qui m'échoit de présenter l'édition de ses œuvres complètes, édition chronologique qui inclut des variantes, états préliminaires ou versions scéniques, m'oblige à me pencher sur les deux facettes : « être pour soi »/« être avec les autres ».

D'une part, je distingue soigneusement la succession des étapes d'écriture : notes disparates, premier jet, manuscrits intermédiaires, première dactylographie, texte soumis aux acteurs, texte joué dans un cadre amateur, texte recorrigé pour des professionnels, texte édité, texte éventuellement revu après publication… Et, ce faisant, j'analyse des processus génétiques. Mais, par ce biais, j'accède aussi à des événements autobiographiques profonds comme le divorce parental. La mère quitte le foyer familial lorsque Jean Louvet a treize ans et il passe son adolescence avec son père. Il écrit :

> En fait, c'est pendant la petite enfance que les rapports ont été très durs. Après : la supériorité intellectuelle de l'enfant atténue.[8]

Sa mère n'assistera à aucune représentation de ses œuvres. Un jour de colère, elle lui dit, parlant d'un fils né avant terme et décédé : « Il était mieux que toi ». Pour Jean, ce « José » demeurera un fantôme qui innervera son inspiration et accompagnera son destin de « créateur de personnages ». D'où l'accumulation de prénoms commençant par « J » dans son œuvre. Jusqu'à ce qu'un jour, il « tourne la page ». Dans l'ordre chronologique, il y a Julien de *Mort et résurrection du citoyen Julien T.* : il demande à sa femme, Maria, d'avorter. Il y a Jo de *L'aménagement*, substitut charnel du mari de Hilde, une snob qui a « eu » des enfants mais n'en veut plus. Il y a Jonathan de *Conversation en Wallonie*, *alter ego* autobiographique de l'auteur, et qui part à la recherche de son « double viril », non pas professeur de français, mais militant socialiste. Il y a la statue en morceaux de Julien Lahaut dans *L'homme qui avait le soleil*

---

[7]   Vincent Radermecker, « Contact avec l'artiste en vie. Rôle et responsabilité » dans Nicole Leclercq & Jan Van Goethem (ed.), *Du document à l'utilisateur. Rôles et responsabilités des centres spécialisés dans les arts du spectacle – From Document to User. The Roles and Responsibilities of Specialised Centres for Performing Arts*, 25e Congrès SIBMAS, Barcelone, 2004, Bruxelles, P.I.E. Peter Lang, 2008.

[8]   Document conservé aux Archives & Musée de la Littérature sous la cote MLT 2977, p. 167.

dans sa poche, qui entre en scène dans une charrette d'enfant. Il y a Jérémie d'*Un homme de compagnie*, homme de gauche sans enfant et qui simule l'accouchement d'une enfant-chien lorsqu'il adopte une petite fille rejetée. Il y a encore Joseph dans *Le grand complot* et surtout Jacob du monologue *Jacob seul*.

Part mystérieuse du processus créatif, la multiplicité de ces « J » nous fait sentir l'irréductibilité du « J » de Jean Louvet. « J » se retrouve dans « Je ». Que notre auteur soit aussi philologue explique ce jeu onomastique.

Les métaphores obsédantes de Charles Mauron nous aident à mieux comprendre. Ce qui frappe, c'est l'origine biblique de la plupart de ces prénoms masculins. Les noms de Jésus et Judas se retrouvent aussi dans diverses notes. *Jacob seul* est écrit en 1989 lorsque l'écrivain a 55 ans. Ce personnage parle comme si le silence allait sceller sa mort. Il converse avec un inconnu qu'il sait ne pas exister. Cet Autre, c'est aussi ce « José ». La fracture est ici émouvante en ce que le public donne sens à cette « parole dans un vide qui n'est pas tout à fait un vide ».

À ces « J » font face des personnages féminins aux prénoms en « a » et « i »[9] : soit Maria, Alice, Marie, Hildegarde, Madeleine… La mère de Louvet s'appelait Augustine Hanoulle. Mais surtout, sa femme s'appelle « Janine ». Jean et Janine ; Louvet et Laruelle. La figure de son épouse, Janine, s'invite à travers ces personnages féminins. Elle chasse le fantôme de la mère, en inspirant, voire en interprétant, des figures de femme qui ont concilié vie familiale et vie militante.

On l'aura compris, se pencher sur ces manuscrits, c'est toucher au « mystère » de l'individualité tout en écoutant la généralité humaine et artistique d'où le tout est né.

Dans notre premier cas d'étude, l'archiviste devait son efficacité au rythme soutenu et presque mécanique d'un traitement pièce par pièce ; dans ce second, il ne s'agit plus seulement d'identifier les documents mais de peser le poids artistique et humain qu'ils recèlent. Écho peut en être donné dans la rubrique « résumé » de nos fiches d'encodage. Entre une vision scientifique/biographique et une appréhension humaine/ philosophique, l'alternance s'instaure comme entre le latent et le manifeste chez les Chinois.

Peinte en 1560, *L'allégorie de la prudence* du Titien montre deux tricéphales : d'hommes et d'animaux. Avec, pour chacune, une figure de face encadrée de deux profils. Au-dessous, deux profils – un chien (à droite) et un loup (à gauche) – mettent en relief la figure d'un lion. Au-dessus, la face du fils du Titien, un Orazio âgé de 50 ans, chevelu,

---

[9]   Pour un essai d'analyse de l'union de ces voyelles, voir Jean Louvet, *Théâtre 2*, Bruxelles, AML Éditions (Archives du futur), 2008, p. 495.

barbu et déterminé, est flanquée de l'œil unique de son père âgé de 75 ans (lorsqu'il peint le tableau), à sa droite, et, à gauche, de celui du petit-fils adoptif, Marco. Une inscription latine associe prudence et les trois « parts » du temps. Entre l'étourderie de la jeunesse et la distraction de la vieillesse trouve place la vigilance. Entre l'expérience des vieux et la vigueur des jeunes, l'âge mûr unit de ses deux yeux, le « clan », qu'il soit carnivore ou iconovore.

Cette image caractérise les trois temps de l'archivage que nous avons apparentés à la vision temporelle de saint Augustin. N'est-ce pas unis que l'acquisition, le traitement et la valorisation d'un fonds actent une « mémoire » ? Acquérir et valoriser sont les deux profils qui permettent au traitement de nous « regarder dans les yeux ». Car ils l'humanisent. Acquérir ne consiste pas seulement à « aller chercher » mais favorise un contact privilégié avec le créateur, ses héritiers ou le dépositaire. On découvre le cadre de vie et/ou de travail. Des anecdotes mettent un visage sur des écrits.

Après un contact privilégié avec madame Françoise Rouleau, veuve du célèbre acteur (cinéma et théâtre), mais surtout du grand metteur en scène que fut Raymond Rouleau, j'ai reçu « comme un cadeau » les archives de son mari. Elle m'a « donné » ce qu'elle détenait. Je l'ai interviewée. Des photographies qu'elle m'a commentées ont nourri mon approche. Elle m'a raconté qu'une des expressions favorites de l'artiste face à une bonne prestation était « c'est du sucre », aussi comme il dormait peu, travaillait intensément, soignait ses distributions. Ses démêlés amoureux passés ont aussi été évoqués. Sans ce témoignage, je n'aurais pas accordé la même attention aux documents, parfois en piètre état, qui me sont passés par les mains. J'ai voulu « travailler » à sa mémoire. S'il ne fut pas encore possible de mettre sur pied une exposition ni d'écrire une biographie, j'ai proposé à une étudiante, dans le cadre d'un cours au Conservatoire royal de Bruxelles, de le choisir comme sujet de travail. Lors de son exposé, elle s'est demandé pourquoi aucune salle de ce Conservatoire ne porte son nom. Oubli peut-être bientôt réparé.

Raymond Rouleau a révélé de jeunes acteurs, dont de nombreuses jeunes actrices : Isabelle Adjani, Corine Luchaire, Pascale Petit, Micheline Presle, Mylène Demongeot, etc. Plus inattendu, Audrey Hepburn a aussi profité de sa direction d'acteur. Lorsqu'il monte *Gigi* de Colette à New York, l'écrivain impose Audrey, alors inconnue, dans le rôle principal. Rouleau se rend toutefois compte que le mode de vie dissipé de la jeune actrice les conduit à l'échec. Il l'affronte. Elle doit travailler. Sa force de caractère en viendra à bout. Et, dès lors, c'est comme « naturellement » que j'identifie, perdue au milieu de documents en mauvais état, une lettre comme étant écrite par la mère d'Audrey. N'y a-t-il pas matière à réflexion lorsqu'on sait que le nom de Raymond

Rouleau est étrangement absent des biographies de l'actrice ? Aucune référence dans les lignes sur *Gigi* d'une biographie de plusieurs pages consultable sur internet. Audrey est alors âgée de 21 ans. Le 26 décembre 1951, via New York, sa mère envoie de Londres à Raymond Rouleau ces mots écrits en français :

> Je voudrais vous présenter mes vœux les meilleurs pour l'année 1952 et vous remercier de tout cœur d'avoir fait de ma petite Audrey une Gigi applaudie ! Quel chef d'œuvre de votre part ! Vous avez su, en grand artiste, faire vibrer cette âme adolescente de toutes les émotions vraies et profondes, et vous avez su les sortir, exprimées et extériorisées, comme aucun autre ne l'aurait pu. Je ressens l'occasion que le ciel a bien voulu accorder à Audrey, de vous rencontrer sur son chemin, comme la chose la plus importante dans sa vie d'artiste et je vous serai reconnaissante jusqu'à la fin de mes jours pour tout ce que vous avez voulu faire pour elle ![10]

Le ton parle. Audrey lui écrit aussi, peu après, l'appelant « mon Maître chéri et adoré ». La première de Gigi eut lieu le 3 octobre 1951 au Fulton Theater. Il y eut 217 représentations. Ce succès public et commercial, une phrase le résume qui cache une dure réalité de travail : « Les critiques furent séduits par le charme, l'élégance et la beauté d'Audrey ». Des « notes aux acteurs » témoignent, elles, des difficultés partagées :

> As Gigi gives the line, "I am going to propose something myself", this is a new argument. It must have new strength and not be dropped. Audrey has a tendency to return to early errors in the scene so it must be watched.[11]

D'autres réceptions « personnalisées » d'archives, suivies d'autres valorisations, seraient à mentionner. Je suis allé chercher les archives d'André Frère sur les berges de la Loire, chez un vieil homme qui avait partagé avec lui quarante ans de sa vie. Comme Raymond Rouleau et Audrey Hepburn, cet artiste est né à Bruxelles. Après dépouillement du fonds, ses photographies de scène ont été restaurées et mises en ligne. Le tout a été l'objet d'un travail d'étudiant ainsi que d'une « chronique du musée [Archives & Musée de la Littérature] » consultable sur notre site.

Qu'une personne prenne en charge la totalité du processus comporte toutefois des risques. Un « effet-entonnoir » est à craindre. « Posséder » une mémoire impose des devoirs : répondre aux demandes internes et externes à l'institution, traiter des compléments qui se greffent peu à peu, participer à une exposition, réaliser une expertise… Cumulées, ces obligations pèsent sur le temps à consacrer à de nouveaux fonds.

---

[10] Lettre conservée aux Archives & Musée de la Littérature (Bruxelles), sous la cote MLT 3239/5.

[11] *Ibid.*, MLT 3239/7.

Or, l'archiviste a besoin d'une intemporalité, d'une sérénité besogneuse comme celle si caractéristique des salles de lecture. Le plasticien Michel Seuphor, dont les Archives et Musée de la Littérature conservent une part des archives, vante les bienfaits de la nuit, ici une « nuit des mots ». Ces phrases sont à méditer :

> Où sont les impatiences, les gestes fous, les joies truquées, les peurs ? Où est passé le pain amer, tout arrosé de larmes ? Le jour est sinistré. La nuit, très calmement, répare les dégâts sans nul effort. Elle a pour elle toute la patience du ciel et cette bénédiction aux ailes indéterminées.[12]

Trois visions du temps ; trois manières d'archiver. Dans la pratique, aucune n'est absolue.

En lien avec notre titre, « les acteurs des archives », nous avons tenu à relativiser ce que le mot « archive » peut avoir de poussiéreux. S'y cachent aussi des liens, des contacts, une communion visible et invisible qui a son charme.

Que l'archive vive avec et par ses acteurs – tant ceux d'hier, d'aujourd'hui que de demain, tant les oubliés que les mémorables –, cela ne rejoint-il pas la magie du théâtre ?

Abstract

Three visions of time; three ways to archive. In practice, no method is perfect.

There is a vision of the three concepts of time of Saint Augustin. It corresponds to a work which is tied not only in the processing of these documents, but to their acquisition and to their future worth. There is a dualistic vision of the Chinese: Yin and the Yang, the obvious and the hidden. In our analysis, a work which consists, not only to develop the uniqueness of a person, but also the necessary links which unites this person with his or her contemporaries. Finally, the discovery of the Big Bang has made us become aware that time also means a "moment of balance" within a process. For an archivist of theatre collections, this point of balance is left to the processing of the document. Is it not this process which will outlive us?

---

[12] Michel Seuphor, *Biens*, Nantes, Convergence, 1990.

Behind the Scenes at the Museum

A Look at the Challenges of Presenting an Exhibition of Theatrical Material in a National Museum of Art and Design

Jane Pritchard

Theatre Collections, Victoria & Albert Museum
(London – United Kingdom)

Two years ago I spoke about the Victoria & Albert's (V&A) collection of Ballets Russes costumes and how, in anticipation of our exhibition this year, we were re-assessing them and asking questions about their identity. Now on the eve of that exhibition which opens on 25 September 2010, I would like to address the challenges of putting together such an exhibition within a major national museum. I would stress that mounting a Ballets Russes exhibition in the V&A is a very different situation than it would have been mounting it within our old Theatre Museum. What we have to constantly remember is that the V&A is a leading London tourist attraction drawing on visitors with hugely varied interests – yes, for some that interest will be theatre but we need to attract many others.

Firstly some general observations on the Ballets Russes exhibition scene. As those of you who attend SIBMAS on a regular basis are aware there have been – and will be – a host of exhibitions throughout the world from 2008-2011, all in some way celebrating the centenary of Diaghilev's Ballets Russes. I have no problem with the range of dates as precisely dating the birth of a performing company is often hard. 1909 saw the first full evenings of ballet presented by Diaghilev in Paris, but in 1909 and 1910 it was a "pick up" company of dancers from Russian Imperial Theatres of Saint Petersburg, Moscow and Warsaw performing for lucrative salaries during summer vacation from theatres operating on a seasonal basis. The Ballets Russes as a year-round operation is not established until 1911. Previously I had liked to claim that the V&A's exhibition would be the grand finale (heralding the centenary of the Company's first visit to London in 1911) but we have been usurped into that position by the National Gallery of Canberra who open their exhibition in December.

Since the last SIBMAS conference, I have seen more than a dozen Ballets Russes exhibitions ranging from magnificent displays of costumes to library exhibitions focusing on documents, designs, photographs and ephemera. For me, three have really stood out – all highly focused. Firstly, the Dance of Colours: Nijinsky's Eye and Abstraction at the Hamburg Kunsthalle, which presented and contextualised Nijinsky's art work largely created in 1918 and 1919, drawing on John Neumeier's amazing collection. Secondly, Diaghilev the Beginning at the Russian Museum, Saint Petersburg, which focused on Diaghilev's career in Russia before turning to ballet and included an excellent evocation of Diaghilev's 1905 Tauride Palace exhibition of portraits. And finally the Russian Opera exhibition at the Centre national du costume de scene at Moulins-sur-Allier which investigated a previously poorly documented aspect of Diaghilev's work. As you have now missed all those exhibitions I would sincerely recommend their catalogues. I should also like to add a word of appreciation for the exhibition mounted jointly by Munich and Vienna as it has been the only one to really place the elusive art of choreography at its heart – and don't I know how difficult it is to include movement in an exhibition. What was very clear from seeing the exhibitions was the importance of clarity in respect of the story being told.

When I arrived at the Theatre Museum as Curator of Dance, I knew that there was a real probability that it would mount a Ballets Russes exhibition given it houses a truly varied and fabulous collection of material on the company. The re-absorption of Theatre & Performance Collections into V&A from the satellite Theatre Museum has enabled the exhibition to have a higher profile and it has become a significant element in promoting the Theatre & Performance Collections in their new context following on from the opening of our new permanent galleries last year.

As I mentioned this means we have to attract a wide range of visitors. Yes we hope the theatre/art/dance/design specialist will come – but on top of that we must attract the visitor who goes to Britain's leading museum of art and design and may never have heard of Diaghilev although will know some of contributory figures – Nijinsky, Stravinsky, Picasso, Matisse, Chanel, etc. We need to cater for the non-specialist. Those passionate about the subject will come anyway.

This major exhibition is possible because we have such a fabulous collection of Ballets Russes material. Indeed, 70% of the exhibition's content is from V&A collections and it is always necessary to remind researchers that there is material in the V&A's Word and Image department and in the National Art Library. Thirty percent are loans from private collectors and museums and libraries in America, France and Stockholm. However this is not an exhibition that has come out of an individual curator's passion for a collection and desire to put forward an alternative story as was the scenario behind the quilt exhibition which preceded us and on which the curator had been working for nine years.

Because of a need for substantial visitor figures the V&A undertakes research on title and "identity" (lead image) for an exhibition. I will not go into the full rigmarole but as a result we ended up with the title Diaghilev and the Golden Age of the Ballets Russes 1909-1929, and a poster with an orange-tinted photograph taken in December 1924 by the British photographer "Sasha" showing the creators of the four leading roles in *Le train bleu* dressed in their Chanel designed clothes posed on stage at the London Coliseum in front of Larionov's cloth for *Baba Yaga*. In fact market research on the "identity" was based around only two options and I am told that this image will appeal to trendy young visitors and the "fashionable" orange (at least we stopped it from being pink) will make it stand out in advertising campaigns. If anyone thinks a curator has any influence they do not – our exhibition "identity" is one of the images I had asked the Marketing Department not to use as I felt it had been over-exposed in the British press and the photograph is not in the exhibition. I will, however, acknowledge that V&A Publications have made the identity look quite elegant on the dust-jacket of the book to accompany the exhibition.

In respect of the title, *Diaghilev and the Golden Age of the Ballets Russes* 1909-1929 tells you what you will be seeing (if you know who Diaghilev was and why the Ballets Russes matters). The V&A likes its "Golden Ages" just as it likes its "isms" (Surrealism/Modernism, etc.) I did suggest we just called the exhibition "Diaghilevism" and, although I was unaware of it at the time, that word was used as the title of an article in 1979. The V&A is also quite keen on dates so visitors know the time-span they are looking at and here, in respect of the informed visitor, they will know we are looking at the first and not successor companies.

But this title has proved something of a straitjacket – Oh, for a liberating title such as Theatre of Marvels used in New York or Étonne-moi! used in Monte-Carlo. The title is problematic as it places Diaghilev the man – the catalyst impresario who brought the creative teams together and ran and promoted the company – at its heart. Here we have a man who, when asked by the King of Spain what he did, replied "I am like your Majesty, I do nothing but I am indispensable" or on another occasion replied simply "I supervise the lighting". How the hell do you show such a man in an exhibition? Portraits and personal objects help – but there are not so many of these and we were unsuccessful in securing the loans of portraits we wanted from Russia. Our own collections about the man himself are not rich although we do have some useful items – ranging from a contract with Chaliapin in Diaghilev's hand and his penultimate hotel bill from the Grand Hôtel des Bains, Venice Lido, for the week before he died. I would, here, like to acknowledge the assistance given to us by the Paris Opéra in agreeing to lend personal material from Diaghilev's passport to his iconic top hat.

One way that we can foreground Diaghilev is in our labelling and we have been greatly assisted by our text editor who has kept saying – "well can't we reference Diaghilev with this or that object". Labels at the V&A have to be very precise – we have a 60-word limit, how much will a visitor read? It's a real discipline. In each of our three galleries we tried to find points that the man dominates. In the first we briefly introduce the man and his early life in Russia including details about Russia during the period 1872-1906 when Diaghilev was based there. We include Diaghilev's early life in Perm, his periodical and art exhibitions with The World of Art, and the dance scene in Europe and Russia "before Diaghilev". This is followed by the early Saisons Russes.

In the second gallery we move backstage deconstructing the elements of production beginning with a section we call "Inspiration". Although, of course, not all the ideas for productions came from Diaghilev himself he had to approve them and we include a large screen of digitised images to reference the multiplicity of sources he drew on. This animated collage is deliberately not explained but includes literary, musical, historical, and visual sources. Some visitors may be bewildered – which at this point we do not mind – but I hope that this will be the only bewildering moment. Knowledgeable visitors may have great fun playing spot the clues to recognise the ballets.

In the third gallery we include a section inspired by the dinner at the Majestic Hôtel, Paris, after the May 1922 first night of *Aurora's Wedding* and *Le Renard*. This was hosted by Sidney Schiff who wanted the opportunity to sit down with the artistic genii of the day – his principal guests were Diaghilev, Stravinsky, Picasso, James Joyce (who arrived drunk) and Marcel Proust. We are using this to establish Diaghilev's status within the creative arts in the 1920s – also my co-curator has the opportunity to fulfil an apparent life-long ambition to display manuscripts by Joyce, Proust and T.S. Eliot together[1]. I should stress that contextualising the Ballets Russes throughout is important to us and this occasion certainly shows Diaghilev's status in his cultural milieu.

---

[1]   Eliot was not at the dinner but was a commentator on the Ballets Russes and supported by Schiff.

Finally just before the end we present the death of Diaghilev (including his death-mask loaned from Stockholm) and his penultimate hotel bill – his company collapsed with his demise but we still have to indicate that his influence continues – one of my favourite quotes about Diaghilev is Prokofiev's observation that Diaghilev "was a giant... whose dimensions increase the more he recedes into the distance". Again positioning this element is important as we need to emphasise Diaghilev's ongoing influence, although to some extent I hope it comes through as the exhibition progresses rather than just appearing as a post-script at the end.

So we have a large exhibition space but the shape of the exhibition itself is dictated by our desire to include two actual set cloths – the Goncharova backcloth for the 1926 *The Firebird* and the Schervashidze realisation of Picasso's painting for the front cloth for *Le train bleu*. This led us to focus on process at the heart of the exhibition and in its overall design. Our designer – the stage designer, Tim Hatley – is giving the whole a theatrical backstage feel. From the start we emphasised that we were not mounting an art show – it was to be an exhibition about theatre. I was not interesting in ticking off all productions which strikes me as a very old fashioned approach; I get frustrated when the history of the Ballets Russes is simply a series of first nights.

From 1911 the Ballets Russes was a touring company, its fortunes dependant on many external factors. From 1914 to 1918 the First World War interrupted the company's work and it found new performance arenas in America, in Spain and in Italy. In the early years of the company it operated in what we in Britain would call an Edwardian world, by the 1920s it is a chic modern world. Certain ballets are performed throughout the company's existence – the Polovtsian Dances from *Prince Igor* was performed at a quarter of all Ballets Russes performances – others, more experimental works with more complex stagings – have a far more limited life. I do acknowledge it is hard to show all this in an exhibition but I am encouraged that research around the exhibitions has included the publication of three versions of the full itinerary and the first really focused biography of Diaghilev (not just an account of his company) which enable researchers to look at the work of the Ballets Russes afresh. Unlike many exhibitions which are the culmination of research I think the exhibitions, symposia and publications around the Ballets Russes have proved a catalyst for further research and fresh thinking.

In our exhibition we present a wide range of material. It is not, like Stockholm and I believe the forthcoming Canberra exhibitions, a display of a costume collection with some supporting material. I hope our costumes (and we are displaying over 70 as well as accessories and additional fashion items) will appear to be integrated with designs, drawings, prints, sculpture, and archives.

At the last SIBMAS conference I spoke about the process of selecting the costumes. Some I discussed made the final selection but we had to balance my wish list with the cost of the undertaking. We have had a fabulous team working to stabilise the costumes. Only occasionally have we had to replace significant elements.

Lopokova's Cancan costume from *La boutique fantasque* has a replacement skirt and the bodice is slightly problematic because of earlier treatment which is hard to reverse. The Prince from the final act of *The Sleeping Princess* has a new sash but reuses the trimming. A sash had in fact been remade before but this costume looks very different from when it was last shown as in mounting it we studied designs and production photographs to get as true a result as possible. Our *Le dieu bleu* costume had to have a huge amount of work with the pink infill being restored. I am still making up my mind about how much we remake the belt. With our costumes we no longer go for a window dressing approach – the stresses, the repairs, the wear is a significant part of the story.

Initially we feared more costumes would have to be displayed flat because of their fragility but careful conservation has made it possible to show the Chinese conjuror from *Parade* on a mannequin for London although it will be shown on a T-bar with its hat on a stand nearby for tours and future display. Eventually it was also agreed that the bathing costumes designed by Chanel for *Le train bleu* could also be presented on mannequins. We still have a few shown flat including Adolph Bolm's outfit as the Polovtsian chief and Sokolova's dress as the Hostess in *Les biches*. All costumes will be shown with a photograph on the label of the costume as worn by a dancer.

The types of mannequin used also required considerable discussion. In our opinion the costumes are too fragile now to be shown in dancing positions although I hope the lighting will bring a theatricality to their presentation. For two costumes we have had stylised "ballerinas" created by H&H Sculptors who specialise in modelling conservation grade figures including for the display of dance costumes. These are for Flore from *Zéphyre et Flore* and the Garçonne from *Les biches* which are skimpy costumes with which tights are important – where legs come into play one is certainly faced by different challenges. Generally we have given an abstraction to the figures by using more abstract and considerably cheaper mannequins made by another British company, Proportions. We are only giving the mannequins heads where needed and using stylised wigs where these are required.

Further challenges have arisen as accessories were not always acquired or catalogued with the correct costume and we have had huge discussions about open versus cased display. Dust in London falling on open displays of fragile costume with elaborate decoration means that delicate material must be cased. The more robust costumes on open display will require cleaning twice during the 3½ month duration of the exhibition.

I would also mention that during conservation our costumes undergo serious analysis – and would draw attention to the fact that mercury has not surprisingly been found in the hats and arsenic in the paint. It really is very important to wear gloves when handling Ballets Russes costumes. While on unstable materials – we were hoping to include Naum Gabo's stunning helmet for *La chatte* in the exhibition. In fact we have not secured the loan much to the relief of the Conservation department as it is made of Celluloid (Cellulose nitrate) and other Gabo sculpture of similar age and materials have suddenly degraded spectacularly. If we had included it would have required its own ventilated case because the gases it can produce would damage other costumes.

Planning the exhibition required a long selection process. We went through three pin-ups, displays of images of the proposed content arranged to indicate the narrative of the exhibition, during which potential material was commented on and criticised by our colleagues from our own and other departments. At the end we had reduce the number of objects to roughly 300 which of course causes a great deal of heartbreak and modifies the exhibition. One of our biggest challenges is how to include music – such an important element in productions. Today background music is simply regarded as "Muzak" so we have invited Howard Goodall, a multi-award-winning composer and respected broadcaster, to create a series of short films to punctuate the exhibition, explaining and illustrating the important contribution music made to the Ballets Russes. There will not be an audio gallery guide. These at the V&A are an optional extra but we believe would add confusion when the audio-visual elements are an integral part of the show.

There are many other issues I wish I had time to mention including copyright. I know it comes as a surprise that most Ballets Russes material – designs and photographs are still in copyright, although I am aware that for some exhibitions curators have turned a blind eye to this. I was, however, quite alarmed when the V&A began investigating the possibility of there being a copyright in costumes; I think because of the major artists involved in their design[2].

---

[2]   In 2013 the V&A policy is that individual theatre costumes are covered by copyright as works of art and that this includes rights for both designer and maker of the costume.

It is curious to discuss an exhibition which is about to open – next week the installation of the cloths takes place and it begins to come together. I can only end by saying I hope that at least some of you will make the journey to London to see the exhibition and I will welcome your feedback on what you see.

Figure 1. "Diaghilev and the Golden Age of the Ballets Russes 1909-1929": View of costumes designed by Bakst in the first gallery. © V&A images 2011.

Figure 2. "Diaghilev and the Golden Age of the Ballets Russes 1909-1929": Costume for Flore on purpose sculpted mannequin. © V&A images 2011.

Abstract

À la veille de l'ouverture de l'exposition «Diaghilev et l'Âge d'or des Ballets russes 1909-1929» au Victoria and Albert Museum à Londres, cette présentation porte sur les défis posés par une telle exposition dans un musée d'art et de design. Cela soulève plusieurs questions telles que: comment rendre accessible au grand public un sujet aussi spécialisé? Comme replacer une entreprise innovante dans son contexte culturel? Comment donner vie à des costumes fragiles? Comment transformer une telle exposition en une expérience théâtrale?

Cet article fait suite à la présentation que Jane Pritchard avait donnée au congrès de la SIBMAS en 2008, afin de révéler l'évolution du projet depuis le concept initial.

"Having a Good Hectic Time…"

Project Based Research on The Ballets Russes Tours to Australia and New Zealand

Richard STONE

Performing Arts Researcher (Australia)

In a paper at the SIBMAS conference in Vienna in 2006 I described the Ballets Russes in Australia Project which had been operating for a year. Now, four years later, I can report the Project has been successfully completed. It has been a "good hectic time".

The title for this paper comes from a letter written from Melbourne in December 1936 by Elisabeth Souvarova a dancer with the first de Basil company to tour Australia and New Zealand. Her real name was Betty Scorer and her letters to her parents in England are candid and informative, conveying a vivid sense of touring far from home with an international ballet company. Scorer's letters are in the Manuscript collection of the National Library of Australia. They have all been digitised and can be read on-line through the National Library website. The Scorer collection and its treatment is an indicator of the success of the Ballets Russes in Australia Project.

This Project grew out of plans to celebrate, in 2006, the 70th anniversary of the arrival of the first Ballets Russes company to visit Australia and New Zealand. Formed by Colonel Wassily de Basil in Europe the company named the Monte Carlo Russian Ballet opened in Adelaide in October 1936. It toured Australia and New Zealand for nine months and was so successful that two more Ballets Russes companies formed by de Basil visited Australia and New Zealand between 1938 and 1940.

The Australian Ballet company traces much of its ancestry to the Ballets Russes companies through people such as Helene Kirsova and Edouard Borovansky, both of them dancers who stayed in Australia and founded professional companies. The Borovansky Ballet directly led to the formation of The Australian Ballet in 1962. The Australian Ballet planned to celebrate this legacy in conjunction with the Ballets Russes anniversary.

In 2004, The Australian Ballet, the National Library of Australia and the Elder Conservatorium of Music in the University of Adelaide developed a research partnership and sought funding for the Ballets Russes in Australia Project. This unique partnership brought together a national heritage collecting institution, an academic teaching body with a specialist theatre arts library, and the national flagship ballet company.

All three partners contributed substantially to the Project, which was largely funded by a research grant from the Australia Research Council (ARC), the federal government agency dedicated to advancing Australia's research excellence. The success of the ARC application was significant as it came from the fields of performing arts and dance history. ARC grants are usually awarded to the fields of economics, science or technology, rarely to the performing arts.

A committee drawn from the three partner institutions managed the Project with a support officer based in Melbourne in The Australian Ballet. A research assistant position based in the National Library in Canberra focussed on research and documentation.

Three platforms underpinned the Project: Research, Documentation, and Celebration. In effect, the three Ballets Russes tours between 1936 and 1940 comprise one continuous major event in the cultural history of Australia and New Zealand. The aim of the Project was to research this event as thoroughly as possible. This research would support and inform anniversary celebrations, notably performances of Ballets Russes repertoire. During the entire research period the Project would gather a significant treasury of documentation for the future.

The Project presented the considerable challenge of researching large-scale tours combining the inherent complexities of touring by any performing arts company with the special demands of a large ballet company. Allied with these are the magnified proportions of travelling to the southern hemisphere and specifically around Australia and New Zealand in the 1930s.

To do justice to the three tours, research necessarily extended beyond the footlights to include aspects of social, business and cultural history as well as music. A very wide resource net was cast embracing published materials, manuscripts both personal and business, official archives, oral history interviews, photographs, trade union records, music scores and ephemera. These were sourced in collections across Australia and New Zealand and further afield in London, Toronto, New York and San Francisco. Libraries, government archives, museums, galleries and performing arts collections at national, state, or local levels were accessed, as well as private collections and special collections in university libraries and archives.

The basic facts of the tours are impressive. The time scale alone meant that during the four-year period October 1936 to September 1940, a Ballets Russes company was performing somewhere in Australia or New Zealand for over 50% of the time. The repertoire performed totalled 44 different ballets offered to an enthusiastic public in an ever-changing programme of triple bills, often with additional overtures and divertissements.

The success of these mammoth undertakings can be credited to the fact that they involved two formidable business organisations. Since 1932 Colonel de Basil had successfully toured ballet companies around Europe and Britain, and across to North America, four years before he headed to the southern hemisphere. (In an intriguing footnote research staff discovered that plans for a Ballets Russes tour to Australia were first mooted in 1932 but negotiations at the time came to nought.) In Australia, the ballet tours were energetically sought by the leading entrepreneurial firm, J.C. Williamson Ltd. This firm was very experienced in importing performing arts companies and artists to Australia and New Zealand, including the tours of Anna Pavlova in 1926 and 1929, as well as a series of opera companies featuring Nellie Melba. They possessed the administrative and financial strength to manage large-scale tours with ready access to a circuit of theatres in both countries.

The intricacies of moving people and sets and costumes to the southern hemisphere and around Australia and New Zealand were revealed through newspapers, letters, and shipping and immigration archives. A set of cable books, which cover the negotiations between Australia and London for the tours, was one of the few significant business records located in the National Library of Australia.

These epic tours began with boarding a ship in Tilbury near London, or some cases in Marseilles. The month long voyage to Australia followed, visiting exotic ports en route and rehearsing on board. Some adventurous individuals flew to Australia, which in those early days of commercial aviation was an eight-day journey. Dancers Serge Lifar and later Anton Dolin made this epic flight. Travel between Australia and New Zealand was also by ship over the Tasman Sea, potentially one of the roughest crossings in the world. There are vivid testimonies to this in dancers' letters, but the *Regisseur* of the company Serge Grigorieff appears to have found it relaxing. Movement around Australia and New Zealand was predominantly by train, including the hiring of Special Trains travelling overnight to ensure the company was ready for the next opening night. Arrivals and departures attracted great attention. The pattern of touring in Australia and New Zealand mixed lengthy stays in the larger Australian cities (e.g. two and half months in Melbourne in 1940), with shorter stays elsewhere, including a series of one night stands in provincial New Zealand in 1937. Arranging accommodation is one of the inescapable practicalities of the travelling life. Letters and newspaper reports reveal that most members of the companies had to find their own accommodation upon arrival in a city, usually sharing in boarding houses or flats. However, the stars and senior management stayed in salubrious hotels.

Wherever the companies were, accommodation provided publicity opportunities as the press coverage of the tours was large. It emerged as one of the most important resources documenting the tours. Every town and city on the schedule had at least one newspaper. In Melbourne and Sydney, Australia's largest cities, four daily newspapers vied for readership. The J.C. Williamson publicity machine placed a massive amount of advertising and fed publicity stories and photographs to the newspapers. They responded enthusiastically adding interviews, social reporting, gossip columns, articles and reviews of a high standard. This coverage was accompanied by a barrage of press photographs capturing the glamorous dancers at a large number of publicity events. New "action" photography techniques captured them on stage in rehearsals and in performance.

The visual record of the tours is extensive. A total of nearly 3,000 photographs were identified by the Project. As well as press photos, leading Australian photographers such as Max Dupain took studio and *en plein air* images. Others captured the dancers at work and play. In addition artists painted, sketched and drew dancers backstage. The National Library has major holdings of photographs and art works. The Hugh P Hall collection alone contains 1,200 performance photographs taken in Melbourne between 1938 and 1940, all of which have been digitised and are available on the Library's website.

A photographic gem unearthed during the Project is a group photo taken in February 1938 on the roof of a department store in Auckland, New Zealand. After much research, it surfaced in the collection of English dancer, Brigitte Kelly, who danced as Maria Sanina. Ms Kelly kindly donated the negative of the photograph to the National Library.

It includes members of the Covent Garden Russian Ballet Company – dancers such as Irina Baronova, Tatiana Riabouchinska, and Anton Dolin; the choreographer Michel Fokine; conductor Antal Dorati. And significantly, stage crew, management and musicians. Assisted by people who were actually in it, or their descendants, we have been able to identify most of the people in this remarkable photo. No other similar group photo has been found for the other two companies.

Movies were shot by amateur cinematographers, including two doctors, Joseph Ringland Anderson in Melbourne and Ewan Murray Will in Sydney. These films of dancers performing and relaxing are housed in the National Film and Sound Archive in Canberra. They were used extensively in the American documentary *Ballets Russes* released in 2005. Discoveries continue and last year a 4-minute colour film sequence from a performance of *Coq d'Or* in Melbourne in 1939 was added to the collection.

It was fortunate that the Ballet Russes Project coincided with the widespread use of digitisation. The National Library of Australia made a major contribution to the Project by digitising a wide range of materials relating to the tours – letters, photographs, art works, oral histories and ephemera including a near-complete set of cast sheets for the Australian tours.

The research team has produced many documents such as bibliographies, chronologies, narratives, indexes, and transcripts. Of particular note are complete chronologies and performance listings for each of the tours. Some published accounts of the tours included partial listings, but there was no complete list of performances and New Zealand tours were particularly neglected.

Ballet Russes companies went to New Zealand in 1937 and 1939. They did not go there on a third tour in 1940 because of growing wartime travel restrictions. The New Zealand chronology is based entirely on newspaper research and incorporates a comprehensive index to the newspaper coverage. The New Zealand research unearthed the fact that the second company performed in one of the southern-most cities in the world, Invercargill, situated at the bottom of the South Island. In a splendid late Victorian theatre on March 20, 1939, the company did two performances of a triple bill comprising *Carnaval*, a one act version of *Swan Lake*, and *Aurora's Wedding*. They then packed up the sets and costumes and left by ship at 1.00 am bound for Melbourne.

Another major compilation is a list of nearly 80 Australian musicians who played in orchestras for Ballets Russes performances between 1936-1940. Previously nothing at all was known about the size of the orchestras or who played in them because musicians were not listed in programmes. The orchestras were locally recruited from a pool of musicians who alternated between theatre work, such as the ballet orchestras, and the concert hall. The research by the Project has advanced knowledge on the development of Australia's music industry and culture in the 1930s. On the other hand, the conductors of Ballets Russes orchestras were well documented. They were recruited in Europe by de Basil as part of the companies and as such were the subject of publicity. For example, Antal Dorati came to Australia twice and was popular with the press, particularly when his daughter Tonina was born in Melbourne in 1940.

During the last four years, the documentation collected by the Project, in conjunction with the rich resources in the National Library, have been used in various forums:

- Exhibitions in 2009 in the National Library of Australia, The Arts Centre, Melbourne, and in 2008, the Art Gallery of South Australia and the Festival Theatre, Adelaide.
- A major television documentary and two radio documentary series were broadcast nationally in 2009.
- Theatre programme essays, journal articles and popular magazine features about the tours, as well as multiple audiovisual presentations to staff of cultural institutions and the public.

As a parallel to these events, research by the Project supported major celebratory outcomes. A three day Ballets Russes Symposium in Adelaide took place in 2008 with international speakers such as Professors Stephanie Jordan and Lynn Garafola, and veteran British television producer Bob Lockyer, along with local academics, artists and dancers, discussing the Ballets Russes heritage internationally and locally.

A book titled *The Ballets Russes in Australia and beyond*[1] was published in 2011 It is a lavishly illustrated collection essays on the Ballets Russes tours and their significance.

Between 2006 and 2009, the Australian Ballet provided a major focus of celebration with its staging of twelve works from the Ballets Russes repertoire. As part of restaging two of the works, *Les Sylphides* and *Les Présages*, The Australian Ballet engaged ballerinas who had danced in these ballets during the 1930s tours: Tatiana Leskova, Anna Volkova, Irina Baronova and Valrene Tweedie provided guidance to a new generation of dancers. The National Library recorded oral history interviews with these venerable ladies and acquired the personal collections of Irina Baronova and Valrene Tweedie. Public presentations were given, including a wonderful interview and dialogue with Irina Baronova, and another with Anna Volkova, both held in the National Library. Contact was also made with other Ballets Russes ballerinas living overseas, Tamara Tchinarova Finch, Jean Haet (stage name Kira Bounina) and Brigitte Kelly (stage name Maria Sanina). It was a great privilege to meet these gracious ballerinas. Their involvement added a poignant human dimension to the research task.

To ensure that the documentation collected by the Project team is available for future researchers, two archives exist. One, in paper form, is housed in the National Library of Australia's Manuscripts Collection. A detailed Finding Aid for this collection of source notes, research trip

---

[1]   Mark Carroll (ed.), *The Ballets Russes in Australia and beyond* Adelaide S.A., Wakefield Press, 2011.

reports, photocopies of key newspaper and magazine, etc. will be available on line in due course. The other archive is an online website hosted by the National Library. Developed using blog technology it includes indexes, compilations, bibliographies, chronologies and narratives on the tours to Australia and New Zealand.

The Ballets Russes in Australia Research Project demonstrates how dedicated research energies have connected a major historical performing arts event to contemporary practices and technologies, ultimately providing a facility for future research needs.

Abstract

Un important projet coopératif de recherche sur les Ballets Russes en Australie, d'une durée de quatre ans, a été mené à bien, à l'occasion du 70ᵉ anniversaire de la tournée en Australie de trois compagnies de Ballets Russes, sous la direction du Colonel de Basil, entre 1936 à 1940. Trois institutions différentes ont travaillé de concert sur ce projet : la Bibliothèque nationale australienne, l'Australian Ballet et l'Edler Conservatorium of Music de l'Université d'Adélaïde. C'est grâce à cette collaboration que le projet a pu se concrétiser.

Grâce à une équipe de recherche dédiée et active, une très large variété de ressources ont été identifiées en Australie et à l'étranger. Les bibliothèques, les centres d'archives, les galeries et les collections privées ont été soigneusement exploitées, et de nouvelles sources importantes ont été découvertes.

Le projet a abouti à l'enrichissement des ressources à la Bibliothèque nationale australienne non seulement à propos de l'histoire du ballet en Australie, mais aussi dans le contexte plus large de l'histoire sociale, de l'histoire de l'art et de la culture musicale australienne.

Un effort concerté a été consacré à la numérisation des documents portant sur les Ballets russes en Australie, notamment dans les collections de photos, les livres, les journaux, les documents éphémères, les albums et les récits oraux. Cela a également permis à la Bibliothèque de rassembler les différents aspects de ces collections, grâce à des bases de données en ligne et de trouver des aides à la recherche.

Les nombreux documents de la Bibliothèque à propos des Ballets russes ont servi à des expositions, à des films documentaires et ont été utilisés par des auteurs qui ont réalisé un volume d'essais sur les Ballets russes en Australie, intitulé *Art at the Frontier : Ballets Russes and beyond*. Les travaux effectués pour le projet de recherches ont essentiellement bénéficié au Ballet australien. Il a en effet, au cours des quatre années du projet, porté à la scène plusieurs œuvres du répertoire des Ballets russes en profitant, pour leur préparation, de la documentation mise à jour dans le cadre du projet.

Pour mettre à la disposition des chercheurs les documents collectés, deux types d'archives ont été réalisés. L'une, au format papier, est conservée dans la Collection des manuscrits de la Bibliothèque nationale australienne. L'autre est un site internet hébergé par la Bibliothèque nationale. Développé selon la technologie du blog, il comporte des index, des compilations, des bibliographies et des chronologies sur les tournées des Ballets russes en Australie. Les deux archives sont connectées électroniquement.

Le projet de recherche sur les Ballets russes en Australie montre comment les énergies de recherche spécialisées ont lié un événement historique majeur des arts du spectacle à des pratiques et technologies contemporaines pour aboutir à un instrument au service des futurs chercheurs.

L'émigration russe des artistes du ballet et son influence sur l'évolution de la danse dans le monde

Irina GAMULA

Musée d'État de Théâtre A. A. Bakhrushin (Moscou – Russie)

À la suite de la révolution de 1917, de nombreux savants, écrivains et artistes quittent la Russie pour l'Europe qui bénéficie ainsi de l'affluence de ces talents.

Au début du XXe siècle, la France et le Danemark possèdent déjà des troupes de ballet, mais c'est en Russie que cette discipline a connu son véritable épanouissement. Bien avant la révolution, les Européens ont eu l'occasion de connaître l'école de danse russe, car les artistes russes ont effectué de fréquentes tournées dans les capitales européennes. En outre, dès 1909, l'énorme succès des Saisons russes de Serge de Diaghilev ouvre une nouvelle ère. Se déplaçant en Europe de l'Ouest, mais aussi en Amérique du Nord et du Sud, sa troupe exerce, pendant les vingt années qui suivent, une grande influence sur la danse dans le monde.

Chopiniana, *Schéhérazade*, *L'oiseau de feu*, *Le spectre de la rose* (dans les chorégraphies de Michel Fokine), *L'après-midi d'un faune*, *Le sacre du printemps* (dans celles de Vaslav Nijinski), *Apollon musagète*, *Le fils prodigue* (dans celles de George Balanchine) tout comme les ballets de Léonide Massine et Bronislava Nijinska, sont des chefs-d'œuvre de grands maîtres russes qui ont été présentés (et le sont encore) sur les scènes internationales.

Anna Pavlova, Vaslav Nijinski, Tamara Karsavina, Vera Karalli et bien d'autres artistes de la troupe des Ballets russes de Diaghilev sont issus du Théâtre Bolchoï et du Théâtre Mariinski.

Dans les années 1920, de nouveaux artistes intègrent la troupe de Diaghilev. Ils viennent, pour partie d'entre eux, des studios et écoles de ballet ouverts à Paris et à Londres par des émigrés russes. Parmi les plus célèbres, citons ceux de Mathilde Kschessinska, d'Olga Preobrajenskaya et de Lioubov Egorova.

Un simple regard sur le parcours biographique de la plupart des Étoiles de la première moitié du XXe siècle – telles Irina Baronova, Tatiana Riabouchinska, Tamara Toumanova, Nina Vyroubova, Yvette Chauviré, Pierre Lacotte, Marika Bezobrazova, Liane Daydé ou Georges Skibine – indique clairement qu'elles ont été formées par des maîtres russes.

Après la mort de Diaghilev en 1929, ses chorégraphes jouent un rôle important dans le développement de l'art du ballet dans le monde entier. George Balanchine, par exemple, est invité par Lincoln Kirstein en Amérique pour créer une école de ballet américaine et la troupe de l'American Ballet, qui travaille quelques années au Metropolitan Opera. Le même Balanchine collabore avec le Ballet russe de Monte-Carlo entre 1944 et 1946, puis crée avec Kirstein la troupe qui devient célèbre sous le nom de New York City Ballet.

Serge Lifar, quant à lui, consacre trente ans de sa vie à la direction de la troupe de l'Opéra de Paris. Le musée théâtral Bakhrushin conserve des lettres et documents qui constituent une bonne source d'informations sur le travail de Lifar à l'Opéra ainsi que ses articles et les textes de ses cours à la Sorbonne. S'y trouvent aussi des lettres d'Irina Kondratievna – élève du maître de ballet Alexandre Alexeïevitch Gorski –, au critique Yuri Alexeïevitch Bakhrushin[1], mentionnant à plusieurs reprises Serge Lifar, avec qui elle entretient des relations difficiles, tout en reconnaissant son importance pour le développement du ballet en France. Les lettres de Kondratievna, qui, au cours de sa vie à Paris, a bien connu plusieurs danseuses russes (Mathilde Kschessinska, Olga Preobrajenskaya, Alexandra Balachova) donnent par ailleurs des informations sur la vie des danseurs émigrés de cette époque.

Jusqu'à l'arrivée de Serge Lifar à l'Opéra de Paris, les ballets constituent une sorte de supplément aux spectacles d'opéra. En créant ses célèbres Mercredis de la danse, il contribue largement à la renaissance de la danse en France et à l'expansion de l'école russe. Il raconte dans *Les mémoires d'Icare* qu'il insistait pour que les danseuses françaises prennent des cours auprès des danseuses russes[2]. En 1945, Lifar, obligé de quitter l'Opéra, part à Monte-Carlo où il fonde le Nouveau Ballet russe de Monte-Carlo qu'il dirige avec toujours le même succès. À l'automne 1947, il signe un contrat avec l'Opéra de Paris et le Nouveau Ballet est racheté par le marquis de Cuevas. Tout en travaillant à la promotion de l'art de la danse, Lifar fonde en 1947 l'Institut de la

---

[1]   Musée théâtral Bakhrushin, fonds 1, numéro d'inventaire 2029, 2020.

[2]   Serge Lifar, *Les mémoires d'Icare*, Monaco, Sauret, 1993, p. 59.

Chorégraphie et commence à donner des cours d'histoire et de théorie de la danse.

La France et le gouvernement français apprécient les mérites de Serge Lifar qui est élu membre correspondant de l'Académie des Beaux-Arts et décoré de l'ordre de la Légion d'honneur.

Le Ballet de Monte-Carlo est lié, lui aussi, à Serge Diaghilev : en 1911, l'imprésario se fixe à Monaco avec sa compagnie. Cette dernière disparaît à sa mort, en 1929, mais le directeur du Théâtre de Monte-Carlo, René Blum, grand amateur d'art et ami de Marcel Proust, s'inspire de l'expérience de Diaghilev et lui rend hommage en fondant Les Ballets russes de Monte-Carlo quelques années plus tard avec le colonel de Basil.

C'est sous la direction de ce personnage que l'Opéra russe se produit à Monte-Carlo au printemps 1931. Le colonel W. de Basil, de son vrai nom Vassili Grigorievitch Voskressenski, mérite une attention particulière : Élizabeth Souritz s'est penchée sur sa biographie et y a découvert des éléments curieux qui montrent de lui une facette inconnue. Officier des cosaques de l'armée impériale russe, il participe à la guerre du Caucase avant d'émigrer en France, en 1919, en compagnie de sa femme, Nina Leonidovna et d'une parente, Valerya Elanskaya. Toutes deux ont été élèves de la chorégraphe et danseuse plastique, Ellen Knipper Radeneck. Voskressenski, qui gagne d'abord sa vie à Paris comme conducteur de camion pendant que les deux femmes se produisent dans les cafés-concerts, décide bientôt de fonder une petite troupe de danse et, dès 1921, donne en Suisse un premier spectacle sous le titre de *Danses plastiques*. La compagnie est bientôt renforcée par l'arrivée de danseurs classiques et son répertoire évolue. Voskressenski lui-même joue des rôles mimés, comme celui de Rothbart dans *Le lac des cygnes*, et il lui arrive d'écrire des arguments de ballets. Pendant quelques années, la troupe survit en effectuant des tournées dans les petites villes de France mais, en 1925, une nouvelle étape commence pour le colonel de Basil : il crée avec le prince Alekseï Tsereteli et Ignaty Zone une agence artistique, Tserbazone, puis prend la direction administrative de l'Opéra russe à Paris.

À l'occasion du passage à Monte-Carlo de l'Opéra russe (où se produit Chaliapine) et du Ballet de l'Opéra russe de Paris (où travaillent Michel Fokine et Bronislava Nijinska), le colonel de Basil fait la connaissance de Blum et décide de créer une troupe de ballet unique.

En 1932, Blum et de Basil fusionnent donc le Ballet de l'Opéra de Monte-Carlo et le Ballet de l'Opéra russe de Paris et marquent ainsi le début de l'histoire des Ballets russes de Monte-Carlo, l'une des troupes de ballet les plus célèbres des années 1930 à 1950, dont l'influence se fait sentir en Europe, en Amérique, mais aussi en Australie. Plusieurs danseurs de la troupe de Diaghilev intègrent la nouvelle compagnie, parmi lesquels

George Balanchine, devenu maître de ballet, Serge Grigoriev, en qualité de directeur de la troupe, et Boris Kochno, comme consultant artistique. Sont invitées également de jeunes danseuses des studios privés russes de Paris, qui entrent dans l'histoire sous le nom de Baby Ballerines.

Les spectacles de la troupe ont toujours fait grande impression. Le peintre Constantin Somov, qui a beaucoup travaillé avec Diaghilev, a assisté aux spectacles en 1932 et 1933 et s'en est montré très satisfait. Balanchine quitte bientôt la troupe et il est remplacé par Léonide Massine. Au même moment, en 1935, Blum et de Basil rompent officiellement leurs relations, ce qui entraîne la création de deux troupes distinctes, le Ballet de Monte-Carlo et le Ballet russe de Monte-Carlo du colonel de Basil, qui prend diverses appellations (Original Ballet russe, Educational ballet…).

Le chorégraphe principal du Ballet de Monte-Carlo est Michel Fokine, qui y remonte ses anciens ballets et y fait de nouvelles créations. En 1938, il passe au service de la troupe rivale du colonel de Basil. Massine est engagé par Blum, mais ce dernier abandonne le ballet la même année. Le banquier d'origine russe, Serge Denham (de son vrai nom Serge I. Dokuchaiev) reprend alors la direction de la compagnie de Blum et l'intitule Ballet russe de Monte-Carlo. Denham travaille en France avant de s'installer aux États-Unis en 1939[3]. La composition du répertoire et le choix des artistes incombent à Léonide Massine, qui réalise par ailleurs pendant cette période un grand nombre de nouveaux ballets, dont la série des « ballets symphoniques » de Brahms, Berlioz, Tchaïkovski et Hindemith. Toutefois, la troupe de Denham a de plus en plus de mal à rivaliser avec les troupes américaines, comme celle du New York City Ballet, fondée par George Balanchine. L'année 1962 voit la fin du Ballet russe de Monte-Carlo[4], compagnie qui a grandement contribué au rayonnement de l'école de danse russe aux États-Unis et a fait connaître aux artistes et au public américains les ballets de Fokine et de Massine et le répertoire des Ballets russes de Diaghilev. Toutefois, dès 1940, le Ballet russe de Monte-Carlo s'est emparé de thèmes et de musiques de compositeurs américains et a confié la chorégraphie du ballet *Rodéo* (1942) à une artiste américaine, Agnes de Mille.

La troupe du colonel de Basil quitte également Monte-Carlo au début de la Seconde Guerre mondiale et effectue des tournées en Australie avant de s'installer, en 1942, en Amérique du Sud, sous le nom de Original Ballet russe. Son répertoire se compose essentiellement de ballets de Fokine, mais aussi de ceux de Massine ; Irina Baronova en est la vedette. La troupe n'a pas de chorégraphe attitré, mais David Lichin crée régulièrement pour elle des ballets, dont *Le bal des cadets*, qui connaît le succès. Dans le but

---

[3]   Resté en France, René Blum est arrêté en 1941 et meurt à Auschwitz en 1942.

[4]   Serge Denham meurt à New York le 30 janvier 1970, âgé de 73 ans.

d'inventer des ballets qui s'accordent au pays dans lequel il se trouve, le colonel de Basil se met en rapport avec des compositeurs et des peintres locaux. C'est ainsi qu'il fait représenter au Théâtre municipal de Rio de Janeiro, en 1946, un ballet intitulé *Yara* sur le thème traditionnel brésilien de la légende de la déesse des eaux, Yara, et du dieu du soleil, Guarani. C'est le compositeur brésilien Francisco Mignone, qui est l'auteur de la musique. Les décors sont commandés au peintre brésilien Candido Portinari et la chorégraphie au danseur tchèque Ivo Vania Psota.

La discipline et les traditions russes règnent dans la troupe (composée essentiellement d'artistes russes) grâce à l'activité de Serge Grigoriev – qui a été le régisseur de la troupe de Diaghilev pendant vingt ans – et de sa femme, Lubov Tchernicheva. La troupe se produit dans tous les pays d'Amérique latine, mais en 1946, ces tournées prennent fin. Les spectacles n'ont pas connu le succès à New York devant la rude concurrence que lui imposent le Ballet russe de Monte-Carlo, installé dans cette ville et qui peut compter sur la collaboration de George Balanchine, ainsi que le Ballet Théâtre, fondé en 1937 par Lucia Chase, et d'autres groupes de danse qui cherchent à rivaliser sur le terrain de la modernité. Le colonel de Basil décide de retourner en Europe mais sa tournée à Londres en 1947 est un fiasco. Celles à Paris et en Espagne remportent un peu plus de succès, mais il lui est de plus en plus difficile d'entretenir une grande troupe de ballet. De plus, il est souvent malade. Toutefois, il n'abandonne pas et poursuit toujours de nouveaux projets dont certains connaissent le succès. Sa troupe cesse d'exister lorsqu'il décède, le 27 juillet 1951.

En dehors du Ballet russe de Monte-Carlo et du Ballet russe original du colonel de Basil, de nombreuses compagnies de danse sont dirigées par des chorégraphes russes. Certaines sont nées alors que Diaghilev était encore vivant : Le Théâtre romantique russe (1921-1926), fondé à Berlin par Boris Romanov ; le Ballet intime (1917-1920) fondé aux États-Unis par Adolph Bolm ; les troupes successives fondées par Ida Rubinstein (1885-1960) tout au long de sa carrière ; la compagnie d'Anna Pavlova (1910-1931). Citons aussi, parmi les plus célèbres, le Ballet de Mikhail Mordkin aux États-Unis, à la fin des années 1930, le Ballet de l'Opéra russe de Paris, le Ballet de Vera Nemtchinova, le Ballet russe de Boris Kniazev, les Ballets 1933 de George Balanchine, le Théâtre de la danse de Bronislava Nijinska et bien d'autres.

Il convient aussi de mentionner le développement du ballet anglais, très influencé par Diaghilev. Marie Rambert, Alicia Markova et Ninette de Valois ont en effet débuté dans sa troupe, avant de créer respectivement le Ballet Rambert, la troupe du London festival Ballet (créée par le couple Alicia Markova-Anton Dolin et devenue aujourd'hui l'English National Ballet), et le Vic-Wells Ballet (qui devient The Royal Ballet) ainsi que l'école Academy of Choreographic Art (devenue en 1956 la Royal Ballet School) qui forma la grande star du ballet anglais, Margot Fonteyn.

Le fonds de manuscrits du Musée du Théâtre Bakhrushin possède des lettres de Nadezda, épouse de Nicolas Legat, qui révèlent l'implication de la famille Legat et des artistes russes dans le développement du ballet anglais. Maître de ballet russe et premier danseur au Théâtre Mariinski, Nicolas Legat est surtout connu pour son activité de pédagogue : Michel Fokine, Vaslav et Bronislava Nijinski, Agrippina Vaganova et Fedor Lopoukhov ont été ses élèves. Il quitte la Russie en 1922, commence par enseigner dans la troupe de Diaghilev puis part pour l'Angleterre où il ouvre une école qui devient très populaire. Après sa mort en 1937, c'est sa femme, ancienne ballerine du Mariinski qui reprend son l'école, dirigée après 1968 par leur fille. Dans ses lettres, Nadezda Legat parle de l'école mais aussi de l'activité de Ninette de Valois et d'Arnold Haskell ainsi que des débuts d'Anton Dolin dans leur troupe, le Moscow Art Ballet[5]. Elle évoque aussi ses rencontres avec Nijinski, Tamara Karsavina et d'autres artistes de la troupe de Diaghilev. Malgré leur subjectivité, ses lettres permettent de préciser quelle influence les Russes ont eue sur le ballet en Europe. Nadezda Legat y décrit notamment la situation de la danse à Bucarest et à Belgrade où, dès 1916, elle vint avec Nicolas Legat donner des spectacles et des concerts. Selon elle, il n'y avait pas de troupe de ballet dans les théâtres de ces capitales et les danseurs étaient engagés pour la création de certains opéras. Elle atteste de l'importance de l'enseignement de Léna Polyakova en Serbie et de l'immigration des danseurs serbes, désormais bien formés, dans toute l'Europe[6].

Dans son article consacré au devenir de l'opéra et du ballet au Théâtre national de Belgrade, Mirka Pavlovic confirme les faits mentionnés dans les lettres de Legat[7]. Toutefois, en 1920, une petite école de ballet est créée à Belgrade et dirigée par la célèbre ballerine Klavdya Lukianovna Isatchenko qui entre bientôt à l'École des artistes de Ballet du Théâtre Populaire. Les cours de chorégraphie y sont donnés par Elena Dmitrievna Polyakova qui, avant la révolution, dansait comme soliste au Théâtre impérial Mariinski et dans la troupe des Ballets russes de Diaghilev. Quand l'école ferme ses portes en 1927, Elena Polyakova ouvre son propre studio.

---

[5] Musée théâtral Bakhrushin, fonds 666, numéro d'inventaire 57.

[6] *Ibid.*, numéro d'inventaire 54.

[7] M. Pavlovitch, « Devenir de l'opéra et du ballet au Théâtre Populaire et les artistes russes », dans Arsen'ev, O. Kirillov, M. Sibinovich (ed.), *L'émigration russe en Yougoslavie*, Moscou, Indrik, 1996, p. 306-307.

Pendant plusieurs années, le Ballet de Belgrade est dirigé par des danseuses russes qui cumulent les fonctions de chorégraphe et de danseuse. Grâce à ces chorégraphes, le Ballet de Belgrade monte une quarantaine de spectacles en dix ans ! Outre Elena Polyakova, Nina Kirsanova, Mikhail Panaev, Anatolii Joukovsky et Margarita Froman figurent parmi les danseurs russes du Ballet. Soulignons que ces artistes ont parfois introduit dans leurs chorégraphies des éléments de danse nationale, Joukovski allant même jusqu'à créer un style particulier de ballet.

On peut donc affirmer que le professionnalisme des danseurs russes a permis au Ballet de Belgrade de s'élever au niveau européen.

Au sujet du ballet en Roumanie, Nadezda Legat écrit :

J'ai dansé à Bucarest en 1936. Ils n'avaient pas encore de vrai ballet. Vera Karalli, notre ballerine moscovite y dansait. Elle avait des élèves et donnait de temps en temps des spectacles mais ils n'avaient pas de vrai ballet.[8]

Parlant de la vie de Vera Karalli à Bucarest, Guenady Kogan mentionne aussi le nom d'Anton Romanovskii, chorégraphe principal de la troupe de l'Opéra royal de Bucarest, ayant travaillé dans de nombreuses troupes de ballet en Russie et en Pologne. Il est à l'origine de la création d'un Ballet national à Bucarest, où seul l'opéra était prospère. À l'arrivée de Karalli, la troupe de ballet est encore assez mal préparée. Elle y donne *Le lac des cygnes* et y représente un ballet de sa création sur une musique de Schubert. Karalli regrettera la brièveté de son séjour à Bucarest où elle a néanmoins ouvert une école de danse pour les enfants[9].

Il est malheureusement impossible, dans ce court exposé, de mentionner toutes les troupes et écoles fondées par les émigrés russes : la liste pourrait en être poursuivie longuement. Mentionnons cependant encore deux noms célèbres : Marika Bezobrazova, directrice de l'école de ballet Académie de danse de Monte-Carlo, élève de Julie Sedova et membre de la troupe du Ballet russe de Monte-Carlo, et Ethéry Pagava, Géorgienne d'ascendance russe, qui a travaillé au Nouveau ballet de Monte-Carlo avec Lifar et a fondé à Paris sa propre compagnie, le Ballet Ethéry Pagava, actif pendant plus de vingt ans.

Signalons pour terminer que si Diaghilev et les Ballets russes ont eu une forte influence sur de nombreux pays d'Europe et d'ailleurs, le Danemark a échappé à ce courant, en restant fidèle à l'esthétique de son grand chorégraphe national, Antoine-Auguste Bournonville.

---

[8]   Musée théâtral Bakhrushin, fonds 666, numéro d'inventaire 54.

[9]   G. Kogan, *Vera Karalli. La légende du ballet russe*, Saint-Pétersbourg, Amphora, 2009.

Abstract

This paper discusses the history of emigration of Russian Ballet dancers to Europe in the 1920s, referring to material at the Bakhrushin Museum in Moscow.

Plugging the Gaps

Documentation of Fringe Theatre
at the British Library

Stephen CLEARY

The British Library (London – United Kingdom)

The wave of fringe theatre and experimental performance that began in the late 1960s went largely undocumented; this was a time before portable video equipment was widely available. This paper looks at current initiatives aimed at documenting the working methods and personal stories of companies and performers of that era through interviews and oral histories.

The use of the word "fringe" in relation to theatre and with the meaning "outside the mainstream" dates from the Edinburgh Festival of 1948. This paper does not go back quite that far. The fringe theatre I will be talking about here is the wave of experimental performance born in Britain in the 1960s in the wake of the first US happenings, and contemporaneous with the burgeoning of radical countercultural ideas about politics and society.

The People Show, Britain's first underground theatre group, gave its debut performance in December 1966, at Better Books in Charing Cross Road, London. Stocked with hard-to-find imported US small-press and underground publications. Better Books occupied a place at the centre of the emerging counterculture. The bookshop doubled as a venue for poetry readings – beat generation figures Allen Ginsberg and Lawrence Ferlinghetti had both read there in 1965 (both readings were recorded and issued subsequently on LP) – and other cultural events such as the documentation exhibition that followed the Destruction in Art Symposium presented by Gustav Metzger and other artists at the Africa Centre in September 1966.

Alternative theatre performances such as the People Show debut and other performances in the same general field given in the late 1960s and through the 1970s went largely undocumented by moving image formats. The hobbyist 8mm film format was inadequate to the task of performance documentation, both in terms of its short maximum running time per reel and its limited image quality, and the relatively affordable portable video equipment that is so widespread today did not yet exist. This paper surveys some of the current initiatives aimed at documenting the working methods and personal stories of companies and performers of that era through the generation of new audio-visual material.

In Britain especially, 1968 was a key year in the story of 20th century theatre, for it was then that state censorship of theatre through the Office of the Lord Chamberlain was finally abolished. Prior to 1968 it had been a legal requirement that all play scripts be submitted to the Lord Chamberlain's Office for examination and licensing prior to public performance. In the years leading up to the eventual repeal of the law the censor's famous blue pencil was often employed to excise bad language, expressions of political dissent or blasphemy, and treatments of sexual subjects – in particular homosexuality. A 1958 memorandum issued by the Lord Chamberlain states unequivocally that "We would not pass a play that was violently pro-homosexuality" and, absurdly and risibly, as is often also the case with comments in the Reader's Reports on submitted playscripts, "We will allow the word 'pansy', but not the word 'bugger'".

The original submitted playscripts and the accompanying Reader's Reports are preserved in the British Library Play Collections and are among the key research resources that have been explored by a recent Arts and Humanities Research Council funded collaboration between the British Library and the University of Sheffield[1]. Its title is the Theatre Archive Project. This project, which began in 2003, was conceived as a scholarly reinvestigation of British Theatre from 1945 up to the end of theatrical censorship in 1968 – up to the beginnings of the new wave of fringe theatre in other words. It has had various outputs, including published monographs; conferences and events; and – most significantly in this particular context – the generation of new research material in the form of more than 200 audio interviews conducted with playwrights, actors, backstage staff and ordinary theatregoers. These audio recordings, together with transcripts of the interviews, searchable by key words and phrases, can be found on the British Library's website.

Although full of interest, these interviews are quite short, around an hour long on average, and not really oral history interviews in the sense

---

[1]   Since late 2010 the Library's partner institution in the project has been De Montfort University, Leicester.

that a professional in that field would understand the term. To a purist, an oral history interview is a lengthy life-story interview, conducted over several recording sessions. The British Library has an interview with the artist Ian Breakwell that runs for 31 hours in total and one with Richard Demarco – Edinburgh Fringe Festival stalwart and co-founder of the city's Traverse Theatre – that is even longer.

Harriet Devine, daughter of English Stage Company founder George Devine, is currently a project interviewer for an ongoing oral history project on the legacy of the English Stage Company. The project is supported by the charity National Life Stories, which is based within the British Library's oral history department.

Harriet Devine has said this about the distinctive oral history interview format:

> My previous interviewing experience had been focused recordings no longer than two hours in duration, for a book, *Looking Back: Playwrights at the Royal Court, 1956-2006*. National Life Stories recordings, I discovered, are quite different, covering the entire lifespan of the interviewee, and can last anything from ten to twenty or more hours. It has been fascinating to delve into the childhoods of these people, to hear about their family backgrounds, their education and their paths into working in theatre, the highs and lows of their careers, and the experiences of their later lives.

Harriet Devine's completed interviews can be heard at the British Library. In this excerpt, recorded in 2008, theatre director Max Stafford-Clark describes a show he created for the Edinburgh Festival in the late 1960s, when he was Artistic Director at the Traverse Theatre.

> Max Stafford-Clark: We did one show called *U2*. It was a one-person show, that is to say the audience was one person. People would ring up and book and we would say sorry it's absolutely booked out but if you leave your name and phone number we will call you back if a spare ticket comes up. The only rule was: it had to be somebody none of us knew. We would call back this person and they would arrive and as they came into this empty theatre the lights would go down and this girl [Linda Goddard] would dance in a kind of spangly silver costume. That was the only thing you could see – it was complete darkness. She would come down a rope, although it looked as though she was flying, and then take this person by the hand and lead them out through the streets of Edinburgh. Various incidents would be played out in the streets: a row about car-parking; a couple arguing about shopping, in front of them. Then they would lead this person into the old Traverse and the first thing they looked at – this member of the audience – was through a keyhole, and in this room – brilliantly lit – was this couple getting undressed and going to bed, and it was the same couple that had been arguing in the street earlier. So, it ended, for some reason, with a kind

of biblical... there was a girl in the company with very long hair... and we got hold of... what were Jesus's feet washed with? Um... frankincense and myrrh, right. We got hold of some frankincense and myrrh and washed this member of the audience's feet with frankincense and myrrh, and then if you remember Mary Magdalene dries his feet with her hair, so this woman dried his feet with her hair. The band by this time had learned to play – it was the Beatles' phase with Indian music – they learned to play the tabla and the sitar, so it ended with sitar music and tabla, him having been through all these sensuous experiences. I remember one night we let this gentleman out into the streets of Edinburgh and it was the same time as the Edinburgh Tattoo had finished, and there was a Fijian band that year and these Fijian pipers and drummers were pouring down the street, to get to their coach, to take them back to their barracks, and he obviously thought that this was part of the show too – that we'd organised these drummers...

Harriet Devine: Now whose concept was that show?

Max Stafford-Clark: Oh that was mine.

Harriet Devine: And how long could that continue, just with the one person coming?

Max Stafford-Clark: Oh it wasn't economic but um... I think we did it for about ten days. The idea was – and it was a worthwhile experiment – that the smaller the audience the more potent your control over them was.

In the UK, the Oral History Society offers a one-day "Introduction to Oral History" course several times a year. Several of these courses are held at the British Library. The course covers the history of the discipline, interview techniques, ethics and equipment, and is useful to anyone considering an oral history project. Financial constraints and other influencing factors mean that not every project will necessarily generate lengthy life stories of the type I have described, but a grasp of oral history principles provides a solid basis from which to shape any project of this general type.

Non-British Library projects such as Unfinished Histories, led by theatre historian Susan Croft and theatre director Jessica Higgs, have made use of this introductory training in the formulation of their project methodology. Unfinished Histories is an ongoing project to record British alternative theatre of the period 1968-1988 through video interviews with practitioners, and the collecting of archive material. A set of the DVD interviews created in the first phase of the project, which focuses on Women's Theatre of the 1970s and 1980s, has been deposited with the British Library, the V&A in London, and Bristol and Sheffield Universities.

**Figure. 1 Stills from Cindy Oswin's video interview with
Laura Gilbert, 2004.**

A project covering similar ground, though in a different fashion, is
Cindy Oswin's On the Fringe. Jim Haynes, for example, who in 1967
founded the Drury Lane Arts Lab in London, having previously been
involved in the inception of the Traverse Theatre in Edinburgh, has been
interviewed for both projects.

Cindy Oswin is a performer who began her career acting in traditional
rep, making the switch to fringe and experimental theatre in the late
1960s. Latterly she has also taken on the role of fringe theatre archivist,
making video interviews with many of her peers from the alternative
theatre scene, initially with the help of a bursary from the Artsadmin
organisation.

Cindy made her first video recording for the On the Fringe project
on 1st May 2004: this was the Memorial Service for People Show co-
founder Jeff Nuttall. Subsequently interviews were filmed with fellow
People Show member Mike Figgis (now better known as a film director),
Richard Demarco (again), both David Gale and Hilary Westlake of theatre
company Lumière & Son, performance artist Ian Hinchliffe, theatre
director Geraldine Pilgrim and many more.

Cindy's video recordings were created both for the benefit of posterity and for use as illustrations in Cindy's autobiographical one-woman theatre show, also called *On the Fringe*. The interviews do not follow many of the rules of traditional oral history methodology. In addition, the handheld camerawork, in the early interviews at least, is often very shaky. However, much of the content is invaluable and fascinating. Here is performer Laura Gilbert, filmed outdoors on her allotment in June 2004, talking about an early performance by the People Show:

Cindy Oswin: Say something about the one where you had to hang upside down.

Laura Gilbert: Oh God, that was a [Jeff] Nuttall script, and – I didn't realise at the time – but it was to do with the Moors Murders thing, and I was chased – there was this motorbike in it. It was very terrifying. I took everything personally, it was just like it was happening to me. This was real. This was real stuff mate. And you were chased around this audience by these two persons, who were Mark [Long] and John Darling, and then there's this motorbike roaring round and all this noise and it's pretty horrifying, and you got captured and then you got strung up by your ankles. It was absolutely excruciatingly painful.

Cindy Oswin: How long were you upside down for?

Laura Gilbert: Oh, bloody ages, and I'd be in absolute agony – I'm going Oh my God, Oh my God – and you're trying not to sort of go out of character but it was so painful. And then some of the people in the audience could see that you were absolutely in agony, and were coming up to cut you down, and of course they weren't allowed to by Mark and John, so I had to hang there with this excruciating agony, and deliver this bloody bit of dialogue that Nuttall had written, which was a bit not-quite-correct actually because he was relating it to my father and I thought, no, that's not quite true actually Nuttall, but anyway it did the job for what he was after.

Cindy Oswin's videotaped interviews from the On the Fringe series and the subsequent On the Edinburgh Fringe series are now part of the British Library collection.

In reference to the area of activity I have been discussing today, it hardly needs remarking that time is not on our side. A performer who was aged 20 or so in 1968 will now be over 60 years old. Many influential performers and directors of the period under review will be considerably older, if they are still alive. Many of course are no longer with us. So it is important that stories from the era are collected before the opportunity to do so is gone forever. They offer much more than a dry addition to the historical record. These first-person accounts have the qualities to delight and inspire those who hear them.

Abstract

La première vague du théâtre marginal, née à la fin des années 1960, est restée fortement non documentée. Les équipements vidéo n'étaient pas disponibles à l'époque en dehors du domaine professionnel.

Cet article se penche sur les initiatives en cours, visant à documenter les méthodes de travail et les histoires personnelles des compagnies et des artistes de cette période, par le biais d'entretiens et de récits oraux.

Bibliography/Further Reading

Harriet Devine, "The Legacy of the English Stage Company," National *Life Stories Review and Accounts 2008-2009*, p. 10-11.

Michael Kirby, *Happenings*, New York, E. P. Dutton & Co., 1965.

Jackie McGlone, *Behind the Fringe*, Edinburgh, Festival Fringe Society, 2003.

Barry Miles, *In the Sixties*, London, Jonathan Cape, 2002.

People Show, <http://peopleshow.co.uk> (accessed May 2010).

Philip Roberts and Max Stafford-Clark, *Taking Stock: The Theatre of Max Stafford-Clark*, London, Nick Hern, 2007.

Theatre Archive Project, <http://sounds.bl.uk/Arts-literature-and-performance/Theatre-Archive-Project> (updated link: accessed October 2012).

Unfinished Histories, <http://www.unfinishedhistories.com> (accessed May 2010).

À la recherche d'un chemin perdu

Les archives du théâtre Činoherní klub : 1965-1972

Petra Honsová

Činoherní klub (Prague – République tchèque)

Le Činoherní klub (Club dramatique), toujours en fonction aujourd'hui, a été fondé à Prague en 1965. Pendant ses sept brillantes premières années, il a été façonné par un groupe d'hommes de théâtre dont la majorité avait étudié à l'AMU (Conservatoire national) dans les années suivant le « dégel », après la mort de Staline. Ils avaient eu l'occasion de rencontrer des personnalités de la culture d'avant-guerre ainsi que ceux qui, après février 1948, ont utilisé le théâtre à des fins de pouvoir. En 1956, après « la dénonciation du culte de la personnalité », la tension sociale diminue lentement : Otomar Krejča est à la direction du Théâtre national et Alfréd Radok est metteur en scène ; Ivan Vyskočil, à la Redoute, ouvre avec ses *text-appeals* la voie à d'autres petits théâtres. En 1958, le Piccolo Teatro se produit à Prague avec *Arlequin, serviteur de deux maîtres.* À nouveau, au théâtre, se multiplient les événements, où l'art du comédien peut se manifester librement dans une ligne de jeu qui trouve son origine dans le mime, l'imagination ludique de l'acteur, le désir et le besoin d'exprimer de tout son être sa propre idée sur le monde.

En 1962 naît le Studio théâtral d'État dont le directeur Miloš Hercík favorise en 1965 la création de deux théâtres désireux d'explorer de nouvelles possibilités théâtrales : au Théâtre za branou (Théâtre derrière la porte), l'auteur Josef Topol, le dramaturge Karel Kraus et le metteur en scène Otomar Krejča se consacrent au drame poétique, le Činoherní klub tournant son attention vers les acteurs.

Tandis qu'au Théâtre Na zábradlí (Théâtre sur la balustrade), Václav Havel et Jan Grossman mettent l'accent sur l'effet du système social sur l'individu, au Činoherní klub, le directeur artistique et dramaturge Jaroslav Vostrý élabore un programme « pour le jeu des acteurs » : « La découverte des possibilités de l'acteur est, d'après nous, la découverte des possibilités de l'être humain. Et c'est de lui qu'il s'agit dans l'art théâtral. » L'examen des rapports de l'homme à la réalité, du point de vue de l'homme lui-même, et sous tous les angles possibles (dans un État socialiste derrière le rideau de fer, à un moment historique intense : avant et après l'occupation en 1968), dans un esprit communautaire extrêmement ouvert et tolérant, comme si tout le monde était d'accord d'avance. Le Činoherní klub repose sur la base du volontariat et offre à chacun le droit d'être co-auteur. L'auteur dramatique et metteur en scène Ladislav Smoček, auteur du spectacle d'ouverture *Pique-nique*, a récemment décrit son expérience d'un tel travail de création en commun comme étant « la certification de son propre "moi" par le "moi" de quelqu'un d'autre, par le jeu, le vrai contact avec les autres ».

La qualité d'auteur en tant qu'expression créatrice « venant de soi et au nom de soi » est la ligne même de la dramaturgie : Ladislav Smoček a présenté, dans les premiers temps, quatre de ses pièces, Alena Vostrá a écrit deux pièces sur mesure pour les acteurs, une pièce de l'acteur Pavel Landovský a été jouée ainsi que de remarquables adaptations scéniques de *Crimes et châtiments* de Dostoïevski, du *Candide* de Voltaire, et une adaptation du *Précepteur* de Lenz. Parmi les autres pièces jouées pendant les sept premières saisons, citons *Pension pour les jeunes hommes* de Sean O'Casey, *Zoo Story* d'Edward Albee, *Les justes* de Camus, *La mandragore* de Machiavel, *Le revizor* de Gogol, *L'anniversaire* de Pinter, *Sauvés* de Bond, *La cerisaie* de Tchekhov, *Les bas-fonds* de Gorki. C'est là que débutent au théâtre les cinéastes Jiří Krejčík, Jiří Menzel et Evald Schorm. Le duo Jan Vodňanský et Petr Skoumal, compositeur attaché au théâtre, y a donné trois programmes musicaux. Après l'année 1972, beaucoup doivent quitter le Činoherní klub, dont Jaroslav Vostrý. Pendant les années de « normalisation » qui suivent, le théâtre lutte pour survivre, soutenu par un public fidèle.

Les archives des années 1965 à 1972 comportent une très riche collection de critiques et d'articles écrits par d'éminents spécialistes, de New York jusqu'à Tokyo. Le tout est rassemblé dans vingt grands dossiers noirs, classés selon les mises en scène et les saisons en deux parties, l'une pour les critiques tchèques, l'autre pour les critiques étrangères, traduites en tchèque. Elles constituent un témoignage de ce que le Činoherní klub a apporté au théâtre européen au tournant des années 1960-1970.

La première tournée à l'étranger a lieu en mai 1966 à Munich où les pièces en un acte de Ladislav Smoček, *Le labyrinthe* et *L'étrange après-midi du docteur Zvonek Burke* ainsi que *La mandragore* de Machiavel sont jouées au Theater in der Brienner Strasse Le célèbre critique allemand Herbert Ihering écrit à ce sujet :

> Une expérience audacieuse sans bases mais avec une imagination mimique sans précédent. C'est une représentation qui se meut véritablement à la limite

d'une conception inamicale de l'œuvre, car ce n'est pas le contenu de *La mandragore* de Machiavel que l'on joue ici, c'est plutôt un tourbillon de baladins autour de l'année 1500. [...] Les Pragois jouent de façon si libérée que l'on oublie le sens de la pièce et que l'on suit avec passion la manière de jouer. La maîtrise artistique est remarquable. Ce qu'a réalisé Jiří Menzel, le metteur en scène, avec les comédiens František Husák, Jiří Hrzán, Petr Čepek, Jiří Hálek, Věra Ferbasová, Jiřina Třebická, Jana Břežková et Josef Somr, est proprement phénoménal.

En 1967, les pièces en un acte de Ladislav Smoček sont présentées avec succès en Suède et au Danemark. Elles sont présentées en 1969 à la Biennale de Venise, où Raul Radice écrit :

Dans *L'étrange après-midi du docteur Zvonek Burke*, les racines de l'œuvre sont compatibles avec les schémas de la commedia dell'arte, mais elles se nourrissent en réalité de moyens farcesques qu'utilisaient les créateurs de films grotesques muets dans la première décade du siècle. Nous devons aussi rendre compte que, dans la personne de Burke, telle que Smoček l'a créée, nous pouvons trouver un parent important du répertoire contemporain de Courteline à Ionesco. [...] Nous avons rarement pu voir jouer des acteurs avec un enthousiasme, une intelligence et une bravoure pareils.

Dans le journal *Die Welt*, Friedrich Luft écrit en 1969 à propos de *L'anniversaire* d'Harold Pinter dans la mise en scène de Jaroslav Vostrý :

Le potentiel artistique des acteurs est merveilleux. Ils ont tous d'énormes capacités dans les rôles de caractère, tous sont parfaitement à leur aise à l'extrême limite de la farce. Pas même en Angleterre, Pinter n'est joué de cette façon à la fois comique et effrayante. [...] Au début on ne fait que rire, jusqu'au moment où l'on se sent subrepticement pris à la gorge.

En mars 1970, le Činoherní klub ouvre le festival World Theatre Season, où il présente à côté de *La mandragore* et de la pièce d'Alena Vostrá *Sur qui tombe le sort (Na koho to slovo padne)*, *Le revizor* de Gogol dans la mise en scène de Jan Kačer. Citons la critique d'Irving Wardle :

Chez les acteurs de Kačer, le grotesque prend la forme d'une sorte de super réalisme : des personnages humains examinés au microscope, gonflés dans des proportions gargantuesques, mais jamais au détriment de leur lien avec le naturel. Le résultat en est un style de farce épique, aussi éloigné de la tradition anglaise que française, instrument idéal pour communiquer une œuvre qui est à la fois mortellement sérieuse et hystériquement comique.

Une autre pièce d'Alena Vostrá est jouée à Bergen et à Oslo. À son sujet, Sigmund Torsteinson a écrit :

Le spectateur commence tout de suite à s'intéresser au destin des personnages de la pièce *À couteaux tirés (Na ostří nože)*, tous les personnages sont finement caractérisés, dans chaque mouvement on peut sentir une grande culture théâtrale, les solutions scéniques sont tout aussi remarquables. […] Nous gardons souvenir des visages qui nous ont parlé depuis le plus profond de la nature humaine – et celui de monsieur le Héros en tout premier lieu, avec son éternel regard impuissant de voyageur sans but.

La cerisaie de Tchekhov est présentée à la Biennale de Venise en 1970. Dans vingt-quatre quotidiens italiens, les critiques admirent tout particulièrement la Ranevskaïa de Věra Galatíková, le Lopakhine de Pavel Landovský et le Trofimov de Josef Abrhám. Dans la traduction sans lyrisme de Leoš Suchařípa, et sous la direction de Jan Kačer, la mise en scène révèle l'ambiguïté de la langue de Tchekhov et s'ouvre aux éléments comiques. En 1972, Ritva Särkisilta écrit en Finlande : « Quelque part entre les traditionnels Tchekhov et Gogol se trouvent les personnages du Činoherní klub. Ils sont trop risibles et mortels pour être vus à travers une forte sentimentalité ».

En 1973, le Činoherní klub ne peut plus répondre à l'invitation de Peter Daubeny, pour le jubilé à Londres du World Theatre Season. Les instances officielles finissent même par interdire le déplacement, alors que le secrétaire du ministre des Affaires étrangères avait expressément promis à Daubeny que personne ne s'opposerait à la participation du théâtre.

Sur les mises en scène d'alors, beaucoup de critiques et de célèbres praticiens de théâtre ont écrit : je ne citerai que Kenneth Tynan, Peter Roberts, Hilary Spurling, John Barber, Peter Ansorge, Hanns Braun, Georges Schlocker, Jarl W. Donnér, Göran O'Eriksson, Carin Mannheimer, Arturo Lazzari, Roberto de Monticelli, Paolo Emilio Poesio, Jarka M. Burian, Anatolij Efros, Alexandr Svobodin, Jan Pavel Gawlik, Elżbieta Wysińska, Helmut Kajzar, Éva Mezei, Gábor Mihályi parmi d'autres.

Cette précieuse partie de nos archives a survécu grâce à Jaroslav Vostrý qui l'a conservée dix-sept ans dans son appartement privé. Treize albums contenant les contacts et les négatifs des excellentes photos de Miloň Novotný ont également été conservés. Grâce aux soins de l'historienne d'art Anna Fárová subsistent de superbes affiches du graphiste Libor Fára qui est aussi l'auteur du logo du théâtre, utilisé jusqu'à ce jour. Les documents télévisés nous informent par ailleurs de façon très complète : la télévision suédoise a filmé *La mandragore* en studio en 1971 et la Télévision tchécoslovaque *Le revizor*. Il existe un disque 33 tours de 1968, aux éditions Supraphon, reprenant des extraits de sept mises en scène, mais il s'agit principalement d'enregistrements en studio. C'est pourquoi nous sommes heureux d'avoir conservé les bandes magnétiques que l'ingénieur du son Richard Bouška a réalisées pendant les représentations. Elles sont actuellement en cours de restauration, en collaboration avec l'association Mluvící kniha (Le livre parlant), laquelle produit des livres audio pour les non-voyants et malvoyants. L'ingénieur du son, Pavel Musil, les numérise et les nettoie. Nous possédons déjà cinq enregistrements audio *live* sur CD. Ce sont d'excellents documents sur l'histoire récente du théâtre, officiellement ignorée pendant vingt ans. Ce n'est que deux décennies seulement après 1989 que l'on se met à la recherche du chemin perdu.

Le premier directeur du théâtre, Jaroslav Vostrý, aujourd'hui professeur et directeur de l'Institut de recherches sur les créations dramatiques et scéniques du DAMU et fondateur de la Société scénologique tchèque, est revenu au théâtre pendant trois ans, après la « Révolution de velours », et a écrit en 1996 le livre *Činoherní klub 1965-1972/Dramaturgie dans la pratique.*

Vladimír Procházka, directeur depuis 1999, soutient l'activité des archives : pour le quarantième anniversaire du théâtre, nous avons préparé, avec les dramaturges Roman Císař et Radvan Pácl et avec le graphiste Joska Skalník, le livre *Činoherní klub 1965-2005*, dans lequel se trouve le matériel photographique de cent douze mises en scène, huit études de théâtrologie et plusieurs dizaines de souvenirs et de déclarations de créateurs et de proches du théâtre. Chaque mois, nous publions une revue publicitaire *Činoherní čtení (À lire sur le Činoherní)*, qui revient fréquemment sur les personnalités et les réalisations de la troupe d'origine.

À côté des archives des années 1965 à 1972, nous possédons des fragments de ce qui a été conservé du temps de la normalisation : des programmes, des photographies, des adaptations de pièces, quelques vidéos. Les documents écrits de cette époque sont toutefois peu nombreux et souvent de qualité inégale, dans la mesure où le point de vue idéologique l'emportait sur l'esthétique. Aujourd'hui, nous sommes en mesure d'offrir aux étudiants et aux chercheurs divers documents à propos de 123 mises en scène. Nous avons le sentiment que cela prend aujourd'hui tout son sens, dans la mesure où le théâtre tchèque porte aujourd'hui encore les traces de son évolution, peu naturelle depuis les années 1970. Cela parce qu'ont été très longuement réduits au silence ceux qui avaient su librement lui donner sa forme et son essence et ceux qui avaient écrit sur lui en connaisseurs.

À la fin de la 45e saison, il est réjouissant que la pièce de Ladislav Smoček *L'étrange après-midi du docteur Zvonek Burke* soit toujours au répertoire. La jeune génération a connu une expérience d'acteur prometteuse en 2002, avec la mise en scène par Ondřej Sokol de la pièce de Martin McDonagh *L'Ouest solitaire*. Dans le contexte de l'histoire de notre théâtre, *La plaisanterie (Ptákovina)* de Milan Kundera (écrite en 1966) est mémorable : le prix Alfréd Radok-Théâtre de l'année

2008 lui a été décerné, dans la mise en scène de Ladislav Smoček au Činoherní klub. Dans un avenir proche, nous prévoyons de participer à l'exposition rétrospective de Luboš Hrůza, scénographe au Činoherní klub qui, à l'époque de l'émigration de 1968-1990, était décorateur en chef du Théâtre national de Norvège et artiste de renommée européenne. Une occasion peut-être de rencontrer à Prague les membres de la SIBMAS.

Abstract

The theatre in Prague known as the Činoherní klub (Drama Club) has existed since 1965. It was founded by two former students of the Academy of Performing Arts: Jaroslav Vostrý, theatre historian and dramaturge, and Ladislav Smoček, dramatist and director. This small venue, seating only 200, became one of the leading Czech theatres during its first seven years. It inherited the sophisticated theatre culture of pre-war Czechoslovakia and created an independent and inspiring form of modern drama. Its original plays (by Ladislav Smoček, Alena Vostrá and Pavel Landovský) and its approach to classical works (O'Casey, Albee, Camus, Machiavelli, Dostoyevsky, Gogol, Pinter, Chekhov, Voltaire, Gorky and Lenz) were an inspiration for European audiences. In January 1970, it was invited to open the World Theatre Season in London. During these years, nearly thirty outstanding artistic personalities worked at the Činoherní klub including authors, actors, dramaturges, translators, directors, designers, musicians, and photographers. The archives from 1965-1972 are a remarkable testimony to these people and the art of the theatre. These archives are also a great source of the history of Czechoslovakia, a country forcibly deprived of its sovereignty through occupation by troops of the Warsaw Pact in August 1968. In 2015, the Činoherní klub will celebrate its fiftieth anniversary.

Aux sources de la création du département de la Musique

Le rattachement de la bibliothèque de l'Opéra à la Bibliothèque nationale

Mathias AUCLAIR

Bibliothèque-musée de l'Opéra (Paris – France)

Les travaux de Nicole Wild[1] et de Valérie Gressel[2] ont mis à la disposition du public une somme considérable d'informations sur la création, le statut et la formation des collections de la bibliothèque de l'Opéra au XIXᵉ siècle. En revanche, aucune étude n'a été consacrée au plus profond changement qui affecte cette institution au XXᵉ siècle : son rattachement à la Bibliothèque nationale, en 1935[3]. En effet, par cette décision, le Législateur donne à la bibliothèque de l'Opéra une nouvelle naissance. Il provoque aussi une mise à jour, parfois douloureuse et pleine d'errements, de ses missions et de son fonctionnement, comme le laissent transparaître les sources peu exploitées, conservées à la Bibliothèque-musée de l'Opéra et à la Mission pour la gestion de la production documentaire et des archives de la Bibliothèque nationale de France. Il l'implique, enfin, quelques années plus tard, dans la création du département de la Musique.

Le décret de 1935 et la fusion des bibliothèques musicales

Le changement de statut du directeur de l'Opéra plus encore que la construction, à la même époque, d'une nouvelle salle de spectacle par l'architecte Charles Garnier, est à l'origine de la création officielle des

---

[1]   Parmi les nombreux travaux de Nicole Wild, citons *Décors et costumes du XIXᵉ siècle*, Paris, Bibliothèque nationale, 1987-1993, 2 vols.

[2]   Valérie Gressel, *Charles Nuitter : des scènes parisiennes à la bibliothèque de l'Opéra*, Hildesheim, G. Olms Verlag, 2002 (Musikwissenschaftliche Publikationen ; 18).

[3]   Voir tout de même l'article-témoignage d'Yvette Fédoroff et Simone Wallon, « Le département de la Musique : naissance et premiers pas », in Michel Nortier (dir.), *Études sur la Bibliothèque nationale et témoignages réunis en hommage à Thérèse Kleindienst*, Paris, Bibliothèque nationale, 1985, p. 85-95.

postes de bibliothécaire et d'archiviste de l'Opéra. En effet, le décret du 22 mars 1866 réforme l'exploitation de l'Opéra qui s'apparente dès lors à une entreprise privée confiée « à un directeur-entrepreneur administrant à ses risques et périls »[4]. Un arrêté du 16 mai 1866, portant réglementation du cahier des charges du directeur de l'Opéra, institue donc dans ses articles 37 et 38 un bibliothécaire et un archiviste, détachés de l'autorité du directeur de l'Opéra et directement placés sous la tutelle du ministre de la Maison de l'Empereur et des Beaux-Arts. Ainsi, des garants de l'inaliénabilité et de la bonne conservation du patrimoine de l'Opéra – qui reste la propriété de l'État – sont officiellement créés[5].

Grâce à ses appuis politiques et à son implication dans le commissariat de l'exposition théâtrale présentée lors de l'Exposition universelle de 1878, l'archiviste Charles Nuitter obtient l'installation d'un musée, en 1881, et d'une salle de lecture, en 1882, dans les espaces du Palais Garnier prévus pour Napoléon III[6]. Cependant, l'ouverture de la nouvelle salle de lecture a conduit au recrutement d'un personnel supplémentaire[7] et s'accompagne donc de dépenses élevées que le rapporteur du budget des Beaux-Arts ne manque pas de constater :

> L'administration de l'Opéra subit encore les frais d'une bibliothèque publique en ce qui concerne le chauffage, le balayage et le paiement d'employés dont quelques-uns pourraient être utiles au public (si le public y venait), mais qui sont absolument inutiles à la direction.[8]

Certains bibliothécaires et archivistes fortunés – tels Charles Nuitter ou Charles Malherbe – se conduisent donc, jusqu'au début du xxe siècle, en

---

[4] *Recueil des lois, décrets, arrêtés, règlements, circulaires, se rapportant aux théâtres et aux établissements d'enseignement musical et dramatique*, Paris, Imprimerie nationale, 1888, p. 19. Voir également Jean Gourret, *Ces hommes qui ont fait l'Opéra*, Paris, Albatros, 1984, p. 138-139.

[5] BMO, PA 1 (15 mai 1866). *Cf.* également Pierre Vidal, « La Bibliothèque-musée de l'Opéra, carrefour entre deux institutions », in Nicole Leclercq et Jan Van Goethem (dir.), *Du document à l'utilisateur : rôles et responsabilités des centres spécialisés dans les arts du spectacle : Société internationale des bibliothèques et musées des arts du spectacle (25e congrès : Barcelone, 6-10 septembre 2004)*, Bruxelles, P. Lang, 2008, p. 87-92.

[6] Valérie Gressel, *Charles Nuitter : des scènes parisiennes à la bibliothèque de l'Opéra*, *op. cit.*, p. 135-157.

[7] *Ibid.*, p. 163-165.

[8] BMO, PA 15 juillet 1886 : Antonin Proust, *n° 1102 : Chambre des députés [...] Rapport fait au nom de la commission du budget chargée d'examiner le projet de loi portant fixation du budget général de l'exercice 1887 : ministère de l'Instruction publique, des Beaux-Arts et des Cultes : 2e section : Beaux-Arts*, Paris, Imprimerie de la Chambre des députés, 1887, p. 94.

mécènes mais, après-guerre, l'institution est en crise. Son fonctionnement a pourtant été réformé à la suite du décès de Malherbe, en 1911 : l'archiviste et le bibliothécaire ont été placés sous l'autorité d'un chef unique, l'« administrateur » ; Antoine Banès, qui occupait les fonctions d'archiviste, est nommé à cette fonction à compter du 1er janvier 1912 par un arrêté du 30 décembre 1911[9]. Cependant, la situation matérielle de l'institution se détériore et la presse musicale s'en fait l'écho. Dès 1920, dans un article publié dans *Le Courrier musical* sur « les bibliothèques musicales », Jean Chantavoine stigmatise :

> les conditions déplorables qui sont faites à nos recherches, non pas même les plus minutieuses, mais les plus élémentaires, par la dispersion des bibliothèques musicales à Paris, les pratiques surannées de leur fonctionnement, les lacunes de leurs fonds, etc.

Il réclame donc la « fusion » de la bibliothèque du Conservatoire, de la bibliothèque de l'Opéra et de la Bibliothèque nationale afin de dresser « un inventaire sérieux et un catalogue pratique » des collections de ces trois institutions et d'utiliser au mieux les crédits qui leur sont accordés[10].

La réduction des moyens consentis à la bibliothèque de l'Opéra et à celle du Conservatoire dans les années qui suivent participe à une nouvelle dégradation de la situation que regrettait Jean Chantavoine. Ainsi, deux décrets du 7 octobre 1926 et du 18 octobre 1927 diminuent, respectivement, le personnel de la bibliothèque du Conservatoire de douze à huit personnes et le personnel de la bibliothèque et du musée de l'Opéra de six à quatre personnes. Un décret du 26 février 1935, pris en application de la loi de finances du 28 février 1934, réduit finalement le personnel total des deux bibliothèques à « un seul fonctionnaire technique : l'administrateur de la bibliothèque de l'Opéra chargé des deux établissements » assisté d'un secrétaire (au Conservatoire), un commis et deux gardiens (à l'Opéra)[11]. En effet, depuis le 1er janvier 1934, Jacques-Gabriel Prod'homme, administrateur de la bibliothèque de l'Opéra, a pris la succession d'Henri Expert, admis à la retraite, à la tête de la bibliothèque du Conservatoire[12].

---

[9]   BMO, Arch. bibl. 16 : État des services du personnel de la bibliothèque, des archives et du musée de l'Opéra.

[10]   Jean Chantavoine, « Les bibliothèques musicales », *Le Courrier musical*, 22e année, n° 3, 1er février 1920, p. 45-47.

[11]   BNF, Archives, A 65/5 : « Note préparée pour M. André Honnorat sur le personnel des bibliothèques musicales », [ca. 1935] et note du 12 février 1936 relative au budget de 1937 des bibliothèques musicales. Voir aussi Julien Cain, *La Bibliothèque nationale pendant les années 1935 à 1940*, Impr. des Journaux officiels, 1941, p. 96-97. [En ligne]. URL : <http://gallica.bnf.fr/ark:/12148/bpt6k497616c.r=.langFR>. Consulté le 10 août 2010.

[12]   BNF, Archives, dossier Jacques-Gabriel Prod'homme : arrêté du 30 décembre 1933.

La suppression de l'unique poste de bibliothécaire du Conservatoire pousse d'ailleurs Henry Prunières, au nom de la Société française de musicologie, à faire une démarche auprès du ministre de tutelle :

> Il y avait avant la guerre au Conservatoire : un bibliothécaire, un sous-bibliothécaire, un conservateur de musée, et à l'Opéra : un bibliothécaire, un archiviste et un conservateur du musée. Après des réductions successives, on se propose aujourd'hui de remplacer ces six personnes occupées dans des locaux distincts, par un seul administrateur dont on ne conçoit pas comment il pourrait suffire à tant de tâches en des lieux différents [...]. Si on supprime successivement les rares places officielles que peuvent occuper en France des musicologues qualifiés, comment espérer que des jeunes gens de valeur consentent à s'orienter vers une carrière où ils ne peuvent espérer occuper aucune situation où leur compétence trouve à s'exercer ?[13]

La démarche de Prunières échoue, mais l'appel de Chantavoine est entendu. En juin 1931, Pol Neveux préside une commission qui siège à la direction générale des Beaux-Arts et estime :

> qu'il serait désirable d'envisager en effet la réunion complète de ces trois fonds en un seul qui serait rattaché à la Réunion des bibliothèques nationales, et qui pourrait même former un département de la Bibliothèque nationale.[14]

Destinée à rejoindre la Bibliothèque nationale, la bibliothèque de l'Opéra n'a plus vocation à conserver ses compétences archivistiques et la plus grande part des archives administratives de l'Opéra qu'elle conserve est transférée aux Archives nationales en 1932[15]. Par ailleurs, au cours de l'été 1932, en prévision de la fusion et grâce à un crédit annuel de 75 000 francs, Pol Neveux constitue une équipe de musicologues sous la conduite de bibliothécaires pour dresser le catalogue des bibliothèques musicales, et plus particulièrement des fonds musicaux du Conservatoire[16]. Dans une note à l'administrateur général, Pierre Josserand, qui dirige l'équipe du Conservatoire, rapporte comme a été constituée cette équipe :

---

[13] BNF, Archives, A 65/4.

[14] BNF, Archives, A 65/4 : Note sur « La fusion des bibliothèques musicales » du 21 août 1935.

[15] Julien Cain, *La Bibliothèque nationale pendant les années 1935 à 1940, op. cit.*, p. 98.

[16] BNF, Archives, A 65/5 : note budgétaire, octobre 1936. BNF, Archives, A 65/4 : Note sur la fusion des bibliothèques musicales, 21 août 1935 ; état des travaux de cette équipe à la bibliothèque du Conservatoire par Yvonne Rokseth, 1936 ; lettre d'Yvonne Rokseth à Julien Cain, 4 octobre 1938 ; note de Josserand à Julien Cain, 2 décembre 1938 ; note de Gastoué sur la bibliothèque du Conservatoire de musique, 25 janvier 1939. Sur cette équipe, voir également Yvette Fédoroff et Simone Wallon, « Le département de la Musique : naissance et premiers pas », art. cit., p. 88-89.

Quant à la compétence musicale, j'entends encore M. Pol Neveux me dire, au moment de la formation de l'équipe et comme je lui avouais mon ignorance : « Mais, c'est ce qu'il nous faut ! Quelques bibliothécaires, pour diriger des musicologues… La bibliothèque du Conservatoire est en train de crever des services compétents des spécialistes ! Ils ont tous des idées de génie et ils n'oublient que deux choses : ce qu'est une bibliothèque, et en particulier celle du Conservatoire ».[17]

Le 30 octobre 1935, le décret-loi « relatif à la fusion des bibliothèques musicales » est finalement promulgué : afin de mutualiser les crédits de bibliothèques aux missions voisines et de concentrer au sein d'un futur département de la Musique les ressources documentaires parisiennes en un seul lieu et sous une seule gestion, la bibliothèque de l'Opéra est rattachée, avec la bibliothèque du Conservatoire national de musique et d'art dramatique, à la Bibliothèque nationale. Prod'homme est nommé « administrateur des bibliothèques musicales » avec autorité sur les bibliothèques et musées musicaux faisant partie de la Bibliothèque nationale.

Le rapport au président de la République motivant la promulgation du décret envisage de « réunir dans un même local l'ensemble des collections […] dans des constructions à élever près de la bibliothèque de l'Arsenal »[18] ; il s'agit de rapprocher ainsi les collections musicales de la collection Rondel :

> La construction d'une bibliothèque unique où les trois fonds seraient réunis a été envisagée et plusieurs solutions ont été proposées. L'une, la plus rationnelle, serait celle qui utiliserait les terrains récemment libérés à côté de la bibliothèque de l'Arsenal où sont déjà conservées d'importantes collections concernant l'art théâtral, la danse, etc.[19]

Cependant, la « construction d'un bâtiment sur l'emplacement de l'immeuble de la place Louvois » pour une « bibliothèque musicale » est examinée et évaluée dès le 19 novembre 1935[20].

La situation difficile dans laquelle se trouvent la bibliothèque de l'Opéra et celle du Conservatoire n'est pas résolue par le décret de 1935 : la fusion n'a pas été accompagnée d'une augmentation sensible des crédits et du

---

[17] BnF, Archives, A 65/4.

[18] Références et texte intégral du rapport et du décret de 1935 en annexe.

[19] BnF, Archives, A 65/4. Note du 21 août 1935 sur la fusion des bibliothèques musicales.

[20] BnF, Archives, A 65/5 : « Bibliothèque musicale. Évaluation approximative par l'architecte en chef de la construction d'un bâtiment sur l'emplacement de l'immeuble de la place Louvois », 19 novembre 1935. Depuis 1964, le département de la Musique est établi dans des locaux spécialement construits pour lui au 2, rue Louvois.

personnel attribués à la Bibliothèque nationale[21] ; les moyens exceptionnels consentis pour accompagner la fusion des bibliothèques musicales avec un travail sur les catalogues ont même été divisés par deux :

> En ce qui concerne le catalogue des bibliothèques musicales, il a été constitué il y a 4 ans par une équipe d'auxiliaires spécialisés, excellents musicologues pour la plupart ou bons bibliographes. Grâce à eux quelques-uns des fonds les plus précieux (manuscrits, musique ancienne) ont pu être catalogués. Ce travail doit être poursuivi, mais il faut pour cela que le crédit, qui était à l'origine de 75 000 francs et qui a été réduit à 37 698 francs, soit rétabli à son chiffre primitif.[22]

Une note du 12 février 1936 relative au budget de 1937 des bibliothèques musicales expose aussi que, « dans leur situation actuelle, les deux bibliothèques musicales sont pratiquement inutilisables »[23]. Une autre note du 24 février 1936 sur les « bibliothèques musicales » se fait d'ailleurs l'écho de réserves formulées à la Chambre quant à l'application du décret du 30 octobre 1935 :

> Dans son rapport pour son budget des Beaux-Arts au nom de la Commission des finances de la Chambre des députés, M. Georges Monnet à propos du chapitre 29, sans examiner dans son ensemble la question, a cru devoir indiquer que la mise en pratique de la mesure prise le 30 octobre appelait les plus « expresses réserves ».[24]

En accord avec les musicologues, et notamment avec le conseil d'administration de la Société française de musicologie qui s'est exprimé à ce sujet, il est entendu que l'application du décret de 1935 doit se faire progressivement : l'achèvement et la fusion des catalogues ainsi que la coordination dans les acquisitions[25] constitueraient une première étape ; le rattachement des personnels de l'Opéra et du Conservatoire au personnel des Bibliothèques nationales serait prévu dans un second temps, dans le cadre du budget de 1938[26].

---

[21] BnF, Archives, A 65/4 : note de Julien Cain relative au « crédit du personnel des bibliothèques musicales », octobre 1936. BnF, Archives, A 65/5 : note du 5 août 1937 à la direction de l'Enseignement supérieur : « [La Bibliothèque nationale] doit faire assurer le fonctionnement des bibliothèques musicales du Conservatoire et de l'Opéra avec une subvention de 53 000 frs. dont on ignore si elle couvre les frais de chauffage de ces établissements ».

[22] BnF, Archives, A 65/5. « Budget de l'Éducation nationale -- chapitre 49 », octobre 1936.

[23] BnF, Archives, A 65/5 : note du 12 février 1936 relative au budget de 1937 des bibliothèques musicales.

[24] BnF, Archives, A 65/4.

[25] De nombreux documents sur la coordination des acquisitions sous les cotes BnF, Archives, A 65/4 et A 65/5.

[26] BnF, Archives, A 65/4 : note du 24 février 1936 sur les « bibliothèques musicales ».

Pour mener les travaux sur le catalogue, des ressources spéciales sont mises à disposition sur les fonds de Grands Travaux et par l'Entr'aide des Travailleurs intellectuels : elles permettent de poursuivre l'inventaire et la préparation du catalogue des fonds de musique ancienne conservés au département des Imprimés[27]. Toutefois, afin d'accroître les moyens de fonctionnement des bibliothèques musicales et d'accélérer les travaux sur le catalogue, l'administration de la Bibliothèque nationale essaie d'obtenir des subventions des services de radiodiffusion et des théâtres nationaux.

Dans une note au ministre des Postes, téléphones et télécommunication du 6 mars 1936, l'administrateur expose que :

> les services de la radio-diffusion ne disposent à l'heure actuelle que d'un matériel très insuffisant pour la préparation des émissions dramatiques aussi bien que des émissions musicales. Ils se trouvent ainsi dans l'obligation de faire appel aux bibliothèques, et avant tout aux fonds spéciaux des Bibliothèques nationales.

Il demande aussi, sur trois ans, une subvention annuelle de 150 000 francs « inscrit[e] au chapitre des bibliothèques théâtrales et musicales » pour dresser le catalogue de la collection Rondel de l'Arsenal et des fonds musicaux de la bibliothèque du Conservatoire et de la bibliothèque de l'Opéra[28].

La demande n'a pas de suites et la Bibliothèque nationale cherche aussi à impliquer les théâtres nationaux – l'Opéra au premier rang de ceux-ci – dans le financement des bibliothèques musicales.

La création de la RTLN et les relations nouvelles avec l'Opéra

Au moment où la bibliothèque de l'Opéra est rattachée à la Bibliothèque nationale, sa situation évolue vis-à-vis du théâtre dont elle conserve le patrimoine. En effet, les conditions qui ont motivé la création de la bibliothèque et des archives de l'Opéra en 1866 se sont évanouies avec la fin du système du directeur-entrepreneur et la création de la Réunion des théâtres lyriques nationaux (RTLN) par la loi du 14 janvier 1939 (qui prend effet dès le premier janvier)[29]. Ni la loi de 1939, ni aucun

---

[27] BNF, Archives, A 65/4 : projet de note, 1938. Voir également Yvette Fédoroff et Simone Wallon, « Le département de la Musique : naissance et premiers pas », art. cit., p. 92-93.

[28] Julien Cain, *La Bibliothèque nationale pendant les années 1935 à 1940, op. cit.*, p. 97.

[29] Loi du 14 janvier 1939 portant réorganisation des théâtres lyriques nationaux (Journal officiel du 21 janvier 1939, p. 1074-1075). Sur la création de la RTLN, voir Pascal Ory, *La Belle illusion : culture et politique sous le signe du Front populaire (1935-1938)*, Paris, Plon, p. 319-320.

de ses décrets d'application (ni aucun texte législatif ou réglementaire ultérieur modifiant le statut de l'Opéra de Paris), ne vient redéfinir quelles missions patrimoniales incombent à la bibliothèque – rattachée désormais à la Bibliothèque nationale – et à l'Opéra de Paris, devenu établissement public[30].

Alors que le projet de RTLN est en cours d'instruction, la Bibliothèque nationale essaie de faire participer le théâtre à l'effort financier que réclame la fusion des bibliothèques musicales et rédige donc une note, le 24 décembre 1937, au ministre de l'Éducation nationale exposant « la situation difficile des bibliothèques musicales (Conservatoire, Opéra) et de la bibliothèque théâtrale (fonds Rondel de l'Arsenal) » :

> Par suite de l'extrême faiblesse des crédits et de la réduction ininterrompue du personnel, ces établissements, dont la richesse est partout reconnue, sont hors d'état de rendre les services que les musiciens, les historiens de la musique et du théâtre, les metteurs en scène, les artistes de tout genre sont en droit d'attendre d'eux.[31]

La note n'est pas envoyée mais un aide-mémoire est remis à Jean Cassou, membre du cabinet de Jean Zay. Le ministre accepte « le principe d'une contribution des théâtres aux frais des bibliothèques, sous forme d'un prélèvement de un pour cent de la subvention versée par l'État à la Réunion des théâtres lyriques nationaux ». Dès l'adoption du projet de loi créant la RTLN par le Sénat, lors de sa séance du 27 décembre 1938, la Bibliothèque nationale rappelle l'accord ministériel au cabinet par une note du 30 décembre 1938. Un projet de décision ministérielle est bien rédigé mais n'est jamais promulgué :

> Le Ministre de l'Éducation nationale à Monsieur le Directeur général des Beaux-Arts.
>
> Désirant mettre fin à la situation difficile des bibliothèques musicales et théâtrales (bibliothèque du Conservatoire et de l'Opéra, fonds musicaux de la Bibliothèque nationale, fonds Rondel de la bibliothèque de l'Arsenal) et considérant les services qu'elles rendent et sont appelées à rendre davantage à l'art dramatique, j'ai décidé de faire participer les théâtres nationaux, qui vont disposer de ressources très importantes, aux frais de ces établissements. Dans les dispositions que vous allez avoir à me proposer en vue de l'application de la loi que le Sénat vient d'adopter, je vous prie en conséquence de bien vouloir tenir compte de cette décision. Il conviendra que vous invitiez les directeurs de théâtres à faire abandon de un pour cent de la subvention de l'État au profit des bibliothèques musicales et théâtrales. Cette contribution sera versée

---

[30] BnF, Archives, A 65/4.
[31] BnF, Archives, A 65/5.

à la Réunion des bibliothèques nationales qui a l'administration de ces établissements.[32]

À défaut de pouvoir bénéficier d'une subvention du théâtre, il importe de montrer à l'Opéra que la Bibliothèque reste l'institution de conservation de son patrimoine, et notamment de l'iconographie théâtrale. Il convient aussi de profiter de la création d'un établissement public réunissant l'Opéra et l'Opéra-Comique pour faire entrer la conservation du patrimoine de ce second théâtre dans la compétence de la bibliothèque de l'Opéra. Le 9 janvier 1939, quelques jours seulement après la création officielle de la RTLN, Jean Cordey demande donc à l'administrateur général de la Bibliothèque nationale s'il accepte :

> pour bien marquer les services que les bibliothèques musicales rendent et sont appelées à rendre aux théâtres lyriques [...] d'écrire une lettre à M. Rouché[33] et à M. Mariotte[34] pour leur proposer officiellement de recueillir dans l'un des locaux de la bibliothèque de l'Opéra les archives et les éléments divers (en particulier les maquettes de décors et les dessins de costumes) que l'Opéra-Comique a grand peine à conserver, faute de place.[35]

Les difficultés d'application du décret de 1935

Le départ à la retraite, prévu le 30 septembre 1937, de l'« administrateur des bibliothèques musicales », Jacques-Gabriel Prod'homme[36], pousse l'administration de la Bibliothèque nationale à procéder à la deuxième étape de l'application du décret de 1935 : le rattachement des personnels de l'Opéra et du Conservatoire au personnel des Bibliothèques nationales. Le 3 juillet 1937, le président de la Société française de musicologie, Amédée Gastoué – qui est chargé par ailleurs du classement du fonds musical de la bibliothèque de l'Opéra – a adressé ses remerciements renouvelés à l'Administrateur général pour avoir obtenu le rattachement des bibliothèques du Conservatoire et de l'Opéra à la Bibliothèque nationale et lui conseiller de profiter du départ à la retraite de J.-G. Prod'homme pour supprimer les postes propres à ces deux bibliothèques et les remplacer, dans chacune d'elles, par un bibliothécaire et un « aide » : « Ainsi les services seraient à la fois centralisés, simplifiés et unifiés, avec une plus grande aisance financière ». L'Administrateur lui

---

[32] BNF, Archives, A 65/5.

[33] Jacques Rouché, administrateur de la Réunion des théâtres lyriques nationaux.

[34] Antoine Mariotte, directeur de l'Opéra-Comique.

[35] BNF, Archives, A 65/5.

[36] BNF, Archives, dossier Jacques-Gabriel Prod'homme : arrêté du ministre de l'Éducation nationale, 4 juin 1937.

répond le 24 août que ces suggestions lui paraissaient « particulièrement importantes » et qu'il s'en est « inspiré dans la préparation du budget de 1938 ». Il souhaite, en effet, procéder à la suppression des « emplois anciens » des bibliothèques musicales par voie budgétaire et a adressé une proposition en ce sens à la direction de l'Enseignement supérieur, le 5 août. À l'appui de sa demande, il relève :

> Le titre d'administrateur des bibliothèques du Conservatoire et de l'Opéra ne correspond à aucun emploi dans les Bibliothèques nationales ; son traitement est inférieur à celui des bibliothécaires. L'appellation elle-même est impropre en ce sens que les bibliothèques musicales sont gérées directement par l'administration de la Bibliothèque nationale. D'autre part, il importe d'organiser pratiquement le rattachement des bibliothèques musicales à la Bibliothèque nationale, sans aucune création d'emploi. Je compte le faire en chargeant l'un des conservateurs-adjoints du département des Imprimés d'adapter l'administration de ces établissements aux règles de la Bibliothèque nationale, et en particulier de coordonner les acquisitions.[37]

Les circonstances sont contraires aux volontés de l'administration de la Bibliothèque nationale : une erreur de transmission empêche l'inscription de la réforme au budget de 1938 et le président de Conseil ne permet d'inscrire aucune création ou transformation d'emploi au budget de 1939[38].

La création du département de la Musique

La guerre diffère les réformes souhaitées par l'administration de la Bibliothèque nationale pour une meilleure intégration des bibliothèques musicales au sein de l'établissement. D'août à octobre 1939, une partie des collections de la bibliothèque de l'Opéra, contenue dans 43 caisses, est transportée par mesure de sécurité au château d'Ussé[39] tandis que sept caisses d'objets d'art appartenant aux collections du musée étaient adressées le 1er octobre 1939 au château de Trévarez, dans le Finistère[40]. Jean Cordey s'occupe de faire revenir les 31 caisses de documents entreposées à Ussé entre novembre 1940 et juin 1941. Les objets abrités au château de Trévarez ne reviennent à Paris qu'en

---

[37] Jean Cordey fut chargé de cette mission.

[38] « Budget de l'Éducation nationale, chapitre 6 (ancien 27) », 25 novembre 1938.

[39] Vingt et une de ces caisses furent transportées de juin à août 1940 au château de Castelnau-Bretenoux.

[40] La BMO conserve un projet d'évacuation des collections, préparé par Amédée Gastoué en septembre 1939, qui prévoyait 75 caisses. BmO, Arch. bibl. 61.

mai 1942 même si dès décembre 1941, les forces d'Occupation ont demandé leur évacuation[41].

Jean Cordey, qui a demandé à l'Administrateur général dans une note du 9 janvier 1939 « de continuer […] la préparation du regroupement des collections musicales avec le Conservatoire, et non musicales avec les bibliothèques nationales de Paris »[42], tente de remédier à l'exiguïté et à l'encombrement des magasins en s'attachant à classer et à ranger méthodiquement les collections mais aussi en faisant transférer aux Imprimés, aux Estampes, aux Monnaies et médailles, à la Mazarine et à l'Arsenal des ouvrages et des périodiques « qui n'ont rien à faire à l'Opéra », en organisant des échanges avec des libraires et en faisant déposer une collection d'instruments exotiques au Musée de l'Homme[43]. Officiellement mis à la retraite le 16 octobre 1941, Jean Cordey fait dès le 28 novembre 1941 la demande de pouvoir continuer à travailler au classement des collections artistiques et au catalogue du musée (auquel il travaille pendant les deux années suivantes)[44].

La nouvelle administration de l'établissement mise en place par le régime de Vichy décide de reprendre en main les bibliothèques musicales et place à leur tête Guillaume de Van[45]. Le 5 janvier 1942, l'administrateur général de la Bibliothèque nationale, Bernard Faÿ, décide :

M. Guillaume de Van, chargé de la direction technique des catalogues musicaux, se mettra en rapport avec M. Cordey et recevra de lui toutes indications propres à lui permettre d'assurer techniquement le fonctionnement de la bibliothèque [de l'Opéra]. La direction administrative de celle-ci sera assurée directement par le secrétariat de la Bibliothèque nationale.[46]

L'administration générale de la Bibliothèque nationale parvient enfin à supprimer les vestiges légaux du régime de la bibliothèque de l'Opéra

---

[41]   BNF, Archives, 2006/086/01 et BmO, Arch. bibl. 64 (15 juillet 1940, 26 juin 1941, 24 décembre 1941, 7 mai 1942, 21 mai 1942). Dans une lettre de Jaujard, directeur des Musées nationaux, à Jean Cordey du 24 décembre 1941, il était question de trois caisses d'objets que les autorités d'Occupation demandaient que l'on évacue du château de Trévarez. En mai 1942, il est question de sept caisses.

[42]   BNF, Archives, A 65/5.

[43]   BmO, Arch. bibl. 64 : Rapport sur le service de la bibliothèque de l'Opéra et lettre du 17 décembre 1941 pour les opérations de transfert ; lettres des 30 septembre et 6 octobre 1941 pour le dépôt d'instruments exotiques au Musée de l'Homme).

[44]   Dans sa note du 9 janvier 1939 à l'administrateur général, Jean Cordey avait déjà demandé à pouvoir s'occuper « du musée qui reste à l'abandon ». BNF, Archives, A 65/5.

[45]   Sur la Bibliothèque nationale pendant l'Occupation, Martine Poulain, *Livres pillés, livres surveillés : les bibliothèques françaises sous l'Occupation*, Paris, Gallimard, 2008. En particulier, p. 133-219.

[46]   BNF, Archives, dossier Jean Cordey.

antérieur à 1935. La loi du 7 mars 1942 relative à la réorganisation de la Réunion des bibliothèques nationales met à la disposition de la Bibliothèque nationale, par ses articles 2 et 3, un personnel nouveau et nombreux et rend possible la création d'un « département de Musique » mais n'unifie pas encore le personnel puisqu'elle ne prononce pas la suppression des anciens emplois des bibliothèques musicales de l'Opéra et du Conservatoire[47]. Un décret élaboré en avril 1942 doit créer officiellement un « département de Musique » à la Bibliothèque nationale et supprimer les emplois « d'administrateur des bibliothèques musicales, de secrétaire de la bibliothèque du Conservatoire et de commis de la bibliothèque de l'Opéra » :

Nous, Maréchal de France, chef de l'État français,

vu le décret du 30 octobre 1935,

vu la loi du 7 mars 1942,

sur le rapport du Ministre Secrétaire d'État à l'Éducation nationale et à la Jeunesse,

décrétons :

Art. 1° – Les bibliothèques musicales de l'Opéra et du Conservatoire national de musique et d'art dramatique, les fonds musicaux conservés dans les divers départements et établissements placés sous l'autorité de l'administrateur général de la Bibliothèque Nationale, seront groupés en un département de Musique.

Art. 2° – Les emplois de conservateur, conservateurs-adjoints, bibliothécaires du département de la Musique sont compris dans les effectifs du personnel des bibliothèques nationales de Paris.

Art. 3° – Les emplois d'administrateur des bibliothèques musicales, de secrétaire de la bibliothèque du Conservatoire et de commis de la bibliothèque de l'Opéra sont supprimés.

Art. 4° – Les frais de matériel occasionnés par le fonctionnement du département de la Musique sont inscrits aux différents chapitres du budget de la Réunion des bibliothèques nationales.

Art. 5° – Est autorisé par voie de mise en dépôt temporaire et permanent tout transfert de collection nécessaire à la conservation, à l'entretien, au regroupement et à la spécialisation des différents fonds musicaux.

Art. 6° – Le secrétaire général aux Beaux-Arts et l'administrateur général de la Réunion des bibliothèques nationales sont chargés, chacun en ce qui le concerne, de l'exécution du présent décret qui sera publié au Journal officiel.[48]

---

[47] BNF, Archives, 2006/038/01 : Loi n° 355 du 7 mars 1942 relative à la réorganisation de la Réunion des bibliothèques nationales (*Journal officiel* du 8 mars 1942, p. 955).

[48] BNF, Archives, A 65/5 : Projet de décret « reçu au classement le 19-V-42 ».

Le décret n'est jamais promulgué mais la suppression est décidée dans le cadre du budget de l'exercice 1943[49] tandis que le décret du 30 juillet 1942 fixant les cadres du personnel de la Réunion des bibliothèques nationales de Paris officialise l'existence du département de la Musique à compter du 16 mars 1942[50]. Guillaume de Van prend la tête du nouveau département tandis que la bibliothèque de l'Opéra est placée sous la responsabilité de Denise Launay.

Nouveau statut et nouvelles missions de la bibliothèque de l'Opéra

Les premières années du rattachement de la bibliothèque de l'Opéra à la Bibliothèque nationale sont marquées par un important travail de remise à niveau des catalogues. Dans ce cadre, les collections musicales font l'objet d'un soin tout particulier : depuis 1934, Amédée Gastoué est chargé non seulement de corriger et de compléter le catalogue rédigé par Théodore de Lajarte dans les premières années de la création de la bibliothèque[51], mais aussi de coter la riche collection musicale de l'Opéra et de la munir d'un catalogue détaillé sur fiches[52]. Gastoué termine son travail en mars 1942 alors que la bibliothèque connaît l'un des pires moments de son histoire.

En effet, la période pendant laquelle Denise Launay est chargée de la bibliothèque, de janvier à décembre 1942[53], coïncide avec la mise en place des mesures à caractère antisémite tant à l'encontre des personnes que des œuvres. Le 9 juillet, une note de service de l'administrateur général Bernard Faÿ stipule que « MM. Les conservateurs et chefs de service voudront bien réserver soit une table spéciale, isolée, soit, de préférence,

---

[49] BNF, Archives, A 65/5 : Note de l'administrateur général de la Bibliothèque nationale au directeur de l'Enseignement supérieur du 19 août 1942 : « Je vous exprime tous mes remerciements pour la mesure que vous m'annoncez avoir proposée dans le budget de l'exercice 1943, portant suppression des emplois propres aux bibliothèques musicales dans la nomenclature du personnel de la Bibliothèque nationale. Il y avait là, en effet, une anomalie qu'il est très satisfaisant de voir disparaître ».

[50] BNF, Archives, Dossier Jacques-Gabriel Prod'homme, note du 29 mars 1945 : « L'existence légale du département de la Musique part du 16 mars 1942, suivant le décret du 30 juillet 1942 fixant les cadres du personnel de la Réunion des bibliothèques nationales de Paris (*Journal officiel* du 6. VIII. 42) ».

[51] Théodore de Lajarte, *Bibliothèque musicale du théâtre de l'Opéra : catalogue historique, chronologique, anecdotique*, Paris, librairie des bibliophiles, 1878. Voir aussi Julien Cain, *La Bibliothèque nationale pendant les années 1935 à 1940, op. cit.*, p. 102.

[52] BMO, Rés. 797 (1), p. 15-16 bis : notice manuscrite sur la révision du catalogue de Théodore de Lajarte, par Amédée Gastoué.

[53] BNF, Archives, dossier Denise Launay et A 13/13 ; BMO, Arch. bibl. 64.

une pièce à l'écart des locaux fréquentés par les autres lecteurs, pour y placer les juifs porteurs de l'étoile jaune »[54]. Le 20 octobre 1942, c'est une note du conservateur en chef du département de la Musique, Guillaume de Van, qui établit que :

> en application d'une circulaire émanant des autorités d'Occupation, il est désormais interdit de communiquer aux lecteurs, sauf sur autorisation de Monsieur l'administrateur général de la Bibliothèque nationale, les ouvrages des catégories suivantes : 1. toute musique d'un auteur juif ainsi que les livres auxquels les juifs ont collaboré ; 2. toute biographie même rédigée par un aryen consacré à un juif ; 3. tous ouvrages traduits de l'anglais.[55]

Une série de scandales a lieu à la bibliothèque au même moment : organisation d'un tripot parmi les membres du personnel, vols de livres, d'estampes, de dessins, de tableaux (dont un Corot, *La pergola des moines*, appartenant à Émile Henriot) et de costumes appartenant au théâtre. Totalement étrangère à ces délits, Denise Launay est pourtant tenue responsable de cette situation et son peu d'aptitude à l'encadrement est stigmatisé. La situation est en fait plus complexe : Guillaume de Van ne cache pas le peu d'estime dans lequel il tient Denise Launay et pense, avant même la constatation des désordres, mettre fin à ses fonctions de responsable de la bibliothèque de l'Opéra au 1er janvier 1943. Le rapport à l'administrateur du 6 décembre 1942 par lequel il dit avoir décidé, pour faute professionnelle de la plus haute gravité, du remplacement immédiat de Denise Launay par Annette Dieudonné, ajoute à l'encontre de la première :

> Je ne peux pas non plus me fier à elle pour l'observance des consignes les plus formels [*sic*] de l'administration ; car, malgré la circulaire concernant les livres juifs, non seulement elle continue à en communiquer, mais elle en recommande à ceux qui viennent chercher une bibliographie.[56]

Guillaume de Van annonce également qu'il congédie toutes les équipes d'étudiants qui travaillent à la bibliothèque et qu'il procède à une redistribution du personnel affecté à cette bibliothèque[57].

En 1946, dans une « note sur les affaires de vol dans les bibliothèques musicales en 1942 », Jean Cordey donne une tout autre version des événements de cette époque :

> Il n'y a dans les archives du département de la musique aucun texte relatif à ces affaires, qui ont été traitées avec une extrême discrétion par MM. Fay et de

---

[54] BMO, Arch. bibl. 64.

[55] BMO, Arch. bibl. 64.

[56] BNF, Archives, A 13/13.

[57] Sur cette affaire, voir également Martine Poulain, *Livres pillés, livres surveillés : les bibliothèques françaises sous l'Occupation, op. cit.*, p. 500, n° 36.

Van, à l'exclusion de toute autre personne du département. Les collaborateurs présents en 1942 que j'ai interrogés, n'ont eu connaissance des méfaits causés, que par les propos d'une femme de ménage [...] qui en fut témoin : vol d'estampes, parties de poker dans des locaux annexes de la bibliothèque de l'Opéra, etc. Les bibliothécaires n'ont donc été renseignés que par ouï-dire. Personnellement j'ai eu l'occasion de constater l'extrême brutalité de l'équipe des soi-disants étudiants introduits par M. de Van dans son département, et pour laquelle il manifestait une sympathie toute particulière. J'ai noté les dégâts que cette équipe a causés dans les dépendances du musée : deux bustes de plâtre mutilés (nez cassés), une statue de plâtre abîmée (doigt cassé) ; un portrait a les yeux crevés, un dossier de fauteuil a été cassé, un tabouret de piano et une chaise démolis. La presque totalité des dessins de costumes pour *Sylvia*, par M. Dethomas, a disparu bien qu'encadrés et estampillés [...] Il me semble que pour avoir des précisions plus détaillées sur les vols de 1942, il y aurait lieu de recourir aux interrogatoires de la commission d'épuration.[58]

Une apostille de Thérèse Kleindienst du 7 janvier 1946 ajoute cependant : « Il n'a pas été fait mention de cette affaire dans les procès-verbaux de la commission d'épuration car le grief n'a pas été retenu : il est impossible d'établir une responsabilité quelconque de M. de Van à ce sujet ». En revanche, une lettre tapuscrite du 18 décembre 1942, sans auteur ni destinataire [certainement Guillaume de Van] clairement désignés, atteste d'une volonté de sélection manifestement antisémite des pièces présentées dans le musée :

Monsieur,

J'ai fait la visite du musée que vous m'avez demandée. Voici la liste des objets qui sont je pense à éliminer : Rosine Bloch (buste marbre), Ed. Colonne (*id.*), Meyerber [*sic*] (buste terre cuite, médaillon, habit d'académicien), Lucienne Bréval (buste, portrait), Halévy (un jeton d'entrée, maquette de *La Juive*). Voulez-vous bien me dire si vous êtes d'accord ? D'autre part, y a-t-il lieu d'éliminer ce qui a trait à Litolf [*sic*], Reyer, Gabrielle Krauss, Hérold, Vestris ? Je vous remercie.

Bien sincèrement vôtre.[59]

Il ne semble pas faire de doute que la personnalité de Denise Launay était incompatible avec celle de Guillaume de Van et que les vols et désordres de 1942, dont les responsabilités sont difficiles à établir de façon certaine, offrent en tout cas un bon prétexte pour remplacer un chef

---

[58] BNF, Archives, A 13/13.

[59] BMO, Arch. bibl. 64. Voir également Jean Laran, *Rapport sur la Réunion des bibliothèques nationales pendant les années 1943 et 1944*, Paris, Impr. des Journaux officiels, 1946, p. 40. [En ligne]. URL : <http://gallica.bnf.fr/ark:/12148/bpt6k 4976184.r=.langFR>. Consulté le 10 août 2010.

de service qui n'applique pas les consignes à caractère antisémite qu'on lui donne. Denise Launay n'est cependant pas révoquée définitivement, comme le réclame Guillaume de Van, mais affectée au service de l'Inventaire. Elle est remplacée par Annette Dieudonné de décembre 1942 à décembre 1943 puis par André Ménétrat qui dirige le service dès la fin du mois de décembre 1943 mais n'en est officiellement chargé qu'à partir du 1er janvier 1944[60].

Les dernières ambiguïtés du statut de la bibliothèque de l'Opéra nées du décret de 1935 ne sont résolues qu'après la guerre. Dès 1939, Jean Cordey a réussi à conforter la mission historique de la bibliothèque de l'Opéra – la conservation du patrimoine de l'Opéra et aussi de l'Opéra-Comique –, mais le statut du musée reste mal défini à la Libération. Guillaume de Van a été suspendu et Jean Cordey accepte d'interrompre sa retraite pour prendre à titre provisoire la direction du département de la Musique de la Bibliothèque nationale à partir du 1er septembre 1944[61]. Il prend définitivement sa retraite le 1er juin 1947 et il est remplacé dans ses fonctions, le 1er juin 1949, par Louis-Marie Michon[62]. Dès les premiers mois de son mandat, le nouveau chef du département de la Musique alerte l'administration de la Bibliothèque nationale sur la situation de la bibliothèque de l'Opéra et demande à ce que le statut du musée soit précisé :

> À la bibliothèque est venu s'adjoindre, depuis 1879, un musée, dont aucun texte ne semble préciser le statut. […] Pour la bibliothèque proprement dite (qui devrait comprendre aussi les fonds de dessins et d'estampes, costumes et décors) et pour le musée, il serait utile que des conversations soient engagées avec la direction générale des Arts et Lettres pour préciser leur statut. Il n'est pas indispensable que les deux services restent liés, et, dans l'avenir, si la bibliothèque doit continuer à s'accroître, peut-être sera-t-on amené à en faire un organisme distinct.[63]

Cette demande reste lettre morte, mais l'entrée du fonds des Archives internationales de la danse dans les collections de la Bibliothèque-musée de l'Opéra en 1952, la création connexe – bien qu'éphémère – d'un musée de la danse dans le Palais Garnier, l'extension des locaux

---

[60]   BNF, Archives, dossiers Annette Dieudonné et André Ménétrat.

[61]   BNF, Archives, dossier Jean Cordey et Martine Poulain, *Livres pillés, livres surveillés : les bibliothèques françaises sous l'Occupation, op. cit.*, p. 342.

[62]   BNF, Archives, dossier Louis-Marie Michon. *Cf.* également Julien Cain, *La Bibliothèque nationale pendant les années 1945 à 1951*, Paris, Impr. des Journaux officiels, 1954, p. 154. [En ligne]. URL : <http://gallica.bnf.fr/ark:/12148/bpt6k497619h.image.f1. langFR>. Consulté le 10 août 2010.

[63]   BMO, Arch. Bibl. 10 : Louis-Marie Michon, Note sur les archives, la bibliothèque et le musée de l'Opéra, 11 août 1950.

de la bibliothèque de l'Opéra dans le théâtre pour accueillir ce fonds et déployer ce nouveau musée renforcent l'institution et lient plus que jamais bibliothèque et musée. L'institution adopte d'ailleurs à cette occasion une nouvelle dénomination, « Bibliothèque-musée de l'Opéra », qui confirme que bibliothèque et musée sont désormais indissociables[64].

Entre 1935 et 1952, la bibliothèque de l'Opéra connaît donc l'une de ses plus profondes réformes : son rattachement à la Bibliothèque nationale et la transformation simultanée de l'Opéra de Paris en établissement public ont contribué au réexamen de ses compétences archivistiques, bibliothéconomiques et muséales. Cependant, sa mission historique – collecter, conserver et valoriser le patrimoine de l'Opéra – n'a pas été fondamentalement remise en cause. Elle est même renforcée. La structure de la RTLN, qui réunit l'Opéra et l'Opéra-Comique, conforte son rôle d'institution patrimoniale des deux théâtres (et non plus du seul Opéra) tandis que le maintien de l'indépendance de la bibliothèque-musée vis-à-vis de la direction du théâtre crée les conditions favorables à une conservation pérenne du patrimoine de l'Opéra et de l'Opéra-Comique.

Annexes

Rapport au président de la République et décret-loi relatifs à la fusion des bibliothèques musicales, 30 octobre 1935[65]

Rapport au président de la République

Paris, le 30 octobre 1935

Monsieur le Président,

Les bibliothèques musicales de l'État comportent actuellement trois dépôts :

l'un à la Bibliothèque nationale,

l'autre au Conservatoire national de musique,

le troisième à la bibliothèque de l'Opéra.

---

[64] Mathias Auclair, « Le fonds des AID à la bibliothèque-musée de l'Opéra : histoire d'une collection », in Inge Baxmann, Claire Rousier et Patrizia Veroli (dir.), *Les Archives internationales de la danse*, Pantin, Centre national de la danse, 2006, p. 168-191 et Mathias Auclair, « L'association des amis de la Bibliothèque-musée de la danse et de la Bibliothèque-musée de l'Opéra (ABMD) », in Ulrike Dembski et Christiane Mühlegger-Henhapel (dir.), *Performing Arts Collections on the Offensive = Les collections d'arts du spectacle passent à l'offensive : 26th SIBMAS Congress, Vienna 2006 = 26e Congrès SIBMAS, Vienne 2006*, Frankfurt am Main, P. Lang, 2007 (Schriftenreihe des Österreichischen Theatermuseums ; 2), p. 137-152.

[65] Texte transcrit d'après le *Journal Officiel* du 31 octobre 1935, p. 11526.

Depuis plusieurs années, les musicographes et les nombreux chercheurs français et étrangers qui s'intéressent aux études musicographiques demandent que ces trois dépôts soient réunis en un seul. Leur travail en serait facilité. D'autre part, les dépenses que comporte l'entretien de ces trois collections seraient atténuées par une réunion des fonds.

Après une étude approfondie, il est apparu qu'il serait désirable d'envisager la réunion complète de ces trois fonds en un seul, qui serait rattaché à la réunion des bibliothèques nationales de Paris et qui pourrait former un département de la Bibliothèque nationale. La fusion de ces trois dépôts facilitera le travail des musicographes et atténuera les dépenses de fonctionnement.

La fusion des personnels pourra être réalisée ainsi que l'exécution d'un catalogue général. Enfin, on pense pouvoir réunir dans un même local l'ensemble des collections, dont l'installation dans les locaux de la Bibliothèque nationale pourra être envisagée lorsque les agrandissements en cours seront achevés ou, si les circonstances le permettent, dans des constructions à élever près de la bibliothèque de l'Arsenal.

Tel est l'objet du projet de décret que nous avons l'honneur de soumettre à votre haute approbation.

Nous vous prions d'agréer, monsieur le Président, l'expression de notre profond respect.

Le président du Conseil, ministre des Affaires étrangères, Pierre Laval.

Le ministre des Finances, Marcel Régnier.

Le ministre de l'Éducation nationale, Mario Roustan.

Le Président de la République française,

Sur le rapport du président du Conseil, ministre des Affaires étrangères, du ministre des Finances et du ministre de l'Éduction nationale,

Vu la loi du 8 juin 1935 autorisant le Gouvernement à prendre par décrets toutes les dispositions ayant force de loi pour défendre le franc ;

Le Conseil des ministres entendu,

Décrète :

Article 1er – Les bibliothèques musicales de l'Opéra et du Conservatoire national de musique et d'art dramatique seront réunies à la Bibliothèque nationale et placées sous l'autorité de l'administrateur général des bibliothèques nationales.

Art. 2 – Un décret contresigné par le ministre de l'Éducation nationale et le ministre des Finances réglera les conditions d'application du présent décret, et notamment les conditions dans lesquelles les personnels de la bibliothèque de l'Opéra et de celle du Conservatoire national de musique et d'art dramatique seront rattachés au personnel des bibliothèques nationales.

Art. 3 – Le présent décret sera soumis à la ratification des Chambres, conformément aux dispositions de la loi du 8 juin 1935.

Art. 4 – Le président du conseil, ministre des Affaires étrangères, le ministre des Finances et le ministre de l'Éducation nationale sont chargés, chacun en ce qui le concerne, de l'exécution du présent décret, qui sera publié au *Journal officiel*.

Fait à Paris, le 30 octobre 1935

Albert Lebrun

Par le président de la République ;

Le président du Conseil, ministre des Affaires étrangères, Pierre Laval.

Le ministre des Finances, Marcel Régnier.

Le ministre de l'Éducation nationale, Mario Roustan.

Abstract

During the 20th century, the Bibliothèque de l'Opéra national de Paris underwent significant administrative transformations: the establishment of an administrator responsible for the "library", the "archives" and the "museum", the transfer of the archival powers of the library to the Archives nationales, etc. The return to the Bibliothèque nationale de France in 1935 in accordance with French law is the most profound of these changes: with this decision, the Bibliothèque de l'Opéra national de Paris is given a new beginning and the creation, a few years later, of the Music department. It also brings up the sometimes misguided ways of its missions, and its functioning until the entry of the collection into the Archives internationales de la danse in 1952. This collection is given a new name, stability and plan to the institution. It is this poorly known history which brings to light sources that have been barely used, that are now preserved in the Bibliothèque-musée de l'Opéra – and in the Mission for the management of the documentary production and the archives of the Bibliothèque nationale de France.

Past – Present – Future

The Austrian Theatre Museum and its Collection of Autographs and Bequests

Christiane MÜHLEGGER-HENHAPEL

Österreichisches Theatermuseum (Vienna – Austria)

Past – History

Performing arts have always been of particular importance in Vienna and the Austrian capital always liked to see itself as one of the leading European centres concerning the field of theatre. But up to the year 1918 not even a separate theatre collection existed among the departments of the Austrian National Library. A huge amount of theatrical materials was spread among different institutions and although, e.g. the collection of manuscripts often purchased theatrical items there was not any intention yet to concentrate all the existing material in one designated place. But in November 1918 things changed when the young Germanist, musicologist and theatre scientist Joseph Gregor started to work at the National Library. From the beginning he focussed on bringing together all existing objects relating to the performing arts. He used the reorganisation of the former imperial and now state-owned possessions to start uniting the theatrical objects of the former imperial library and emphasised on the scientific importance of the archives of the suburban theatres.

In 1920 a large music and theatre exhibition was organised as part of the Vienna Festwochen and on this occasion a huge amount of material was brought together and theatre literature and visual material presented in a very illustrative way. The next step towards the foundation of a separate theatre collection happened in 1921 when the National Library decided to acquire the private collection of the actor and former director of the Burgtheater, Hugo Thimig.

Thimig was one of the first collectors of theatrical items and after more than 50 years of intensive collecting he owned one of the most extensive private collections concerning the German speaking theatre. About 120,000 objects including almanacs, books, biographies, publications concerning the history of theatre and dramaturgy, journals, drama texts, leaflets, theatre bills, manuscripts and graphic objects. In winter 1921-1922 the official decision about the foundation of a separate theatre collection was finally made. The Thimig collection should become its impressive basis and Joseph Gregor its first director. Due to his tireless personal commitment the holdings of the theatre collection increased to a considerable amount within only a few years. The main aim of the theatre collection and later on that of the museum concerning acquisition was a complete as possible documentation of performing arts (above all in Austria). Over the years new objects – most of them through bequests of theatre members, theatre directors or actors such as Josef Kainz – contributed to the expansion of the collection. These contributions were often items which normally were not among library holdings such as costumes, paintings, statuettes or mementos. Joseph Gregor, who made his enquiries in all possible geographic and contextual directions, also soon realised the increasing importance of the new media of that time, above all film. With consent of the general director of the National Library he affiliated the "Archiv für Filmkunde" to the theatre collection in 1929 and started a collection of all possible kinds of film items – except the reels. This collection quickly increased and in 1949 the archive became the "Institut für Filmkunde" but shortly afterwards was disbanded again. In 1955 – again in collaboration with Gregor – the Österreichische Filmarchiv was founded and consequently the collecting domains were separated: presently, the Filmarchiv is the only institution to collect film items.

In connection with the theatre collection and its successive expansion the foundation of a separate theatre museum was discussed for many years. In 1931 some rooms in the Burgtheater were finally dedicated to a "National Theatre Museum" – but closed again in 1938.

It was only in 1975 when an "Austrian Theatre Museum" was founded with the main task to organise exhibitions by using the materials of the departments of the National Library. This museum was situated in the Hanuschgasse near the State Opera but rather soon the rooms proved to be too small. Therefore the Republic of Austria bought the nearby Palais Lobkowitz and had it completely refurbished. On October 26th 1991 the Austrian Theatre Museum was officially inaugurated and the holdings of the former theatre collection of the national library were merged with those of the theatre museum in the Hanuschgasse. This finally was the birth of one of the world's largest museums of performing arts which has the opportunity to present the various collections in beautiful and representative exhibition rooms. At the beginning of the year 2001 the

Austrian Theatre Museum finally became part of the Kunsthistorisches Museum[1].

Present

This survey on the history of the Theatre Museum presents a successful past and promising future of this institution. But in the course of analysing the future prospects one also has to take a closer look at a number of questions which are results of former decisions with a considerable impact on the current working conditions.

Let me now in greater detail explain the actual situation from the view of my field of responsibility – the collection of "Autographs and bequests".

As a result of Joseph Gregor's busy collecting activities the theatre collection had to deal with a rapidly growing number of objects within a rather short time and on the other hand a permanent lack of staff. Gregor had most of the time only two permanent staff members and the situation did not get any better over the following decades. In relation to the huge amount of items we are in charge of within the different collections of the museum we are also understaffed today.

Everybody taking part in this conference knows about the basic problem of performing arts collections: the diversity of objects and the overlap of the different fields within the various collections. The name "Collection of autographs AND bequests" already shows these difficulties.

In general extensive bequests always have been and still are divided between the different collections within the museum. As a consequence often no complete and precise reconstruction is possible. For only a few important and valuable collections were catalogues established but most of the time these remained single projects. In order to achieve a complete record of the collections of the theatre museum there still is a long way to go.

A publication about the National Library dating from 1987 describes the holdings of the collection of autographs as follows:

> The collection contains about 65,000 autographs which originally mostly belonged to bequests. Such a bequest not only includes hand written or typed correspondence, manuscripts or notes, etc. but also different documents such as visual material or collections of newspaper cuttings, etc. The range

---

[1] *Cf.* Christiane Mühlegger-Henhapel, «Die Sammlung als Denkmal: Joseph Gregor und das Österreichische Theatermuseum,» in Christiane Mühlegger-Henhapel (ed.), *Joseph Gregor: Gelehrter – Dichter – Sammler*, Frankfurt/Main, Peter Lang, 2006, p. 33-45.

of autographs comprises hand- or machine written letters, post cards and telegrams but also manuscripts, notes and scripts of plays.[2]

This description shows both the huge content of the collection and the difficulties in treating such diverse material. As a consequence one first started to take a comprehensive inventory only of the most valuable, interesting or requested objects, such as, for example, the correspondence. The remaining items were only physically sorted in labelled boxes without any inventory numbers.

Dividing an extensive bequest seems inevitable concerning its preservation but at the same time it presents new problems.

The collection of autographs and bequests holds a special position within the museum as we tend not only the autograph and manuscript collection of the museum but are also responsible for all incoming bequests and their distribution – that's why we often serve as a "focal point" for all objects that can't be classified clearly. Because of holdings such as the bequest of Hermann Bahr or Stefan Zweig's autograph collection we also have to serve as a literary archive. For a more precise description of the contents of the collection the curators would prefer the name "Collection of autographs" but so far this couldn't be solved internally.

Another discrepancy results from the fact that since the theatre collection was founded autographs have never been systematically or consistently acquired. For Gregor one point was certain: "Autographs came to the theatre collection only in combination with a collection, an archive, a bequest or a donation"[3]. As a consequence musical items were handed over to the music department of the National Library, valuable manuscripts to the manuscript department. While the theatre collection was still part of the National Library the interconnection between the departments worked well, catalogue entries referred to each other easily. But presently after the separation of the theatre collection from the national library and its autonomy as a museum with respect to its affiliation to the Kunsthistorisches Museum this increasingly became a problem. The original unity of a bequest can often hardly be reconstructed; research work becomes considerably complicated.

The staff of the museum often suggested the installation of a registrar but because of financial straits it does not seem to be realistic any time soon.

---

[2]   Peter Nics, « Vorhang auf! Die Theatersammlung, » in *Ein Weltgebäude der Gedanken Die Österreichische Nationalbibliothek*, Graz, *Akad. Druck- u. Verl.-Anst.*, 1987, p. 233-259 (trans. by Christiane Mühlegger).

[3]   Joseph Gregor, « Entwicklung der Theatersammlung der Nationalbibliothek in Wien, » in *Zentralblatt für Bibliothekswesen* 57 (1940), p. 36-44 (trans. Christiane Mühlegger).

The desirable procedure should work as follows: the registrar organises the incoming collections, meaning he issues the entry number, roughly sorts out the items before handing them over to the different departments of the museum for further working steps: assignment of inventory numbers, entry into the database, etc. With the help of a recorded entry number on every single object the provenance of the total stock of the original bequest can easily be reconstructed if necessary.

The current situation again presents the same questions: currently the staff of the collection for autographs and bequests fulfils the task of the registrars – this means issuing the entry number, sifting through the material, categorising, handing it over to the other departments etc. In the best case only the written material remains in the autograph collection. The further handling of the documents is then within the responsibility of each department. The next decision which has to be taken within the collection concerns the extent to which the bequest needs to be edited – this depends on the importance of its content or the urgency of conservation. Because of the huge amount of single objects and the backlog of work this often means only physical categorisation with labelling the archive boxes, less often extensive inventory or data entries and digitisation.

Besides working on bequests, i.e. collection maintenance, the curators of the Austrian Theatre Museum have the following tasks:

– Conceptual planning of exhibition and exhibition catalogues
– Support of researchers and readers in the department
– Answering requests
– Handling loan requests

Because of the actual urgency of these tasks the workup of the collections often needs to be postponed due to the lack of urgent necessity. As a result the backlog of decades can only slowly be managed. In the first place we always try to handle new accessions and not to increase the backlog of work.

This implies the often discussed problem how to treat the researchers in the collection. To what extent may the documents be provided for research? Should it only imply the inventoried material or also the documents without inventory number? We decided not to act too restrictively in order to guarantee constant research work. But still these decisions always are a balancing act. On the one hand researchers appreciate our cooperation and the possibility to get access to unknown archive documents. But on the other hand concerning the vast number of un-inventoried material and possible losses this approach seems to be somewhat precarious. It is always a matter of confidence and the subjective impression of a person:

we have personally known some of them for years and they even often make valuable contributions to our work.

What is the current approach in order to ensure the future preservation and use of our documents?

In the age of new media one of the most important and absolutely essential steps is the digitisation and/or digital provision of our objects.

In 1999 the Austrian Theatre Museum started into the "digital age" with the introduction of the database M-BOX which made possible a data entry that was perfect for the special needs of the museum and its various collections. Only two years later the theatre museum was affiliated with the Kunsthistorisches Museum and therefore had to take over another new database, TMS – The Museum System. This system unfortunately started with an enormous data loss because the import of data from the M-BOX didn't work. At first TMS didn't seem suitable for the needs of the theatre museum as it was customised for fine art museums. But the staff of the museum participated actively in adapting the database for the needs of the different collections. The user interface and data fields were adjusted – a rather complicated and time-consuming process and unfortunately not entirely satisfactory. But after some initial reservations TMS has now been accepted and is being utilised accordingly. The number of data records now stands at about 160,000. The more data recorded the more possibilities that result from an optimal link of contents become clear: loans, preparing exhibitions, conservation and restoration work, and researchers benefit from the database.

Regarding the collection of autographs we chose the following approach: currently 2.5 staff members are confronted with a huge amount of un-inventoried material as well as busy exhibition activities – during my first six years as curator in the theatre museum I was either responsible for or collaborated in seven exhibitions and catalogues. Because of this time-consuming work which has to be done simultaneously to all the current tasks we decided to act project-related in order not to lose track. Decisions are taken according to the contextual/historical importance of the objects. The main goal always has to be to ensure findability and accessibility of the material – and there we have already been rather successful. For the future we will realistically continue to be very selective in order to handle the backlog and at the same time advance digitisation.

Projects

The bequest of Hermann Bahr, one of the few complete bequests, is of particular importance within the collection of autographs. A large part of the current projects and requests focusses on this material. It is certainly among the best inventoried material of the collection. All projects are accompanied by a checking of inventory numbers, database entry and – if possible – digitisation of the objects.

- Correspondence between Hermann Bahr and the Czech author, theatre personality and politician Jaroslav Kvapil (Kurt Ifkovits, published 2007)
- The diaries of Hermann Bahr until 1908 have already been published. A further sifting of the bequest now found new, additional material, therefore a supplemental volume is planned; the edition of the diaries from the period 1909-1911 is in progress.
- Correspondence between Hermann Bahr and Hugo von Hofmannsthal – this is a project of the University of Basel in Cooperation with the team of the critical Hofmannsthal edition, the editors of the correspondence between Hofmannsthal's parents (Freies Deutsches Hochstift Frankfurt), the editors of the Hermann Bahr diaries and the staff of the Austrian Theatre Museum
- An Internet project of the University of Vienna. The aim is a catalogue of Hermann Bahr's more than 3,000 articles and essays published during his lifetime as well as a 23 volume edition of his most important critical writings. Referring to the bequest material in the autograph collection, it is planned to scan newspaper cuttings and copies of letters. The digital images will be available on the Internet; the homepages of the theatre museum and of the Bahr project will refer one to another. <www.univie.ac.at/bahr>

Further Projects

- Edition of the correspondence between Alfred Roller and Hugo von Hofmannsthal (Mühlegger/Giacon).
- The Austrian Theatre Museum owns Alfred Roller's artistic and written bequest with a large number of letters from Hugo von Hofmannsthal. The annotated edition will also include the letters of Alfred Roller which are kept in the collections of the Freies Deutsches Hochstift in Frankfurt.
- Since the revision of the homepage of the Kunsthistorisches Museum we are able to supply even more information concerning our collections via the Internet. The autograph collection benefits from that fact through linking already existing content lists of bequests with the information on the homepage. Most of them

are only word documents but nevertheless provide interesting additional information for the users. The benefit of these links becomes noticeable as we get much more direct requests and at the same time the collections of the theatre museum are available to a wider audience and stay present in the digitised public consciousness. (Fig. 1)

<http://www.theatermuseum.at/sammlungen/handschriften-und-nachlaesse/verzeichnis-der-nachlaesse/>

– The Register of Artistic, Literary, Academic and Cultural-Political Estates in Austria is a project of the Austrian National Library with the theatre museum as one of the financing partners. The aim of the project – in collaboration with more than 50 partner institutions – is the central and comprehensive documentation of bequests within the field of culture and science in Austria. A specially installed OPAC system (available from mid-2010) will offer user-friendly search entries and requested information can easily be obtained. In addition there will also be links to biographical information. After the completion of this project the database will manage several thousand data entries. (Fig. 2)

<http://aleph20-prod-acc.obvsg.at/F?CON_LNG=ger&func=find-b-0&local_base=nlv>

Future Prospects

The Austrian Theatre Museum keeps collections of enormous thematic and formal diversity. Unexpected finds of relevance may still be possible. And therefore the primary concern for the future should be to continuously record the museum's collections and to make them accessible to a wide public. The interest in the contents of the collections should increase and despite financial straits lead to a targeted collection policy in order to continuously develop the content of the collections. Despite great treasures the theatre museum suffers from the over-use of its holdings, contemporary items are rarely acquired. Focussing only on the great theatrical past of the last centuries will not work in the future. Time consuming and cost intensive exhibitions can make one blind to the needs of the collections. Despite successful, scientifically founded and well attended exhibitions – which of course greatly increase the name recognition – the theatre museum needs to preserve its self-conception as a theatre collection in order to find its way into a successful future.

Figure 1.

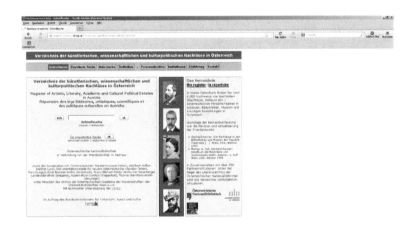

Figure 2.

Abstract

Le Musée autrichien du Théâtre est l'un des plus grands parmi les musées et collections mondiaux de sa catégorie. Depuis sa fondation, en 1922, jusqu'à nos jours, l'institution doit gérer un très grand nombre d'objets tout en faisant face à un manque permanent de personnel. Sa position intermédiaire entre archives et musée du théâtre, qui organise des expositions plusieurs fois par an, pose des défis supplémentaires. La collection d'autographes et de legs du musée est un bon exemple de l'effort fourni pour conserver des objets du passé en vue d'être présentés à un public actuel et pour pouvoir répondre à des demandes futures.

Second Session

Deuxième session

Connecting Platform

Theatre Institute in Warsaw

Agata ADAMIECKA & Dorota BUCHWALD

Theatre Institute (Warsaw – Poland)

The Theatre Institute was founded as an institution meant to link the past and future of Polish theatre. Since the beginning of our seven-year history we have been committed to overcoming the traditional distinctions and separations between disciplines and institutions dealing with theatre. For example, it is the largest national theatre archive and information centre for contemporary theatre in Poland; it hosts academic programmes and carries out international programs of workshops for professionals in the theatre industry and trains specialists in the subject of theatre pedagogy and theatre dramaturgy. The Institute is actively involved in contemporary theatre life: it organises one of the largest national festivals, carries out a staging competition sponsored by the Ministry of Culture and implements a programme financed by the Ministry aimed at increasing the mobility of theatre productions to places in Poland without permanent theatres. Through meetings, discussions, conferences, and readings, the Institute moderates the debate on contemporary Polish theatre and creates a space where various members of the community can meet: academics, professionals, critics, and fans. Our activities are geared towards three main target groups: contemporary theatre, the academic community and schools.

Contemporary Polish Theatre Projects

Polish Theatre

The aim of the project is to reach those who do not have contact with the theatre and to encourage theatres themselves to be active outside of their own cities and physical buildings. The inspiration for this so-called network of theatre tours was the activities of the Reduta Theatre, which existed in between the First and Second World Wars and was established by the famous actor Juliusz Osterwa. Osterwa was also a pioneer in the fields of geology, theory of theatre and Mieczyslaw Limanowski's philosophy. Reduta travelled all over the territory of Poland, which had recently been united after 123 years of annexation. It had a special repertoire dedicated to inhabitants of small cities and town comprised of staged international and Polish classics as well as contemporary plays that dealt with social issues.

The project, funded by the Ministry of Culture and National Heritage, takes the form of a two-tiered competition: theatres submit the staging of certain plays from their repertoire along with the budget needed to send the play on a tour and a special artistic commission selects their choices which it then submits to an Organisational Committee who makes the final decision on who to fund. Seventy-seven plays were submitted to the first edition of the program in 2009 from which the commission chose twenty plays. Out of those, sixteen theatres were selected by the Organisational Committee to be funded. The tours took place from September to December and the theatres visited seventy-three towns in Poland, one hundred and seven plays were staged which were viewed by over 21,000 audience members.

An additional benefit of the project was the promotion of cultural centres that exist outside of large metropolitan areas and have professional theatre halls.

Słowacki – All Dramas

The year 2009 saw two anniversaries connected to the dates of one of Poland's Romantic poets: the 200th anniversary of Juliusz Słowacki's birth and the 160th anniversary of his death. Therefore 2009 was declared the Year of Słowacki resulting in a new publication about him, modern performances of his dramas and other methods to include him into the contemporary cultural debate. We took the term "include in the debate" literally here at the Theatre Institute and proposed to "read out" his dramas which are quite prolific as there are twenty-three of them, though most are only known by a small group of literary researchers. However we weren't concerned with a simple dictation of the texts but a reinterpretation to find a language for them which would reflect contemporary sensitivities and which would spark a discussion about their current value. Experts were paired up with each other, comprised of directors and dramaturges, literary experts, historians of theatre, culture and philosophy academics, etc., who met an average of once a week from June 2009 to May 2010 and together with actors presented Słowacki's work through performative readings after only a few analytical rehearsals. The commentary after the reading, as part of the contemporary interpretation, often took the form of an academic lecture or a discussion on the emotional reactions to the play.

Competition

In order to encourage theatre directors to enrich their repertoire and to find inspiration in forgotten literary works, the first edition of the *National Competition of Staging Old European Literary Works* was launched in 2004. Drama theatres (institutional and non-institutional) along with puppet theatres were eligible to submit their plays under the condition that the material on which they base their play on was written before 1969 and that it hasn't been staged within the last nineteen years (in order to ensure that it is authentically "old").

The entries are judged by a special jury that decides on the quality, quantity and amount of the award (awards are granted in categories of the whole play, for staging, music, direction, and actor's roles). Apart from financial awards, there are also recommendations to professionally register their plays and to show them during the Institute's Warsaw Theatre Meetings. The Ministry of Culture and National Heritage finance the competition of which five editions have taken place so far.

Warsaw Theatre Meetings

Warsaw Theatre Meetings (WTM) is one of the oldest and most important theatre festivals in Poland. It started in 1965 and from its beginning the festival was a non-competitive event – a showcase of the best and most fascinating plays from theatres outside of Warsaw. Acclamations were granted and its hierarchy in the league of theatres across the country was established. There were years when it did not take place, most often due to political and historical circumstances and since 2008, the meetings have been organised by the Theatre Institute by request of the City Hall of Warsaw City, with Institute Director Maciej Nowak as its artistic director. Apart from the main idea of presenting the best plays of the season, the artistic director has also included many other side events such as a parallel thematic festival. In 2008, it was an overview of independent theatre from Wroclaw; in 2009 saw a series of plays from Bialystok's Lalek Theatre while 2010 was planned to showcase the best of Walbrzych's Drama Theatre. Unfortunately the 30th edition of the WTM was cancelled. This was the very difficult decision of the director after the catastrophe in which the presidential plane of Poland crashed, killing all 96 passengers which included the President and First Lady along with the whole head of the armed forces and many other prominent political leaders. The accident occurred a day before the festival was to begin. A national mourning was announced on that day, while funerals were constantly held in Warsaw for the following two weeks. The independent decision of the director was accepted by city government officials as well as the Minister of Culture but was extremely controversial in the theatre community, especially amongst its younger members. They argued that cancelling the event during a national mourning denigrates theatre to the rank of simple entertainment while theatre could and should be one of the places where people can collectively work through traumatic experiences. Theatre, with its ability to react to the changing contexts in which it exist and with the strong presence of death and transience, could create an alternative community space in this country dominated by the Catholic Church's stronghold over community space. Those in favour of cancelling the festival argued that this was one of the rare events in the history of the nation in which being alternative and a diversity of voices were not higher values than the collective mourning. Two other historic moments were mentioned in which Polish theatres were closed: during World War Two and during martial law in 1981. We decided to open up the issue to a public debate by organising discussions with philosophers, cultural studies scholars, and sociologists to talk about the interpretation by Poles of mourning and the role of the theatre during these specific times.

Dramaturge Forum

Not long ago, only a few years back, a new position was introduced into Polish theatres which had been known outside of the country for years, that being the dramaturge: someone different than the literary director who was traditional present in our theatres and different than the playwright who would supply the theatre with a repertoire. For this reason, our Institute organised special workshops for those who sought to attain or improve their skills in this field by exposing them to various models and ways of working as a dramaturge in the theatre. The sessions were lead by excellent foreign and Polish experts, including Hans-Thies Lehmann, Carl Hegemann (dramaturge for, amongst others, Frank Castorf) and Synne K. Behrndt (a dramaturge involved in the British Devised Theatre movement).

Our goal was to, on one hand, offer an opportunity to meet with outstanding dramaturges, and on the other hand to support the development of the dramaturge profession in the context of the Polish theatre. The meetings took place monthly throughout the year of 2009. Ninety people applied for the workshops although there was only space for thirty-two.

Academia Project

As the archives housed by the Theatre Institute mainly serve theatre scholars and students, the academic community is a main target group of our activities. From our very beginning, the aim of the Institute was not only to create a modern, open and accessible archive but also to include an element of academic analysis through research and publishing projects. We set out to research both past and current Polish theatre practice and creating a theatre studies programme inspired by contemporary humanities. Our programmes serve to support the theoretical and methodological methods not widely present or represented in the domestic research on theatre. We have been carrying out the *Different Stage* programme for five years now and which attempts to apply an interdisciplinary methodology including gender studies and queer theory to the scholarly work on the Polish theatre. An annual conference is held in this programme as well as workshops and seminars. A book is published after each conference and the series already contains three volumes, with the fourth in progress.

The New History programme was constructed in a similar way, with an aim to enhance and modernise Polish theatre history in its meta-critical and methodological aspects. The project is a response to the long-term and repeatedly diagnosed impasse in Polish research on theatre history. The first conference, which was organised as part of the project, took place last year entitled Establishing History. Creating the History of Theatre. The purpose of the conference was to reflect on the issue of the conscious, and what might be more important, unconscious creation of the history of theatre by those who study it. As planned, theoretical analysis on the conditions of the history of theatre was linked with the analysis of historical theatre practice, so that an important theme throughout the conference became an examination of the achievement of Polish theatre history, the definitions and hierarchies included in it, as well as the issues that are absent. We invited experienced scholars to comment on their own achievements but also young academics that represented methodologies not present in Polish theatre history. During the next conference we would like to continue to critically reflect on what is traditionally considered the "facts" of history. The conference is entitled The Meaning of Facts. We encourage participants to reflect on the facts present in the historical-theatrical discourse not only theoretically, but also through a study of specific examples connected directly to the history of theatre.

Apart from long-term research projects, the Institute carries out a publishing programme which includes an on-going, open contest. We base our decisions on the same criteria as with the conference: we support projects which deal with issues not present or not well represented in Polish theatre studies and which introduce a native theatre studies inspired by the influences of aesthetic, cultural and social theories of contemporary humanities. All of the publishing projects at the Institute are made up of two phases. During the first phase the author of the project presents their thesis and research results in an event open to the public, a lecture or workshop. The second phase consists of publishing a written document. This format activates and integrates the academic and theatre communities, ensures a public debate and allows for a confrontation of the research hypotheses before they are finally sent to print. An example of an outcome from this process is the latest synthesis of Polish theatre written by Dariusz Kosinski entitled *Polish Theatre. History*. This is the first book published in the last 30 years that includes the whole history of Polish theatre, taking into account performance studies, new historicism and other poststructural inspirations. Without being modest, this can be considered one of the most important publications of Polish academia on the subject of theatre. We are currently working on its international version and we hope that it will be available on the international market soon.

Program for Collaboration with Schools and (Very) Young Audiences

One of the goals of the Institute is to reach those who are interested in theatre and to create the opportunity for dialogue and to get in touch with each other. Which is why we spend as much time and energy within the academic community as we do on theatrical pedagogy. This manifests itself on all levels of education, including a pioneer programme of theatre workshops for infants and their parents, in creating partnerships between schools and professional theatres, and workshops for employees of theatres who lead educational programmes. The fundamental concept of the project is to ensure a real participation of children and youth in the creative process of the theatre as well as establishing a professional theatre for young audiences where they will be able to get to know not only the repertoire but also how the theatre works. Our educational programme consists of several projects:

1. *Theatre and School* is a pioneering project in Poland creating a stable partnership between schools and theatres. As part of the project, youth get to know the specifics of the theatre as an institution and art form. Each school-theatre pair carries out their own programme however each one has the common feature of classes in writing plays and attending the shows of the partner theatre.

2. *TISZ Annex* is a separate branch of the *Theatre and School* project. It is a series of specialised workshops for theatre employees who create educational projects in their institutions. The workshops are lead by experts in the field of theatrical education from various countries and have a practical format containing substantial, organisational and financial aspects of educational initiatives. This

series offers the only opportunity in Poland to complete a full, 130-hour course in theatrical education.

3. Another educational project is the *Summer in the Theatre* project, heavily subsidised by the Ministry of Culture, which takes the form of a semi-summer camp for children and youth. Theatres prepare two-week long artistic workshops on different themes having to do with the production of a theatre show: acting, costume and stage design, music, PR and journalism and technical support. The workshops conclude in presenting what the participants have learned once in a theatre and another time in another venue in a certain city. This is an opportunity to take part in educational theatre workshops in the summer, which include creative workshops, meetings with artists and collectively preparing a theatre play. It creates a space where an intensive dialogue can take place between artists and children and youth as well as between young artists and amateurs with society in which they function on a day to day basis.

4. Theatricals are weekly theatre games for children and their parents. The outstanding aspect of this idea is having a group for children below the age of 1. The sessions for infants are movement and musical games in tandem with parents or parent/child. They include elements of physical training and voice work to assist the child in its development and supply the parent with a new activity to play with their child and build their relationship.

All of the activities of the Institute are ruled by the conviction that the history of theatre will only be interesting when contemporary theatre itself is fascinating. That is why we have such a diverse range of activities and a healthy balance between documentation, conservation and research of the past in theatre and constructing its contemporary elements. The Theatre Institute in Warsaw was created as and is developing as a connecting platform, uniting the past, present and future of Polish theatre.

Abstract

L'objectif initial de l'Institut du Théâtre de Varsovie était d'être une institution unissant le passé et le futur du théâtre polonais. Après sept années d'activités, l'idée est venue de dépasser les traditionnelles distinctions et divisions entre les disciplines et institutions relatives au théâtre. L'Institut œuvre à la constitution des plus importantes archives théâtrales nationales, tout en étant un centre d'informations sur le théâtre contemporain ; il propose des programmes académiques visant à étudier l'histoire du théâtre polonais ainsi qu'à appliquer à la réflexion sur le théâtre les méthodologies interdisciplinaires des sciences humaines contemporaines ; il organise des ateliers internationaux destinés aux professionnels du théâtre et aux praticiens, dans les domaines de l'enseignement du théâtre et de la dramaturgie.

L'Institut s'implique fortement dans la vie théâtrale contemporaine, en organisant l'un des plus grands festivals polonais ainsi qu'un concours pour la mise en scène d'œuvres classiques de la littérature européenne. Conjointement avec le ministère de la Culture, il réalise en outre un programme relatif au financement de tournées des meilleurs spectacles de la saison, permettant à ceux qui n'ont habituellement pas de contact avec le théâtre de s'y confronter. Il permet également aux compagnies de théâtre polonaises de travailler avec les centres culturels locaux implantés en dehors des grandes villes.

Par le biais de réunions, de conférences, de lectures publiques, l'Institut modère le débat sur le théâtre polonais contemporain et crée un espace de rencontre pour les différents cercles engagés dans les arts de la scène : les chercheurs, les professionnels, les critiques, les amateurs. Toutes les activités de l'Institut sont guidées par l'idée que l'histoire du théâtre ne sera attrayante que si le théâtre contemporain l'est également. C'est en quoi l'Institut du Théâtre de Varsovie a été pensé et agit comme une plateforme reliant le passé, le présent et le futur du théâtre polonais.

The Theatre Subject at the Art Library

From Collection to Users' Expectation

Yulia KATKOVSKAYA

Russian State Art Library (Moscow – Russia)

The Russian State Art Library, a keeper of historical and art properties, is a leading scientific and informational organisation in Russia. In 1991, the State Central Theatre Library was reorganised and now is a main library collecting documents on all aspects of art and theatre. The Russian State Art Library is part of Russia's cultural history and still plays a great role in today's cultural life.

The Library's life has long been connected with the famous Maly Theatre, originating from its theatre book collection. The Russian State Art Library was founded on the initiative of the famous theatrical teacher, the Dean of the Maly's theatrical school, Professor Alexandr Alexandrovich Fomin, who was also the Library's Director. He united the famous scientists of his time and put the minds of politicians to creating the library, including well-known Commissar of Education, Anatoly Lunacharskiy. The ceremonial opening of the Library was held in the centre of Moscow in the Higher Maly Theatre Workshop on May 24th, 1922. Many prominent theatrical masters who participated in opening ceremony left their autographs in the memory book. The future of the Library was bright. The Library has been serving Moscow theatres since 1925 and counts among their users major masters of the stage such as E. N. Gogoleva, N. M. Dudinskaya, Yu. A. Zavadsky, I. S. Kozlovsky, I. M. Moskvin, N. P. Ohlopkov, V. N. Pashennaya, P. M. Sadovsky, A. K. Tarasova, E. D. Turchaninova, N. P. Hmelev, famous artists such as P. V. Wiliams, E. E. Lansere, I. I. Nivinsky, Yu. I. Pimenov, A. G. Tyshler, V. A. Schuko, K. F. Yuon and many others. The Library wasn't closed during the Second World War, but the rooms were almost unheated, stocks were kept carefully and work was not interrupted while he Library served military theatres, propaganda brigades and ensembles, *Sovinforburo* correspondents, and soldiers.

Today, the Library stocks consist of books, magazines, newspapers and cuttings, theatre programmes, prints, drawings, watercolours, postcards, and photographs. These materials reflect the nature of the Library; they are in active use by the creative professionals and they are a unique base for art researchers and the general humanitarian. The Library became a laboratory for art and science; and now, creative groups and artists use it to create films, plays, television programmes, books, and art and architecture projects. Over time the Library's activities have been expanded including the ability to serve readers. The Library is an information, science and consultation centre for art and positions itself as a research centre on theatrical problems.

The Library holds one or two biennial conferences. One conference, held for the first time in November 1995, was A Theatrical Book Between the Past and the Future, in which two inseparable cultural themes sound in the problems of scientific readings of the theatre and the book. Over the years, the readings focused on the creation and existence of a theatrical play, history of theatrical libraries and their collections, presence and reflection of the theatre in the so-called literary monuments, places of theatre in book and electronic environments.

Another, the conference, Michoels Readings, held for the first time in December 1997, attracts many specialists involved with issues of national theatre problems and international theatrical connections. In contrast to the first Michoels Readings, which was dedicated to the life and works of S. M. Michoels, later readings became to cover wider spectre of problems such as existence of national theatre in a foreign language environment, the sources of the theatre and theatrical and literature monuments, and archives and collections of national theatre history.

Among the authors of publications in conference proceedings are famous scientists and also Russian State Art Library specialists such as theatre critics and art historians, philologists and linguists. The majority of them actively participate in cultural and public life of Moscow and Russia, publish reviews and professional critical articles on art and theatre, and teach at universities. The conference proceedings are highly appreciated in the press.

The Russian State Art Library actively participates in contemporary theatrical life by finding new names in contemporary theatrical art and literature. The Russian State Art Library, together with the Moscow theatre, School of Modern Drama is a co-founder of annual contest *Dramatis personae*. The contest started in 2003 when the Russian national awards for achievements in the field of drama was established by initiation of the theatre School of Modern Drama. Following the competition, the top ten pieces are published in the annual publication *Contest* "Dramatis personae".

Additionally, the Russian State Art Library maintains an active exhibition programme. The Library's exhibition projects are always the current response to events in the domestic and foreign cultural space. For example, there was an exhibition of the 200th anniversary of the birth of Alexandr Pushkin titled A. S. Pushkin. *Boris Godunov*: The History of the Creation and Dramatic Realisation on the Russian Stage; an exhibition of the 200th anniversary of the birth of Nikolay Gogol named *Revisor* of Gogol. Realisation: Theatre and Cinematography, and an anniversary exhibition of one of the largest publishers – Cambridge Publishing.

The Russian State Art Library also holds exhibitions specifically dedicated to conferences in the Library such as "Shot literature". Jewish writers in Lazar Ran graphics and Reading the fate of the stage… the unknown materials on Jewish theatre history in Belorussia. Twentieth Century.

There is always one aim of the library: how to show the theatre in all its diversity to interest and educate the user. Library stocks keep many materials on which interesting and complete exhibitions can be based such as unique graphics, sketches, photographs, postcards, and rare books, but in the modern world cooperation and partnership is extremely important, and they can develop interactively and in a virtual space. One example is professional relationships on the Internet, such as large-scale projects like the Union Catalogue of Russian Libraries. The exhibition activity of RSAL is not only aimed to open the library stocks to the reader, although this is the primary goal, but also to show documents from other collections.

Perhaps one of the most spectacular kinds of theatrical art is scenography. The Library held various exhibitions devoted to the scenographers, O. Sheinzis, and the Brothers Volskiy. Also, the sketches of Saint Petersburg's theatrical artists M. Azizian, V. Dorrer, E. Kapelush, M. Kitaev, E. Kochergin, and O. Savarenskaya were exhibited. All original material is available to users.

The exhibition, Directing Space: the Scenography and Painting of Oleg Sheinzis introduced readers and library guests with the works of one of the best scenographers of late 20th-early 21st centuries. The great artist only once managed to show his works on a personal exhibition. The exposition in RSAL was the first after he was passed away. Oleg Aronovich Scheinzis was among the RSAL readers since 1972 – since his enter in Moscow Art Theatre School, and he died at 57 in 2006. Among the works presented at the exhibition are sketches of costume and scenery sketches for the outstanding performances of the Moscow State Theatre *Lenkom*: *Juno and Avos*, *Memorial Prayer*, *Hamlet*, and also for the performances of the other theatres such as *Love for Three Oranges* in the Bolshoi Theatre; *Marriage* in the Moscow Academic Theatre of V. Mayakovsky and *Theatre on Pokrovka*; *Madame Butterfly* in the London Opera House, etc. On exhibition one can also see portraits, urban landscapes, joke greeting cards, posters of guest performances, and photographs from the family archives. Some of the exhibits where placed on the walls of one of the RSAL reading rooms, and the readers have got opportunity to do their work while surrounded by the works of outstanding master. This idea was welcomed by Mark Zakharov, who is the Chief Director of the Lenkom theatre, in which Oleg Sheinzis worked as director of scenography for more than twenty years: "I believe that buildings have their own memory, and this walls, in which so many people accustomed to the arts, learning their secrets, are very well suited to exhibit the works that Oleg gave us". The Library widened the exposition by the art and archive materials from its own stocks: drawings for the performances *Zoyka's Apartments*, *Optimistic Tragedy*, and *Dictatorship of Conscience*, theatre programmes, magazine and newspaper articles, written by O. Sheinzis, and interviews with him.

The exhibition became a notable event in the cultural life of Moscow. Prominent theatrical figures took part in it. With great warmth M. A. Zakharov, A. M. Smelyanskiy, S. M. Barkhin, B. M. Poyurovskiy talk about extraordinary talent of Oleg Sheinzis and his deep sincere love for his profession, his country, his friends and students. His colleagues were called him "Composer of the space". He knew how to make his imagination to work quickly and clearly. He even taught students learning about scenography in the Moscow Art Theatre School to dream before design. Do not miss the memorable performance *Juno and Avos*, designed by Scheinzis. The expressive graphics of this performance is unforgettable: two lighted podiums, caravel contour, the sails flap and the grins of golden masks. That's all has been really spectacular, while not being vulgar embellishment: with all beauty of the performances decorated by him, Oleg Sheinzis didn't make simple prettiness, he created another emotional reality on stage, transition to another dimension.

Great interest was the presentation of the book *Oleg Sheinzis. Why Does One Need the Artist?* Curator and author of the project, a great friend of artist's family, A. V. Oganesyan spoke about how the book was created, who helped in the selection of material and in design, highlighting the role of the artist S. M. Barkhin. Exhibition hall of the RSAL took the unprecedented number of visitors that day: colleagues and friends of Oleg Sheinzis, his students and graduates, admirers of his work. Many noted that the exposure helped them to see new aspects of the remarkable talent of the master. That's what written in the guestbook by a theatre researcher, specialist in scenography, book's author L. Oves: "The exhibition extends the idea of the artist and shows with clarity the chamber, lyrical, intimate nature of his work."

In 2006, the exhibition Fairy Tale in Theatre was organised for the 250th anniversary of the Saint Petersburg Theatre Library in conjunction with the RSAL. Visitors from the northern capital brought costumes and scenery for performances based on the fabulous stories staged at the Mariinsky Theatre in late 19th and early 20th centuries, by works of famous and other artists. The exposition provided an opportunity to follow the changes in the artistic principles of a performance for half a century. The works of I. A. Vsevolozhskiy were first shown to the public here. Today, he is mostly known as a director of the Imperial theatre and author of plays and librettos, but rarely as a designer although he designed twenty-five performances for the Mariinsky theatre. The famous ballet, *Sleeping Beauty*, was born thanks to Vsevolozhskiy – he wrote a libretto and interested P.I. Tchaikovsky and M. I. Petipa in the idea of creating a magnificent ballet *á la* Versailles resembling a Louis XIV spectacle. The sketches by Vsevolozhsky for Tchaikovsky's ballets *Sleeping Beauty* (1890), *Nutcracker* (1892) and *Iolanta* (1892) were part of the exhibition. The sketches by Konstantin Korovin for the ballet *Sleeping Beauty*, revived in 1914 in the same theatre, allows us to compare different approaches of artists in the creation of a holistic image of the performance. While not being a professional artist, Vsevolozhsky was an excellent connoisseur of the stage and, in fact, the first Russian costume designer: he was always making costume sketches not only historically true and beautiful, but also comfortable for performers.

The richest Library stocks helps to discover the history of various types and genres of art. The history of the Russian ballet to the mid 1920s was spectacularly represented at the exhibition *La Sylphide, Swan, Faun...* Colourful French lithographs form the middle of the 19th century introduced the reader-viewer into the world of European ballet, where Marie Taglioni, Fanny Elssler and others reigned. The original photos of the outstanding choreographer, M. I. Petipa (from the Petipa family photo archive kept in RSAL), famous artists M. Kshesinskaya, T. Karsavina (photo by M. Sherling), M. Mordkin, O. Spesivtseva acquainted viewers with the brilliant era of Diaghilev's Russian Ballet Seasons. Among the photographs of ballet star Anna Pavlova, in life and on stage, one had never been published before. Of equal rarity was the programme of the 1897 ballet performance *Thetis and Peleus* of Mariinsky theatre (staged by Marius Petipa, the performers were M. Kshesinskaya and P. Gerdt), and programme-booklet *Russian Seasons* of various years in Paris, London and Monte-Carlo. Among the books on the history of ballet were some unique editions: the hand-written copy of Part IV of S. Khudekov's monograph *History of Dances* – Saint Petersburg, 1918; *Lettres sur la danse, sur les ballets et les arts* by Jean-Georges Noverre published in Saint Petersburg, 1803 in French; and the Paris edition of 18th century book *Chorégraphie ou l'art de décrire la dance, par caractères, figures et signes démonstratifs...* by R. A. Feuillet.

Historical perspectives were important aspects of various Russian theatres activities, not only Moscow theatres but also of other Russian cities with exhibitions such as, Father of the Russian Theatre to the 250th Anniversary of the Oldest Theatres in Russia – Feodor Volkov in Yaroslavl, the exhibition Taganka – 40. Just the facts – a round date with the theatre established in 1964, and the exhibition Fomenko on Both sides of the Wings, dedicated to productions and actors of the Peter Fomenko Theatre. The spirit of 1960s was the time of creative renewal of the language of theatre and its creativity. Renewal of the artistic language is not just in theatre, but movies and other art forms, and could be felt at the exhibition Ottepel. Theatre in Moscow. There were costumes, models, sketches, photos and personal belongings of the actors represented in the exhibition.

Photographic exhibits are the most frequent at expositions. The RSAL stocks contain photos from various times that have historical and artistic value and a large part of them gives us an idea about performances of various theatres. Photographs are extremely important for theatre researchers, scenographers, directors and actors. A professional theatrical photographer knows the fabric of the play very well and his pictures always speak to the audience. From the photo, we can judge the appearance of the actor and the power of his emotions. Among those names is a famous photographer, Miron Sherling (1880-1958). His photographs are more like reproductions of paintings, due to the master's developed understanding of the composition, his ability to find the most significant thing in the image to convey the motion of the character. The protagonists of the Sherling's remarkable photographs are the opera singers and the ballet dancers of Bolshoi Theatre. To be photographed by Sherling was considered a great honour. Amongst his friends were famous figures of literature and art: A. M. Gorky, I. E. Repin, F. I. Chaliapin, I. G. Ehrenburg. The RSAL has one of the biggest collections of photographs by M. A. Sherling.

It is said that the "walls are teaching" – the good Old Russian proverb about schools with creative profiles. If we talk about Russia, especially the pre-revolutionary times, remember the Imperial Academy of Fine Arts (Saint Petersburg), where prints and drawings of the best Russian and foreign artists were hanging on walls of classrooms, and being carefully collected by patrons specifically for visual education of future architects and artists. Thus, in a modern sense, the Academy was both the school and the open, living museum. Modern cultural institutions continue the tradition of knowledge and skills by passing through the demonstration of the best of the collections, through the systematic disclosure of assets, through involvement, and the RSAL is among them. The uniqueness of the RSAL is in the richest illustrative material in the library collection. Besides the books and modern multimedia that, as one may know, not always attracts the contemporary reader who thinks that he can find them on the Internet, our library exhibits the original documents of the era, whether it is from the 18th or beginning of the 21st century. The rich collections of sketches, photographs, postcards, and works of applied graphics, with all of those stored in special library stock, the Complex Department of Iconographic Materials, allows the library to implement such exhibition projects. The interior of the library exhibition room, which remains unchanged since the building by architect M. F. Kasakov, also helps to maintain the atmosphere of "teaching walls". RSAL moved into this building, which is an architectural monument, in 1948. The library carefully keeps the monument and the theatrical history of which counts for more than two hundred years. The owner of the building during Kasakov's time was the vice-governor of Moscow, N.E. Myasoedov. It is known that in Myasoedov's house there was a "serf" theatre, where serf actors played. In the 1829 the palace was bought by the treasury for the theatre school and later, there was a Directorate of the Imperial Theatres – state institution that manages the Imperial Theatres.

The building is filled with theatrical atmosphere. In addition to its administrative offices, the apartments of actors and employees of Moscow theatres were located here. For example, the family of the I. M. Lapitskiy (Mikhailov) lived here. Lapitskiy was a Russian director and actor, organiser and leader of the Theatre of Musical Drama (1912-1919, Petrograd) and also worked in Bolshoi Theatre. His granddaughter, who is one of the oldest library employees now, donated photographs and documents from the family archives to the library. Thanks to a donation by another library employee, E. S. Kulikova, the library has part of the Petipa photo archive that was kept by her relative. These archives include 400 photographs of Petipa family from 1860 to 1960. Thus, the link of times has been established, continuing the existence of the theatre in the walls of the Library and increasing the values of the Library collections.

The history of Complex Department of Iconographic Materials' creation (the research of which was started by Elena Khaplanova) is tightly bound to the honoured artist of the USSR, Professor Pavel Pavlovich Pashkov (1872-1952). In 1930, P. Pashkov worked as a stage designer in the Academic Maly Theatre. He was one of the best experts in the field of theatrical scenery and costume and he led the research, study and description of materials related to the theatre. With him, not only a collection of iconographic material began to take shape, but also the method of service to readers. P. Pashkov accurately identified that the main task of the department was to provide knowledge and wake up an artist's imagination. Art documents must meet the individual approaches of the artist, his demands, and be the driving force of fantasy.

The engravings and lithographs from the Imperial Maly Theatre collection served as the basis of the library stock. The collection contains European and Russian materials from the 16th to the 20th century, and Japanese and Chinese materials. The most common are the publications from the 19th century. The collection also contains rare and valuable documents, including some that are unique. For example, the engravings by the architect I. A. Fomin (1912) with the notes of the author, portraits of actors engraved by E. F. Sievert (1913) with pencil marks of the author concerning the circumstances of the creation of prints and he collection of Russian etchings from the 1880s, including Victor Vasnetsov's works, is very interesting. The collection of unique graphics and sketches by artists of theatre and cinema was created at the same time as the main stock. Drawings of furniture, genre sketches, cartoons, sketches were included in the library stock by P. Pashkov. The Russian State Art Library has a interesting collection of works by M. Azizian, N. Akimov, S. Barkhin, T. Bruni, N. Voinova, V. and R. Volskiy, V. Dorrer, E. Kapelyush, P. Kaplevich, M. Kitaev, E. Kochergin, O. Kruchinina, S. Maklakova, B. Messerer, L. Novi, V. Ryndin, O. Savarenskaya, V. Khodasevich, N. Schneider and other artists.

The Library's photography collection consists of documents reflecting social, political, economical and cultural life of Russia, the USSR and foreign countries from 1850 to 2000. The largest part of the department stock comprises theatrical photographs, represented by works of famous artist such as I. Aleksandrov, S. Bergamasco, I. G. Dyagovchenko, A. Lorens, E. Mrozovskaya, V. Petrusov, B. Fabisovich, K. Fisher *et al.* In the 1970s, the Library received a gift of the photo portraits by wonderful master M. Sherling. This stock may be called a photographic encyclopaedia of the theatre. The collection of consumer photography covers the period from 1850 to 1960. There are very valuable pictures in the collection that introduce the earliest method of photography, the daguerreotype. RGBI holds three daguerreotypes dating from the years 1850 to 1853 in his stock. The most valuable examples of the stock are signed photographs of eminent theatrical personalities. The Department's collection has documents from the private collections of M. Zagorskiy, S. Mokulsky, S. Zimin, I. Lapitski, P. Pashkov etc.

The postcards collection is incredibly broad in its topics and contains domestic and foreign publications. Of special interest are the sections devoted to views of Russia and foreign countries. There exists a large collection, of more than two thousand postcards, reproducing the images of old Moscow and Saint Petersburg, the modes of life and types of Russia. Among the postcards on costume history is the Russian

Folk Costume collection from the beginning of the 20th century by N. L. Shabelskaya.

All the collections are stored in the Library and are loaned out to specialists on special request. Each storage unit receives the individual bibliographic description and subject headings. Thus, based on a collection of prints, photographs, and postcards, one can get an idea of the types of towns and regions, some depicted objects, costumes, actors, historical themes, everyday life of peoples, and the diversity of subjects and themes.

Since 1989, the Library collects the masterpieces of native and foreign theatre and cinema. The cinema- and video-documents and multimedia service department was organised in the RSAL. Its stock contains movies and cartoons, records of dramatic productions, ballets, operas, musicals, pop concerts, and circus performances. The largest part of the collection is the documentaries and popular science films and videos on architecture, painting, sculpture, graphics, applied arts, ethnography, costume history, literature, music, and religion. Profile collecting was produced with the participation of teachers of creative institutions.

In the middle of 1930s, the Library began to gather current news stories, as well as books and offset duplicator reprints of old newspapers, representing the development of theatrical process in the country. Since 1974, the Library began to systematically collect theatre programmes of performances of domestic and foreign theatre groups touring the Soviet Union. Most valuable are newspaper articles about the theatres of 1920s. Reviews of performances are the basis of the "Theatre" section. The "People" section contains interviews, creative portraits of actors, directors and artists of theatres, movies, pop music, circus, of poets, playwrights, composers, conductors, choreographers, choirmasters, sculptors, painters, architects, speakers of radio and television, theatre and music and movie critics. All articles are categorised by topics and issues, including the information about competitions and festivals.

Categorisation and analytical processing of a document's content is one of the main prerequisites for a successful search in the library. This condition has been met by every collection in the Library: the collection of books, including reference ones, graphic materials, electronic resources and video media. As a special library, the RSAL has some unique files and electronic databases, which allow readers to quickly and efficiently find the necessary information by performing specific requests (search by author, title and other bibliographic data) as well as extensive enquiries by various topics. For example, is the file "Scenery" with card indexes and databases to search for plays by title, various forms of the author's name, number of actors, scene of action, scenarios of events, and systematic list of magazines, such as domestic and foreign fashion magazines, are available in the library.

The wide profile of the RSAL collection of art enables us to give costume history classes within the walls of the Library with students, technologists and stage managers of Moscow Art Theatre School. As a result, the circle of users, such as the library friends is expanding, while students are forming the habit of working in a library with books, microfiche, and other various kinds of documents. And then the next step is a joint exhibition projects that demonstrates the work of students, possibly future masters of the art scene, in the creation of theatrical scenery and costume. One of the last exhibitions of this profile was called *Théâtre trompe l'œil* and was devoted to simulating texture of a variety of materials, creating accessories, jewellery, lace and embroidery from paper and other similar materials. Of great interest are the students' coursework projects and dissertations, for the preparation of which, the era, the historical costumes, particularly its finish, texture, fabrics and colour must be studied in detail. Moreover, a detailed study of the era preceding the creation of theatrical costume in varying degrees of stylisation, as it is a prerequisite for an authentic appearance of the characters.

The library isn't just a repository, but an institution open to a wide range of users. There are:

- contacts with the art, literature, theatrical museums, schools, universities, and theatres, and relations with them contribute to a better understanding of the challenges faced by users.
- coordination with other libraries (our methodical works is accepted by the main Russian methodical centre for subject cataloguing – Russian National Library, Saint Petersburg).
- cooperation with theatre community, providing full conditions for work of specialists and researchers of the theatre.

So, RSAL helps to realise the user's expectations that are related to:

- their professional occupation. Their interest depends on who the user is – the specialist or the student.
- educational activity.
- self-educational activity.
- leisure time activity.

The library supports the interests and wishes of readers.

For better understanding of a user's expectations, the interests of readers and the degree of their satisfaction were monitored and analysed, and users working remotely on the Internet were also counted. To increase the interest of users, the Library conducted outreach and educational work with readers of all categories, as a part of the current project Library Square of Arts. The Library holds seminars, discussions on art, meeting with leaders of the scene, the playwrights, directors and others, and presentations of new books. In 2003, the Library launched a project specifically focused on student audience – Increasing information literacy of students of creative university. This project is focused on fundamental principles of the UNESCO Information for All Programme. The Library has developed a series of seminars to help students of creative professions to learn how to use informational resources in the field of culture.

Additionally, for many years, fundamental bibliographies on theatrical subjects were being published to help the reader. Initially, in 1970s to 1980s publishing in the Library developed in two directions – for professionals and to help self-education. For example, a series of *What to read about the theatre* (1976-1980s) has been published for self-education. For professionals, retrospective indexes and bibliographies were published: *Yearbooks dramas*, indexes on the history of the Soviet Russian drama theatre (1977-1978), children's theatre in the USSR (1978-1979), African theatre (1982), Armenian drama theatre (1983), Estonian theatre (1986), systematic indexes of specialised magazines *Theatre* (1984-1985, 1992), *Libretto 18* – beginning of the 20th century from the RSAL collection (2008); bibliographies devoted to individual theatres and theatre companies: the Moscow Theatre Sovremennik (1971), Theatre of V. Mayakovskiy (1982), Moscow Theatre of Drama and Comedy on Taganka (1989), Theatre of Anatoly Vasilyev (1991), Theatre At Nikitsky Gate (2007) and others. The library was working on personal bibliographic index devoted V. Mayakovsky (1973), M. Chekhov (1994), S. Mikhoels (2003), M. Levitin (2003), M. Bulgakov (2008) and others, and also produces indexes that contain information about theatrical libraries, collections and archives.

There are many genres and types of arts in the RSAL stock, including theatre in all its diversity. There are not just traditional forms of the theatre like drama and ballet, but also contemporary trends. To be able to speak on the modern scientific language one should constantly keep track of terminology changes. Some terms don't even have an established interpretation in the Russian language yet, and they do not only lack adequate translation, but also merge with new semantic variations, or get included in a more narrow sense of the term. So specialists have the task of how to include the term into the subject heading system by keeping both the sense of term and the document meaning. Because of that and by being a serious informational institution, RSAL has, among others, a problem of strengthening the research component in the library.

To expand the circle of friends and users of the RSAL, the Library works on the content and design of its Internet portal, publishing information about new acquisitions, the exhibition programme, providing links to useful resources: sites of museums, libraries, art groups and associations, as well as advertising Library stock and collections, publishing booklets and pamphlets, indexes, creating a system of directories and files available to remote users via the Internet.

The goals and objectives of libraries can be achieved by the process of innovation aimed at the modernisation of the library. To improve services to readers and to preserve actively used valuable documents, the Library started a digitisation project. For the same purpose, the Library's card index was also digitised and made available on the Internet. However, despite this, the personality of the librarian as a competent assistant continues to play an extremely significant role. One proof of this is the unique project The Museum of the Reader, an idea of Director of the RSAL, Ada Kolganova that opened at the end of 2009. The opening ceremony was attended by the artistic director of the Maly Theatre Y. M. Solomin, rector of the Shchepkin Higher Theatre School B. N. Lyubimov, Head of literary department of the Moscow Art Theatre N. M. Sheiko *et al.* The first exposition of the Museum was devoted to the history of the RSAL, which was established in the depths of the Maly Theatre.

The museum's archival material includes records, letters, orders, photographs and other documents that represent the first decade of the life of the library. For the first time unique documents were exhibited – written requests by readers' to the Theatre Library. The Museum of the Reader exposition exhibits readers' requests by A. A. Ostuzhev, V. N. Paschennaya, I. V. Iinskiy, B. A. Babochkin, I. M. Smoktunovsky, V. M. Solomin, Y. M. Solomin and other famous actors. The Museum of the Reader is the quintessence of the reader searches in the library. Publication of the rare book collection completes exposition of the Museum. These are rare and valuable books of 19th and 20th centuries on art and costume history, art history, costume, geography, arts, architecture, which are important to create performances and movies. The unique part of this stock are personal collections of books, which reflect the reading interests of the professional actor V. V. Gvozditskiy and artist and researcher V. N. Kulikov, former employee of the RSAL, and a foremost authority in military costume. The Museum space is expanded by a virtual exhibition, which shows the search for sources by librarians in the preparation of the Maly Theatre productions of *Othello* (1935), *I az vozdam* (*To me belongeth vengeance and recompense*, 1991), and *Corsican* (2001); these materials were accessed by A. A. Ostuzhev, N. A. Belevtseva, V. G. Konstantinov and other figures of the Maly Theatre. In the future, there will be exhibitions devoted to the creation of the performances in the Bolshoi Theatre, Moscow Art Theatre, Moscow Sovremennik Theatre, Moscow Theatre of Drama and Comedy on Taganka, and other creative groups in Moscow.

In the past years, the Library has become more attractive to the user thanks also to the permanent exhibits telling the history of contacts between organisations and individuals who formed the glory of the national theatre. To date, strong, long-term friendships continue to grow and the Library continues to keep the atmosphere of the theatre world and always ready to accept a new, active viewer-reader.

Abstract

La Bibliothèque d'art de Russie, gardienne du patrimoine historique et artistique, est une organisation scientifique et d'information éminente en Russie. En 1991, la Bibliothèque centrale d'État du Théâtre a été réorganisée. Elle est devenue une bibliothèque majeure, qui collecte des documents portant sur tous les aspects de l'art et du théâtre. La Bibliothèque d'art de Russie fait partie de l'histoire culturelle et joue toujours un grand rôle dans la vie culturelle d'aujourd'hui.

Au cours des dernières années, la Bibliothèque est devenue plus attrayante pour l'utilisateur, grâce notamment aux expositions permanentes racontant l'histoire des contacts entre les institutions et les individus qui ont fait la gloire de notre théâtre national. Aujourd'hui, des relations fortes et durables continuent de se nouer. La Bibliothèque préserve l'atmosphère du monde du théâtre et est toujours prête à accueillir un nouveau spectateur-lecteur actif.

Spectacle vivant et patrimoine : une relation ambivalente

L'exemple de la Comédie-Française

Agathe Sanjuan

Bibliothèque-musée de la Comédie-Française (Paris – France)

La Comédie-Française est un théâtre public, riche d'une histoire de plus de trois siècles. La tutelle étatique qui préside à sa création en 1680 et à son fonctionnement depuis lui confère d'emblée une valeur patrimoniale, au même titre que les grands établissements créés à la même époque (l'Académie royale de Musique et de Danse, l'Académie française…).

Aujourd'hui, la situation des collections de la Comédie-Française est atypique. À l'exception de la bibliothèque-musée de l'Opéra, désormais rattachée à la Bibliothèque nationale de France, la Comédie-Française est le seul théâtre de France à conserver et à administrer lui-même ses archives depuis aussi longtemps. Les collections, gérées depuis la fin du XIXᵉ siècle par des bibliothécaires attachés au théâtre, étaient auparavant sous l'emprise des comédiens eux-mêmes. C'est peut-être ce qui, encore aujourd'hui, explique le lien très fort qui unit la Troupe à son patrimoine, le théâtre en devenir au théâtre du passé. Le destin de ce théâtre revêt un caractère patrimonial à plusieurs titres : la Comédie-Française est d'abord garante d'un patrimoine littéraire (son répertoire qu'elle a pour mission d'enrichir) ; sa longue histoire lui a par ailleurs, permis d'accumuler un patrimoine matériel très important, tant archivistique que muséal. La position très particulière de ces collections, au sein d'un théâtre en activité et d'une troupe constituée en « société », pose la question du statut des œuvres (collection publique ou privée), celui du musée lui-même et de son public.

Un théâtre dépositaire d'un patrimoine littéraire

L'origine de la Comédie-Française tient dans la volonté du roi Louis XIV en 1680 d'opérer la fusion entre deux troupes rivales pour « rendre la représentation des comédies plus parfaite ». Cette jonction, qui s'effectue dans la douleur pour les comédiens de l'une et l'autre troupe, a pour contrepartie de défendre à toute autre troupe de jouer en français dans Paris et ses faubourgs. La troupe désormais « unique » obtient donc le monopole du répertoire en français ; charge à elle de l'enrichir. Les comédiens, en leurs assemblées, lisent alors les pièces et établissent le répertoire, dont ils sont responsables et garants de la qualité littéraire[1]. Toute œuvre jouée en leur théâtre, entre au Répertoire, dont le caractère consécratoire pour l'auteur est manifeste dès le XVIIIᵉ siècle. Les comédiens ont donc reçu naturellement un certain nombre de manuscrits : peu de manuscrits d'auteurs, mais beaucoup de manuscrits de souffleurs, parfois corrigés par l'auteur lui-même, visé par le censeur et portant les marques de l'adaptation dramaturgique, qui naît à l'épreuve du plateau et du public. Ces manuscrits sont d'une importance considérable pour l'établissement des éditions de textes car ils en nourrissent l'analyse dramaturgique et littéraire.

Citons deux manuscrits qui suffiront à donner une idée de l'importance de ce patrimoine : le manuscrit de copiste de *La commère* de Marivaux, pièce considérée comme perdue, redécouvert par l'archiviste de la Comédie-Française, Sylvie Chevalley, en 1965[2], le manuscrit autographe d'*Hernani* de Victor Hugo. Il convient de s'arrêter sur le destin de ce dernier. Victor Hugo avait décidé de léguer l'ensemble de ses œuvres dans son codicille testamentaire du 31 août 1881 qui stipule : « Je donne tous mes manuscrits et tout ce qui sera trouvé écrit ou dessiné par moi à la Bibliothèque nationale de Paris qui sera un jour la Bibliothèque des États-Unis d'Europe ». Néanmoins, il avait formulé oralement le vœu, auprès de Paul Meurice, son exécuteur testamentaire, que le manuscrit d'*Hernani* revienne à la Comédie-Française. Il fut donc offert à la Troupe qui avait accueilli l'auteur en 1830 pour livrer à ses côtés une des plus célèbres batailles littéraires du théâtre français. À l'occasion d'un prêt pour une exposition de la Bibliothèque nationale au XXᵉ siècle, le manuscrit a pourtant été tamponné et coté aux Nouvelles acquisitions françaises, célèbre série du département des manuscrits, la Bibliothèque nationale le considérant désormais comme un dépôt auprès de la Comédie-Française[3], au grand dam des comédiens. On voit là combien ce manuscrit acquis

---

[1]   Le Comité de lecture qui existe encore aujourd'hui remplit cette fonction : il est à la fois composé de comédiens et de personnalités extérieures, appartenant au monde littéraire et artistique.

[2]   Ms. 2019 : *La commère*, comédie en un acte, copie manuscrite, 49 p., Bibliothèque Pont de Vesle n° 1078.

[3]   Ce manuscrit autographe doit être comparé au manuscrit de souffleur de 1830, ainsi qu'aux épreuves de l'édition de 1836, également conservées à la bibliothèque de la Comédie-Française. *Cf.* l'édition de John J. Janc, *Hernani*, Lanham, New York, Oxford, University press of America, 2001.

de haute lutte par les Comédiens-Français lui fut par la suite disputé. L'entrée au Français d'*Hernani* témoigne en effet d'une bataille littéraire et dramaturgique qui démontre la valeur symbolique de la notion de répertoire : faire entrer le romantisme dans le temple du théâtre français était en quelque sorte en reconnaître la valeur et la portée. Aujourd'hui encore, le répertoire fait débat et l'entrée de certains auteurs est contestée.

Un patrimoine archivistique amassé « par nécessité »

En dehors de ces archives littéraires, le fonds de la Comédie-Française est également riche d'un patrimoine archivistique touchant toutes les activités du théâtre, tant artistiques qu'administratives : manuscrits de rôles se faisant le miroir des traditions de jeu et des filiations d'interprétations qui se transmettent au sein d'un même emploi, mémoires de décorateurs, sans oublier la fabuleuse série des registres journaliers, reflet au jour le jour des activités de la Troupe.

Le patrimoine archivistique de la Comédie se constitue en quelque sorte « naturellement », et pendant longtemps sans que les comédiens y apportent le soin nécessaire, comme l'atteste en 1779 Delaporte, secrétaire souffleur de la Comédie qui décrit le dépôt d'archives comme un « galetas », s'attarde sur le désordre de ces « liasses de papier faisant un monceau couvert de poussière et d'ordures de souris et de rats, auxquels [*sic*] on n'ose pas toucher »[4]. De fait, il faudra attendre la seconde moitié du XIXe siècle pour que les bibliothécaires sortent ces richesses du chaos.

A contrario, en 1785, les comédiens font l'acquisition d'une pièce d'archive exceptionnelle touchant leur histoire, le « Registre de La Grange ». Le registre est acheté pour la somme de 240 livres, auprès de Madame Varlet, parente de La Grange, comédien et compagnon de Molière qui tint dans ce registre un véritable journal de bord de la troupe de Molière dès 1659 et jusqu'après la mort de celui-ci en 1673, ainsi que des débuts de la Comédie-Française à partir de 1680 et jusqu'en 1685.

Pendant la Révolution, les comédiens se félicitent de cette acquisition alors qu'elle sert de pièce justificative pour la revendication de leur droit de propriété sur certaines pièces de théâtre qu'ils disent avoir « achetées », au premier rang desquelles, les pièces de Molière. À la suite de l'arrestation des comédiens en 1793 par le Comité de salut public, leurs archives sont mises sous scellés. Lorsqu'en 1809, dix ans après la renaissance de la Comédie-Française, les comédiens se soucient enfin de rapatrier leurs « papiers » dans leur théâtre de la rue de Richelieu, le registre de La Grange manque.

---

4   Cité par Joël Huthwohl, « Du galetas au musée. Les collections de la Comédie-Française du XVIIIe siècle à l'entre-deux-guerres », in *Revue d'histoire du théâtre*, n° 2008-1, p. 27-36. Cet article trace l'histoire des collections.

Les pérégrinations du registre pendant tout le XIXᵉ siècle sont difficiles à suivre. Redécouvert à la mort de Mᵐᵉ Suin, comédienne qui l'avait conservé précieusement, il est ensuite prêté à un archiviste du théâtre (Lemazurier), puis à un moliériste (Taschereau), et enfin au ministre Fould qui l'exhibait comme « curiosité » pour ses visiteurs !

La Comédie-Française, devant le développement des études moliéresques, se décida à le publier en 1876[5]. Le registre de La Grange acquiert alors une valeur symbolique très forte auprès des comédiens, ce qui contredit l'apparente désinvolture qu'ils manifestent à son égard, le prêtant sans scrupule à des amateurs, au risque de le mettre en danger, mais peut-être aussi par générosité et pour encourager son étude. Cette forte portée symbolique perdure de nos jours : le registre journalier de la troupe, tenu encore aujourd'hui, porte le nom de « registre La Grange », hommage au premier d'entre eux. Depuis la dernière édition du registre chez Minkoff en 1972, un exemplaire du registre en fac-similé est offert à chaque nouveau sociétaire, passage de témoin du « patron », Molière, aux jeunes générations. La valeur exceptionnelle du Registre de La Grange, comme témoin de la présence symbolique de Molière au sein de la Comédie-Française explique sans doute l'attention particulière qui lui est portée par les comédiens. C'est une des rares pièces d'archives citées dans le premier catalogue du Musée : celui de René Delorme en 1878[6].

Le registre, malgré ces aléas, fait figure d'exception quant à l'intérêt que les comédiens portent à leurs archives, jusqu'à l'arrivée d'un premier bibliothécaire professionnel en 1855, Léon Guillard (1855-1878), auquel succède Georges Monval (1885-1908). Tous deux mènent un travail de défrichage salutaire pour les collections et fondent le service de la bibliothèque[7]. Alors que pendant longtemps, les archives s'accumulent sans ordre, au risque d'en perdre des parts importantes, les comédiens ont eu une politique volontariste concernant leur patrimoine muséal.

Une troupe « habitée » par son patrimoine, un théâtre « meublé » par son musée

En 1759, les comédiens se préoccupent de décorer leur salle d'assemblée avec les bustes de Corneille, Racine, Molière[8]. L'initiative vient de Lekain, mais n'aboutira qu'en 1775 grâce à Caffiéri qui offre le

---

[5] *Note sur Lagrange et son registre*, par Sylvie Chevalley, faisant suite à l'édition en fac-similé du registre, Genève, Minkoff, 1972.

[6] René Delorme, *Le Musée de la Comédie-Française*, Paris, Ollendorf, 1878, p. 158.

[7] *Cf.* Joël Huthwohl, « Du galetas au musée. Les collections de la Comédie-Française du XVIIIᵉ siècle à l'entre-deux-guerres », *op. cit.*

[8] Cité par Émile Dacier, *Le Musée de la Comédie-Française*, Paris, Librairie de l'Art ancien et moderne, 1905, p. 4.

buste de Piron en échange d'une entrée à vie à la Comédie-Française. Le buste de Piron est le premier d'une longue série illustrant les grands auteurs de la Comédie. Ces œuvres sont offertes en échange d'entrées à vie. Tout un « mobilier » est ainsi conçu par les plus grands sculpteurs du temps (Huez, Caffiéri, Foucou, Boizot, Pajou, Berruer, Houdon), pour la future salle du Faubourg Saint-Germain qui ouvre ses portes en 1782 (actuelle salle de l'Odéon). La notion de « musée » n'est pas encore d'actualité et il s'agit bien là de « meubler », de « décorer » le théâtre, en faisant certes appel aux plus grands artistes du moment. Le premier inventaire général, daté de 1815[9], mentionne « L'État des statues, portraits » parmi les « glaces et autres objets appartenant à l'ancienne Comédie-Française ou acquis depuis ». Contrairement aux pièces de serrurerie, aux meubles et aux éléments de costume, la valeur de ces objets particuliers n'est pas mentionnée, il n'en est question que « pour mémoire ». La sécheresse de la description étonne (« la statue en pied de Voltaire par M. Houdon », « Dufresny par Pajou, en marbre ») par rapport à la description des glaces dont on précise les dimensions, dans la même section de l'inventaire.

Jusqu'à une époque relativement récente, les œuvres sont donc considérées comme des meubles ou même parfois des accessoires de scène. Le portrait de Montfleury attribué à Antoine Durand (1645), une des peintures les plus anciennes de la Comédie-Française, « jouait » encore en 1956, dans la mise en scène de *La machine à écrire* de Jean Cocteau.

Limitées à vingt bustes et statues et douze peintures en 1815[10], les collections s'enrichissent considérablement à partir de 1830. Le 8 décembre 1835, *Le Moniteur universel* annonce pour la première fois la fondation, au foyer du Théâtre-Français, d'un Musée Molière, projet qui ne s'est pas réalisé[11]. Arsène Houssaye (1850-1856), le premier administrateur nommé par le gouvernement à la suite d'une réforme statutaire qui dépossède en partie les comédiens de l'administration de leur théâtre, s'intéresse à la possibilité d'ouvrir un musée et écrit au directeur des Beaux-Arts pour solliciter une subvention spécifique[12]. C'est donc grâce à l'administration des Beaux-Arts, c'est-à-dire grâce à une subvention publique dédiée aux collections, que la Comédie-Française peut acheter le portrait de *Talma en Néron* par Delacroix en 1856.

Dans la seconde moitié du siècle, le ministère des Beaux-Arts passe une série de commandes de bustes d'auteurs et de comédiens pour le compte de

---

[9]   Registre 569.

[10] Inventaire des collections en 1815.

[11] Georges Monval, *Les collections de la Comédie-Française, catalogue historique et raisonné*, Paris, Société de propagation des livres d'art, 1897, p. 7-8.

[12] René Delorme, *Le Musée de la Comédie-Française, op. cit.*, p. 16.

la Comédie-Française. À partir de la fin du XIXᵉ siècle, on réclame l'ouverture d'un musée, pouvant rivaliser avec le Garrick-Club. Alexandre Dumas fils déclare : « Le Théâtre-Français n'est pas un théâtre comme les autres. Quand on y apporte un manuscrit, il y a les Bustes qui vous regardent »[13]. Il est assez logique de constater que de la même manière que l'État intervient directement dans l'administration du théâtre à partir de 1850, il s'implique également dans la politique d'acquisition du théâtre, notamment en termes de financement. Les comédiens continuent de valider l'entrée des œuvres au sein du comité d'administration, mais l'apport d'un financement extérieur nous fait dire qu'ils n'en ont plus tout à fait l'exclusivité.

Citons quelques œuvres emblématiques appartenant au musée. Le Doyen en est sans conteste le « fauteuil de Molière », objet emblématique s'il en est, puisqu'il est justement à l'origine un vrai meuble de scène, le fauteuil de malade dans lequel Molière interpréta son dernier rôle le 17 février 1673[14]. Le fauteuil, symbole de la présence spirituelle de Molière, le patron de la Troupe, fut longtemps utilisé sur scène avant d'être retiré du magasin des meubles, eu égard à sa noble origine. Il accueille encore aujourd'hui le public avant son entrée dans la salle. Il est ainsi décrit dans l'inventaire de 1815 : « Un fauteuil de Molière à crémaillère et couvert de peau noire (pour mémoire, parce qu'il n'a pas de prix) ».

Autre pièce emblématique pour l'attachement que lui témoignent les comédiens, le *Voltaire assis* de Houdon, offert par la nièce du poète, Madame Denis, et de nombreuses fois disputé aux comédiens, notamment lorsqu'il fut « saisi » pendant la Révolution française et l'incarcération des comédiens, « comme objet appartenant à la nation ».

Au XIXᵉ siècle, les comédiens procèdent à de belles acquisitions qui font aujourd'hui la renommée de la collection. Les modes d'acquisitions varient : le portrait de *Mˡˡᵉ Duclos en Ariane (Ariane de Thomas Corneille)* par Largillière, est acheté par les comédiens en 1815, le portrait de *Rachel en allégorie de La Tragédie* par Jean-Léon Gérôme, est attribué à la Comédie-Française par arrêté ministériel en 1861, *Molière à la table de Louis XIV* de Jean-Dominique Ingres est offert par l'artiste en 1858 en échange d'une entrée à vie, dans la tradition instaurée au XVIIIᵉ siècle.

Statut de l'œuvre, statut ambivalent du musée

La question du statut des œuvres est loin d'être aisée à trancher en raison d'une certaine confusion du statut juridique de la Comédie-Française et de la Société des Comédiens-Français jusqu'à une époque

---

[13] Cité par Jules Claretie dans Émile Dacier, *Le Musée de la Comédie-Française, op. cit.*, p. VIII.

[14] Georges Monval, *Le Musée de la Comédie-Française, op. cit.*, p. 2.

très récente. À la création de la Troupe en 1680, les comédiens signent un acte d'association, comme le voulait la tradition au xviie siècle. Cet acte détermine le fonctionnement de la troupe. De nombreux décrets et ordonnances viennent ensuite modifier cet acte fondateur, en particulier le décret « de Moscou » (1812) qui est toujours le texte fondateur de l'établissement. Comme nous l'avons vu à travers les quelques exemples cités, les œuvres ont été acquises tantôt par les comédiens eux-mêmes, parfois sur leurs propres deniers, tantôt pour le compte de la Comédie-Française en tant qu'établissement. Certaines hésitations sur la propriété des œuvres ont malheureusement autorisé des déclassements d'œuvres et leur vente, au profit parfois de certains comédiens. Certaines œuvres sont ainsi sorties des collections, d'autres ayant pu être rachetées, comme le *Portrait de Mounet-Sully* par Charles-Auguste Mengin, legs de Charles Alexandre Mathis (1889), revendu en 1952, acquis par le comédien Robert Manuel auprès d'un antiquaire, et finalement racheté par la Comédie-Française à Robert Manuel en 1987. On voit là que le caractère inaliénable des collections était loin d'être acquis, ce qui a donné lieu, dans les années 1950, à des ventes catastrophiques de pièces parfois majeures.

Dans les années 1980, la bibliothèque-musée a enfin obtenu l'autorisation de préempter en vente publique. Ces dernières années, elle a aussi pu bénéficier de l'aide du fonds du patrimoine pour l'acquisition de pièces exceptionnelles, ces deux dernières procédures attestant le statut de collection publique des pièces ainsi acquises, et de ce fait, inaliénables.

La publication du décret du 1er avril 1995, conférant à la Comédie-Française le statut d'établissement national à caractère industriel et commercial, vient confirmer le dispositif, même si certains dons sont faits au seul bénéfice de la Société des Comédiens-Français. La question de la propriété des œuvres est néanmoins loin d'être tranchée.

Autre ambiguïté, le musée se trouve *in situ* : la collection n'est pas accessible au public extérieur mais constitue un exemple intéressant d'une collection vivante, une collection dont le personnel du théâtre, les comédiens y compris, a une connaissance intime et quotidienne, une collection avec laquelle il entretient une relation affective forte, mais qui est en quelque sorte « subtilisée » au public extérieur. Les trop rares visites organisées dans les espaces privés du théâtre ne parviennent pas à satisfaire un public toujours plus pressant de connaître les collections. En 2010, on peut faire le même constat qu'Émile Dacier en 1905 dans son ouvrage *Le Musée de la Comédie-Française, 1680-1905*[15] :

---

[15] Émile Dacier, *Le Musée de la Comédie-Française, 1680-1905*, Paris, Librairie de l'art ancien et moderne, 1905, p. 3.

Dans l'état actuel, le musée de la Comédie-Française n'est pas « visitable », et non seulement les pièces qui le composent ne sont pas réunies et groupées avec méthode, mais elles se trouvent éparpillées aux quatre coins du théâtre. On a bien fait place à quelques sculptures dans la partie accessible aux spectateurs : vestibules, escaliers et foyers du public ; mais tout le reste des œuvres d'art est dispersé dans l'intérieur du monument. On en rencontre, dès les premières marches, aux murs de l'escalier de l'administration et dès le palier ; là, prenez un couloir : qu'il conduise au foyer des artistes, du foyer à la scène, de la scène à la salle, vous passez entre une double haie de tableaux et de bustes ; ouvrez une porte – celle du foyer des artistes ou du foyer des travestissements, – pénétrez dans une antichambre – celle de l'administrateur, des secrétaires, du comité, – introduisez-vous dans le cabinet de l'administrateur, dans celui du secrétaire général, dans la salle du comité, partout, des cadres et des socles ! On dirait que les vieux serviteurs de Molière, délaissant le paradis où les comédiens glorieux se racontent pendant toute l'éternité leurs succès d'antan, sont revenus sur terre et qu'ils se sont embusqués, pour mieux veiller sur la « tradition », dans les coins les plus sombres de leur théâtre aimé !

On ne pourrait mieux décrire, aujourd'hui encore, le charme désuet de cette collection conservée non dans un musée traditionnel, mais dans un lieu dont la fonction est tout autre.

Le terme même de « musée » est aujourd'hui souvent récusé par le théâtre. À juste titre, la Comédie-Française refuse d'être considérée comme un conservatoire de traditions, voire un musée des pratiques théâtrales ou de l'interprétation, elle revendique au contraire d'être un théâtre de création et d'avant-garde qui se projette dans le futur. Le véritable « musée » qui habite ses murs est parfois trop facilement rendu responsable de cette image patrimoniale, archaïsante, voire poussiéreuse de l'institution. Souvent refoulé, le passé de l'institution habite pourtant totalement les pratiques institutionnelles du présent : le fonctionnement du comité de lecture qui fait entrer les pièces au répertoire, le fonctionnement du comité d'administration, l'autorité du Doyen (le plus ancien sociétaire au sein de la Troupe, qui la représente et incarne une certaine autorité morale), la cérémonie de l'hommage à Molière (le 15 janvier, jour anniversaire de son baptême, toute la Troupe lui rend hommage sur le plateau de la Salle Richelieu). La Comédie-Française a conscience de la responsabilité qui lui incombe en tant que gardienne d'une certaine mémoire du spectacle vivant et ne dédaigne pas d'utiliser son patrimoine, notamment en le citant dans certains spectacles : le fauteuil de Molière, sous forme de réplique, est utilisé dans la mise en scène de Denis Podalydès de *Cyrano de Bergerac* d'Edmond Rostand, à titre d'exemple.

En conclusion, on ne peut que souligner le caractère ambivalent des collections de la Comédie-Française. Ayant le pressentiment de leur responsabilité patrimoniale, les comédiens ont gardé leurs archives tout en les laissant végéter pendant des décennies, sans doute faute de temps et de moyens. Lorsqu'ils se préoccupent de constituer un patrimoine muséal, c'est plus certainement dans le but de « meubler » leur théâtre, de le « théâtraliser » encore un peu plus en le peuplant des figures de grands auteurs. La propriété et le statut des collections sont eux-mêmes ambigus, entre collection publique et collection privée appartenant à une collectivité. Enfin le musée lui-même n'est ouvert dans sa totalité qu'au personnel du théâtre, ce qui en restreint nécessairement l'audience et la portée en dépit de la qualité des collections. Peut-on rêver de l'ouverture d'un musée de la Comédie-Française ou d'un musée du théâtre prenant en compte ces œuvres ? C'est un vœu qui sera sans doute formulé lors du prochain colloque organisé à Paris au mois d'octobre, intitulé « Quel musée pour le théâtre »[16].

Abstract

The Comédie-Française, the French national theatre, houses a collection of works of art, a library and archive collection dating back to the 17th century. A heritage inseparable from its theatrical tradition, the status of its collections is no less as paradoxical as an in situ museum housed in a working theatre. The heritage mission of the Comédie-Française must therefore coexist with its primary mission, artistic creation.

---

[16] « Quel musée pour le spectacle vivant ? », colloque international INHA BnF, Paris, 21-22 octobre 2010. Actes partiellement publiés en russe dans *Сцена / La Scène / The Stage*, n° 1 (69) 2011. [Note ajoutée en 2012 en vue de l'édition]

What's Going on Behind the Scene?

The Point of View of an Information Specialist

Margret SCHILD

Theatre Museum (Düsseldorf – Germany)

Introduction – a Short Look Back

Since 1988, located in a historical building in the Hofgarten, the largest green space in the city centre of Düsseldorf, the museum had to face challenges and changes – as other museums. The concept of the permanent exhibition changed: the chronological presentation of theatre history in Dusseldorf was substituted by focusing on the location of the theatres and their meaning concerning the role of theatre in its historical context (SchauPlätze). Later this approach has been changed to the concept of an exhibition platform (Museum für Zuschaukunst), explaining the different aspects of producing and presenting theatre as well as the reception. Instead of a fixed permanent exhibition the aspects of theatre work are presented by presenting changing protagonists: by the presentation the life and work of actors, directors, costume and stage designers, dedicated to subjects. Information technology became more important as well: since 2004 the museum has offered a website[1] and became a participant in the project d:kult (Digital Archive of Art and Culture Düsseldorf). In 2005, because of the growth of the holdings and with regard to changes in the regulations concerning fire protection, the collection had to move to a separate site. Last, but not least the relation to the theatre practice has been enforced heavily, for example by presenting performances and other theatrical events, by offering workshops and seminars about acting, by initiating projects and festivals. The museum has now two sites: exhibition, stage, library in the city centre and the collection, located near by the university.

---

[1] <http:/www.duesseldorf.de/theatermuseum>.

This paper will focus on aspects of information management and its role to serve as an interface between past, present and future. Collecting and recording can be mentioned as support to the preservation and improvement of the cultural heritage in the field of the performing arts. On the occasion of the conferences in 2002 and 2006, the role of the library within the process of introducing information technology and the expected benefits of participating in a collaborative project of collection management on the local level have been already presented.

D:kult – Now a Permanent Task of the Cultural Department and of the Participating Cultural Institutions

The aims of d:kult are still the same as at its implementation in 2005:

- to establish an unified digital archive of the cultural heritage within the institutions, funded by the city of Düsseldorf;
- to record and manage the complete holdings;
- to organise a workflow to enable data recall for collections and cross over enquiries.
- to present the collection together on the Internet.

The status of the project and the number of participants has changed over the years. In 2009 d:kult became a long-term project and, step-by-step, other cultural institutions, such as the City Museum and the Film Museum, became participants.

One important step was the establishment of the d:kult team in 2007 in which a central unit of museum documentation was created. Beside the project manager, three people were employed to provide support to the project manager and the staff within the cultural institutions. These colleagues are professionals in the field of documentation and media design and they are specially trained in the facilities of TMS and other related tools. They are responsible for the administration of the database, introduce and train new users, give advice and help during the implementation and afterwards. They are also the intermediaries to the City's Department of Information Technology and the software producer.

Since 2008, besides recording, d:kult offers the possibility to present the objects on the Internet – called d:kult online[2]. Each institute defines the objects, made available via d:kult online. A minimal standard for the description of the objects and copyright issues have to be taken into consideration.

---

[2]   <http://dkult.duesseldorf.de/>.

Colleagues in the German and international museum community as well as in other communities, dedicated to the digitisation, the protection and preservation of cultural heritage benefit from the experiences and expertise of the colleagues involved. For example, the head of the project became member of the competence network for the German Digital Library – one potential provider to Europeana[3]. Members of the former project team share their experience and ideas with other users of the same software (user's meeting on the local and the international level) and colleagues, using other collection management software to reach and implement professional standards in general (for example within the Working Group of Collection Management (AG Sammlungsmanagement), affiliated to the Special Interest Group Documentation (Fachgruppe Dokumentation) as part of the German Union of Museums (Deutscher Museumsbund).

Objects and Related People, Institutions, and Media within d:kult

Within the Theatre Museum a data model was developed to reflect the complex information structures in a reasonable way. The main access point is the performance (*Inszenierung*). Around the performance we collect many objects (costumes, text books, posters, theatre programmes, play bills, press clippings, images, autographs and letters, audiovisual media, stage and costume design, stage models, requisites) related to the performance. Other important access points are people (*Personen*) and institutions (*Körperschaften*), which are related to the theatre and may be related to a special performance. We also have objects (*Objekte*) without any relation to a performance but have a certain relation to the collection's profile.

The Museum System (TMS), i.e. the implemented software, offers the possibility to create "virtual objects", which we use to record the performances and will be used in the Film Museum to handle cinematographic information concerning a film, independent from the physical objects within the collection.

Because of the importance of documenting performances we started to record the current ones in North-Rhine Westphalia, together with theatre programmes and press clippings for each show. After two seasons the clippings are transferred to the collection, including the change of location within TMS. If we have additional personal resources we record performances from the past – going back, step by step, season by season. At the moment we have recorded performances since

---

[3]   <http://www.europeana.eu/portal/>.

the 1996-1997 season, but unfortunately not all of them are accessible online because some checking work has to be done. Further resources include theatre programmes or play bills and books, published at the end of a director's era in order to document their activities or on the occasion of an anniversary. Additionally, we record performances in the context of projects, for example a touring exhibition about Gustaf Gründgens, an exhibition on the life and work of Karlheinz Stroux (Director of the Düsseldorfer Schauspielhaus between 1956 and 1972), in the context of recording costumes of the German Opera on the Rhine (Deutsche Oper am Rhein Düsseldorf-Duisburg), the documentation of the production archive of the Kom(m)ödchen (a cabaret in Düsseldorf, founded by Kay and Lore Lorentz) or the project Hamlet – European Transfer (H.E.T.).

TMS allows the creation of recording forms by the users, adapted to their needs without changing the database structure as a whole. So we have developed a form for performances and forms for the objects showing directly the related performance on the top of the screen. We defined core elements of description, too: author/composer of the piece, (music) director, and set and costume designer have to be recorded as well as the location and the date of the first presentation. If pictures of the performance are available (for example on the theatre's website), a choice of images are archived within the media module to get a first impression of the performance. These pictures are normally only for internal use, but we put the information about the resource of the images and – if mentioned – the name of the photographer into the database. So we establish, for the long term, an information tool about theatre photography in the context of our collection. Recording and indexing of photographs belonging to the visual archive, is the task of the colleagues within the collection – these images are handled like objects as other visual objects, for example paintings, graphics, sculptures and other objects of art.

Other workflows are possible as well, such as the recording of objects shown in an exhibition – without any relation to a performance, importing data on autographs and assets from already existing digital resources (i.e. the finding aids to the assets of the Schauspielhaus Düsseldorf Dumont-Lindemann, of Karlheinz Stroux and a part of the asset of Gustaf Gründgens), and press clippings about various people.

Adding media can enrich all kinds of objects: they (i.e. images, data files, audio visual media, etc.) can be connected to virtual and physical objects as well as to the constituent module (people/institutions) and to exhibitions. These media objects can be made accessible for both internal as well as external use through d:kult online.

At the moment (June 2010) we have recorded 1,770 performances, about 35,000 objects and about 5,000 media. Within the constituent module about 18,200 people/institutions have been entered by the staff of the Theatre Museum.

Archiving Activities and Exhibitions within d:kult

TMS supports all aspects of workflow within a museum. One important aspect is the documentation of activities and the establishment of an electronic archive. A part of the electronic archive can be found within the website of the museum. For each exhibition presented by the Theatre Museum, at least one page has been created and is accessible[4] even if the exhibition has closed and disappeared. This kind of presentation offers the user only an impression of the activities. Another approach is the publication of an exhibition catalogue or an accompanying publication – but not every activity or exhibition can be documented by a printed publication. The exhibition module within TMS offers the possibility to prepare exhibitions as well as to document them afterwards. Since only a little part of our collection has been recorded in the database, the preparation of an exhibition within TMS is still difficult – it's possible, when the curator and other involved staff preparing the exhibition use TMS during this part of the workflow. We are still working on this aspect. If we work with freelancers or foreign curators, they need an introduction on how to use the database and a time-restricted account. Meanwhile the use of Office Programs is quite normal, but the use of collection management software and the data exchange between different management systems is not so easy.

At the moment we use the exhibition module as a substitute for an exhibition catalogue (for example the exhibition of graphics by Ingrid Mizsenko, inspired by her visits of the workshops behind the scenes of Düsseldorf theatres) or for retrospective documentation. One exhibition on the occasion of the 60th anniversary of the Kom(m)ödchen and on the 100th anniversary of Schauspielhaus Düsseldorf have been recorded in the exhibition module after the closure. One member of the curatorial staff has taken over the task to record the objects and document the exhibition by photographs within TMS. Other current projects are the documentation of the basic concept of the exhibition Museum für Zuschaukunst (presented in Düsseldorf from October 2009 to January 2010) and a poster exhibition about theatre buildings in North-Rhine Westphalia, presented in the summer of 2010 in connection with the Festival of Theatres in North-Rhine Westphalia at Düsseldorf.

---

[4]   <http://www.duesseldorf.de/theatermuseum/th_mehr/tm_archiv.shtml>.

Another point of importance is the presentation of projects going on behind the scene, especially within the collection, which are normally not visible to the public. In the past, records or research projects presented as finding aids, exhibitions or publications may be in printed or electronic form and sometime as reports on the state of the material during conference projects or in order to get a funding extension. In this context TMS and the web presentation d:kult online offers a look behind the scenes. If one work package has been terminated, a project milestone has been reached and this part can be made accessible to the interested public and may raise interest to the progress of the ongoing project. Colleagues involved in the recording of and the research concerning the production archive of the Kom(m)ödchen, present their results step by step via d:kult online and inform the public by press releases within this context. By creating permanent links, a connection between information via the website (Neues aus dem Museum) and via d:kult online was made.

Using TMS for this kind of public relations has many advantages for the museum. On one hand, the permanent, normally hidden, process of recording can be made visible to the public. On the other hand, the presentation via d:kult can be seen as a motivation to enforce the activities in the field of documentation internally. Furthermore it supports the transparency internally and externally as well as the quality. Expertise and knowledge within the museum and within the whole project about cultural heritage can be exchanged via d:kult as a platform. One example in this context is the constituent module, containing information about people and institutions, which is established and maintained by all participating institutions.

Forwarding Information to Projects on the National and International Level

Within d:kult professional (principally librarian) standards and rules are used. Authority files for names (PND for people, AKL for artists, and GKD for institutions) are implemented as well as the authority file of subject headings (SWD), the Classification of Iconography (ICON Class[5] in the field of fine arts, and the Thesaurus of Geographical Names (TGN). The software itself includes the Art and Architecture Thesaurus (AAT), which has unfortunately not yet been translated into German, and meets the requirements of the British Spectrum Standard (i.e. the minimal standard for museums in Great Britain[6]. The discussion and participation within relevant communities enable the transfer of data into other information services on the national and international level.

---

[5]   <http://www.iconclass.nl/>.

[6]   <http://www.collectionstrust.org.uk/stand>.

The head of d:kult is a member of the Working Group for Data Exchange, another group affiliated with the Special Interest Group of Documentation. After the implementation of d:kult online, the forwarding of data to the common portal of libraries, archives and museums (BAM[7]) is taken into consideration. This portal provides an Internet-based access point to cultural information in Germany. After a search within the portal, BAM, the user gets a list of hits and is redirected to the resources themselves in order to present the content in the original context. The integration of the data into BAM has not yet been realised.

Within the context of providing information to Europeana, the German Digital Library (Deutsche Digitale Bibliothek[8]) has been developed as the German contribution towards more digitisation. The aim is to enable access to 30,000 cultural and scientific institutions (libraries, archives, museums). The concept and the project plan were developed between 2009 and 2010 and the implementation and realisation will follow in 2010-2011. A network of competence has been established because of the federal structure of Germany and the fact, that culture is a voluntary duty of the states, and the regional and local bodies. d:kult is member of this network and has the chance to take active part within the development of the German Digital Library.

Additionally, participation offers the chance to get in contact with other important projects in the field of the preservation and documentation of cultural heritage, for such as Kalliope[9], the union catalogue of autographs and assets, maintained by the State Prussian Library (Staatsbibliothek Preußischer Kulturbesitz). Autographs and assets, owned by Düsseldorf's cultural institutions are or will be recorded there – the data of the Heinrich-Heine-Institut, another participant within d:kult, are already imported to TMS, and data from the Theatre Museum will follow as well as data of the Goethe Museum. From another point of view, an interface has to be created to enable the export of data from d:kult to Kaliope in the future – for example autographs from the production archive of the Kom(m)ödchen.

The Theatre Museum, as a small institution, had the chance to join collaborative projects on the local level from which the participation enabled the museum to make the recorded information accessible and visible in diverse contexts. Furthermore, the implementation of such tools and active participation influences the workflow and the development of the staff internally and enables a high degree of transparency, i.e. the documentation of the existing knowledge in the database, the intensive

---

7 <http://www.bam-portal.de/>.

8 <http://www.deutsche-digitale-bibliothek.de/>.

9 <http://kalliope.staatsbibliothek-berlin.de/>.

occupation with the subject and the collection result in more efficient and higher quality of work and increased staff competencies.

Collaborative Projects – in the Field of the Performing Arts, too?

In the German museum community the collaboration between the museums collection management policies has been reinforced during the last years. The Special Interest Group of Documentation serves as a platform for the exchange of knowledge and expertise and puts tools for common use at the disposal of their members (i.e. the development of thesauri and classifications). On the international level a data format for the exchange of data (Lido – Lightweight Information Describing Objects) has been developed together with important institutions like the Getty Institute and collection management software providers.

Within the International Federation of Film Archives (FIAF[10]) a working group has been established to have a look to new trends within the field of cataloguing such as the Anglo-American Cataloguing Rules (AACR) changing into Resource Description and Access (RDA[11]), and rules for the description of items in the field of archives, libraries and museums and the widespread data format for libraries, MARC, changing into an object-oriented approach. The working group wants to know how the data, relevant for recording cinematographic information and related collections, can be recorded on the basis of these new rules and the functional requirement for bibliographical records (FRBR[12]). In the past librarian rules and principles have been successfully used in the field of cataloguing media, including film and related objects within the FIAF and existing rules based on these principles, have been adapted to the needs of film archives and collections.

In the field of the performing arts no standards and procedures have yet been established to exchange information among archives, libraries and museums. Which rules and data formats have to be used? What kind of information should be exchanged, for example, data concerning the performances? Which information categories in the context of an object are relevant and may be exchanged? Do we have or need rules and data formats as a basis for recording and exchanging records between different institutions on the national or international level? Do other institutions in the field of the performing arts plan to contribute to national or

---

[10] <http://www.fiafnet.org/uk/>.

[11] <http://www.rda-jsc.org/rda.html>.

[12] <http://www.ifla.org/en/publications/functional-requirements-for-bibliographic-records>.

international digitization projects – like Europeana or Athena (provider of museum information)? And how could the collaboration with collections be realised outside of Europe? SIBMAS and its conferences could serve as platform for such a discussion.

Abstract

Le Musée du Théâtre participe, depuis l'origine, au projet d:kult: Digital Archive of Art and Culture in Düsseldorf (Archives numériques des arts et de la culture à Düsseldorf). d:kult est une initiative des institutions culturelles, subventionnée par la ville de Düsseldorf. d:kult encourage l'enregistrement commun, la gestion et l'accessibilité des objets culturels qui sont sous la responsabilité de ces instituts.

Le Musée s'est impliqué dans le projet en raison de la diversité de ses collections, de son intérêt pour la mise en œuvre et l'utilisation des technologies avancées de l'information, ainsi que de sa volonté de se faire mieux connaître et d'offrir à un large public des services utiles et intéressants.

Le Musée tente, à côté de la présentation traditionnelle, de montrer l'envers du décor, par des expositions, des visites guidées, des événements et des spectacles. Il permet au visiteur/utilisateur de voir ce qui se passe dans toutes les parties du musée, particulièrement celles qui sont cachées (la plus grande partie des collections) ou qui ont disparu (comme par exemple les expositions antérieures).

La collecte et l'enregistrement servent de supports pour la préservation et l'enrichissement du patrimoine culturel dans le domaine des arts du spectacle. La base de données peut être considérée comme une interface entre passé, présent et futur. Nous collectons des objets et des documents du passé, nous présentons le théâtre actuel – grâce à la récolte d'objets et documents contemporains ainsi qu'à la création de spectacles –, et nous essayons de structurer l'information de manière à soutenir l'enseignement et la recherche d'aujourd'hui et de demain. L'enregistrement de toutes ces activités implique l'archivage et la sécurisation de la totalité de ces connaissances rassemblées.

Dans le domaine des arts du spectacle, il n'existe pas de normes et de procédures établies pour un échange d'informations entre les centres d'archives, les bibliothèques et les musées. La question reste ouverte pour l'avenir.

The Meyerhold Exhibition in Tokyo

Yoko UEDA

The Tsubouchi Memorial Theatre Museum, Waseda University
(Tokyo – Japan)

Some objects maintain the energy of their former holders after their death. Almost all of the theatre museum collections, more or less visible or invisible, maintain the energy of the performances, which have been played. It is this energy that I wanted to show in the exhibition Theatre and Life of Meyerhold – 70 years after his death, 55 years after his resurgence, which took place at The Tsubouchi Memorial Theatre Museum of Waseda University in March and April 2010. Peter Brook, who was greatly influenced by Meyerhold, said:

> What is necessary, however, is an incomplete design; a design that has clarity without rigidity; one that could be called "open" as against "shut". This is the essence of theatrical thinking: a true theatre designer will think of his designs as being all the time in motion, in action, in relation to what the actor brings to a scene as it unfolds.[1]

Displaying the theatre, the exposition must open the doors leading to the imagined stage. The energy of the exhibition must act on the imagination of visitor-spectator and make him or her penetrate into the exhibiting images.

The Tsubouchi Memorial Theatre Museum at Waseda University is the only museum of theatre arts in Japan whose collection includes objects related to the world history of theatre arts. The Theatre Museum was established in 1928 and architecturally modelled after the English Renaissance theatre The Fortune. The inscription on its façade *Totus Mundus Agit Historionem* was taken from Shakespeare's The Globe Theatre still maintains a principle of Shoyo Tsubouchi (1859-1935), the founder of our museum. Teaching English literature (he also founded the faculty of literature at our university) Dr. Tsubouchi endeavoured to

---

[1] Peter Brook, *The Empty Space*, London, Macgibbon & Kee, 1969, p. 101-102.

modernise Japanese theatre culture. He translated the complete works of Shakespeare for the first time in Asia and donated the royalties from the books for the establishment of The Theatre Museum in Tokyo. It is known that Japan had been a closed country until 1854 by the policy of *sakoku* (seclusion). After the period of isolation from international society, Japan started to seek ways to be "modernised", to bring its culture to the level of the European countries. It was at that time that the first universities modelled after the European institutions were established in Japan. Waseda University was founded in 1882 by the politician Shigenobu Okuma for the purpose of bringing up individuals who might support the further development of the country. Founder of the Theatre Museum of Waseda University Dr. Tsubouchi played a key role in the development of Japanese literature and theatre. European drama in Japan took its first steps with Dr. Tsubouchi's translations of Shakespeare and the performances he organised and directed mainly in his own theatre company Bungei kyokai in Waseda University. (It will not be superfluous to mention here one interesting fact that "modernisation" of Japanese literature and theatre meant to introduce the logic and psychology of realism and to conquer the conventional manner of the Japanese art at that age). Born in 1874, Meyerlold could be considered as the contemporary of Dr. Tsubouchi. Meyerhold's best work *The Government Inspector* premiered in late December 1926 and two years later in 1928 the Theatre Museum was founded in Tokyo.

It was almost by accident that I ended up organising the exhibition on Meyerhold's theatre. One night in September 2008 when I struggled with my doctoral thesis one colleague sent me an email about the lack of plans for exhibitions in the following year and asked if I could offer some project the next day. I agreed without thinking and in one night produced a plan for the exhibition based on a valuable collection related to this great theatre director in our museum (a portrait with his autograph, posters, playbills, booklets and so on). Furthermore 2010 marks the 70th anniversary of his death.

Having finished my doctoral dissertation I began the research for the exhibition. I quickly understood that the required effort for the task was incredible. There was an unhappy situation with Meyerlold studies in Japan – no experts, comparatively few translations of his works and studies on his arts. It was quickly realised; however, that it is the scale and diversity of Meyerhold's genius that stand in the way of the researchers attempts to approach his arts. Additionally, the unstable nature of the theatre arts makes situation even more complicated. The theatre performance consists of various elements, not only artificially fixed ones, such as the text, *mise en scène* or the sets, but also the natural condition of media, for example, actors and spectators, even the weather. When by some miracle all elements act in the best way and form a whole unity, a theatre performance might rise to an incredible height, but we never again can see theatre performances of the past.

A question started to worry me – how can I present such an ephemeral kind of art in an exhibition? Although all of them are worth expositing, actually there is a lack of materials about Meyerhold in our collection (only six posters, one autographed portrait, three manuscript leaves, half a dozen playbills, and about twenty photographs and books). Moreover, the old, fixed, thick glass showcases in our more than 80 years old museum are inconvenient in size and form and can even be an obstacle in designing the exhibition.

At some point I was struck with the idea of obtaining permission to use replicated material from Russia and attempting to visually reconstruct each work with a focus on photographs. Two excellent exhibitions in the Meyerhold Apartment Museum in Moscow (Meyerhold – The Space of Love and Meyerhold the Actor/Actor in the Meyerhold Theatre) assured me that it is possible to present the dynamism of the stage using a large number of stage photographs and portraits. The photographs of Meyerhold Theatre are still stylish. Stage compositions reflect Meyerhold's strong knowledge of art history and fixed in two dimensions they still possess the great visual effect of the performances. In the Meyerhold Theatre they worked out the system of recording the theatre arts and left a vast collection of archive materials. Almost all of the stage photographs were taken during the organised with the purpose of photo-documentation sessions after the performances. I made three research trips to Russia and visited some archives including the Central Science Library of Theatre Union, the Bakhrushin State Theatre Museum and the Saint-Petersburg State Museum of Theatre and Music. During these trips I collected about 170 different items. Also, Professor Masaharu Ura of the University of Tokyo loaned me approximately 150 photographs that were previously held by Professor Yoshio Nozaki (1906-1995) of Waseda University the preeminent expert on 20th century Russian theatre. Materials donated by him make up the largest part of our Russian theatre collection[2]. Finally,

---

2   After the Exhibition there were two significant discoveries to clarify the history of the considerable part of exhibits. The 2011 Great East Japan Earthquake brought us the big finding. There was no damage of the Museum but the seismic reinforcing arms were distorted, walls cracked and contents of the shelves fell. Putting the storages into order, a box of one hundred fifty photographs of Meyerhold Theatre was found, which we identified as the originals of the prof. Ura's cabinet photo collection. Another evidences were found in Meyerhold Theatre Archive at Russian State Archive of Literature and Art (RGALI) – a letter dated 31 January 1930 from the first director of The Tsubouchi Memorial Theatre Museum Umaji Kaneko to The State Meyerhold Museum asking to supply the Theatre Museum with "publications and objects bearing on the theatrical art" and help "healthy growth" of the institution, some negotiation letters from

I gathered so many photo-materials that I had to make a difficult choice between equally interesting images.

The exhibition was composed of 260 items including photographs, a theatre scale model, posters, playbills, postcards and books. We decided to exhibit photographs from several of the Moscow Art Theatre's productions directed by Stanislavsky, where Meyerhold started his career as an actor, such as Tolstoy's *Tsar Fyodor Ivanovich* (1889) and *The Death of Ivan the Terrible* (1889); Chekhov's *Seagull* (1889), in which Meyerhold played Kostya Treplev; the photographs of the productions performed during the so called provincial seasons period, such as Chekhov's *Three Sisters* (1902) based on Stanislavsky's version and Von Chantine's *Acrobats* (1903); and the photographs taken during his work in the Kommisarzhevskaya Theatre – Maeterlinck's *Sister Beatrice* (1906) and Blok's *The Fairground Booth* (1906) and one of the studio productions of pseudonym, Doctor Dapertutto, his own adaptation of Schnitzler's *Colombina's Scaf* (1910). From the works performed in the Imperial Theatres, we decided to exhibit the photos of Molière's *Dom Juan* (1910), Calderon's *The Constant Prince*, Ostrovsky's *The Storm* (1916) and the most remarkable work of pre-revolutionary period – Lermontov's *Masquerade* (1917). From the post-revolution works we choose some pictures of the agitation plays, such as Verhaeren's *The Dawns* (1920), Mayakovsky's *Mistery-Bouffe* (1918, 1921), Tretyakov's *Earth Rampant* (1923) based on Martine's *The Night* (the first performance using a screen on the stage); the masterpiece of constructivist works Crommelynck's *The Magnanimous Cuckold* (1922), another constructivist work Sukhovo-Kobylin's *The Death of Tarelkin* (1922), the agitation revues *D.E.* (1924) based on the novel of Ehrenburg's *Trust "D.E."* and Tretyakov's *Roar, China!* (1926), urban melodramas reflecting life under the NEP (New Economy Policy) Faiko's *Lake Lyul* (1923) and *Bubus, the Teacher* (1925), contemporary adaptations of Ostorovsky's social dramas *A Lucrative Post* (1923) and *The Forest* (1924), masterpieces of contemporary satires Erdman's *The Mandate* (1925), Mayakovsky's *The Bedbug* (1929) and *The Bathhouse* (1930), newly interpreted classics Gogol's *The Government Inspector* (1926), Griboedov's *Woe to Wit* (1928), Duma fils's *Lady of the Camellias* (1934), Sukhovo-Kobylin's *Krechinsky's Wedding* (1934)

Yoshio Nozaki who had lived in Leningrad from 1928 to 1932 to director of State Meyerhold Theatre Museum Valeryan Stepanov and receipts for the photographs. (The Meyerhold Theatre, 1920-1938 [microform]: from the holdings of the State Archive of Literature and Art, Moscow, Russia. Woodbridge, CT: Reasearch Publications, 1999. File No. 963, Inventory No. 1, case No. 1209.) In January 1933 Nozaki organized five days exhibition "USSR Theatre" at Asahi Newspaper Gallery. The second Nozaki collection Soviet Theatre exhibition was held at Tsubouchi Memorial Theatre Museum from 16 November 1989 to 9 February 1990.

and Tchaikovsky's opera *Queen of Spades* (1935) with a new corrected libretto based on the Pushkin's original novel.

Materials on Meyerhold's pre-revolutionary activities are rare than those of his post-revolutionary works, which is why we did not display the photographs of both the plays at the Studio in Povarskaya Street in Moscow nor the operas in the Imperial Mariinsky Theatre in Saint Petersburg. Some materials we could not include due to financial reasons. Nevertheless, we could certainly exhibit materials of all the important works of this extraordinarily productive theatre director. We made an effort to give the synopses of plays and commentaries on directing innovations in the explanation panels and named the scenes, roles and actors in the photo captions.

I was surprised at how clear we could get every detail in the stage photographs when they were printed in large format. I assembled the whole composition of the exhibition with several expressive photographs printed in the maximum size but perhaps the section dedicated to *The Government Inspector*, in the biggest showcase (about 4.5 by 3.5 meters), had the most overpowering energy. It is undoubtedly a masterpiece in the history of 20th century world theatre although the most well known of Meyerhold's work in Japan is *The Magnanimous Cuckold* because of its popularity in the avant-garde culture contexts. On the wall inside this showcase we displayed twenty-eight monochrome photographs in various sizes and a poster of the debate on *The Government Inspector* with radical red letters. We also displayed the playbills, the books and the individual portraits of each actor in their roles from this performance.

On the wall in front of *The Government Inspector* was the section on *The Magnanimous Cuckold*. It was a composition of nine pictures arranged in order with the photo-documents of biomechanics training on either side. It looked like an iconostas and presented an interesting contrast to the baroque and grotesque exposition of *The Government Inspector*. In the centre of this room we put a white scale model of the New Meyerhold Theatre created this winter by the architect Satoru Ito at a request from the Meyerhold research group. The construction of the New Meyerhold Theatre began in the 1930s but was stopped by Stalin in 1938. We made our model based mainly on the plans of architects Vahtangov and Barkhin who worked on this project. We also used posters of Japanese architect Renshichiro Kawakita (1902-1975) that were made for the exhibition of New Meyerhold Theatre in the Haiyuza Theatre in Tokyo in early 1930s and were donated to our Museum in 1934. The scale model was planned and made with precision and a good sense of style. A white square box with an ellipse space inside it asserted itself in the centre of the exhibition room giving an impression as if it is a projector and all the pictures are its projection. The scale model made the whole exhibition to work as an installation. Moreover, it became an embodiment of another form of exposition of the results of the theatre research besides the articles.

To give our exhibition further dynamism, we planned several events beginning with the lectures delivered in spring 2009 by the French authority on Meyerhold studies, Doctor Béatrice Picon-Vallin, who had been temporarily invited to Japan as a senior research fellow of the Theatre Research Centre attached to our museum. I have to mention here the great significance of Doctor Picon-Vallin's visit to Japan. Besides her remarkable lectures, she played a very important role in connecting people by bringing together nearly all of the members of the Japanese Meyerhold research group. In the autumn, we won a collaborative research grant making it possible to produce the scale model and invite theatre director, actor and biomechanics instructor Alexey Levinsky to organise his first ever workshop in Japan (1-5 March, 2010). On the 4th of March 2010 we organised the symposium, Actual Biomechanics where Levinsky, being a student of the original biomechanics training and who learnt it directly from the Meyerhold Theatre actor and instructor, Nikolai Kustov, he discussed it with different representatives of Japanese theatre circles and critics. We also organised the showing of Protozanov's movie *The White Eagle* (1928), thus giving the audience a rare chance to see Meyerhold as an actor with their own eyes. After that, theatre critic Hidenaga Otori, expert on DaDa, Professor Fumi Tsukahara and theatre director and psychiatrist Shigeyuki Toshima discussed the arts of the avant-garde, particularly the relations between arts and politics (12 March, 2010). Finally, as our closing event, we presented Molecular Theatre's performance *Ballet-Biomechanics* directed by Shigeyuki Toshima who tried to express the tension of Meyerhold's struggle for the revolution in arts and declared his determination as an avant-garde successor (24-25 April, 2010). I hope that we were successful in achieving desired high level of "Meyerhold energy" in Waseda.

The exhibition Theatre and Life of Meyerhold gathered in total 5,202 visitors making it a splendid achievement for the University's museum, especially taking into account the spring holydays season in March.

Abstract

Certains objets conservent l'énergie de leurs défunts propriétaires. Presque toutes les collections des musées du théâtre préservent, de manière plus ou moins visible, l'énergie des spectacles représentés. C'est cette énergie que nous avons voulu montrer dans l'exposition : Le théâtre et la vie de Meyerhold – 70 ans après sa mort, 55 ans après sa réapparition, qui a eu lieu au Tsubouchi Memorial Theatre Museum de l'Université de

Waseda en mars et avril 2010. Peter Brook, qui a été très influencé par Meyerhold, a écrit :

> Or, c'est précisément quelque chose d'inachevé qu'il nous faut : un projet qui soit clair sans être rigide, qui puisse être qualifié d'«ouvert» et non de «fermé». C'est le b.a.-ba de la pensée théâtrale. Un véritable décorateur de théâtre concevra ses projets comme toujours en mouvement, en action, en relation avec ce que le comédien apporte à une scène, au fur et à mesure qu'elle se développe.[3]

Pour montrer le théâtre, l'exposition doit ouvrir des portes qui mènent à une scène imaginée. La force de l'exposition doit agir sur l'imagination du visiteur-spectateur et le faire pénétrer à l'intérieur des images exposées.

---

[3] Peter Brook, *L'espace vide*, (trad. Ch. Estienne et F. Fayolle), Paris, Seuil (Essais), 1977, p. 135.

Changes at the Theatre Instituut Nederland

Hans VAN KEULEN

Manager Collection and Documentation Department
Theatre Instituut Nederland
Since 01-01-2013 Curator Performing Arts Heritage Collections
Special Collections University of Amsterdam (Netherland)

Introduction

Theatre cannot be preserved; it has to be seen and experienced. Often, I am confronted with this objection when I enthusiastically speak about exhibitions. To a large degree it is true. The goose bumps, the tremors, the hearty laugh, the emotion – everything that is aroused by a beautiful and exceptional performance cannot be preserved by us as guardians of the legacy of the performing arts. Nevertheless, by conserving abundant data and objects we can, as it were, reconstitute the performance. I would like to relate how Theatre Instituut Nederland currently does this in the digital age. I am currently responsible for the collection and documentation at Theatre Instituut Nederland, or TIN.

The last time that I spoke about Theatre Instituut Nederland was at the Barcelona Congress in 2004.

Now, six years later, much has taken place in the interim. Therefore, I would like to provide you with an update on TIN as an organisation, in 2010: the expectations, wishes and desires of our users; the acquisition of the collection and the digital developments in collection conservation.

Institut del Teatre Barcelona 2004.

Organisation

We left our five buildings on the Herengrach to continue in ordinary office premises on the Sarphatistraat.

The collection was also moved from the Herengracht to the Sarphatistraat. 2009.

With no museum, but with a free and public Media Centre, this library was designed by a theatre designer and a light designer and contains such elements as metal partitions, full of theatre texts, and "theatre backdrops" as ceiling coverings.

The new mediacentre at the Sarphatistraat.

Was the change of address due to economisation factors? No, we had already established that the wonderful 17th century buildings could not satisfy the modern requirements of a museum; the exhibition space was too small in its entirety, somewhat over 500m², so visitors rarely returned.

The outside of the new building tin at the Sarphatistraat.

The exhibition in the Museum De Fundatie Zwolle about musical theatre.

Despite the constantly changing exhibitions, the average visitor had a sense of: "seen it once, done it". We received some 35,000 visitors a year, of which 50% were tourists who came for the canal-side buildings and 6,000 were pupils from primary and secondary education.

Additionally, the educational spaces were too small and the location functioned poorly as office space. In order to visit personnel from my own department, sometimes I had to travel through seven different doors, protected by electronic locks and accessible via stairs and passages – very romantic, but hardly effective. It was enough of a reason for the new director, Henk Scholten, who was appointed in January 2008, to take the difficult decision to leave the building.

Since April 2009 we have been housed in what is also, incidentally, a beautiful renovated bank building in the Amsterdam School style.

We still organise exhibitions, but now on location and no longer only in Amsterdam, but in the whole of the Netherlands. Furthermore, we are aiming to open a national museum for the performing arts in the next 10 years.

In 2009, we organised three exhibitions; two in Amsterdam (in the Amsterdam Historical Museum and in the Jewish Historical Museum) and one in Zwolle, in the north of the Netherlands, on musical theatre.

Dance pioneer Sonja Gaskell in the Jewish Historical Museum.

The theme of the presentations in the period 2009-2012 was forty years in four years, to mark 1969, which was a very important year for Dutch theatre history. The so-called Tomato Action took place in these twilight days of the turbulent period of 1968, whereby a new generation of theatre makers pelted the old with tomatoes. The consequences included the birth of the black box theatre and theatre at special sites. In 2009, 43,000 people visited these exhibitions. In May of this year a touring exhibition about Site Specific Theatre began in Utrecht and will travel to seven different festivals.

Site specific Exposition, here before the Citytheatre in Utrecht.
Design: Teun Mosk.

We are still the sector and heritage institute. Despite a different organisation, whereby the presentation of both services has fallen under the auspices of one department, heritage and the interests of the sector nevertheless remain different entities. This is the way that TIN has organised things since 2009.

Organisational chart

What is now different than in 2004 is that the Media Centre and data collection are no longer separate from the museum collection, and the exhibitions and collection no longer fall under one department. The whole organisation has become flatter: more departments, less intermediary managers. At the time of the move we also streamlined from fifty full-time employees to thirty-seven, so that more money was made available for activities.

Wishes and Desires of our Customers

Heritage organisations are often focused on supply. There is a collection that the public has perhaps not asked for. In order to ascertain the wishes of our users and to inform us about our image tin conducted a study at the start of this year among the members of the Media Centre and the sector.

We have some 3,500 members. These are also members of the Media Centre. Everyone can visit the Media Centre for free and consult books and journals, but anyone who wishes to borrow books will have to become a member.

Who are our members?
–   More often a woman than a man
–   Broad age category: from 17 to 89
–   Only 15% are fulltime students, 60% work, 16% work+ study
–   64% work in art and culture, a third do not
–   Emphasis on artistic positions + education
–   Many freelancers
–   Sector: 1 in 3 are members
–   Students are almost all culture/theatre related

Top 5 reasons for becoming a member:
–   1. Borrow books (76%)
–   2. Interest in Dutch theatre (60%)
–   3. Necessary for study (45%)
–   4. Warm heart for NL theatre (33%)
–   5. Vested interest in theatre climate (31%)

Top 5 in the collection for the members:
–   1. Theatre texts (80%)
–   2. Theatre books (65%)
–   3. Audio and video (38%)
–   4. Reference works (27%)
–   5. Clippings files (24%)

We also asked the members of our sector what they think of us:

Profile of Theatre Instituut Nederland

- Publications and exhibitions score the highest: 80%+
- Media Centre and database: 64%
- The best-known TIN projects are Theatre Prizes (67%) and Blind Date (60%)
- Activities in the area of reflection/education and international promotion are the least well known

According to the members of our sector the core of the Institute is:

* The knowledge and information centre for theatre
* Collection and presentation of heritage

Less "core":

* Promotion of interests, exchange of knowledge, discussion, education, stimulation of theatre visits
* Umbrella: promotion

As a result of these two studies the Management Team concluded that our role as information and knowledge institute should be strengthened in the coming years. This autumn we will discuss how we are going to achieve this and which tasks that will be at the cost of. Furthermore, we scored only moderately for accessibility and inspiration; of course we wish to work hard to improve.

Collection

Our Adlib database now contains the following numbers:

94,128 productions

143 paintings

12,000 digital reviews

408 archives

26,500 posters

21,654 drawings (and graphics)

74,992 books of which 31,661 are texts (scripts)

324 paper theatres

1,729 puppets

10,100 video recordings (of which 1250 are digital)

55,000 photos of which 40,753 also have a digital representation

435 set models

211 masks

366 pieces of jewellery

4,886 costumes

32,100 sound recordings

24,059 programme booklets

These are not all the sub-collections and also not everything is listed in Adlib. You can read through all of this in peace on our website <www.tin.nl> and also search the collection. Except, of course, for the portion that has not yet been digitally described, let alone possesses a digital image; this involves a large collection of photos, cuttings, programme booklets and theatre texts from before 1850.

A. Active Acquisition

The acquisition of our collection can be divided into active, current acquisitions and gifts that we receive retrospectively. We still collect all the details of all professional theatre productions produced in the Netherlands, and this concerns some 1,700 per year, with a peak this year of 2050! It therefore relates to all theatre disciplines, from dance to puppetry and from mime to opera. In order to achieve a representative and responsibly maintained collection, tin decided to create an expert advisory commission in 2003, which makes a selection of productions for the compilation of its collection. The procedure was evaluated and improved in 2009. This selection is now called the TIN Collection Selection. (TCS)

In the case of the acquisition of posters, videos and photos, the tcs Advisory Commission makes a selection of some on hundred representative productions at the end of the theatre season. The Commission consists of fifteen members that have been chosen on the basis of their expertise in the areas of the various theatre disciplines. The ten external members are reviewers, theatre directors or programmers, who through their various positions see many performances. The other five members are personnel from Theatre Instituut Nederland with substantive knowledge of theatre. The chosen productions do not necessarily have to be 'the best' performances; they can also be productions that had an important social theme, or productions that were perhaps not substantively very strong but had a wonderful, exceptional or innovative design. Attention is also paid to the proportional choice of productions by discipline, in relation to the entire offering of the season in question. The selection is supplemented annually with productions that have been awarded important prizes. These posters, videos and photos are digitalised upon arrival.

B. Retrospective

We also try as far as possible to apply these norms to retrospective acquisition. Often this concerns the archives of theatre companies or directors or actors. In each case we try to make a representative selection from the performances that they have presented. We attempt to sketch as complete a picture as possible of these performances: photos, posters, reviews, programmes, scripts, budgets and policy papers- and, of course, video. Not all (sub) collections can be dealt with in this way, which is why we have also drawn up selection criteria to accompany these basic principles; for example, technical requirements, gaps and the numbers per year.

Storage in Amsterdam South-East (Bijlmer).

Projects

Over the last five years the collection department has caught up dramatically in terms of the digitalisation of images. Some 53,000 performance photos, 22,000 prints and drawings, 18,000 posters, 1,500 costumes, 24,000 programmes and 300 files of personal particulars have been digitalised. And 2,500 hours of video have been recorded on the hard drive. Can all of this now be seen on the web? Not yet, but we are working hard on it.

This year the department is undertaking two major projects that are both devoted to the realisation of the digital *Theatre Encyclopaedia*. One project involves arranging the copyrights. We have started with the 4,000 photographers that we have in our files. We write to them asking if they would collaborate for free on a low-resolution image in the Theatre Encyclopaedia. The reactions have been encouraging (400 different and important photographers have signed a contract) but it is an enormous task to trace all of the photographers. This also gives rise to fundamental questions: in the future we will be able to display images on the Internet for which the rights have been arranged; but at the same time we will perhaps not be able to display the most important or interesting images or videos, the ones we most want. Is this a problem? Is this a form of self-censorship?

The other project entails combating the contamination of the database: the operation – clean Adlib. More than 240,000 terms and names are being validated. Some names such as […] appear with more than twenty variations. Which is correct? It involves a great deal of searching and mental work and is extremely labour intensive, but important for correct searches in the *Theatre Encyclopaedia*. Why are we digitalising at such a rapid pace and why are we arranging the rights and validating the names of persons and institutions? We are doing this for one great project that we have been working on for some five years.

Theatre Encyclopaedia

The *Theatre Encyclopaedia*[1] is to be a well-organised reference work on the Internet about the performances, people and institutions in the Dutch theatre field and about the TIN collection. The Theatre Encyclopaedia will present this information in its mutual relationships and context. The Theatre Encyclopaedia will be searchable, will possess multi-media elements and connections to other sources of information on the Internet, it will be reliable (or: will be honest about the degree of reliability), complete (according to clear criteria) and current.

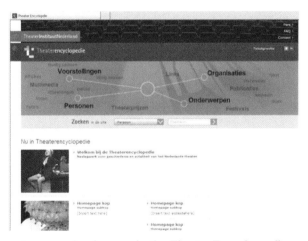

An example of a page in the *Theatre Encyclopaedia*.

---

1   <www.theaterencyclopedie.nl>.

The most important aim of the *Theatre Encyclopaedia* is to introduce a coordinating structure to the entire range of information at TIN. It is the means for the presentation of the knowledge, information and the collection at TIN. All of the data about performances, people and institutions that are currently being collected will of course find its home here. New data sources can be included simply in the structure and new information products and services will originate there.

The *Theatre Encyclopaedia* will be the source for data about professional theatre in the Netherlands from the beginning of the 20th century (and in the future, still further back) to the present day, covering the full breadth of the performing arts, from dance to youth theatre and from mime to musical. It will therefore be a unique reference-work in the world of a living theatre culture. A Wikipedia approach has been chosen for the operating method. Authors will work together on entries. The entries in the *Theatre Encyclopaedia* will appear in the context of Wikipedia and vice versa. Within the context of the encyclopaedia all of the entries will be enriched in a unique manner. The entries that relate to terms that comprise the knowledge model of this information environment will be developed under moderation. It thus relates to terms from the thesaurus, and in the long run, to the terms that will form part of an adopted formal ontology and other meta-data, which are considered to be of structural importance for the field in the Netherlands.

As far as the knowledge model is concerned a number of guiding principles will be laid down. The knowledge model must make three things possible: enclose subjectivity (i.e. the nature of knowledge and experience), from the perspective of an expert and that of an enthusiast into a continuum and finally to make all sorts of relationships possible between knowledge data and files within the encyclopaedia and outside it. In the Wikipedia approach, co-creation is a fundamental component of the process: with experts, with professionals and also with enthusiasts, who in time will form a community, in this context, and also provide value for one another.

The encyclopaedia is being developed by TIN; in the long run this will involve many partners. TIN's mission is to strengthen Dutch theatre with information, inspiration, promotion and reflection. TIN's core values include enterprise and ensuring supplemental value. We think that the *Theatre Encyclopaedia* can strengthen both the mission and the core values.

The *Theatre Encyclopaedia's* target group, in the first instance, includes people who are interested in theatre, with special attention for professionals and students of theatre-related educational programmes. Pupils from the Cultural and Artistic Education Programme, CKV, must also be able to find material in the Theatre Encyclopaedia for their papers. In addition, the *Theatre Encyclopaedia* must become an instrument to inform the general public and to make them enthusiastic about theatre.

Naturally, I would have liked to show you this in operation. Unfortunately, after three years we have (still) not advanced further than a base model; at the end of 2010 a real working model will be on the agenda. In such a lengthy development trajectory it is not always easy to keep both one's own personnel and the financiers convinced. The *Theatre Encyclopaedia* is being developed with many supplemental resources from various funds.

Performing Arts Museum

Will TIN do everything digitally in the future? No, as I have said, in the coming years we will travel through the Netherlands with exhibitions. Not only those for enthusiasts that have previously been mentioned, but also a touring exhibition made especially for theatre education, Backstage

Educational installation Backstage.

Additionally, we are also engaged in the realisation of a performing arts museum and I would like to offer a brief peek behind the veil. The management team has drawn up six basic principles for the realisation of the performing arts museum:

1. The PKM, performing arts museum in Dutch, will first and foremost be an educational museum, complementing the educational work of companies, performance venues and institutions of arts education. It will work closely with schools and educational services in order to achieve optimal engagement.

2. The PKM will also focus on a general public/audience that is interested in the performing arts, offering something to both the 'novice' as well as the more experienced visitor.

3. Central for the PKM will be the experience. The collection will serve the narratives that are told and/or the experience that the visitor will have. The diversity and consequently the various learning styles of the anticipated visitors will be taken into account.

4. The PKM will make the performing arts personal for each visitor. Not only will specifically selected presentations be shown, the museum will also show what the impact of the performing arts can be on the individual. Interactivity will be a basic principle. Visitors will be able to share their experiences of the performing arts. An active website with a web 2.0 component will be essential.

5. Building, presentation and service will be of a high standard, contemporary and provoke comment. They will give the visitor a feeling that is comparable with being in a theatre, concert hall or pop venue. This will necessarily demand high quality staff.

6. Third parties will also employ the PKM. The PKM will be open to the initiative of others precisely in order to return theatre and music to the social debate. These others may well be companies, orchestras and heritage institutions but they may just as well be social organisations. There will be at least one theatre/ auditorium. A combination of PKM and theatre/concert hall is desirable.

We will investigate whether and how these principles can be realised in the ensuing six months. To this end, we have formulated three different scenarios.

Scenario 1. Independent Museum for the Performing Arts.

Scenario 2. Two permanent locations in a major museum plus a number of touring exhibitions

Scenario 3. Touring exhibitions and other presentations, the same as we do now.

In this paper I have told you something about the new Theatre Instituut – our new location, the search for the correct criteria for the acquisition and selection of the collection, the search for the correct paths on the digital super-highway and our wish to achieve a new performing arts museum. Also, I have provided insight into what the clients and users expect of us, in 2010 because this is why we are doing it after all. We, the people who wish to conserve the theatre heritage for posterity, do this in order to be of good service to our present and future clients.

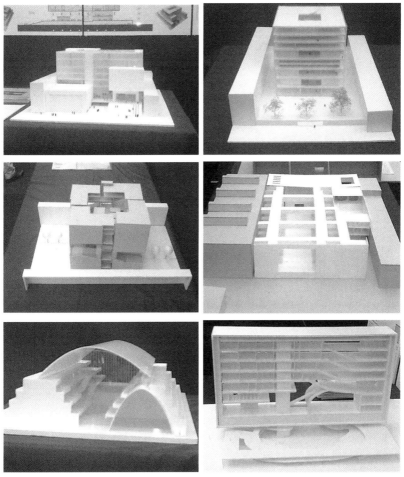

Some results of a completion for a performance art museum by architectural Students Delft.

Abstract

Hans van Keulen relate les changements survenus au Theatre Instituut Nederland, qui a quitté les bâtiments sur le canal pour le centre d'Amsterdam et s'est installé dans un lieu plus approprié. Il évoque aussi les perspectives de travail dans un nouveau musée (avec le patrimoine théâtral et musical) ainsi que le projet de nouvelle encyclopédie numérique du théâtre.

The Development of a Theatre Museum as a Criterion of the Stable Development of Society

Dmitry V. RODIONOV

A. A. Bakhrushin State Central Theatrical Museum
(Moscow – Russia)

The National Theatre History Museum and the Contemporary National Theatre – The Features of the Creation and the Development of The A.A. Bakhrushin State Central Theatre Museum (Principles of the Composing of the Collection, the General Information about the Collection, the Collection in the Pre-Revolutionary Period before 1917, in the 1920s, in the 1930s, to 1980s (USSR), and after 1991 (Russian Federation)

The A. A. Bakhrushin Theatre Museum, the state collection of rarities concerning the theatre art history in Russia and abroad, includes, nowadays, more than 1.5 million items. The famous industrialist and philanthropist Alexey Bakhrushin, who was a member of one of the richest merchant families in Russia, founded the museum as a private collection in the late 19th century. Bakhrushin was an avid theatregoer and he truly honoured the dramatics of the Moscow Maly Theatre and its leading actors, as he was balletomane and never missed a premiere at the Moscow Bolshoi Theatre. His passion for the theatre became the basis of his collecting activities from the one side, and from the other allowed him to become the one of the famous Russian theatrical personalities (Bakhrushin was one of the founders of the Russian Theatre Society, who worked hard for its foundation and development, and later he directed the Moscow Vvedensky National House, where he created a theatrical group for workers, where the professionalism matched its serious repertoire).

Bakhrushin composed his collection on the basis of the principle of the integrated gathering. He believed that only the most extensive consideration of an historical object would help the future generation to learn about a fact or a person in a greater degree of objectivity. That is why he attached a special importance to the memorial items relating to the life and work of an actor, a director, or a theatre painter (scenographer). Bakhrushin also sought to return to the cultural circulation the materials related to the Russian theatre from its inception in Russia and to his contemporary time: that is why the puppet folk dens, the theatre accessories of Pushkin's time of the 19th century, and materials on the country-seat, or serf, theatre of the 18th century had been included in his collection.

Thus, Bakhrushin collected the unique materials, concerning not only the history of the Imperial, i.e. State Theatres, but also the development of the provincial theatres, that appeared in Russia in large number after the abolition of state monopoly on the theatre business.

In 1913, Bakhrushin donated his collection to the state, and his museum was included as a theatrical and literary museum in the institutional system of the Imperial Academy of Sciences, and Bakhrushin was appointed museum director for his lifetime.

It should be noted, that the interest of Bakhrushin as collector was not limited to the field of the theatre, although, of course, they were prevailing: Bakhrushin also collected materials about the history of the Russian culture, associated with famous Russian writers, he also assembled the unique collection of the musical instruments, some of which already in Soviet times had been transferred, in particular, to the Hermitage. Certainly, the contribution of Alexey Bakhrushin in preserving the cultural heritage of Russia is enormous and relates to one of the most prominent acts, which may be done in this domain.

After the Revolution in 1918, the museum, despite of all the complexities of the political time, by the personal order of the People's Commissar Lunacharsky was saved by its nationalisation and by conferring the status of a state museum. Bakhrushin remained museum director during his life, and then the museum was named after its founder. However, the whole private property that belonged to Bakhrushin has been expropriated, and the estate near Moscow has been looted and destroyed. Bakhrushin headed the museum until his death in 1929. In the 1920s the museum collection was enriched by his efforts with the considerable material connected, from the one side, with the landmark productions of that time, in particularly, with Golovin's scenery sketches for the play *Masquerade* staged by Meyerhold, from the other side, with materials on the Russian theatrical avant-garde and Constructivism, that once again testified to the Bakhrushin artistic flair and intuition, who had been able to recognise and to distinguish, within the theatrical practice, the most significant and remarkable events and phenomena.

In 1930s, after the death of Bakhrushin, the museum was repeatedly endangered by closure and the removal of buildings for various state purposes. However, the credibility of the museum in the cultural environment was so high that the most of such attempts, fortunately, ended unsuccessfully. For example, in 1937 Stanislavski wrote a letter to Stalin in defence of the museum, and the museum was left alone. From the 1940s to the 1970s, the state's attention to the museum was minimal: the museum did not receive from the state any means to build a modern storage facility and no successive support for its activities. However, the federal status of the museum made it possible, that the museum received, on the centralised way, the materials from all theatres of the USSR. This circumstance helped to keep the full-scale history of the Soviet theatre of this period. At the same time the museum had been named the Central Theatre Museum, i.e. the main state museum in the field of theatre art.

In the 1980s, the museum had also become the all-union scientific-methodical centre working with all museum departments belonging to theatres of the country.

The years of 1990-2000s were significant for the museum. Several branches, such as the House-Museum of the great Russian actor Mikhail Stchepkin, the House-Museum of the outstanding Russian tragic actress Maria Ermolova, the estate of the famous Russian dramatist Alexander Ostrovsky, the museum-apartments of Vsevolod Meyerhold, of Galina Ulanova, of the actor's family Mironov and Menaker, of the director Valentin Pluchek have been founded and opened. Presently, the first Russian museum dedicated to a theatre artist is preparing to open: the museum-studio by David Borovsky. In 1997, by a special decree by the President of Russian Federation, the A.A. Bakhrushin museum was raised to the status of a particularly valuable object of the cultural heritage of the people of Russia.

Role of the State in the Development of the Museum and the Selfless Work of the Curators of its Collections

In the Soviet times, the relationship between the museum and the State evolved in line with the ideological norms and attitudes prevailing in the society and, naturally, kept the museum's activities within these bounds. In this situation, the State, from the one side, delivered to the museum the archives of some theatres, which had been closed for the ideological reasons – for example, of the State Theatre named after Vsevolod Meyerhold (GOSTIM) in 1938, of the Chamber Theatre in 1949, on the other side, the museum followed the orders of the Ministry of Culture, that prescribed to transfer numerous materials from its collection to other museums, including the newly created national museum institutions. That caused extensive damage to the collection from the standpoint of the principles of its integrity and the legal rights possession.

The Bakhrushin museum has learned from its own experience on the principle of the residual financing prevailing in the Soviet period acts in regard to the state cultural institutions. The salaries of the museum employees, like in all museums in the country, was on the lowest scale, and let them only survive, not live to full value. Therefore, museum workers can be called selfless, as only their deep personal interest and their dedication to the chosen profession left these people remain members of the museum staff.

Nowadays, in the post Soviet times, when the democratic norms have being hardly and arduously established in the Russian society and the economic component of the life, or as we say the market, dominates over all other components, the government and the culture are setting also difficult and arduous the new principles of their relations. The funding of the cultural programmes and museums, in particular, still leaves much to be desired. Also, there is the extremely low level of wages of museum employees; the present economic crisis has only exacerbated the situation. Besides the budget financing, which includes the salary fund, the deduction to the insurance fund, the payment of the public utilities, the expenses of the safeguarding, the museum is able to obtain so-called extra-budgetary funds to implement their innovative programmes. For example, in 2009, the museum received financial means to organise the 6th Bakhrushin festival, to publish the materials to the 200th anniversary of Nikolai Gogol and to restore objects from its collection. Also, in 2009, the applications for carrying out the necessary works to ensure the fire protection measures in all building of the main museum complex have been completely satisfied.

Outstanding Representatives of the Russian Theatre and about the Value of the Theatre Museum

Thanks to Bakhrushin, the museum established, from the moment it had been founded, the close and confidential relations to the theatrical elite of Russia. Bakhrushin enjoyed the veritable authority and respect amidst the actors, many outstanding people of the national theatre attended his "Bakhrushin Saturdays" that he used to arrange in his home. One indicative fact: on November 25th, 1913, when Bakhrushin transferred his collection to the Imperial Academy of Sciences, on this solemn event there were, besides Its Imperial Highness of Grand Duke Konstantin Konstantinovich, the founders of the Moscow Art Theatre Stanislavsky and Nemirovich-Danchenko, actresses of Maly Theatre Ermolova and Jablochkina, the writer Bunin, the dramatist Sumbatov-Juzhin, the heads of private theatres Zimin, Nezlobin, Korsh, the professors of the Moscow university Davydov, Veselovsky and others.

The most eminent Russian intellectuals confirmed the enormous value of a national theatrical museum for Russian culture. Here are some citations:

P.P. Gnedich to A.A. Bakhrushin, September 1924

30 years ago you have modestly begun your collecting. Now your Theatrical Museum has expanded and represents a storehouse of art of huge value. In the West and in America such museums are not present any samples. You are a pioneer in this business. (F. 1, op. 1, storage unit 4481)

A.F. Koni to A.A. Bakhrushin, 6th of November, 1924

Gathering the harvest of the scenic past, the museum makes it a seed for the further manifestations of dramatic art and for maintenance the traditions which are therein necessary. For a thoughtful and sensitive visitor, it presents the richest historical material, giving the chance to peer even into the psychological bases of the creativity of outstanding actors. (F. 1, op. 1 storage unit 4493)

K. S. Stanislavsky, 5th of March 1932

The A. A. Bakhrushin State Theatre Museum exists during 38 years in Moscow. Owing to the completeness of the collections it contains, it is the world scale establishment, and I, being familiar with similar museums in Europe, should put it considerably above the European collections. (F. 1, op. 3, storage unit 289)

And from present day:

F. M. Tchehankov in his book *My Ragged Memory*, 2003

To my dear, unique A. A. Bakhrushin Theatre Museum. Only in Russia there are such a Theatre and such a Museum, which store our life, the theatre life.

Piotr Fomenko and his actors and pupils, so called *fomenkies*, October, 2004

Dear curators of the theatrical history!

You collected, stored and restored all those small strokes to the big portrait of the theatre carefully and with love to your museum during 110 years, doing this portrait not illustrative, but perceived, transferring breath and atmosphere! (F 15, storage unit 323803)

Such appreciation of the activity of the Theatre Museum, of its importance for the modern theatre are one of the bases of its foundation's sense of existence and the guarantee of the successful development to the coming generations would be able from the "first hand" to see and to study the history of the national theatre and its outstanding representatives.

The Place of the Theatrical Museum in the Contemporary Structure of the State Culture Institutions of the Russian Federation

In the Russian Federation (according to the state on the 1st of January, 2006) there are 2,180 Museums, 638 of them are branches. In the immediate competence of the Ministry of Culture of Russian Federation are 57 museums and 5 branches. Other Ministries and State Departments (e.g. the Academy of Sciences, the Academy of Art, the Ministry of Defence etc.) are in charge of 100 museums. The subjects of the Federation administer to other museums by the organs of the self-government, or they are private property. The museums safeguard circa 80 million museum objects and museum collections that are part of the Museum Fund of the Russian Federation; 90% of the total amount of the museum objects and collections belong to the State part of the Museum Fund and are State property.

Currently, the Ministry of Culture of the Russian Federation, the Federal Service for the Supervision of Observance of Law in the Domain of the Protection of the Cultural Heritage of Russia, the Federal Archives Department, the Federal Media Department acting in the domain of the registration and the safeguarding of museum valuables, have been led by the rules of six basic Federal Laws, of three legal normative acts issued by the Government of the Russian Federation, of five Department statements and twelve methodical references and appropriate instructive documents. In 2010, the first part of the Instruction about the registration and conservation of museum objects and museum collections has been confirmed. At present, the second part of that Instruction is being completed. In this document, the norms of the conservation of objects and collections belonging to the Museum Fund will be determined.

The Ministry of Culture of Russia, the Ministry of Internal Affairs and the Federal Archives Department have elaborated and inculcated the Instruction about the organisation of the guarding of objects where the cultural values have been kept. The standard demands to the engineering and the technical surety of the cultural institutions as well to their providing with the technical means of guarding, have been confirmed. These demands have been regularly completed by the references expounded in the appropriate circular letters.

According to the existing praxis and to the acting normative acts, the registration of museum valuables is decentralised, i.e. the registration stock documentation isn't being kept at the immediate disposal of the owner, i.e. of the State Federal Centre. The registration and conservation of objects belonging to the Museum Fund has been fulfilled by the museums themselves on the spot. Therefore, it hampers the Federal Centre to realise its tasks concerning the supervision of the condition and the composition of objects from the collection of the State Museum Fund.

The Ministry of Culture of Russian Federation in active collaboration with the museum community continues to work on the drawing of normative documents, concerning the condition of existing technical means of the protection and the supervision of physical removal of objects, and on the creation of the latent marking (identification signing) of objects belonging to the Museum Fund of Russian Federation. Unfortunately, until now, there is no State programme of constructing modern depositories intended to keep the funds of State museums.

A particularly serious problem consists of the following: the registration system at the separate department museums doesn't ensure the appropriate level of conservation and studying of objects, and the collections of these museums haven't been included into the Museum Fund of Russian Federation. So, nowadays there are in the domain of theatre art 72 museums, which belong to the structure of existing theatres and act as theatre departments. These museums are working on the basis of theatre statutes, i.e. they have liabilities in regards the registration and conservation of their museum materials. In 2009, our museum received, from the Moscow Evgeny Vakhtangov Theatre, a donation of approximately 3,000 sketches created for the performances of this theatre in the period from 1920s to the present time. This collection remained safe almost by wonder, and owing to the conscientious work of the theatre employees.

But now, our museum as a Federal museum and as the scientific and methodical centre working with the theatre-owned museums, has no legal basis to fix the collections of these museums, therefore has lost many quite important historical and cultural materials and remains a very disturbing matter. Besides the State Central Theatre Museum A. A. Bakhrushin, nowadays the vast collections of theatre art rarities have been kept in the State Museum of Musical Arts named after Mikhail Glinka, Moscow (a Federal museum), the State Saint-Petersburg Museum of Theatrical and Musical Art (led by the city government of Saint-Petersburg), the Museums of the Bolshoi Theatre and the Maly Theatre (both museums are structural departments of these theatres), the State Literary Museum (a Federal Museum), the Russian State Archives of Literature and Art (led by the Federal Archives department) and some others. They are all significant imitative arts museums (both Federal and municipal) of their own, as a rule, collecting the objects concerning the history of the theatre.

The Forms of the Interaction of a Theatre Museum with the Contemporary Theatre Art People: Short Dialogues and the Philosophy of a Dialogue

Currently, the Theatre Museum A.A. Bakhrushin practically develops some directions of its acting, which make it able to fulfill the main mission of the museum – to keep, study and enrich its collections and, besides, to effect the public promotional work as an integral part of this mission. We pay serious attention to the enriching of our collections, particularly in regards to the contemporary theatre. For example, according to the results of annual exhibitions of theatre painters, we acquire, on the basis of an expert estimation, the most significant artworks. We are also methodically working with proprietors of private archives with the aim to receive materials from these archives as donation to our museum and we arrange expedition trips to different Russian cities to receive materials from the local theatres. Therein the limitations are connected only with the deficiency of financial means that could be used to make acquisitions at the extent, which seems us to be necessary in each particular period. The second limitation is of a technical and technological kind. Since 2009 we began to inculcate at our museum an electronic registration system. We put ourselves a task trended to maximum, i.e. to treat and to put into the electronic catalogue the information about all objects from our collections, and the amount makes, I remind, you, more than 1.5 million of units. Certainly, today all new incoming materials have been immediately put in the electronic base. Our general philosophy consists in the following: we are keeping the history of the national theatre and its representatives and, moreover, we must make this history "live" and accessible to the people.

The museum arranges the multiform enlightening activities. In its rooms, numerous actions have been organised: there are the exhibitions dedicated to actors, artists, directors, dramatists and important cultural events, as well as the concerts, evenings, lectures and clubs. Just these activities let the museum establish a dialogue with the theatre people who are forming its contemporary appearance. The great number of friends and partners of our museum reflects the involvement of the museum and of its employees in the contemporary theatre life.

Nowadays the Russian theatre is testing its strengths in the field between the traditional repertoire theatre, the new drama, the restoration of the classics, and the new European theatre. The formerly practiced escape from the social problems to the amusement of low standard has been a provisional appearance, and today leading theatre people are being taken by more serious artistic and social tasks. The number of successful improvements increases, but it is the theme of another lecture. The fact that the museum is trying to build its own strategy in this process seems us to be very important.

Undoubtedly the scientific activities take the most important place in this dialogue, and namely the research undertaken by the museum employees and, moreover, the possibilities, that we could grant to the researchers, i.e. to the theatre researchers, art historians, music researchers and others. Our problem lies in the room deficiency, so that today we are able to meet visitors – students, postgraduate students, and scientific workers – once weekly if they are coming from Moscow, and as an exception every day, if they are coming from other cities or from abroad. All most significant scientific works concerning the national theatre history are being created and published with participation of the museum, it is another testimony of the worth of our collections and of their public necessity, that is – the grade of the involving of our museum in the socio-dynamics of the national culture is very high. In 2007, at the museum the Scientific Council has been founded, which includes 30 members – there are prominent Russian actors, producers, artists, art historians, and colleagues from other museums and archives. The Council has to examine and to discuss the museum plans and the most significant projects connected with its development. Such a form of a dialogue with the scientific and theatre elite implies a high level of responsibility, but it is also a creative joy to communicate with such significant people. Our present contacts with theatre institutions are of the sporadic character, and probably it is time to determine the forms and tasks of the systematic interaction, because within the current activities of the museum the essential attention is paid to children and youth. The Bakhrushin Festival of 2010, arranged in this year the seventh time, has been also addressed to the youth. Thereat we turn our attention first of all to the children who need a particular social protection, i.e. to the orphans and invalids. In these activities, an actor and a theatre artist invited by us to take part in the festival, become for these children the guides immediately to the world of arts.

In this report I tried to outline only the most important directions of the activities of the A.A. Bakhrushin State Central Theatre Museum. I do hope that even the schematic description let our colleagues imagine the main directions of our work. I hope also, that our common tasks to safeguard the world cultural heritage would further our unification, the exchange of the helpful and important experience, and therefore they would donate us the joy of human contact.

Abstract

Dmitry V. Rodionov se penche sur le Musée national d'Histoire du Théâtre et le théâtre national contemporain, les caractéristiques de la création et du développement du Musée central d'État du Théâtre A. A. Bakhrushin (les principes de la constitution de la collection, une information générale sur la collection; la collection pendant la période pré-révolutionnaire, dans les années 1920, dans les années 1930, jusqu'aux années 1980 (URSS), et après 1991 (Fédération de Russie).

Difficulties of an Institution Collecting the Performing Arts within the So-Called Cultural Scene

Thomas TRABITSCH

Austrian Theatre Museum (Vienna – Austria)

In recent years, in the course of managing an institution that deals with the – not only but also – contemporary performing arts, I have become increasingly aware of "culture" as a term that constantly comes up as part of my work. As a consequence, I have felt obliged to try to define the term in its broadest sense. The present essay is an attempt to find a meaningful definition of culture, but I must stress that it is only that: an attempt.

Culture is the basis of our lives. It is how we handle, create and deal with daily living and the way we react to our surroundings. Moreover, it is the way we deal with and shape our entire existence. And finally, it is the way we preserve the accomplishments of earlier generations, while preserving the work of our generation for the next.

Culture is also a means of including the work of former generations in our lives in a process that is a work of art in its own right. It is the way we accept and deal with research and its findings, at the same time creating the basis for our present life. All of this, if done properly, can provide the basis for future generations as well, although they are likely to have the same kind of difficulties in discovering and understanding their own culture, with results that will likely depend on the prevailing point of view.

In any case, depending on the special field on which our work as so-called specialists is concentrated within our respective museums and the research that emerges from it, we regard the preservation of the past and the present as an important part of our mission. As our work itself is part of the definition of culture, the question again arises: what does the term culture mean in general, and what does it stand for?

I believe we must begin by understanding the term culture in its broadest sense. To provide only a few examples, this should also include the culture of speech and expression (yes, they, too, are part of our culture), the culture of discussion (which involves allowing people to express their opinions without interruption and refraining from talking before they have finished), the culture of writing, of eating, of dressing, and finally to reiterate: the way of preserving that which surrounds us, including our science and research.

I believe it is very important to remain constantly in search of a clear definition of culture. We must remain aware that while the work we do is only a small part of a huge field, it is a very important one. We have an obligation to ensure that the work we do now will not be neglected in the future.

Allow me to suggest an image: culture overall may be seen as a huge mirror that reflects the work, the activity, the existence of a nation. As such, it reflects our museums and the work they do as a consequence of their responsibility to preserve (reflect) the heritage of a nation in its every aspect.

This huge mirror not only reflects what has been done at museums in the past and what is currently being done, but it also shows and reflects what might be or must be done in the future. The mirror indicates and also measures the importance of our work. In doing so it also demonstrates and proves that we have a leading role to play.

You may be asking yourselves why I am making these points, since you may not see the immediate connection between my thoughts and the main topic of our meeting, *Performing Arts Collections uniting past and future*. The answer is simple: we all know that within the so-called "museum scene", theatre museums and other institutions that are supposed to research the performing arts and present the results tend to be at the same time understood and misunderstood. They play a relatively small role in the museum scene, as certain numbers become more and more important as a consequence of the economic atmosphere in which we live.

If too much importance were to be placed on the number of visitors and the revenue they generate, an institution as highly specialised as a theatre museum would be forced to close its doors or at least reduce its exhibition work to a minimum in order to concentrate solely on research and on the digitalisation of its holdings, which, as an important part of our work is done anyway and has to be done in the future, too. Yet the financial benefit of reducing museum activities would be negligible, and at the same time, the museum would more or less disappear as an institution, which presents exhibition in order to present the result of the research, which is being done.

Specialised museums such as theatre museums and their collections should not be compared with large institutions, and that applies equally to visitor numbers, revenue and financial results, a word with rather disturbing implications. Just to give you an example: with respect to the number of visitors the Pinakothek in Munich cannot be compared with the Deutsches Theatermuseum, nor is the number of visitors of the Kunsthistorisches Museum comparable with the Austrian Theatre Museum. In some respects, on the other hand, such a comparison would not necessarily always be to the disadvantage of the smaller institution.

I have used a mirror as the image of culture, reflecting the nation and its life. If we reduce the capacity of our institutions to collect materials from the performing arts or even close these institutions, we may indeed save just a bit of money, but at the same time we risk creating a blind spot on this mirror.

The consequences may not be immediately evident to the present generation, but we must be aware of the consequences this implies for the generations to come. We must carefully consider the amount of money that might be saved and weigh that against the potential loss to our descendants. Can or should we afford that? What is the relationship between the money saved and the disadvantages to later generations?

As you all know, the Austrian Theatre Museum became part of the Kunsthistorisches Museum in 2000. This system works rather well and will continue to work as long as the staff members of both institutions are prepared to accept certain rules, as long as they continue to talk to each other in order to solve problems the moment they arise. Again, the process of discussion is another part of our culture.

As soon as a problem arises, we have to point it out in order to solve it. We are all familiar with these problems: a lack of effective strategies in marketing and public relations, a lack of money to make additions to our collections. The list goes on an on.

In 2008, we were given a new opportunity when the ministry provided the money needed for us to close our permanent exhibition (which had been on display for more than nine years) in order to renovate the first floor of the museum. We now have a new system of display cases, the exhibition space has a new lighting system, and the museum is now both humidity- and temperature-controlled. As one stage designer and exhibition architect said: "Vienna has a new museum". Of course, having a new and enlarged space also means that the costs have risen. This is a problem that will have to be solved, for example, by increasing our cooperation with other similar institutions in order to share some of the costs. This is already being done and will be continued with our friends in Munich.

Of course, we face criticism from people who cite our dependence on the Kunsthistorisches Museum. But we are openly facing this situation. If we were independent, we would need more staff and as a consequence more office place, not to mention the storage problems that we are now already facing. At the same time, we could not expect more financial support from the state. To put things in a positive context: while the Austrian Theatre Museum is not independent, we are allowed to plan our operations with our collections, their content and the aims we have set for ourselves in mind. So while we continue to work within the given structure, we will never relinquish the responsibility we feel in doing our work, presenting our collection, and being part of our nation's culture in the way I described at the outset.

In conclusion, let me propose a few questions: how do we define the role of a theatre museum today – an institution that collects and presents the performing arts? I remember a statement I read in the art magazine *Parnass*: "Kunst rechnet sich nicht!" Difficult to translate, it can mean "Art doesn't pay" but the best translation may be: "Art shouldn't have to pay for itself to be valued."

That leads to my next question: can a theatre museum or any other institution collecting and presenting the performing arts survive in a world that is increasingly dominated by the bottom line? How should a theatre museum, or any other institution that collects and presents the performing arts define its future role – in the future and for the future? And finally: is it acceptable or even conceivable for a nation to fail to support and operate an institution whose task is to document the nation's performing arts?

Update 2013

During this time, these little thoughts mentioned at the Munich meeting in 2010, up to more than two years later, many things have happened and have been changed, all of them with the intention of being in favour of the Austrian Theatre Museum.

First, the storage problem has been solved. We have been provided with a huge storage place within a brand new building, which is also the central depot of the Kunsthistorisches Museum. This definitely benefits all the objects stored there. Additionally, it provides us with new space in our museum in downtown Vienna.

Also, while remaining in the already mentioned museum structure, we are, more than before, able, and actually asked, to go our own way with the budget to be used by us for our very own purposes. We discuss and explain our projects and aims, without being asked how we intend to transform them into existence. The only thing needing to be done is to stay within the budget framework, which we construct in the best possible cooperation with the heads of the museums. As a consequence, and actually needless to say, we are facing a larger responsibility which we, of course, accept, although – not only in our museum – for the last few years, the existing budget remained the same in opposite to the raising overall costs.

To summarise: our museums do know, that they depend on each other and in combination with the most possible way of trusting each other, the system works. Yet we have to be aware of the fact, that this positive construction will only work as long as all partners are prepared to cooperate in a fair way, meaning that there will always be the need of solving situations which have not been expected – and again: this has to be solved by all partners. As long as we are aware of this ever existing situation, I do believe in the continuation of the positive situation, which we are facing right now.

Abstract

Au cours des dernières années, dans le cadre de la gestion d'une institution qui s'occupe – pas seulement, mais aussi – des arts du spectacle contemporain, Thomas Trabitsch a été amené à prendre de plus en plus conscience du mot « culture » qu'il retrouve constamment dans son travail. Il s'est donc senti obligé d'essayer de définir ce terme dans son sens le plus large.

Le présent essai est une tentative de trouver une définition signifiante de la culture, mais l'auteur souligne que ce n'est rien d'autre que cela : une tentative.

Ceci amène la question suivante : un musée de théâtre – ou toute autre institution qui collecte et présente les arts du spectacle – peut-il survivre dans un monde de plus en plus fondé sur les résultats ? Comment un musée du théâtre – ou toute autre institution qui collecte et présente les arts du spectacle – devrait-il définir son rôle futur : à l'avenir et pour l'avenir ? Et enfin, est-il acceptable ou même concevable pour une nation, de ne pas soutenir et faire fonctionner une institution dont la mission est de documenter les arts du spectacle nationaux ?

One Moment in Time

How Theatre History Backs Up the Future of the Theatre

Winrich MEISZIES

Theatre Museum (Düsseldorf – Germany)

Starting Point 1910

On November 1st, 1910 the first German Theatre exhibition opened in Berlin. The exhibition was a joint effort of the Gesellschaft für Theatergeschichte (Society for Theatre History) and the Deutsche Bühnenverein (the organisation of the theatre managers) and aimed at "… representing hundreds of years of German theatre in the shape of the most remarkable personalities and their outstanding efforts by means of documents, pictures, props and relics…" as the Secretary General of the Gesellschaft für Theatergeschichte pointed out.

The majority of objects in the exhibition came from "…court and municipal theatres both looking back on a long, glorious and eventful history, from archives, public libraries and museums as well as private collections and bequests of great artists…" The most efficient documentary work was done by the court theatres because "…they have a sufficient number of officials at hand for registration, documentation and handling…".

Almost equal were the municipal theatres because "… understanding managers have saved objects for a little theatre-museum of their own in archives, libraries, offices, green rooms or workshops throughout a hundred and more years." On the other hand the author also complains that "… owing to responsible managers a lot of objects were destroyed, fell into despair and dissipated".

The description of the exhibition closes with the remark "… that the German theatre does not need a *single exhibition* but a *permanent museum* just like the other arts."

Despite the disappointment of the representatives of the exhibition we have to look closer on the conditions of this first "German theatre-exhibition".

The "Gesellschaft für Theatergeschichte e. V." was founded by authors, journalists, researchers, actors, directors and others devoted to the theatre as a registered organisation in 1902 in Berlin. Their aim was to create an interdisciplinary forum dealing with past and present theatre. Until today it is an independent scholarly organisation publishing research results by members and others.

The "Deutsche Bühnenverein" (founded in 1846) is the federal organisation of the responsible bodies of public and private theatres and orchestras in Germany. It represents the interests of its 430 members in problems concerning political subjects and industrial law.

The two organisations represented the theatre and theatre research, and their joint project "German theatre-exhibition" showed an interest in both past and present of the theatre. Like in a trade fair, supplier and provider gave an overview over products and services. The past of the theatre was an aspect of theatre marketing with equal rights to the present theatre and its work.

At that time the dream of a permanent theatre museum had already partly become true. In 1907 the Royal Bavarian Court actress Clara Ziegler (1844-1909) bequeathed in her will her villa and her considerable fortune for the establishment of a theatre museum. "My foundation aims at creating a distinguished home for our art that does honour to our profession." On June 24th 1910 the museum was opened. In 1979 the museum became an independent state museum within the administration of the state of Bavaria.

To be honest: it was not the first German attempt to create a theatre museum. In 1899 in memory of actress Marie Seebach (1830-1897) her sister Wilhelmine Seebach arranged a "Marie-Seebach-Museum," in two rooms of the Marie-Seebach-Foundation, a retirement home for actors in the city of Weimar that was founded in 1895. In 1902 this museum appeared with entry fee and regular opening hours in the annual records of the "Deutsche Bühnenverein."

Two actresses had one idea, and two times a personal memorial place was chosen with very close personal relations. Following a press release of 1902 the Weimar museum contains "… all the memories of her artistic career, everything she liked and valued… Relicts are affectionately collected in these rooms the Grand Duke called a sanctuary…" Following the terminology we can consider a place of worship for a community of fans conjuring up and reviving their memories.

As we can see from these examples there is a very close relation between the actual theatre and theatre history. At that time theatre history is a genuine part of theatre marketing but we have to look on the way the theatre historiography works in Germany.

German Traditions

Our way of understanding theatre has its basis in the 18th century. From that point on the public debate denies theatre being a means of aristocratic and clerical representation. The "pre-dramatic" time of *ex tempore* theatre was to be replaced by a theatre of the authors. But the theatre only rarely lived up to the demand of the authors of the Enlightenment who wanted the theatre to be a school for moral values and education.

So we must admit: our way of understanding theatre is based on *ideas* about theatre, on programmatic thinking not on an existing practice. The theatre of Enlightment was expected to give up the practice of theatre as a means of entertainment for both the court and the market place. The performance was no longer based on the actor and his mere ability and action but on the literary text and its accurate reproduction.

It took until 1918 when the aristocratic system was deprived of power by the Weimar Republic and lots of the court theatres became civic theatres under municipal or state administration. Theatre became the public mandated means of education, and the gap between education and entertainment opened and became more and more insurmountable for German theatre.

Defining national German identity there are two main developments. First, there was no experience in civic power. The overcoming of the hundreds of independent territories within the borders of today's Germany was not a revolutionary act. The German Empire of 1871 was the achievement of the Prussian chancellor Bismarck. Even the civic dream of civil rights did not come true by a civic uproar but by the generosity of the state authorities. In the course of the 18th and 19th century the civic revolution happened in the heads of German intellectuals, in literature and on stage. As Schiller wrote in the late 18th century: the national German stage has to initiate the German nation. This kind of mission for the theatre sounded very ambitious yet it overcharged and overcharges the theatre until today.

The second experience is the two world wars caused by Germany. The trust in state authorities was on the decrease. After ww i the "lost generation" of sons fought with the generation of fathers and this conflict even became a literary topic in the theatre of the 1920s.

The Nazi regime barred Germany and its cultural development from the rest of Europe and the world. The restart after ww ii could not pick up the aesthetic developments on stage other nations had undergone and the national cultural life started on the basis of the "outlived" traditions of the Weimar Republic. Any other traditions were refused as abused. A lot of artists as well as citizens were suspicious of traditions. Until now the general awareness of historical developments is not very strong. We are living in a throw-away society, we do not know and do not want to know where we are coming from.

Today's Situation of Theatres

After WW II, cultural affairs in Germany figure as an optional public service without statutory regulations. As a whole the budget for cultural affairs of cities, states and the federal government sums up to 8.1 Billion Euro which is 1.62% of the total budget of the Federal Republic. (Up to now the share of private enterprises subsidizing public cultural institutions is 5% of the total German budget for cultural affairs, or 350 to 400 Million Euro.)

With 45% (3.64 Billion Euro) the cities have the highest share, followed by the states of the federation with 42% (3.34 Billion Euro). The Federal Government has a share of 13% (1.02 Billion Euro).

Even though the number of theatre visitors is steady at 30.9 million (2006-2007), the theatres generate 18% of their operating expenses and the public assignments remain constant at 2.08 Billion Euro, the number of performances is slightly increasing up to 63,652, and the number of productions is now up to 4,945 (6.5% more).

We know about 121 municipal and state theatres, 22 regional theatres, 136 orchestras, 150 private theatres and 36 festivals.

As you could see, the money for financing the cultural sector is mainly provided by the cities. Due to last year's economic crisis the cities are going to lose lots of tax revenues from private enterprises. The deficit in the budget of German cities will rise from 4.9 Billion Euro in 2009 up to 12 Billion Euro in 2010. Cuttings of 10% are expected for the optional public service of cultural affairs.

But even though more and more people realise that cutting the budget for cultural affairs will not solve the public financial problems, there are still politicians arguing about the costs of theatre as a public service. We have to consider this kind of debate as ideological. Obviously the crisis of the theatre in Germany is a crisis of its acceptance. National differences may obscure this fact, but we have to face the fact that public interest in theatre is fading and that also will have an effect on the work of theatre documentation.

Theatre Documentation in Germany

Looking at the landscape of theatre museums in Germany there are only three independent institutions with permanent presentations and access, listed in alphabetical order of the cities: the theatre museum of the state capital of Düsseldorf, the theatre museum of the state theatre of Lower Saxony in Hannover, and the theatre museum of the cultural foundation of the City of Meiningen. Even the German theatre museum in Munich only offers in spite of its worldwide renowned collection temporarily operating exhibitions. Its status under direct administration of the state of Bavaria is unique in Germany.

The Academy of Arts in Berlin is a corporation under public law supported by the Federal Republic of Germany. Its mission is to encourage the arts and to give advice concerning arts and culture to the Federal Republic. An essential part of the Academy is its archives with the departments of the arts represented in the Academy.

Under indirect responsibility of different German states are the theatre collections of the universities of Berlin, Bochum, Darmstadt, Hamburg, Kiel and Cologne. Their academic purposes and designation as "collections" restrict their functions to research and teaching and by this are creating an exclusive sphere of activity. The future of some of these collections looks very dark.

Still only one of the German theatres runs an independent, publicly accessible theatre museum: the State Theatre of Lower Saxony in Hannover. The history of this museum dates back to 1927 when a so-called in-house museum was opened in order to intensify the relations between spectator and "his" artists and his theatre.

As in 1910 the municipal theatres, their archives and collections were only one of several "columns" of the theatre exhibition; up to now the importance of the cities for the German theatre has even multiplied. Still there is only a single independent institution run by a city: the Düsseldorf theatre museum. Its collections and exhibitions reflect in a special way the development of the municipal theatre in Germany drawing on the example of Düsseldorf. Currently the Düsseldorf theatre museum is planning a project to provide evidence of the existence of "hidden" theatre archives in theatres and other institutions of the state of North Rhine-Westphalia, of which Düsseldorf is the state capital.

As a specialised institution for dance documentation the German Dance Archive (Cologne) is run by the City of Cologne as well as by the cultural foundation of Cologne Commercial and Savings Bank (a subsidiary company of the City of Cologne), but its mission for collecting and educational work is national. The Cologne Dance Archive is paralleled by the foundation of a German Dance Archive in Leipzig in the former German Democratic Republic.

The Neuberin-Museum in Reichenbach (dedicated to the 18th century theatre reformer Caroline Neuber) is also used as city archive and city museum. Theatre departments can also be found in bigger municipal museum complexes of the City Museum Berlin and the Reiss-Engelhorn-Museums in Mannheim.

The Deutsche Kabarett-Archiv in Mainz is specialised in literary cabaret. The archives are a cultural foundation subsidized by several public institutions. Since 1999, in recognition of their national importance, the Cabaret Archives have been supported by funding from the Cultural and Media Deputies of the Federal Government.

As you could see: there are diverse organizational structures, there are no published missions by the responsible bodies, there is no institution with either a national or a regional responsibility. Everybody is stewing in one's own juice, nobody looks beyond one's own nose. Theatre documentation has no authority in questions concerning theatre – neither by its organizational standing nor by the objects of its collection.

Neither theatres nor politicians take theatre documentation really seriously.

Today's Situation of Theatre Documentation and Exhibition

Even though the 1910 exhibition intended "sacred devotion and mythic shivers of emotion" as effect on the visitor, the author turns explicitly against a "cult of relicts". "Such a cult run by single persons may cause – following the attitude of the assessment – wistful, upraising or ridiculous effects", as the author wrote in his introduction.

We can distinguish different types of exhibitions:

– the representational exhibition is just made to show the opulence of the collection. Everything – shown without any distinction – is important. The visitor is to be struck by the mass and the quality of the objects and should not attempt asking himself questions;

– the memorial exhibition shows real "relicts" sometimes "in situ", on the auratic spot. The staging of this kind of exhibition is based on solemnity along with emotionality and irrationality. The memorial exhibition does not present documents but monuments;

– the documentational exhibition on specific topics shows how much the researcher knows about subjects, persons and circumstances, whether the visitor can follow him or not. Names and objects are dropped like in "The Star-Money". The visitor is forced to process the canon of the researcher who wants him to understand: "We do not show off, we have";

– in the persuading exhibition the objects are just the proof of a thesis and follow the ruling ideas without a possibility for the visitor to start a communication with the objects.

Even though the limits of estimation of theatre exhibitions are (even in 1910) more and more restricted by the aesthetical development of the theatre itself, as "the more and more enhanced demands for the staging in our leading theatres diminish systematically the ability for the perception of theatrical illusion", we have to admit that an exhibition works like a performance: it is an offer to think about a subject.

Even though theatre seems to be the "enemy" of theatre documentation and theatre exhibition we have to ask, what theatre documentation can do for the theatre. As we have heard about the decreasing acceptance of theatre, we shall ask ourselves how can we help to create acceptance for the theatre.

What Kind of Theatre Are We Talking about?

The word "theatre" has its origin in the Greek word "theatron" which only means "a place where you can look at something". Talking about theatre we take our (national) understanding of theatre for granted. Do we talk about the same thing? What do differences in the development of theatre depend on?

The roots of our present theatre are based in the rituals of transformation that can be found in ancient societies. What do we have to know about theatre to record and to collect theatre? What are the essential areas of theatre work and how can they be represented in the theatre collections and how can they be made descriptive?

From numerous talks with spectators, even regular spectators, it became evident that only the contents of the plays are identified as theatre. The statement that this or that play has pleased or displeased a spectator – although the dramatic text is unknown and cannot be known because most of the scripts are not published outside the theatre – shows that it is difficult for the spectator to approach the performing art from the aesthetical side.

Often there is no appropriate description for the essence of the performing arts efforts. For a fruitful discussion on the aesthetical side of a staging, a lot of spectators lack the necessary terms and basic historical knowledge of the change of conditions of performances and the ways of representation.

The striking ignorance of theatre history – often identified with history of drama – shows deficits in dealing with theatre as an independent form of art.

Any programmatic study of the drama and its aesthetics can only be understood in the context of the background of the very theatrical practice. Just the knowledge of theatre history becomes understanding of the very means of theatre.

Theatre studies – until the 1970s devoted to the reconstruction of theatre history – have developed over the years methods of theatre semiotics and offer as well, for the analysis of the single performance and description of the basic relations between the dramatic text and the staging, a helpful approach.

On stage everything becomes a semiotic sign. This kind of sign may be:

– the highly complex expression of the single actor by voice, mimics, gesture and body;
– the arrangement of the actors in the space of the stage;
– costume;
– make-up or masks;
– set;
– props;
– sound;
– and music.

The actor as well as the set are by no means neutral bearers of significance but define and change inevitibly the meaning of a performance. The process of staging has to be understood as a process of transformation where pure words were exchanged into more complex theatrical signs without obtaining an identical meaning: the dramatic text and the performance are distinguished works of art.

Collecting and Exhibiting Strategies

Unlike other kinds of art theatre is never the artistic achievement of a single person. Theatre is a "social" art, a co-operation of a multitude of participants often hidden before the audience who is not or cannot be aware of each share in the art of theatre. Until the beginning of the 20th century they stood back behind the oeuvre, behind the performance. Most rarely they have "big" names known nationally or even internationally – unlike to the pictorial arts with their spectacular exhibitions.

Beyond the intense theatrical experience the audience often forgets that theatre has its history, that the artistic means and the organisational conditions have their development – just like all other kinds of arts. From one moment to the other the theatre event becomes theatre history. In our work of theatre documentation we deal with moments.

In the historically exemplifying presentation, the artistic means of the theatre can be "dissected" like in an experiment. To keep the vanishing moment from the not stoppable process of a performance provides the opportunity to find clarification on the ways how theatre works.

We are the "masters of the moment", our collections represent uncountable moments of theatre art. We are not only responsible for the moments and the objects but also for the flow of time. Our work is to help people to understand theatre or at least to help them to a better understanding of the theatre.

Getting to know the historic changes of the art of theatre can open the mind of the spectator, who learns:

- not to hold on to his learned and appreciated habits of seeing and understanding,
- not to blackguard the new and different on the stage, because it does not correspond with his very own theatre experience and imprinting.

All branches of theatre documentation (museum, collection, library) cannot and are in fact not made to replace the theatre.

Being aware of the fact (even in 1910) that an exhibition or a book about theatre cannot achieve a kind of effect like a theatre performance, we are confronted with the fact that theatre documentation plays the role of "stepchild" unlike the institutions dedicated to the "sisters in art", and I cannot see big changes in the last 100 years.

Abstract

Le théâtre est une « espèce en voie de disparition » de la production culturelle. Dans la compétition des médias, le théâtre bat en retraite. Nous vivons dans une société du jetable. La conscience apportée à l'évolution historique est en train de disparaître. Ce fait peut être occulté par de véritables différences nationales, mais nous allons devoir affronter la réalité de la diminution de l'intérêt du public pour le théâtre et de sa conséquence sur le travail des collections théâtrales. Comment les collections théâtrales peuvent-elles renforcer la situation du théâtre ?

Un aperçu des différentes situations nationales

L'Allemagne est connue pour son financement public du théâtre, mais qu'en est-il de la documentation théâtrale ? Quelle est la nature des relations entre les institutions nationales et, par exemple, les pays européens et leurs instances responsables ?

Des avis différents sur le théâtre

Le mot « théâtre » trouve son origine dans le terme grec « theatron » qui ne signifie rien d'autre que « le lieu où l'on peut regarder quelque chose ». Quand on parle de théâtre, nous tenons pour acquise notre compréhension (nationale) du mot. Parlons-nous bien de la même chose ? De qui dépendent les différences dans le développement du théâtre ?

L'essence du théâtre et son influence sur les collections théâtrales

Les racines du théâtre d'aujourd'hui se trouvent dans les rituels de transformation des sociétés antiques. Que doit-on savoir sur le théâtre pour les enregistrer et les collecter? Quels sont les domaines essentiels du travail théâtral et comment peuvent-ils être représentés dans les collections de théâtre; comment peuvent-ils être décrits?

Les archives de la production

Les collections théâtrales ne devraient pas se limiter à être la mémoire du théâtre mais devraient être tout autant une école de la réception. Comment pouvons-nous faire prendre conscience aux gens de la nécessité de savoir d'où nous venons, aussi bien pour les acteurs que pour le public? Comment pouvons-nous faire en sorte que nos collections soient productives pour le théâtre et pour son public? Comment pouvons-nous montrer les bénéfices spécifiques du théâtre pour la société?

Les stratégies de collecte et d'exposition

Le Code de déontologie de l'ICOM pour les musées publié en 2006 dit que :

Les autorités de tutelles ont la responsabilité de veiller à ce que tout musée possède un statut, une constitution ou tout autre document écrit officiel, conforme au droit national. Ces documents stipuleront clairement le statut juridique du musée, ses missions, sa permanence et son caractère non lucratif.

Les musées qui détiennent les collections les conservent dans l'intérêt de la société et de son développement. (Code de déontologie, deuxième partie). Avons-nous la possibilité, les sources et les compétences nécessaires pour travailler au profit du théâtre?

Les musées travaillent en étroite coopération avec les communautés d'où proviennent les collections, ainsi qu'avec les communautés qu'ils servent. (Code de déontologie, sixième partie).

L'explication de la sixième partie précise que les collections contribuent à diverses formes d'identité. Comment pouvons-nous contribuer à l'identité du théâtre en tant qu'instrument de l'identité culturelle nationale?

Database of Scenography and Photography[1]

Denisa ŠŤASTNÁ

Arts Institute – Theatre-Institute (Prague – Czech Republic)

The Department of Collections and Archives

The Department of Collections and Archives of the Arts and Theatre Institute (ATI) acquires, catalogues, archives and makes available to the public those culturally valuable artefacts and archive documents that are related to theatre primarily in the Czech Republic. In 2009, the Departments of Collections and Archives were established as separate divisions, and in addition to the archives, their primary focus is the artistic and theatre articles of historical value from two distinct fields – theatre set design and photography.

The Scenography Collection

The Institute has collected scenographic artefacts since the organisation was first established in 1959. At that time, the collection was created arbitrarily and grew primarily from the personal connections between the Institute employees and the creators of the theatre productions. It was not until 2006 that the collection of the Theatre Institute, respectively the scenography collection, was registered at the Central Registry of the Collections of the Ministry of Culture, making it is possible to refer to the professional administration of the collection. Its continual and systematic growth is based on the acquisition activities that are overseen by its eight member advisory committee. The acquisitions are primarily donations or purchases from either the authors themselves or from those who have inherited the artefacts.

The aim of the collection is to methodically gather, store, catalogue, and present the significant works of Czech stage design, both from a historical perspective, as well as the current developments in

---

[1]   Updated January 2013.

contemporary theatre. In addition to the works of the personalities who have greatly influenced the development of Czech theatre since 1945, priority of the collection is given to the contemporary works from the 1990s. The collection contains works created by Czech stage and costume designers for the theatres in the Czech Republic and in particular those theatres abroad.

The collection includes primarily original stage and costume designs and models, which combine, not only the value of the work from a theatre perspective, but also as a unique piece of art. Both of these aspects are very important in terms of building the collection: neither the individual creative technique nor the use of materials is paramount during the selection of the subjects. The working papers and sketches have their own significance, as they are the original glance of the work process. Some of the most significant artists represented in the collection include Vlastislav Hofman, František Tröster, Josef Svoboda, Jan Sládek, Adolf Wenig, Ladislav Vychodil, Jindřiška Hirschová, Otakar Schindler, Libor Fára, Luboš Hrůza, Jaroslav Malina, Miroslav Melena, Jan Vančura, Jan Skalický, Jan Dušek, Jana Zbořilová, Marta Roszkopfová, Petr Lébl and Zuzana Štefunková Rusínová.

Information about the basic identification of each artefact – including digital reproductions – is fed into the database (also linked to the *Theatre* database), which was created specifically for this collection. Currently 1,945 objects have been catalogued in the collection. One important aspect of the acquisition activities is not only the assurance of the proper preservation of the artefact, but also that they are accessible to the public. The Department of Collections and Archives will organise together, or individually, a variety of exhibition projects, where the artefacts found in the collection will appeal to the interest of the everyday spectator, as well as those specialising in the theatrical field, at home and abroad.

The Photography Collection

The collection of theatre photography is an entirely specific artistic discipline. This discipline is in its own right an original work of art that reveals the work the theatre production and, in an ideal case, its congenial interpretation. Moreover, its role is the combination of an artistic purpose, as well as a source of documentation. Both of these functions are equally important. Still however, theatre photography remains as a side interest of historians of photography and curators of collective photography exhibitions, as it is still regarded as a mere emotionless recording of the activities that take place on stage. This is also probably one of the reasons why no comprehensive publications that address this unique phenomenon exist here in the Czech Republic or even abroad. Theatre photography has a very long tradition here in the Czech Republic. In the second half of the 20th century, Jaroslav Krejčí and Josef Koudelka cultivated this discipline into an irreplaceable artistic genre and has since become an attractive product that can be "exported".

The Arts and Theatre Institute has approximately 180,000 original photographs, slides and negatives. The systematic cataloguing of the photography collection began in 2008 as a branch of the Preservation and Presentation of Cultural Heritage of Czech and World Theatre that was realised with the support of the Financial Mechanisms EHP/Norway.

Thanks to this, an unprecedented opportunity arose – a chance to capture, describe and make available those images that map the past sixty years of Czech theatre. Each individual photograph is assigned basic identification information that is entered into a database connected to the *Theatre* database. Every entry contains information pertaining to its related production. Together with the visual information, researchers obtain a complete set of data including the names of the authors, the production team, and the performers. Earlier this year, the database was made accessible on the Internet[2]. Currently, the database has expanded to include more than 180,000 scanned photographs from nearly 12,000 productions. This is the work of more than 200 photographers, including Jaroslav Krejčí, Vilém Sochůrek and Viktor Kronbauer.

Abstract

Le recensement de la collection des arts du spectacle à l'Enregistrement central des Collections du ministère de la Culture a donné lieu à la création, en 2006, de l'Institut des arts et du théâtre à Prague. Après la fondation officielle de la Collection scénographique, le travail d'acquisition et de conservation des objets scénographiques, qui se pratiquaient déjà auparavant, est devenu plus systématique et plus ciblé.

La collection s'est spécialisée principalement dans la conception contemporaine des décors (plus particulièrement depuis les années 1990), et se concentre sur le travail des personnes qui ont grandement influencé les arts dans le théâtre tchèque après 1945. Elle consiste en une série d'éléments de décors et de costumes originaux, conçus par des scénographes tchèques à l'occasion de productions tchèques pour des scènes étrangères.

---

[2] <http://www.divadelni-ustav.cz/inscenace.aspx>.

Aujourd'hui, on compte environ 1 500 objets, reliant les valeurs de l'art et celles du théâtre. Parmi ces réalisations, se trouvent celles de quelques-uns des plus grands scénographes tchèques tels que Vlastislav Hofman, František Tröster, Josef Svoboda, Jan Sládek, Adolf Wenig, Otakar Schindler, Luboš Hrůza, Jindřiška Hirschová, Jan Skalický, Jan Vančura, Egon Tobiáš ou Petr Lébl.

A New Idea for a Permanent Exhibition: the History of Theatre in Krakow

From Actors' Domination to the Time of the Auteur Director

Agnieszka Kowalska

Department of History of Theatre
Historical Museum of the City of Krakow (Poland)

The idea to create the Museum of Theatre in Krakow was initiated in 1917 by a writer and curator of the National Museum, Maciej Szukiewicz. Although the cultural elite of the city supported it, Szukiewicz's project was only launched in 1969. At that time the Historical Museum of the City of Krakow opened a Theatre Department in a 13th century building called Dom pod Krzyzem, a former hospital for poor students dedicated to Sain Roch. In the 19th century it was a tenement house. Between 1917 and 1937 it housed the Association of Painters; this is where in 1933 the painter Jozef Jarema founded the experimental theatre Cricot. This avantgarde stage quickly gained recognition among theatregoers. The building was given to the Historical Museum in 1949 and, as mentioned before, devoted to a theatrical exhibition.

The Department of History of Theatre in Krakow in The Historical Museum of the City of Krakow had presented two versions of permanent exhibitions as of 2008. The first was open between 1969 and 1981 and the second existed from 1989 to 2008. Both exhibitions were based on the historical items, theatricalities and artefacts connected with Krakow's actors, directors and scenic designers. Although the old exhibitions were well thought out and elegantly arranged, they drew the attention of the visitors just to the chronological arrangement. The wide selection of the theatrical collection uncovered only the beauty of individual exhibits. On the other hand, it showed the significance of these artefacts as discrete museum objects. In each room, which was devoted to a particular period, exhibits were divided into artefacts illustrating theatrical shows (mostly photographs of actors in costumes), objects belonging to famous artists (personal items, portraits etc.) and production designs. The main idea of the past exhibition was to show the best artefacts of the theatrical collection. Those objects weren't described as elements of theatres work and art. It was a traditional reading of the exhibition as a place whose purpose is to show a part of the museum's collection. The Historical Museum was only meant to be an institution that kept important artefacts and exhibits.

The new idea of the permanent exhibition is also based on the history of the theatre in Krakow. However, the chronology decided upon during work on the scenario results from the Historical Museum's mission, which is to acquaint the visitor with the city's cultural and historical heritage. The Theatre Branch as a part of a greater institution needs to fit into the mode of operation of the whole organisation so that artistic events create a coherent whole, together with the initiatives of other branches. Therefore, one of the aims of the new exhibition is to both show the history of theatre in Krakow and the place of theatre in the history of the city. All the same, the exhibition should not become a pretext to present exhibits only from the aesthetic point of view. That is why the modern, theatrical exhibition should create new meanings and describe the principle and essence of the theatre's existence in each period. The development of the project of the new exhibition started in 2008, when the planning group was called together. Nowadays, this group of theatre historians is creating a new scenario. The boundaries of the work are the year 1781, when the first professional theatre in Krakow opened, and 1989, when political changes greatly influenced the artistic shape and functioning of the theatre. The exhibition will be divided into eleven thematically arranged parts, each of which is going to concentrate on a period in the history of Krakow's theatre. Individual elements were titled:

1) Stage without Theatre, Theatre in the Medieval Times
2) The Beginnings of Professional Theatre in Krakow
3) Actor as the Crucial Creator, Theatre in the Time of Stanislaw Kozmian (1865-1893)
4) The Perfect Actor: Helena Modrzejewska (the Time of Stars)
5) Krakow for the National Art (1893-1918)
6) Stanislaw Wyspianski as the Artist of the Theatre – Complete Artist
7) A Bit of Paris in Poland – the Artistic Cabaret, Zielony Balonik (1905-1912)
8) Eclecticism in Theatre (1918-1939)
9) Fighting for Polish Identity, Underground Theatre (1939-1945)
10) Stage Director as the Undisputed Creator of Theatre (1945-1989)
11) Dressing Room (educational space).

This chronological arrangement constitutes only a starting point for displaying the concept of theatre as the place of clashes and interactions of various artistic fields. It is also a way to present a uniform and clear picture of the most important artistic changes that made Krakow theatre so unique. These twelve topics are only variations of the three main elements of a theatrical show, that is the actor, the director and the stage designer. Generally, in the history of Krakow theatre there were periods when one of the aforementioned groups dominated. In the second half of the 19th century the actor was the most significant, then at the turn of 20th century there was an increase of importance of production design, whereas the second half of the 20th century was the time when theatre was shaped by charismatic directors. Thus the title of this paper is: *From Actors' Domination to the Time of the Auteur Director.* In connection to the exhibition it means that each part is a description and illustration of one or two chosen themes characteristic to each period and tied to the three main parts, such that the time of Stanislaw Kozmian (1865-1893) will be shown through the perspective of an actor and actor's workshop. In the Era of Stars, acting in Poland was based on a strict convention called "idealist realism" as well as on the idea of the actor's employment. With this in mind, the visual arrangement of the exhibition and the choice of exhibits will serve the purpose of illustrating the issues in the most artistic way and including the viewers in the sightseeing process to encourage them to confront their own ideas of 19th century theatre with the reality of it at that time.

Another topic, of Krakow for the National Art, concerns the influence of modern naturalist and symbolist acting and Polish romanticism on the development of production design (or, as it was then called, exposition/ display). Here arises the problem of how to display drama. I decided to draw the viewers' attention to two or three movable models presenting reconstructed fragments of chosen shows, bringing out the importance of scenery and the beginnings and matching it to the individual character of each show. We will also show how a symbolist drama, its foundations and a newly introduced type of character-affected shows. All these changes led to the rise of new professions related to theatre or to the change of directors' responsibilities and what was expected of them. A perfect example of this is the work of Krakow's theatres after 1945, when numerous professional and avant-garde theatres emerged.

Contemporary theatre, based on the harmonious co-operation of artists representing various arts is difficult to categorise. This is why, when creating the concept of the exhibition, I undertook the challenging task of showing the diversity of Krakow's theatre of the second half of the 20th century, not through the official theatres, but rather through individual gifted producers, some of whom are also renowned abroad. I chose seven of them: Andrzej Wajda, Krystian Lupa, Jerzy Jarocki, Konrad Swinarski, Tadeusz Kantor, Jozef Szajna and Mieczyslaw Kotlarczyk, who represent distinct views on the substance of theatre and whose individual styles are still easily recognisable today. Each of these artists will be presented through one representative show.

Other topics I mentioned before, like Zielony Balonik or Eclecticism in Theatre, are other variants of the main theme of the exhibition. They are to complement the main idea of the exhibition as well as to introduce the biographies of actors, producers and directors representing a given trend, like Modrzejewska or Wyspianski, or to present interdisciplinary performances. We also plan to prepare a multi-purpose hall to conduct meetings, film presentations, concerts, conferences, etc. However, not all issues and periods will be presented with the use of traditional exhibits. For instance, the beginnings of professional theatre and underground theatre of 1939-1945 will be shown only with the use of multimedia. This leads to a crucial dilemma in the work on the exhibition.

Currently there is a new tendency to shift the stress from exhibit to artistic vision. A few recent exhibitions (at The Museum of the Warsaw Uprising, The Museum of Chopin in Warsaw, and Oskar Schindler's Factory in Krakow) display exhibits only as elements of a story. This is not about using multimedia, but rather about the creation of an exhibition as a separate reality, which appeals to all senses. There is probably nothing wrong in this. Indeed, the exhibition prepared by us requires multiple staging techniques (lighting, sound, colour, texture, etc.). However, I believe we cannot underestimate the value of an original artefact which is, in my experience, still of fundamental value to the public. Therefore, we aim to use modern technology so that it does not dim what is the essence of the museum – the exhibits. Multimedia are there only to help us envisage, reconstruct e.g. the look of 19th century stage, the way actors moved in a given fragment of a play; or to reconstruct a piece of music or stage decorations. In the case of certain exhibits, a change of perspective is needed; some are valuable not in themselves or because of the person who made them, but take on special meaning when they are contextualised with the stage (given set designs), actor (through photographs and videos of a performance), text (scripts, recordings) and props. Then we get the idea of what the artist looked like and how he moved, which leads to suggestions concerning character description, the concept of the performance, the styles of a play, not to mention attitudes to life in certain periods. For instance, the meaning of footlights, curtain or costume design becomes clear only when they are set in the environment in which they belong and it is shown how they were used. This is why it is vital to display them in the right context.

The new arrangement of a theatrical exposition as described, a blend of multimedia and traditional exhibits must also shift the place of the audience in the museum. The role of the spectator will change in various parts of the exhibition, which has to be interactive and thus it will force the spectators to interact with the exhibition through starting some elements (touch pads) or peeking though a keyhole (Nickelodeon). The spectator will thus take on the role of a researcher who, in order to explore a given issue or extend his knowledge, will have to make an effort, to make a discovery through touching certain elements, reading text on the pads, etc. On the other hand, we would like the spectator to feel like a theatre employee, who is also responsible for the smooth running of a show. He becomes a member of technical staff by turning on stage lights or a wind machine. When asked to place a prop or prepare a costume in the educational area, Dressing Room, he will become a set designer or even an actor. All of this is designed to confront his subjective image of theatre with the historical tendencies presented in the exhibition. The spectator becomes part of our exhibition.

All of the work described, connected with the creation of the scenario and design, is seriously impeded by the size of the exhibition space and by the historic character of the building. Even at the stage of creating the concept we were forced to cut our ideas to the actual capacity of the building. Dom pod Krzyzem consists of three floors with nine rooms in various shapes and sizes (the biggest is only 50m^2). There is no possibility to connect or enlarge any of the rooms. Introducing any changes or renovating would require constant supervision and consent on the part of the director of historical preservation (as it is a 13th century building). In this initial stage of preparation we cannot be sure how many of our ideas will be carried out and whether all technical and multimedia solutions are possible to implement. Therefore even at this initial stage we are trying to create a couple of scenarios, to suggest a few possible solutions to present a given topic. We will have to verify their usefulness while setting up the exhibition.

Finally, underneath the issues discussed lies the question of why we are preparing an exhibition on the history of theatre. Here I can speak only on my behalf. In the history of Krakow's theatre there were people for whom theatre was not only entertainment or a space in which to analyse the existing state of affairs. Krakow's artists believed that through their work they were given the power to change audiences, to create and bring back the audience's national and human identity. Today only a few researchers know most of these artists, and although it may sound pompous, I believe that the duty of every historian of Krakow's theatre is to familiarise contemporary audiences with them. We have the opportunity to do it through our exhibition.

Abstract

Jusqu'en 2008, le Département d'Histoire du Théâtre de Cracovie au Musée historique de la ville de Cracovie avait présenté deux expositions permanentes. La première avait ouvert ses portes en 1969 et s'est prolongée jusqu'en 1981. La seconde a été présentée de 1989 à 2008. Toutes deux se basaient sur la présentation d'objets historiques et théâtraux et sur les souvenirs liés à des acteurs, metteurs en scène et décorateurs de Cracovie. Bien que ces expositions aient été bien pensées et organisées avec élégance, elles proposaient à l'intérêt des visiteurs qu'une présentation chronologique. La riche sélection effectuée au sein de la collection théâtrale ne révélait que la beauté propre des expositions qui ont par ailleurs montré l'importance des artéfacts comme objets de musée à part entière.

Le projet de l'exposition permanente actuelle repose également sur l'histoire théâtrale de Cracovie mais elle ouvre de nouvelles voies et décrit les principes et l'essence de l'existence du théâtre pour chacune des périodes présentées. Le travail sur ce projet a commencé en 2008 au moment où les personnes qui devaient s'atteler à cette tâche ont été désignées.

Globalement, l'objectif principal de la nouvelle exposition est de décrire, grâce à une disposition moderne et à des artéfacts et objets appropriés, les tendances et transformations les plus importantes de l'art du théâtre, du XIXᵉ au XXᵉ siècle, dans les domaines du jeu, de la mise en scène, de la direction d'acteurs et de la scénographie.

Les concepteurs souhaitent offrir aux visiteurs la possibilité de faire partie intégrante de l'exposition, ce qui implique le recours à une technologie moderne et visuelle. Le public pourra « animer » et activer tel ou tel élément de l'exposition. C'est d'une grande importance pour que les visiteurs puissent confronter leurs propres idées et stéréotypes sur, par exemple, le théâtre du XIXᵉ siècle, aux événements réels de cette époque.

Ceci soulève, bien entendu, de nombreuses questions sur la pertinence du concept d'exposition théâtrale, sur les problèmes liés aux répétitions et sur les doutes qui surgissent quand on tente de mettre en rapport un espace moyenâgeux et des expositions traditionnelles avec une technologie scénaristique et visuelle. Les questions les plus importantes concernent la place du visiteur dans le nouveau musée et les raisons qui amènent à monter ce genre d'exposition.

Les archives de Michel Fokine à la Bibliothèque théâtrale de Saint-Pétersbourg

Galina IVANOVA

Bibliothèque théâtrale d'État (Saint-Pétersbourg – Russie)

Un grand nombre de collections mondiales détiennent des documents relatifs à la vie et aux créations de Michel Fokine (1880-1942) – maître de ballet, danseur et pédagogue. En Russie, le plus important dépositaire de l'héritage de Michel Fokine est, sans aucun doute, la Bibliothèque théâtrale de Saint-Pétersbourg (SPbBT).

Historique de la formation et du développement du fonds d'archives

Les documents transmis au début des années 1960 par Vitale M. Fokine (1905-1977), fils du célèbre chorégraphe, constituent la partie essentielle des archives de Michel Fokine. L'historien du ballet Yuri Iosifovich Slonimski (1902-1978) et le directeur de la Bibliothèque théâtrale Sergei Aleksandrovich Mortchikhine (1904-1963) ont contribué au retour en Russie des documents d'archives qui se trouvaient aux États-Unis, où le chorégraphe avait émigré en 1921.

À la mort de Vera Fokina (1886-1958), c'est Vitale Fokine qui hérita des archives de son père. Michel Fokine n'ayant pas eu le temps de terminer ses mémoires – il a rédigé les quelques premiers chapitres décrivant sa vie jusqu'au début du xxe siècle – Vitale les a terminés, en introduisant dans son texte des citations, lettres, articles, notes de création et brouillons de son père. Le livre de Fokine, *Memoirs of a Ballet Master*, a été publié aux États-Unis en 1961[1].

Au même moment, à Leningrad, un groupe d'auteurs préparait un volume consacré à Michel Fokine. Une correspondance s'engagea entre

---

[1] Michel Fokine, *Memoirs of a Ballet Master*, trad. Vitale Fokine, Anatole Chujoy (ed.), Boston, Little Brown, 1961.

Vitale Fokine, Yuri Slonimski et Sergei Mortchikhine, à la suite de quoi, les archives américaines furent transférées à la Bibliothèque théâtrale de Saint-Pétersbourg. La majeure partie de ces documents est incluse dans la version russe du livre. La première édition des mémoires du maître de ballet, Michel Fokine, intitulée *Contre le courant*[2] a paru à Leningrad en 1962. Les mémoires du chorégraphe-réformateur occupent la place centrale de ce volume, *Contre le courant* étant le titre qu'il avait donné à ses mémoires. Vitale Fokine a fait office de collaborateur et consultant, fournissant des informations sur des faits et événements qui ne se trouvaient pas dans les documents reçus.

Par la suite, les lettres et documents conservés chez Sophia M. Kroupitskaya – sœur du maître de ballet – sont venus compléter le fonds d'archives de Michel Fokine. Serge Lifar a par ailleurs offert quelques documents lors de sa venue à Leningrad en mai 1961.

Des documents d'archives

Le recensement et la description scientifique du fonds par les archivistes de la bibliothèque se sont terminés en 1987. Il comporte 270 pièces (7 056 pages), réparties en plusieurs groupes :

– documents biographiques (certificats, diplômes…) ;

– mémoires de Michel Fokine ;

– documents manuscrits de travail (notes chorégraphiques, notes sur la scénographie, articles, scénarios et projets de ballets, documents relatifs aux créations de ballets) ;

– documents relatifs à la production et à la mise en scène des ballets de Fokine, y compris pour les spectacles donnés sur la scène des Théâtres impériaux russes et chez Serge de Diaghilev (contrats, conventions, factures, bulletins de paye et quittances) ;

– correspondance de Michel Fokine avec Anna Pavlova, Serge de Diaghilev, Ida Rubinstein, Serge Rachmaninov, Lincoln Kirstein, Cyril W. Beaumont, etc. ainsi que les lettres de Vitale Fokine (1959-1963) ;

– photos (Michel Fokine et Vera Fokina dans leur vie privée et sur scène) ;

– documents artistiques (maquettes de costumes par Michel Fokine et Léon Bakst ; affiches et programmes des tournées de Fokine et Fokina en Russie (1915-1918) et pendant la période américaine (1921-1942) ; programmes des « Saisons russes ») ;

---

[2]   Mihail Mihajlovič Fokin, *Protiv tečeniâ : vospominaniâ baletmejstera, scenarii i zamysly baletov, statʼi, intervû i pisʼma*, Leningrad-Moskva, Iskustvo, 1962.

   – documents de différentes personnalités (livres et articles de Serge Lifar ; documents relatifs à l'édition du livre de Michel Fokine. *Contre le courant. Mémoires du maître de ballet*).

De nombreux documents conservés dans le fonds sont d'un grand intérêt historique et constituent en outre des témoignages précieux sur la vie de Fokine. Il est important de noter que ces pièces concernent chacune des époques de création du maître de ballet.

Les documents les plus anciens concernent la période d'études à l'École impériale de Ballet de Saint-Pétersbourg. Il s'agit de deux certificats portant sur la conduite et sur les progrès de l'écolier (1895-96 et 1997-98).

Le nom de Fokine est intimement lié au succès des premières « Saisons russes » de Paris. La première Saison présentait le répertoire du Théâtre Mariinski de Saint-Pétersbourg, comportant des créations de Fokine.

De 1909 à 1912 et en 1914, Fokine était premier chorégraphe de la troupe des Ballets russes et le fonds comporte un grand nombre de documents relatifs à Serge de Diaghilev (1872-1929) – fondateur et directeur de la légendaire compagnie. Ces documents rendent notamment compte des relations complexes entre les membres de la troupe. Diaghilev, par exemple, reprochait à Fokine de reprendre ses chorégraphies parisiennes sur la scène de Saint-Pétersbourg alors que le maître de ballet accusait l'imprésario d'engager d'autres chorégraphes sans son accord, et regrettait la manie de Diaghilev de changer le titre de ses ballets.

C'est le travail de création chorégraphique de Fokine qui constitue la partie essentielle du fonds d'archives. Le chorégraphe a créé plus quatre-vingts ballets en un acte et miniatures chorégraphiques, dont dix chefs-d'œuvre immortels conçus pour les Ballets russes entre 1909 et 1914. Les documents permettent de suivre avec clarté l'histoire de la création de quelques ballets, comme par exemple, *Cléopâtre*, l'un des premiers ballets des « Saisons russes ». Créé en 1908 à Saint-Pétersbourg sous le titre *Une nuit d'Égypte*, *Cléopâtre* fut présenté l'année suivante à Paris avec Ida Rubinstein. La notation chorégraphique de la scène d'entrée de Cléopâtre, le devis des costumes pour la création de 1908 au Théâtre Mariinski, la description des costumes des 57 interprètes, des photos et cartes postales du couple Fokine dans ce spectacle présenté à Milan, Berlin et Stockholm font partie du fonds.

Soulignons que le thème de l'Égypte a toujours attiré Michel Fokine. Le fonds comporte un album de dessins et des calques réalisés par le maître de ballet : catalogue original des attitudes, vêtements, ornements, détails d'architecture de différentes cultures nationales.

Une bonne dizaine de feuilles sont consacrées à l'Égypte et nous avons pu établir qu'elles étaient copiées des illustrations de l'*Histoire de l'art dans l'Antiquité*[3].

Il est également possible de suivre l'histoire des créations de Fokine, en collaboration avec des danseuses célèbres. *Le cygne*, solo chorégraphié par Fokine pour Anna Pavlova sur l'andante du *Carnaval des animaux* de Saint-Saëns, a été créé à Saint-Pétersbourg à l'occasion d'un gala de charité en 1907. Ce solo qui conjugue les talents de Fokine-chorégraphe et de Pavlova-danseuse, est devenu le symbole poétique de la chorégraphie russe de cette époque. Par la suite, la version chorégraphique Fokine-Pavlova a pris le titre de *La mort du cygne*. Outre la description qui est faite de ce ballet dans les mémoires, le fonds contient le brouillon d'une conférence du maître ballet en russe : seize pages décrivant le spectacle et l'histoire de sa création de manière détaillée ainsi. Ces notes ont servi de base à la rédaction d'un livre intitulé *Mikhaïl Fokine. La mort du cygne*[4]. D'autres documents concernent Anna Pavlova : des photographies portant la signature autographe de la danseuse et une correspondance à propos de *Chopiniana*, première version de *Les Sylphides*.

Il existe par ailleurs des photographies (36 clichés et 49 photographies) de Vera Fokina dans *La mort du cygne*. En classant dans l'ordre les photos des différentes attitudes du ballet, il est possible de le reconstituer et d'en retrouver le découpage. Ouliana Lopatkina, la danseuse-étoile actuelle du ballet du Mariinsli, a consulté ces photographies lors de son travail de préparation du ballet.

Michel Fokine était passionné par le théâtre dramatique. Deux documents conservés dans le fonds témoignent d'un échange de lettres entre Ida Rubinstein et lui en 1913, à l'occasion de la participation du chorégraphe à la mise en scène du mystère de Gabriele d'Annunzio, *La pisanelle*, au Théâtre du Châtelet, à Paris. Notons que ces documents n'étaient jusqu'ici pas disponibles pour les travaux de recherches consacrés à ce spectacle. Nous possédons, dans les archives, le brouillon d'un télégramme de Fokine à Ida Rubinstein, très vraisemblablement en réaction à une invitation (qui ne se trouve pas dans le fonds) de celle-ci. Le document présente un intérêt évident : il contient en effet la description détaillée d'un des principaux jeux de scène du spectacle, le style précis de l'accompagnement musical, le nombre et la durée des parties dansées.

---

[3]   Georges Perrot et Charles Chipiez, *Histoire de l'art dans l'antiquité. T. 1. L'Égypte*, Paris, Hachette, 1882.

[4]   Traduction en anglais : "*The Dying Swan* music by C. Saint-Saëns ; detailed description of the dance by Michel Fokine; thirty-six photographs from poses by Vera Fokina", New York, J. Fischer & brothe, [c1925].

Au printemps 1913, Vsevolod Meyerhold (metteur en scène), Ida Rubinstein (interprète principale), Léon Bakst (décorateur) et Michel Fokine (chorégraphe) se retrouvaient à Paris pour un travail collectif sur le spectacle. Les danses du troisième acte, chorégraphiées par Fokine, constituaient les moments les plus tragiques de ce spectacle dramatique.

L'œuvre de Fokine est l'illustration même de ses théories. Le fonds d'archives comporte des articles et des lettres dans lesquels Fokine énonce clairement les principes de son esthétique et ses propres conceptions chorégraphiques, notamment, à propos de la danse moderne et des rapports étroits qui doivent exister entre la musique, la peinture et la danse.

Les archives en rapport avec le processus de création : relations avec le théâtre contemporain

Les documents d'archives sont de toute première importance pour les chercheurs, en ce qu'ils donnent des informations souvent uniques sur les spectacles. Ils peuvent être la source de recréation de certains ballets de Fokine et les chorégraphes contemporains se tournent fréquemment vers des documents tels que :

- les notes chorégraphiques pour les ballets *Cléopâtre, L'oiseau de feu, Schéhérazade, Le dieu bleu* ; le scénario du ballet *Daphnis et Chloé* ; des documents sur les ballets *Le carnaval, La bacchanale, Barbe-bleue* ;
- des cartes postales et photographies d'acteurs dans leurs rôles, permettant de retrouver les décors, costumes, accessoires et attitudes des interprètes et donc de reconstituer l'aspect visuel de certains spectacles : Michel Fokine et Vera Fokina dans les ballets *Le Pavillon d'Armide, Le carnaval, Daphnis et Chloé, Cléopâtre* ou *Schéhérazade* ;
- des maquettes de costumes avec leur description, réalisée par le maître de ballet pour *Cléopâtre, Le carnaval* et *La bacchanale*.

Michel Fokine quitta définitivement la Russie en 1918, sans pourtant avoir pu réaliser son rêve de présenter à Saint-Pétersbourg les ballets créés en France pour Diaghilev. La programmation du Théâtre Mariinski – scène natale du maître de ballet – n'a jamais comporté beaucoup de ballets de Fokine, alors même que, pendant treize ans (de 1905 à 1918), il y a réalisé plus de vingt mises en scène, dont la moitié sont des parties dansées d'opéras.

La dernière réalisation de Fokine en Russie porte sur les chorégraphies de l'opéra *Rouslan et Ludmila*. Des annotations chorégraphiques et des commentaires de la main du chorégraphe figurent sur la partition de la « Marche de Tchernomor ».

Dans le courant des années 1990, Andris Liepa, fils du danseur de légende Maris Liepa, aujourd'hui directeur artistique de la troupe des « Saisons russes du XXIe siècle », a réalisé le rêve de Fokine en montant des créations jusque-là inconnues à Saint-Pétersbourg et à Moscou. Depuis plus de vingt ans, en effet, il remonte les ballets de Fokine, en s'inspirant des documents d'archives du fonds, et en s'attachant à une reconstitution minutieuse de ses chorégraphies. Il a ainsi pu recréer sur la scène du Théâtre Mariinski, *Petrouchka*, *Schéhérazade* et *L'oiseau de feu ;* en collaboration avec le ballet du Kremlin de Moscou, *Le dieu bleu* et *L'oiseau de feu* ; et dans le cadre de son activité aux « Saisons russes du XXIe siècle », *Le pavillon d'Armide*.

Isabelle, la petite-fille de Michel Fokine, a par ailleurs elle aussi pris connaissance des archives du chorégraphe à la Bibliothèque théâtrale de Saint-Pétersbourg.

Au début des années 1990, le Ballet russe de l'Âge d'argent a présenté sur la scène du Théâtre musical du Conservatoire de Saint-Pétersbourg, sous la direction de Nikita Dolgouchine, un programme de ballets comportant *Le pavillon d'Armide*, des fragments de *Petrouchka* et *L'oiseau de feu*. Dolgouchine, chorégraphe saint-pétersbourgeois et grand connaisseur de la chorégraphie du siècle passé, œuvre à la reconstitution de ballets de Fokine, en donnant à ses chefs-d'œuvre une forme raffinée, grâce à la collecte scrupuleuse de documents chorégraphiques et iconographiques.

Des projets d'expositions et une participation aux projets internationaux

La Bibliothèque théâtrale organise des expositions et participe à des projets internationaux. En 1997, elle a ouvert l'exposition Les Saisons russes de Serge Diaghilev, l'une des manifestations organisées à l'occasion du 125e anniversaire du fondateur de la célèbre troupe. Parmi les pièces exposées – dont la plupart l'étaient pour la première fois – se trouvaient des croquis et des livres ainsi que des documents rares appartenant au fonds Fokine (lettres, photographies, dessins). Un catalogue de l'exposition, édité sous le même titre, décrivait 70 pièces appartenant majoritairement au fonds d'archives.

Les mérites de Michel Fokine, largement reconnus par le public parisien et le gouvernement français, ont valu au maître de ballet et artiste des Théâtres impériaux russes, l'attribution d'un diplôme d'Officier de l'instruction publique du ministère de l'Instruction publique. Ce document a été présenté au Musée national russe en 2003, à l'occasion de l'exposition Les Français à Saint-Pétersbourg.

Le centenaire des Saisons russes de Serge Diaghilev a été célébré dans le monde entier par des expositions et des festivals de musique et de danse.

Des documents du fonds Fokine ont été montrés dans de nombreuses expositions internationales. Par exemple, quatre documents (copies) comportant des notations chorégraphiques pour le ballet *L'oiseau de feu* en 1910, un plan de répétition et des croquis des personnages ont été prêtés en 2009 au Deutschen Theatermuseum München et à l'Österreichischen Theatermuseum Wien pour leur exposition conjointe.

Une restauration et une conservation des documents d'archives

Notons que les lecteurs de la Bibliothèque théâtrale ont une spécificité : dans la plupart des cas, ils sont animés par l'envie de travailler avec des originaux plutôt que des copies, avec un livre imprimé plutôt qu'avec sa version numérisée. Mais le papier de la plupart des documents, anciens, est fragile et délabré. Le souci de leur préservation est donc en conflit avec l'objectif de l'archivage de ces documents, qui est de les mettre à la disposition du lecteur.

La Bibliothèque se fixe un objectif de protection et de conservation des documents d'archives dont l'état de conservation est menacé par une manipulation trop fréquente. La restauration des photos d'archives a été entreprise dans le cadre du Programme national pour la conservation des fonds de bibliothèques. Des mesures de désinfection ont été prises et des copies de sauvegarde ont été réalisées. Ce travail de restauration d'archives a été long : pratiquement deux ans. L'étape suivante est la numérisation de ces photos.

Nouvelles technologies et accessibilité des sources pour le grand public

Le développement des techniques de numérisation offre de nouvelles possibilités de garantie de conservation des fonds. Dans le cadre du projet Réserve électronique que la spbbt a lancé en 2006, 105 documents d'archives de Michel Fokine ont ainsi été numérisés, à commencer par les autographes du maître de ballet (lettres, notations). La base de données des archives de Michel Fokine est accessible sur DVD.

Pour chaque document, on dispose de la description détaillée de l'archive, avec des annotations, et une image pouvant être agrandie ou réduite. La recherche se fait à travers plusieurs index : titres des mises en scène, noms, personnages, institutions, et également par mots-clés. Il est par ailleurs possible de limiter la recherche en fonction du type de document (lettre, dessin, photographie, brouillon, etc.).

L'objectif de ce travail est évidemment de préserver les documents originaux tout en donnant au grand public un accès aux richesses des archives de Michel Fokine. Le travail sur l'enrichissement de notre Réserve électronique est appelé à se poursuivre, la mise en place de nouveaux projets, comme la poursuite des anciens, dépendant naturellement des budgets disponibles.

Pour conclure, soulignons que la Bibliothèque théâtrale de Saint-Pétersbourg a pour mission de contribuer à la conservation du patrimoine chorégraphique, de mettre toutes les informations nécessaires à la disposition de tous les publics et de soutenir la recherche dans le domaine de la danse.

Abstract

The Saint Petersburg State Theatre Library houses the Mikhail Fokine archives. Vitali Fokine donated the family archives of the ballet master Mikhail Fokine to the library in 1960.

This paper presents:

- A historical record of the creation and development of the archives.
- Documents depicting all the different periods of the ballet master's life and illustrating the different stages in the creation of some of his ballets.
- Archives referencing the creation process, the relations with contemporary theatre, the library's contribution to the various revivals and re-creations of Fokine's ballets.
- Exhibition Projects and international participation in projects: the archives have participated in many exhibitions on Les Saisons Russes.

Theatrical Materials in the Municipal Library of Prague

Marie Valtrová & Helena Pinkerová

Municipal Library of Prague (Czech Republic)

The first public library in Prague opened on the 1st of July 1891 and has, in a sense, continued the activities of society libraries of the second half of the 19th century. The Public Municipal Library of the King's City of Prague was established on the basis of a municipal ordinance as a library for all citizens of Prague. The Municipal Library was first based on Na Zderaze Street, however in 1903 it was relocated to the corner of Platnérská Street and Mariánské náměstí in the Old City of Prague where the current Central Library building is located. From the beginning, the original Central Library building was inadequate to the needs of the Prague book network. The Municipal Insurance Company of Prague agreed to help the library and provided financial means for a new building – and so, between 1925 and 1928 a new building was designed by Frantisek Roith and constructed on Mariánské náměstí. This was the first purpose-built library building in the Czechoslovak Republic, and at the same time, one of the most modern buildings in Europe, sized to accommodate a wide variety of library, concert, educational and exhibition activities. Extensive, and modern, storage facilities allowed for dynamic growth of the library collection.

The theatre and film section of the Municipal Library of Prague was opened on 1st November 1942. Paradoxically, its operation began during one of the hardest periods for the Czech nation – during German occupation and the Protectorate of Bohemia and Moravia. The period was also characteristic of a fresh interest in Czech theatre and film. The inauguration ceremony was attended by many celebrities of that time, such as Adina Mandlová, Růžena Šlemrová, Hana Vítová, Blanka Waleská, actor František Vnouček, film critic Bedřich Rádl, violin virtuoso Jaroslav Kocian and many others.

Currently, the theatre and film section is one of the specialised sections in he Municipal Library of Prague; it was opened on 20th April 1998 after the full automation and renovation of the library and matches the original architecture. On the 8th of June 1993 the theatre and film section of the Municipal Library of Prague joined SIBMAS and it is also represented in the Dramaturgical Society since February 1997.

The purpose of the theatre and film section of the Municipal Library of Prague is to provide reader services from the areas of dramaturgy, costume design, film, radio and television. When it opened, its collection only contained 1,865 volumes, now, however, this has increased to approximately 60,000 items, including circa 20,000 items of Czech and foreign plays, 1,000 film and television scripts, 3,000 volumes of theatre, film, television and radio journals and 36,000 volumes of secondary and specialised literature on the history of theatre, film and other aforementioned areas.

The structure of the collection has changed proportionately to the changes in Czechoslovak society. The first official intervention occurred in 1940 by the then Minister of Education Emanuel Moravec and the Ministry of Interior Affairs. Still, most of the collection was saved with the silent consent of the Czech police. Further purges continued after February 1948, when a so-called "purging committee" was established and in total was responsible for the removal of almost 124,000 items from its establishment to 31st December 1952. The last notable external intervention was the purge of various pieces of literature during the so-called normalisation era based on the Directive on special collections of the Ministry of Culture in 1972. This purge focused especially on work from the 1960s, mainly by foreign authors and those who have emigrated. In total 1,700 works were purged.

Despite these repeated external interferences, the structure of the theatre and film section collection was essentially preserved. The base of this collection, with substantial historical value, is formed by texts of Czech plays from the 19th century and the first half of the 20th century, which are located in the storage facilities of the Central Library on Mariánské náměstí and include the first editions of plays by famous as well as less known playwrights and translators. The oldest of these are from the first half of the 19th century and include plays of Jan Nepomuk Štěpánek, Václav Kliment Klicpera, Josef Kajetán Tyl, Matěj Kopecký and others. The collection of international plays includes first and foremost the work of William Shakespeare, Johann Wolfgang von Goethe and Friedrich Schiller in their first Czech translations. Another valuable part of the collection are the first editions of work by famous authors from the 1930s: the Čapek brothers, František Langer, Fráňa Šrámek, Vítězslav Nezval and comedies by Jiří Voskovec and Jan Werich. Based on a resolution for protecting the collection, it is only allowed to borrow theatre plays appearing in type before 1920 on site.

A portion of the plays published before 1860 were moved to the new section of precious prints on Ortenovo náměstí after 1989. Original plays in foreign languages (the oldest being Molière's *The Misanthrope* from 1749, Racine's *Alexander the Great* from 1779 and plays by Shakespeare and Schiller translated by Karel Ignác Thám from the 1880s) and original Czech plays from the first half of the 19th century have been provided proper placement and care by specialists. The collection was located in the relative safety of air-conditioned areas with a special depository and strict borrowing conditions until the Prague floods of 2002, which also affected the section of precious prints. Approximately 800 plays were damaged and the restoration efforts comprised several distinct methods (drying in wood dryers, in vacuum packs and the vacuum chamber in the National Library of the Czech Republic) and took several years. After the section was moved to another building in 2004, the whole department and section of precious prints was renovated thanks to several donations (improvements include restoration workshops, air conditioned depositories and a cataloguing centre). Now, in cooperation with the restoration section of the National Library, the saved precious prints (including plays) are gradually being restored.

Another manner of preserving historically valuable work in the collection of the Municipal Library of Prague is digitisation. The Municipal Library of Prague has long been pursuing a digitisation centre. In 2005, a unique opportunity arose – the idea could be developed as a project in the Financial Mechanisms of the European Economic Area and Norway. The project was named HISPRA – Preservation of Historical Pragensia and other rare documents from the collection of the Municipal Library of Prague. After a tough approval process in the autumn of 2006, the project was accepted for realisation. The project is planned for four years with the possibility of continuation and a budget of 507,740 EUR. In November 2007, the Municipal Library of Prague began the digitisation process for precious and historical prints in its new centre. In the first year the department of digitisation focused on processing approximately 1,000 pragensia, and in 2009-2010 1,200 plays were digitised. The selection includes not only the most popular plays (medieval plays, Czech and foreign plays) and film scripts (the new film wave) but also significant historical and theoretical work from these areas and certain theatre and film magazines (*Divadlo* from the 1960s and others).

In conclusion we state that the goal of this contribution is to document how the Municipal Library of Prague takes care of its collection and makes sure that rare plays are preserved for future generations, thus adopting the mission connecting all participants of this international conference: to keep the memories of theatre alive.

Abstract

Il est ici question du passé, du présent et de l'avenir du Département théâtral et cinématographique de la Bibliothèque municipale de Prague, fondée en 1942. Elle est la seule bibliothèque publique spécialisée dans ces domaines à Prague. Sont décrits la structure, la déposition, l'importance historique et les chances de rénovation et de numérisation des rares écrits de la collection, par exemple, les premières éditions remarquables des pièces tchèques, des traductions de classiques étrangers, etc.

The Scientific Research Portal

Media, Stage, Film

Ann Kersting-Meuleman

University Library at Frankfurt/Main (Germany)

Since the end of 2008 a new research tool is available for scholars of theatre and film studies in Germany: the Virtual Subject Library Medien Bühne Film (media stage film[1]). Medien Bühne Film is a central information portal for the subjects of communication, media studies/journalism, film and theatre studies. It is primarily intended for students and for scholars (research and teaching) but also for interested laymen, pupils and professionals in related areas. It is primarily intended for German users, but large parts of it can also be accessed free of charge from abroad.

What Is a Virtual Research Library/Internet Library?

[An] internet library is a portal that offers an integrated access to relevant scientific conventional and digital information resources [on certain subjects]. Information scattered on private or institutional websites, databases or library catalogues are brought together in order to facilitate research. Without [an internet library] this information has to be collected in a laborious and time-consuming process.[2]

In other words, a virtual research library is a complementary offer to the service supplied by real libraries: it is a portal to provision of digital information and it offers search options across heterogeneous data sources.

---

[1] <http://www.medien-buehne-film.de/en/>.

[2] Modified from ilissAfrica, "About the Project," <http://www.ilissafrica.de/en/about/iliss-project.html> (accessed 24.06.2012).

DFG **Programme Supra-regional Literature Supply**

The German Research Foundation (DFG) serves science in all its branches by giving financial support to research projects and by promoting cooperation among researchers. It places special emphasis on the international collaboration of researchers and knowledge transfer.

One of the programmes serves to improve literature supply in Germany. Different from other countries, the German National Library, which was only founded in 1912, collects primarily German publications or publications on Germany. This is why literature published before 1913, as well as literature in foreign languages, has to be supplied by other research libraries: by state and university libraries. The DFG gives a central means for extending collections to those libraries which have been declared responsible for one or several special subjects because of their extensive older holdings[3].

Besides printed literature and microforms it also supports the establishment of so-called Virtual Subject Libraries (i.e., Internet libraries).

There is a cross-disciplinary portal for about forty German virtual libraries called Vascoda[4].

Literature on theatre is collected in the University Library of Frankfurt. The rich historic collections of the Rothschild Library and of the Museum for Music and Theatre History founded by Friedrich Nicolas Manskopf provided the basis. Since 1950 the library has received special funding from the DFG for the acquisition of books and journals in foreign (European) languages. Up to now the collection comprises about

---

3   "The DFG funds projects hosted by scientific libraries, archives and other scientific service and information centres in Germany. The aim is to set up nationwide high-performance research information systems. Through this programme, the DFG aims to facilitate the provision of a comprehensive range of highly specialised literature collections and digital sources of information for use in scientific research in Germany. The goal is to satisfy the demand for access to specialised scientific information by creating a system that goes beyond those provided by individual university libraries. The programme is supported by a number of universal scientific libraries that manage DFG special subject collections. Although not funded by the DFG, the three German specialist national libraries (for Applied Natural Sciences and Technology, Economics and Medicine) form a third pillar of this system by covering the applied subject areas. The literature and information collections are available to all scientists and academics in Germany without restriction. Internet-based services for bibliographical research, interlibrary loans, document delivery and direct online access to those collections available in digital form, are being set up by the participating libraries as part of their virtual subject libraries." From DFG website, <http://www.dfg.de/en/research_funding/programmes/infrastructure/lis/digital_information/library_licenses/index.html> (accessed 31.05.2010).

4   Former web address <www.vascoda.de>, now integrated into webis.sub.uni-hamburg.de/webis/index.php (accessed 23.01.2012).

125,000 books on film and theatre, 620 current journals, more than 100,000 theatre programmes from German stages, and special material such as theatre-related bequests, including the archive of the Municipal Theatre and Opera House of Frankfurt, an opera collection consisting of performance material for more than 1,000 works from 1780, scene stills, scene and costume design sketches, libretti, prompt books, playbills, etc.

What Is the Virtual Subject Library Medien Bühne Film? What Are the Aims?

The Virtual Subject Library Medien Bühne Film is an interdisciplinary research tool and information portal for the areas of communication studies, journalism and media studies, and theatre and film studies. In addition to the conventional media offered by libraries it gives access to online digital resources. Internet sources are selected for scientific relevance, and following quality criteria, the content is recorded by library standards. Researchers, students and interested persons who are looking for information on a certain subject can thus start parallel searches in different data sources, get information, or access full-text resources from a single starting point with a single search order.

Establishing this Internet library is a project in two parts which belongs to the program "Supra-regional Literature Supply/Virtual Libraries" funded by the DFG. The Virtual Subject Library Media Stage Film is a collaborative project of the Leipzig University Library (SSG[5] 3.5 Communication and Media Studies/Journalism), the University Library Johann Christian Senckenberg Frankfurt am Main (SSG 9.3 Theatre and Film Arts), the University of Music and Theatre "Felix Mendelssohn Bartholdy" Leipzig, and the Academy of Film and Television "Konrad Wolf" in Potsdam. Its first funding period was from September 2007 to August 2009; the second has started in March 2010 and will continue until mid-2014.

Access Points

Due to the different subjects represented in this portal we give the possibility of searching all at a time or of limiting the search to sources related to one of the subjects right from the start.

Within each entry point you can choose the search of all sources ("meta search") or click further to a special search in one of the integrated modules:

– Library catalogues
– Internet sources
– Journal article titles

---

[5] A Sondersammelgebiet is a special subject collection funded by the DFG.

– Nationwide licensed databases
– Electronic journals
– Databases

Meta Search

Meta search allows simultaneous searching in the following electronic sources:

Library Catalogues (Free Access)

– State and University Library Bremen subject catalogue Publizistik, Journalism, Press (responsible library up to 1998)
– University Library Frankfurt subject catalogue broadcasting, television (responsible library up to 1998)
– University Library Leipzig subject catalogue communication and media studies, journalism (responsible library from 1998 on)
– Library of the Hans-Bredow-Institut for media studies
– Library of the Friedrich-Ebert-Stiftung (political and social sciences)
– University Library Frankfurt subject catalogue theatre and film studies
– University Library Frankfurt digitized card catalogue (all subjects, up to 1986)
– Union Catalogue Film

Internet Sources (Free Access)

– Internet guide all subjects
– Internet guide communication and media studies, journalism
– Internet guide theatre studies
– Internet guide film studies

Database of Journal Article Titles (Licensed, Free Access)

– Online Current Contents communication and media studies (OLC KMW) (Licensed)
– Online Current Contents film and theatre studies (OLC FTW) (Free Access)

Nation-wide Licensed Databases (Licensed)

– Periodicals Index Online/PIO 1739-2000
– Periodicals Archive Online/PAO 1802-2000
– Later: Early English Books Online/EEBO

Internet Sources

Core themes of the collection profile of the Internet Resources Theatre Guide are theatre studies, playwriting, dance studies, and cabaret (circus, vaudeville, cabaret). All aspects are covered: historical, aesthetic, psychological, sociological, technical and economic. Non-artistic areas such as theatre technology or management aspects of theatre are also included as well as sources with an enlarged view of the subject, such as forms of paratheatrical behaviour, theatricality, or performance theory.

The focus is on sources that examine the regions Europe, USA, Canada, Australia and New Zealand; to a lesser extent sources of other regions are also collected.

The regional and thematic limits of the collection profile are not drawn too strictly for the sake of unrestricted interdisciplinary research.

The Internet sources are either taken from link lists of renowned institutions like the Zentral- und Landesbibliothek Berlin or the Hochschule für Film und Fernsehen Potsdam, or they are systematically searched in the Web by scholarly assistants of our project.

Only websites of scientific interest are selected for the Virtual Library. The website is described in bibliographic categories following Dublin Core. They are described (free text) and indexed thematically following modified versions of RVK (Regensburger Verbundklassifikation, a very common classification in German University Libraries) and DDC (Dewey Decimal Classification).

You can use either the simple search or the combined search, or search by theme, region, source or time.

Library Catalogues

In this presentation I'll focus on the library catalogues interesting for theatre studies, the last three ones in the existing list, as well as two others which will be added to it within the next two years. For the moment you'll find the title data and local information on the shelf numbers. During the next months a reference to availability in all German (maybe even European) libraries will be added (via a link to Karlsruher Virtueller Katalog KVK).

At first, a link to World Cat was not planned because not enough German regional union catalogues were involved in it, but it was added in 2011.

- University Library Frankfurt subject catalogue theatre and film studies
- From 1986 on, over 80,000 books on film and theatre, about 650 current journals. The search is possible in the following

categories: author, title, keyword, and standard identification number.

- University Library Frankfurt digitised card catalogue (all subjects, up to 1986)
- About 30,000 books on theatre and film. The search is limited to the categories author and title.
- Union Catalogue Film (hosted by the KOBV, Berlin)
- Union catalogue of audio-visual media from about thirteen institutions.
- Union catalogue of literature on film from about eleven institutions.
- Later: Library of the Deutsches Theatermuseum/Clara-Ziegler-Stiftung Munich
- Later: Library of the Theatre Collection of the University of Cologne.

You can find lists of recently acquired media in the folder "service"; the lists are published monthly in alphabetical order of authors' names and book titles.

E-journals

Electronic journals can also be accessed via the host of the University Library of Regensburg. Each title is marked in one of the traffic light colours:

- Green: free product, accessible from everywhere
- Yellow: licenced product, accessible from institutions which acquired the licence
- Red: not licenced in own institution

In June 2010, 132 titles of online theatre journals were listed, half of them with free access.

Databases

A link to the DBIS system hosted by the University Library of Regensburg gives access to about thirty databases. They are marked according to their availability:

- F: free product, accessible from everywhere (eleven titles)
- L: licenced product, accessible from institutions which bought the licence (sixteen titles)
- Red: not licenced in own institution
- D: nation-wide licence (three titles)

The different types of data bases included are article databases (8), inventory (1), databases without specification (2), biographical databases (2), bibliographies (9), facts databases (2), portal (1), full-text database (8), and dictionaries, encyclopedias, reference books (5).

Journal Articles: Online Contents Service (Swets Data, Own Data)

Online Contents Film and Theatre Studies is a service free of charge from the Special Collection Film/Theatre at Frankfurt University Library. The database contains the tables of contents of about two hundred film, theatre, dance, and media journals.

In the first half of 2010, bibliographic descriptions of approximately 164,000 records of journal articles and reviews from the areas of Theatre, Dance, and Film were listed, with publication year from 1990 until today. Online Contents Film/Theatre is based on a product by Swets Information Services and is updated daily. Frankfurt University Library continuously adds to it the article titles of eighty more journals. Access is free of charge worldwide; registration is not required.

Publications on theatre, dance and film from Latin America, Africa, Asia and the Baltic countries are not defined within the field of collection but can be occasionally found in this list.

Online Contents Film and Theatre Studies can be used as a bibliographic database as well as an access point to Inter Library Loan (ILL) and the document delivery service subito[6].

Free Electronic Full Texts (National Licences, DFG Collections, etc.)

The Frankfurt and Leipzig University Libraries are both building up a document server on which full text articles are collected, indexed and archived long-term. The DFG funds scholarly assistants who contact institutions and scholars to collect electronic publications not archived by the German National Library.

What Is Available from Abroad?

From abroad you have free access to:
- Internet sources
- Library catalogues

---

[6]   See <www.subito-doc.de/?lang=en> (accessed 24.06.2010).

- Online Contents
- Free electronic full texts

Not available are:

- Licensed databases and e-journals

Staff

The staff working for the Virtual Library project is half in Leipzig, and half in Frankfurt/Main:

- Scholarly staff: 1.75 full time employees
- Scholarly assistants: 1 full time and 2 half-time employees (film: 19 hours/week; theatre: 19 hours/week; media/communication studies: 38 hours/week),
- Student assistants (KMW/UB Lpz.: 10 hours/week, Film/Theater/UB Ffm.: 10 hours/week),
- Subject librarians with 10% of their full working time (KMW/UB Lpz.: 1 librarian with 4-5 hours/week, Film/Theater/UB Ffm.: 1 librarian with 3.5-4 hours/week)
- IT specialists: two part-time employees

Next Steps /Future Plans

During the next two years we want to improve the usability of the Virtual Library Medien Bühne Film. There will be an evaluation by students within a university project.

There will also be:

- An improvement in quantity of sources
- The integration of more library catalogues
- The integration of more subject-specific nationwide licensed databases
- Enhancement of the Internet resources database
- Enhancement of the document servers
- Enhancement of the Online Contents database

Quality improvement will take place, with information on local availability for all of Germany (maybe beyond).

New features will be added:

- A research database in cooperation with the German Society of publishing and communication science DGPuK)
- At least one digitised subject-specific bibliography
- The installation of a web search engine

- Development of new service tools (for example personalising functions)
- An English user interface

Another important field is public relations: we have to make our product better known in universities, scholarly communities and the general public.

Last but not least, and this will be one of the most difficult tasks: we have to prepare the standard operation of the portal after the end of funding by DFG.

Abstract

La Bibliothèque virtuelle Medien Buehne Film (Média, scène, film) est un portail de recherche scientifique portant sur les études de théâtre et de cinéma, de communication et d'études des médias et de journalisme. Le portail, via l'URL <www.medien-buehne-film.de>, donne accès à de nombreux catalogues de bibliothèques sectorielles, bases de données et revues électroniques.

Les informations concernant les ressources disponibles gratuitement sur internet sont également collectées et indexées dans une base de données. Contrairement aux listes habituelles de liens de ressources internet, ceux-ci sont catalogués en catégories répondant aux critères du Dublin Core et sont régulièrement contrôlés quant à leur disponibilité et leur intégrité. Avec plus de 4500 sources enregistrées à partir du World Wide Web, le Guide internet de la Bibliothèque virtuelle représente déjà la collection la plus vaste d'études de théâtre, film et média en Allemagne disponible en ligne.

Ceux qui n'ont pas la possibilité de se rendre dans la « vraie » bibliothèque seront particulièrement heureux de disposer de ces nombreuses sources en ligne : sites internet thématiques et portails, documents scientifiques plein texte en pdf, bases de données bibliographiques, cinématographiques et journaux en ligne, pour ne mentionner que les sources les plus courantes…

En tant que projet commun des bibliothèques de l'Université de Leipzig (chef de projet) et de Francfort, de l'Académie du film et de la télévision de Potsdam et du Collège de musique et de théâtre de Leipzig, l'élaboration de la Bibliothèque virtuelle Medien Buehne Film est financée, depuis septembre 2007, par la Fondation allemande de la recherche. Le financement de ce projet se poursuivra jusqu'en avril 2012, date à partir de laquelle le fonctionnement régulier du portail sera pris en charge par les bibliothèques.

Common Panel on Curating

Compiled by Claudia BLANK

German Theatre Museum (Munich – Germany)

The joint conference of SIBMAS and IFTR offered not only a number of meetings on a social level (joint evening meal of both EXCOMS, guided tour and garden party at the German Theatre Museum, joint reception in the Gartensaal (Garden Hall) of the Prinzregententheater (Prince Regent Theatre) and joint state reception at the Museum of Antiquities). Before the reception in the Prinzregententheater there was also a joint session with participants from both organisations holding discussions on the podium.

Christopher Balme, Munich host of the IFTR World Congress, had the idea of making "curating" the theme of this round of the conference. He launched this theme as follows.

Introduction to Curatorial Practices and the Public Sphere

The term "curation" has gained in recent years a new plurality of meanings and applications. What was once an occupational title referring to the keeper or custodian of a museum or other archival collection is now applied to a wide range of different activities in the visual and performing arts. "To curate" something may refer to the conceptual work on an exhibition but can equally mean the organisation of a performing arts festival. In the context of contemporary art, curation implies the combination of different art forms under a guiding idea to be displayed or exhibited for the public. Thus curation has become a key practice at the interface of critical theory and practice, exploring the changing relationships between the arts, exhibition and performance spaces, and audiences.

Our aim in this panel is to bring together representatives from SIBMAS and IFTR to exchange ideas about curation today and in the future. We wish to explore how better cooperation and more lines of communication can be established between academic scholarship on the one hand and the professional practices in libraries and museums on the other. Both activities are coming under increasing pressure to communicate with the wider public and it is here that new forms of curatorial practices provide an important point of intersection. What is the relationship between specialist and public interest? How does one bridge the gap between live and archived performing arts? What are limits and common denominators of curatorial practices between museum and festival?

This was the blueprint for creating the basis for this round of the discussion. The Curating Panel participants were: Claudia Blank (SIBMAS), Gabriele Brandstetter (IFTR), Jane Pritchard (SIBMAS) and Richard Stone (SIBMAS). Birgit Wiens assumed responsibility for moderating. In preparation for this task she had drawn up the following notes (this list of questions was sent to the participants in advance):

Possible Topics and Course

1. Please describe your institution briefly

2. Questions to the representatives of Theatre Museums

   a. Shifts in Contemporary Theatre Practices

      Theatre, as we know, is an ephemeral art form, and theatre museums cannot collect the art work "itself", but only remaining elements (director's notes, biographies of the actors/actresses, fotos, models of the stage design, programmes, articles, etc.). Contemporary theatre practice might require new categories and strategies of collecting.

      Practice in the performing arts has changed. Traditionally, the role and responsibilities of writers, directors, and performers (*virtuosi*) were separate, whereas in current practice we see more and more that responsibilities are overlapping or shared. Also, the aesthetic forms of theatre/performance pieces are no longer limited to a "stage work" but have enfolded a spectrum of performative practices. The advent of new media and intermedial practices has added to this diversification. And also, we see complexity on the institutional level (emergence of international production networks, co-production and touring, interweavings of theatre culture/"theatrical trade routes"/globalisation).

      How does your institution react to these changes; what are your principles for collecting and archiving?

   b. Curatorial Principles and Practices

      How would you describe/summarize the curatorial principles and practices of your institution? Please give examples of key projects that you have been working on during the last years.

c. Audience/Public Sphere

As a museum, what kind of audience do you address? What kinds of presentation formats do you usually choose: traditional formats such as exhibitions, lectures? Discursive, performative and process-oriented formats such as forums, interventions etc.? In which ways can the audience become involved? How would you describe the public sphere that you address/generate with your activities?

d. Curating as Science/Curating as Art?

Please outline the kind of research done in your institution. Do you see curating as a scientific task, or can it also be artistic?

e. Networks and Collaborations

Please describe your context and network (discourse network as well as production network). Which are the institutions and partners you collaborate with?

f. New Media, Digital Archives, Transnational Networks

In which ways do you make use of new media in your museum (for archiving and for presentation)? How do you envision the possibility of a "digital archive of theatre history", and which examples of digital notation make sense to you (e.g., William Forsythe, "Improvisation Technologies"; Waseda University/zkm, "That's Kyogen"; R. Beacham, Theatron Visualization Project, just to name a few)?

How do you see your institution within the context of the contemporary "knowledge society"?

According to Yukiko Shitakata, Curator, Tokyo[1]

The whole notion and system of "archive" should be reconsidered beyond cultures and countries, and there will be no one, universal state of "archive", but there will be more de-centralized, multi-perspective approaches to the archive. The digitally networked archive with social taggings by people's participation would be one of the actual, significant forms of archives.

Would you agree?

What is your vision for the future?

3. Questions to Theatre Studies/Institutes at Universities

Applied Research/Curating as Choreography

– Theatre Studies as Applied Research
– Example: Zentrum für Bewegungsforschung (Centre for Movement Research), Freie Universität Berlin

---

[1] "Curating the Future", Yukiko Shitakata, Curator, Tokyo.

- Please describe the concepts and strategies of the applied research at ZBF.

Key Concept: "Curating as Choreography"

- What does "Curating as Choreography" mean: starting a dynamic process within multiple components? (Which ones?)
- How do curators, choreographers, performers and audience interact within this process? What can be the possible tasks? Which modes of presentation (and also analysis and evaluation) are possible? (Please describe a current project.)
- Do you think that art/theatre/dance is epistemological?
- Please describe your network, partners and collaborations.
- The ZBF work is transdisciplinary: which disciplines are involved? Why does it make sense to involve nature sciences (e.g., physics, swarm theory, etc.)?
- In which way do the results of your research reflect back into other disciplines?
- How do you use new media in your research work? What has been the impact of digital culture on contemporary choreography and dance?
- Dance especially (because it does not depend on language/ dramatic texts) has become very much internationalised. Do you see a danger that cultural differences get lost in the contemporary festival scene and "theatre trade routes"?
- "Interweaving of performance cultures": in which way does this phenomenon become visible in dance?
- What is your vision?

Entering the Debate

After a brief address by Christopher Balme, in which he stressed the importance of a joint event held by both organisations, and short welcoming speeches by Claire Hudson, the President of SIBMAS, and Klaus Zehelein, the host and President of the Bavarian Theatre Academy, the presenter Birgit Wiens once again briefly outlined the theme. She then asked each participant to submit a statement on the theme of curating. The first in line was Claudia Blank, whose comments were reported in writing as follows.

Aspects of Curating

Firstly, as to be expected in my profession, I'd like to revisit the concept of curating in the museum context, because with all the diversity of regional linguistic usage this is where its roots lie. In English, the professional title "curator" means being an employee of a museum, where collections are kept, and taking care of the items there – preserving them, preparing inventories for them, looking after and acquiring them. For us here, the title for this professional activity is "Konservator", just as the description "Conservateur" is used in France. There, this feature of the job is given emphasis, whereby the director of a museum often refers to herself, or himself, as the "Conservateur en Chef".

Something develops during the course of such activity, which I call "curatorial knowledge". This is a knowledge of the materials which bear witness to the theatre and which often have their own history, such as stage set and costume designs, playbills and programme booklets or photography, which is my specialist area. For example, the theatrical authenticity of a photograph from the 19th century cannot be properly evaluated until it is known that up until the last decade of that century it can only have originated in the daylight of a photographic studio, which at that time was already ornately fitted out with decorative props.

And incidentally, you'll find such "curatorial knowledge" in the publication presented by the German Theatre Museum for its centenary this year, containing an English-language CD. Please forgive this brief advertisement.

Looking after the items in the collection inventories is a fundamental activity in curating, and indeed the word derives from the Latin "curare", meaning to care for. But that's not all. We museum personnel are also responsible for bringing to life the objects entrusted to us, not only in publications but in exhibitions as well. Designing and staging an exhibition is, for us, an element of the concept of curating. So we also write this into invitations to openings of our exhibitions.

The curating of an exhibition can take an extremely wide variety of forms, depending on the nature of the exhibition to be prepared.

Our thematically oriented exhibitions, which use original materials, often go far beyond the preparation of our own collection objects, which involves a great deal of time and considerable costs. For example, over the past year we also presented an exhibition on the 100th anniversary of the Ballets Russes at the German Theatre Museum, which we were able to stage with the co-operation of the Austrian Theatre Museum, where it was presented for a second time, and whose director, Thomas Trabitsch, is with us today and to whom I am very grateful. Our curators, the dance researchers Claudia Jeschke and Nicole Haitzinger, have undertaken numerous research visits, several times to Moscow and Saint Petersburg, and also to Paris, Stockholm, Hamburg and Vienna, etc. For them it was essential to approach this activity with a clear basic concept, otherwise they would have become hopelessly lost in the abundance of materials to be inspected. The emphasis was placed upon "Russian Pictorial Worlds in Motion", which therefore ruled out ballets such as *Josephslegende* or *Scheherazade* from the outset.

However, we were thus also bold enough to refer to movement in the title, whereby we hit upon the crux of the problems surrounding exhibitions: how is the art of movement to be captured in an exhibition whose very nature is static? Time and again our discussions revolved around this question – particularly in dealing with valuable historical objects. Exhibiting an original costume firstly involves doing justice to the curatorial requirements of the object. Puppets arranged into an elaborate pose will overstrain the sensitive historic textiles. In the end we gained inspiration from the Ballets Russes production of *Petrushka* and placed the curatorially correct costume puppets on a stylized carousel which revolved slowly.

We currently have a very different kind of exhibition taking place, such as those which visited us yesterday evening could have seen. The curator of our exhibition Female Stage Directors, Christina Haberlik, mainly generated the exhibition objects herself, by visiting, interviewing and filming the directors concerned. These film sequences, shown as excerpts, are supplemented by photographic enlargements and quotations on the walls, and likewise originate from the interviews.

A third variant of a type of exhibition on theatrical subjects is the preparation of a biographical exhibition on the basis of an extensive estate, which involves deciphering diaries and correspondence which have remained and, through this time-consuming and laborious work, creating for ourselves the foundation for an exhibition and accompanying publication. This activity, for which my colleague Birgit Pargner is our specialist, is rewarded with exciting, moving and often very intimate insights into a personality, which in her last exhibition was Marianne Hoppe.

Making decisions on what type of exhibition on what subjects is to be prepared and by whom it should be curated is to some extent a meta-level of curating, which – particularly in the case of external curators – also includes the step-by-step accompaniment to the individual working phases of conception and realisation. Therefore, it was a quite deliberate decision to select the abovementioned dance researchers for our Ballets Russes exhibition, because a Fine Art expert will, for example, look at a figurine by Leon Bakst with his professionally trained eye and comment on form, line, colour and decoration. However, the exciting aspect of the figurines by Bakst is the previously sketched movement inherent in them. A dance researcher is able to explain precisely this.

In addition, a dance researcher can decipher dance notations, and we've made use of this to add to the sense of movement in our exhibition.

As we have heard today from our colleague Galina Ivanova, the estate of the Ballets Russes choreographer Mikhail Fokine is kept in the Theatre Library of Saint Petersburg. It contains dance notations, of which we have shown a few reproductions, and have printed a few in enlarged form on the floor, so that visitors can walk along them – and now and then I've observed them doing so. Furthermore, Claudia Jeschke has rehearsed notations on a few sequences from various ballets with a female dancer from the Bavarian State Ballet. These sequences were filmed and could be viewed on monitors, classified according to the relevant original stage and costume designs and other objects.

The planning of exhibitions also involves calculating the chronological lead-in times. This means, for example, that I'm already busy working on planning for up until 2014. The same applies to my colleague in Vienna. Whenever we meet, at some stage during the discussion we always share our thoughts on what we're currently planning for the next three to four years, although this can always be subject to changes due to all sorts of unforeseen circumstances. If this kind of activity is also to be attributed to the term "curating", then I for my part would also like to interpret this concept as broadly as other contributors will do today.

In planning our exhibition programme, the principle aim is to constantly pick different subjects from the great variety of possibilities, in order to expand the circle of people who know about and visit the German Theatre Museum. This happened, for example, with the exhibition of Japanese Nô costumes in 2004, which was clearly visited by people who are not amongst our regular visitors, or the exhibition on Michael Ende, which jointly with the Museum Education Centre we also prepared specially for children and young people, and precisely this group of people brought a wonderful liveliness into the museum.

The most successful are biographical exhibitions on performing artists who are well-known regionally, nationally or internationally, such as Therese Giehse, Marianne Hoppe or Oskar Werner. However, even if we consider a director such as Otto Falckenberg, for example, we no longer attract so many visitors. Simply the presentation of an artist, who although at the hub of operations is in the public's perception of theatre a step behind the performer on stage, is no longer so popular. The top spot as a visitor attraction – which was not surprising but was anticipated – went to our exhibition on Maria Callas. If such a subject cannot draw in a large number of visitors, we really can give up presenting exhibitions. However, our aim is not to limit ourselves just to these biographical exhibitions, but to constantly introduce other subjects, such as the current Female Stage Directors, although unfortunately even they don't attract so many visitors.

Finally, to sum up I should like to mention one last concept: as preparation for the current Gustav Mahler exhibition at the Austrian Theatre Museum, which in the coming year we will take over and adapt for Munich, a team of specialists has been formed who have over many years dedicated themselves to this subject. The person responsible for coordinating all relevant contributions, suggestions and objections, and from these forming a unity, is referred to as the "Head Curator" or "Chief Curator" in the accompanying publication.

Richard Stone and Jane Pritchard

Richard Stone and Jane Pritchard followed. The SIBMAS participants also linked up the debate with a joint theme, as they were each working on historical accounts of the Ballets Russes in their respective countries.

Richard Stone discussed the changing use of the concept of curating as evidenced by changes in management nomenclature in a large collecting institution, the National Library of Australia. This library houses a wealth of material on the theatre in Australia, in collections classified according to the type of materials such as books, programmes and printed ephemera, photographs, designs and drawings. Previously, the employees responsible for this were not called curators. There was a shift in the 1990s, when management-level personnel were now given this job title.

However, a further change occurred later when curators were specifically appointed for the theme areas of music and dance. These curators play a more all-embracing role, and their subject areas now cover not only the collecting and cataloguing of materials but also the interpretation of the collected materials – and this is the essential innovation. These curators are also responsible for arranging presentations and events, and they maintain contacts with other institutions, such as theatre and ballet companies, orchestras, and key individuals in the theatre world.

Jane Pritchard, Curator of Dance at the Victoria and Albert Museum in London, emphasised that the traditional values of curatorship lay in collection, preservation, and making material and information accessible to a wide public. She emphasised that the Museum was offered a wide range of material and that it was important to accept those that would enhance existing holdings. The selection of material is important as museums cannot simply gather up everything that they are offered. The Theatre and Performance Collections had been established in the 1920s as part of the Department of Prints and Drawings and initially focused on collecting works on paper – programmes and related ephemera and designs. By the 1970s the holdings had grown to become a collection of collections and a department in its own right, extending its collections to costumes and three-dimensional objects.

Selecting and collecting material for preservation is central to our work and we recognise that the material may now also be in digital formats. The v&a as an institution is endeavouring to get to grips with such collections. Collections need cataloguing and this task, along with the digitisation of images (beginning with early photographs and designs) has to be a priority. However communication with the public and finding ways of making collections accessible to the public were major concerns. The collection is now largely based in a large repository where we also have our reading room to give access to material to individuals be they scholars or the curious public. This includes access to our recordings of performances (nvap[2]). (The condition of recording is such that these cannot be screened on-line but special in-house screenings will be held in the main museum.) A significant and growing sector of our material may be viewed within the v&a's collections on-line[3].

Finding a range of ways to grant accessibility to the collection is important and these include study sessions focusing on a specific area in which small groups will be introduced to part of the collection. This is a way of showing parts of the collection such as costumes to which access in generally more restricted to interested groups. Sessions will also introduce groups of students to using the collection for individual research. Other ways of giving a profile to objects and collections include publishing papers, contributing to radio and television programmes, and taking advantage of the new on-line media. Here the curators present collections, objects and their history, place them into context and also introduce their research results. This is a traditional part of curatorship but there is a need to be proactive appreciating the growing opportunities in the 21st century and to make material accessible with the ability to reach a much wider audience.

Jane Pritchard also briefly presented the most recent history of the London theatre collection. After 25 years in its own premises in Covent Garden the independent Theatre Museum building had closed three years ago and the collections returned to its parental home of the Victoria & Albert Museum. For Pritchard and her colleagues this had advantages and disadvantages. On the one hand, they missed their former independence and location in London's "theatre-land", but on the other the theatre collection was now placed in a larger context and this was particularly interesting for the curators and provided greater access to resources such as conservation. Within the Victoria & Albert Museum at South Kensington the department had its own galleries, attracting larger

---

2   The National Video Archive of Performance.

3   Search the collections at <http://collections.vam.ac.uk/>.

numbers of visitors than received at Covent Garden. The material on show is only a tiny part of the collection and daily tours are available to enhance the visitor's experience. In addition there is space for changing special displays which are also sent out on tour. To date these have focused on the photographic collections but the next will feature the work of the designer and theatre polymath Gordon Craig. The V&A also has generous space for special exhibitions, and the first of a proposed series focusing on theatre and performance concerns the Ballets Russes which Pritchard curated. She also gave a talk on this exhibition at the present Conference[4].

Gabriele Brandstetter

Gabriele Brandstetter, on the other hand, included a large number of cultural activities within her concept of curating.

First of all she introduced the Center for Movement Research (CMR), which she founded in 2005. Giving more specific details, she reported briefly on two CMR projects. Firstly, she introduced the Prognosen über Bewegungen (Prognoses on Movements) project, and stressed that this brought together scientists and artists working in quite different fields.

The second project Gabriele Brandstetter mentioned was: Theater ohne Fluchtpunkt – Konfigurationen von Raum und Bewegung im Spannungsfeld gegenwärtiger Kunst, Wissenschaft und Politik (Theater without Vanishing Points – Configurations of Space and Movement in the Dynamics of Contemporary Art, Science and Politics) in Hellerau, Dresden, which was organised by the Theatre Studies department at the Academy of Fine Arts Dresden and the CMR.

The central field of activity which also particularly interested Gabriele Brandstetter in connection with the theme of curating was dance dramaturgy. She raised the question of what the dance dramaturg is. Is he a curator in the classical sense described by the previous speakers? Does he curate? Or is he a filter or a mediator? Is he a context provider or even a programme maker?

Finally, she touched upon another interdisciplinary initiative which is supported by Tanzplan Deutschland. This involved organising a series of workshops under the title Rethinking the Curatorial. Here, reflections upon the history of dance dramaturgy led into the subject area of curating. In this connection the plan was to offer, as a pilot project, a Masters programme bringing together Berlin MA students in dance studies, and Leipzig art students studying for the recently introduced MA in curating.

---

[4]   *Cf.* Jane Pritchard, "Behind the Scenes at the Museum: A Look at the Challenges of Presenting an Exhibition of Theatrical Material in a National Museum of Art and Design", p. 57-65.

As a concluding thought, Gabriele Brandstetter emphasised that, for her, composing and cooperation are essential features of dynamic curating.

There followed a short discussion, moderated by Birgit Wiens, in which the individual participants linked up to one another. Focal points here were cooperation and networks, with the SIBMAS participants reporting on their most recent working experiences in connection with their projects on the Ballets Russes (see also in this connection the SIBMAS talk by Richard Stone[5]).

---

[5] *Cf.* p. 67-74.

THIRD SESSION

TROISIÈME SESSION

Le dépôt légal du Web à la BnF

Une nouvelle perspective pour la conservation de la mémoire du spectacle

Cécile OBLIGI

Département des Arts du Spectacle – Bibliothèque nationale de France (Paris)

Contexte et définition

Depuis bientôt cinq siècles, obligation est faite en France à tout éditeur, imprimeur, producteur, distributeur ou importateur, de déposer chaque document qu'il édite, imprime, produit, distribue ou importe, à l'un des organismes dépositaires du dépôt légal. Concernant initialement les imprimés, le dépôt légal s'est étendu au fil des siècles aux estampes, cartes, plans, partitions musicales, photographies, phonogrammes, affiches, vidéogrammes et documents multimédias. Enfin le 1er août 2006, il est étendu à l'Internet par le titre IV de la loi DADVSI (Droits d'auteur et droits voisins dans la société de l'information) : « Sont également soumis au dépôt légal les signes, signaux, écrits, images, sons ou messages de toute nature faisant l'objet d'une communication au public par voie électronique. » Un décret d'application doit venir préciser les conditions de sélection et de consultation[1].

Ce dépôt légal de l'Internet est partagé entre l'Institut national de l'audiovisuel (INA), qui collecte les sites du domaine de la communication audiovisuelle (notamment ceux qui concernent la radio et la télévision) et la Bibliothèque nationale de France (BNF), qui se charge de tous les autres sites.

Contrairement aux autres supports, le dépôt légal n'implique pas de démarche particulière de la part des producteurs d'un site, à qui l'on demande seulement de fournir les informations techniques nécessaires en cas de difficulté à capter leur site. Il s'agit donc d'une collecte davantage

---

[1] Paru en décembre 2011 (décret n° 2011-1904).

que d'un dépôt. Inversement, l'autorisation des producteurs de sites n'est pas nécessaire, c'est la loi qui autorise un robot à collecter.

Méthode et principes de collecte

Pour collecter les sites Web, on utilise le robot moissonneur *Heritrix*. Ce robot, qui est un logiciel libre développé au sein d'un organisme international de préservation du Web, l'International Internet Preservation Consortium (IIPC), moissonne le Web en partant d'une liste d'adresses Web (URL). Il extrait les liens dans les pages de code des sites et les suit comme le ferait un internaute, mais de manière automatique. Il copie ensuite les informations ainsi collectées.

L'objectif de l'exhaustivité, valable pour les autres supports, est impossible à atteindre dans le cas du Web. Plus modestement, l'ambition est de collecter au mieux le domaine français, évalué en 2009 à cinq millions de sites. Deux grands types de collectes sont pratiqués, les collectes larges et les collectes ciblées. Les collectes larges moissonnent tous les sites en .fr, dont la liste est fournie par l'Association française pour le nommage Internet en coopération (AFNIC). D'abord faites en partenariat avec la fondation Internet Archive, elles ont été internalisées pour la première fois en 2010. Dans la collecte large, le robot n'entre pas en profondeur dans le site et se limite à quatre clics de profondeur. Il suit cependant une partie des liens trouvés (à l'exception des sites étrangers) et couvre donc une masse de sites qui va bien au-delà du .fr. Le deuxième type de collecte, dite ciblée, est le fruit de la sélection des bibliothécaires. Ces derniers définissent des listes d'URL qu'ils souhaitent voir collecter. La collecte ciblée descend plus en profondeur dans un site et permet de capter des sites qui échappent à la large : les sous-sites notamment, ou des sites bien trop importants (> 100 000 URL) qui ne pourraient être captés en totalité par le robot, ou enfin, des sites dont la périodicité de mise à jour est importante. Ces collectes ciblées sont internalisées depuis 2007. Il existe enfin des dépôts par les producteurs, mais ce cas est minoritaire.

Pour couvrir également la période où ces collectes n'existaient pas encore (1996-2005), la BNF a acquis – en antiquariat pourrait-on dire par analogie avec les autres supports – auprès d'Internet Archive[2] les sites en .fr que cette fondation avait archivés.

La collection ainsi obtenue atteint des dimensions vertigineuses : 13,6 milliards de fichiers et 182 téraoctets de données au début de l'année 2010.

Les principes qui guident la collecte s'inspirent du modèle du dépôt légal existant pour les autres supports, mais présentent quelques

---

[2]   Voici l'adresse du site de la fondation : <http://archive.org/>.

particularités. L'exhaustivité, irréalisable, a été abandonnée ; en revanche, c'est bien la masse qui est visée, et non une sélection de morceaux choisis. De même que l'on ne faisait pas rentrer un roman en fonction de sa valeur littéraire, un site Web n'entre pas dans les collections en raison de sa qualité. Pour une part, les collections du Web sont la continuité, sous une autre forme, des mêmes contenus. C'est le cas par exemple d'une revue qui passe d'un format papier à une diffusion Web, parfois en abandonnant totalement le papier. La revue de la Société des auteurs compositeurs dramatiques (SACD), *les Actes du théâtre*, qui a abandonné la version papier en 2007, en est un bon exemple. Notons qu'à cette occasion, le rythme de parution, autrefois trimestriel, est devenu variable, parfois plus fréquent qu'auparavant. Cette modification n'est probablement pas un simple hasard. Mais bien plus qu'un changement de support ou qu'un complément des supports traditionnels, le Web est un nouveau vecteur de production de l'information à part entière, avec sa logique propre, différente de celle des supports traditionnels.

Comme pour les supports traditionnels se pose, après la collecte, la question du stockage, puis de l'accès. Le stockage est réalisé sur des baies de stockage sur disques nommées « petabox » qui sont au nombre de cinq et d'une capacité totale d'environ 500 téraoctets. La conservation de données virtuelles a elle aussi une dimension physique. Une copie de sauvegarde est effectuée dans le Système de préservation et d'archivage réparti (SPAR)[3].

Le dépôt légal du Web des sites consacrés aux arts du spectacle

Les sites concernant les arts du spectacle sont captés à la fois par les collectes larges et les collectes ciblées, et ce, dès les débuts du projet. La collecte large ne demande pas de travail préparatoire aux bibliothécaires des départements de collection, leur rôle est d'examiner le produit de la collecte. En revanche, pour lancer les collectes ciblées, la participation active des bibliothécaires de la BNF est requise. Leur travail consiste à sélectionner un certain nombre d'URL qui seront suivies par le robot. Pour procéder à ce travail de sélection, une application, visible uniquement par les agents participants, a été développée. Elle permet la gestion de ce que l'on appelle un « panier » contenant des listes d'URL.

La première participation du département des Arts du spectacle date de 2005. À ce moment, le panier, de taille modeste, était constitué de 25 URL.

---

[3] Présentation disponible ici : <http://www.bnf.fr/fr/professionnels/conserver_spar/s. conserver_SPAR_presentation.html>.

En 2010, deux agents y consacrent chacun cinq à dix jours par an et entretiennent à eux deux 300 URL. Au démarrage du projet, les deux agents ont choisi de s'intéresser d'abord aux sites en lien avec leur domaine. En effet, ces deux personnes travaillaient dans le secteur « Actualités » du département des Arts du spectacle. Ce secteur collecte les documents dits d'actualité émis par une structure lors de la production et diffusion d'un spectacle : programmes, dépliants, dossiers de presse, coupures de presse. En utilisant le carnet d'adresses qui sert à leurs activités courantes, ils ont ainsi constitué un panier qui contenait essentiellement des sites de théâtres français, publics et privés (Théâtre national de la Colline à Paris, Théâtre des Célestins à Lyon, Théâtre de la Tête d'or à Lyon, par exemple).

Dans un deuxième temps, en 2009, l'accent a été mis sur les blogs de critique théâtrale. En effet, très souvent hébergés sur des sous-sites (Armelle Héliot sur le site du *Figaro* par exemple) ou sur des sites personnels, les blogs de critique étaient susceptibles d'échapper à la collecte large. Très significatifs de la vie culturelle, ils constituent une source essentielle et particulièrement volatile pour la recherche en arts du spectacle. Une vingtaine d'URL ont été sélectionnées et captées par la dernière collecte.

À terme, le panier a vocation à recouper tous les domaines traités par les autres supports (cirque, music-hall, arts de la rue, marionnettes…), une extension est donc à prévoir dans les années qui viennent.

Consultation des archives du Web

Il ne suffit pas d'engranger et de stocker des données, il faut aussi pouvoir les lire. Les archives du Web sont consultables uniquement dans les emprises de la BNF dans les salles dites de recherche par opposition aux salles ouvertes au grand public. L'application qui permet de consulter ces archives est nommée *Wayback machine*, machine qui « remonte le temps ». Il n'était pas envisageable de cataloguer le Web, même en se limitant au Web français. En revanche, une indexation automatique a été réalisée et le fonctionnement de la *Wayback machine* en découle. Elle permet d'accéder de deux manières aux archives : par l'URL ou bien en recherchant par mots. Dans une recherche par URL, on aboutit à la liste des années pour lesquelles des collectes existent. En cliquant sur une année, on obtient la liste des dates précises auxquelles les sites ont été capturés. On clique alors sur la date souhaitée et obtient la page d'accueil du site à la date voulue. Ensuite, on navigue comme sur le Web vivant dans la capture du site. Le deuxième moyen d'accès est la recherche par mots. Dans ce cas, on obtient une liste de résultats cliquables, très similaire aux résultats d'un moteur de recherche généraliste sur le Web.

Cette recherche par mots n'est possible que si a eu lieu une indexation plein texte, réalisée en pratique sur une partie des archives seulement, correspondant à la période 2006-2007. Ce mode de recherche, le plus proche des pratiques des usagers sur le Web et le plus intuitif, est le plus attendu. Il est cependant beaucoup plus coûteux à mettre en place.

À l'image d'une archive traditionnelle, les archives du Web sont à replacer dans un contexte. Comme pour un manuscrit ou une estampe, l'archive du Web ment autant qu'elle dit la vérité. Ce que le lecteur a sous les yeux ne correspond pas nécessairement à l'état d'un site tel qu'un internaute l'a vu mais à ce que le robot a pu capturer. Il peut y avoir des pages tronquées (format non lisible ou non capturable par le robot) ou des pages constituées d'éléments distincts les uns des autres et donc captés à des dates différentes. La critique de la source est similaire – mais pour l'instant moins naturelle – à celle que l'on pratique dans le cas d'une archive sur support traditionnel.

En effet, il existe des limites techniques à cette collecte. Certains formats sont particulièrement difficiles à capturer, certains contenus de site relèvent du Web dit profond (contenus protégés par un mot de passe, intervention d'une boîte de dialogue). Le robot est néanmoins de plus en plus performant et capte à chaque collecte de nouveaux éléments. Ainsi la capture des vidéos (très intéressantes pour les captations de scène) a progressé et donne accès à un matériau plus riche. Les vidéos du site du Théâtre national de la Colline en sont un bon exemple.

Perspectives

Nous constituons aujourd'hui la source des recherches de demain. L'archivage a suivi de peu l'apparition du support, ce qui nous permet d'avoir des traces pour les tout débuts de l'internet. Il se trouve qu'une partie de la création en arts du spectacle se fait maintenant sur la Toile directement, parfois sans autre forme de diffusion. Il était donc essentiel de mettre en place les structures permettant d'archiver cette nouvelle forme de production.

Abstract

The scope of legal deposit in France was extended to cover the Internet by the Law of August 1st 2006, and entrusted to the Bibliothèque nationale de France (BNF). Websites belonging to the French national domain can be collected by the (BNF), to be preserved and made available to the public. Website collection by the BNF consists of both a quantitative (large-scale and undeveloped collections) and a qualitative approach (sites selected by librarians) which allows it to keep track of information which may become rare and precious due to the particularly volatile medium that it uses. Thus, the collections from the Performing Arts department are enriched every year with these new documents called "Web archives". Wether the documents are simple paperless contents once produced on another medium, or a completely new genre without equivalent material, these documents are the future records for the future performing arts researchers.

Web 2.0

How Can SIBMAS and Its Members Use It, and What Pitfalls Can Be Expected?

Paul S. ULRICH

Berlin (Germany)

Web 2.0 is a much-talked-about trend in the use of World Wide Web technology and web design that aims to facilitate creativity, information sharing, and, most notably, collaboration among users. These concepts have led to the development and evolution of web-based communities and hosted services, such as social-networking sites, wikis, blogs, and folksonomies. What possibilities exist for SIBMAS and its members to use Web 2.0 to develop new ways for doing both old and new, innovative things? Is everything as wonderful as it is portrayed, or are there problems for us?

Before beginning to talk about Web 2.0, let's take a moment to think about the conditions in theatres. Their energies are focused on getting a performance up. No extensive thought is given to what will happen once the production is taken down. The mandate museums, archives and to a lesser extent libraries have is to collect, to preserve and to make material relating to these productions accessible at a later time to interested persons. Our job is to make the past accessible to the future. Ironically this "secondary" part of our mission has placed us in a position similar to that of the theatres, particularly when we become part of an environment in which the present and perhaps the future is important, but where the past receives little attention. What do I mean by this? Very simple: I assume that you can show me numerous printed copies of activities in which you have been involved in the past, but can you show me what your web presence looked like a year ago? Two years ago? Ten years ago?

By being content providers on the web there is a real danger that we will lose our perspectives for the future, become enamoured by the present, and forget about the past. When we fail to incorporate our professional objectives in our institutions with we are doing to make ourselves visible and interesting on the web, then we have inadvertently transferred our role from museal/archival institution to producing theatre.

"Web 2.0" is currently a hot topic. All over the world institutions are adding what they call Web 2.0 applications to their web offerings. Some are doing interesting innovative things; others are simply making additions to their websites to convince others – both users as well as other institutions – that they are doing something innovative. Unfortunately many of these "Web 2.0" offerings have very little to do with what is meant by Web 2.0. But what is Web 2.0?

According to Wikipedia – which itself is an example of a Web 2.0 application – Web 2.0 refers to web "applications that facilitate interactive information sharing, interoperability, user-centered design, and collaboration"[1]. In other words a Web 2.0 site permits users to interact as contributors to the site's content; this is opposed to websites where users are limited to a passive viewing of information. Examples of Web 2.0 include web-based communities, hosted services, web applications, social-networking sites, video-sharing sites, wikis, blogs, mashups[2], and folksonomies[3].

The important words/phrases here are "interact", "interactive information sharing" and "to interact with each other as contributors to the content". "Interact" means that a two-way transaction takes place: not merely does a site owner provide – and control – the information presented, but users likewise provide content which the owner is unable or unwilling to place there. "Contributors to the content" means that not all the content comes from the site owner; it also means that some control is relinquished – at least for a period of time – over the content which is visible to site visitors.

The user experience with Web 1.0 is passive; the user is a viewer, a consumer. Web 2.0 removes the authority from the content provider and places it in the hands of the user. The user is a participant who helps determine what is on a site, and judges what content is valuable.

---

[1]　See <http://en.wikipedia.org/wiki/Web_2.0> (accessed July 2010).

[2]　A mashup is a web page or application that uses or combines data or functionality from two or more external sources to create a new service. The term implies easy, fast integration, frequently using open APIS (application programming interfaces) and data sources to produce enriching results that were not necessarily the original reason for producing the raw source data.

[3]　A folksonomy is a system of classification derived from the practice and method of collaboratively creating and managing tags to annotate and categorize content; this practice is also known as collaborative tagging, social classification, social indexing, and social tagging.

Social Network

A social network is a social structure made of individuals (or organisations) called "nodes" which are tied (connected) by one or more specific types of interdependency, such as friendship, kinship, common interest, financial exchange, dislike, sexual relationships, or relationships of beliefs, knowledge or prestige.

Social network services focus on building and reflecting social relations among people who share interests and/or activities. Such services consist of a representation of each user (often a profile), his/her social links, and a variety of additional services. Most social network services are web based and provide means for users to interact with applications such as e-mail and instant messaging. Although online community services are sometimes considered as a social network service in a broader sense, social network service usually means an individual-centered service whereas online community services are group-centered. Social networking sites allow users to share ideas, activities, events, and interests within their individual networks. In general, these services allow users to create a profile for themselves, and can be broken down into two broad categories: internal social networking and external social networking. At the forefront of emerging trends in social networking sites is the concept of "real time" and "location based". Real time allows users to contribute content, which is then broadcasted as it is being uploaded – the concept is similar to live television broadcasts. One popular use for this new technology is social networking between businesses. Companies have found that social networking sites such as Facebook and Twitter are great ways to build their brand image.

There are good reasons for using existing social networks: they have massive user bases and it is easier to talk to people in a place where they are already spending time, rather then getting them to come to a new website. But there are may be negative side effects to doing this: some – particularly younger – people consider such sites as their private space and they resent institutions trying to market to them on these sites.

Museums, archives and libraries are well-placed to appeal to the computer generation because they are content rich and can be virtually "cut-up" and stuck back together online in numerous, different ways to reflect the individual taste of each participant. Remixing, reinterpreting and sharing interesting content is the kind of engaging interaction that draws young people to sites like Bebo[4]. To reach this target group, institutions need to look beyond using social networks for marketing and embrace this "everyone is a curator" culture both online and offline.

---

[4] Bebo, an acronym for "Blog early, blog often", is a social networking website. See <http://www.bebo.com/>.

In "Web 1.0" terms, accessibility to museum, library and archive collections means making collections available for online viewing, adopting interoperable online metadata standards (Dublin Core[5]) and respecting accessibility guidelines (w3c[6]). In a digital heritage context, interactivity was primarily associated with clicking buttons and boxes on web pages, with the possibility of enhancing dialogue between museum and audience by allowing users to send emails through websites, or by offering online discussion forums and bulletin boards. User empowerment is interpreted as allowing users to personalise content on mini-websites and saving it for later retrieval[7]. Such online presentations are generally little more than static presentations of digital files.

Objects in museum collections are interpreted and contextualised in exhibitions. Many museums offer further layers of interpretation in a variety of media, such as audio guides, publications and educational events. Online museum collections, however, generally provide very little metadata. The low level of interpretation and the lack of a theoretical, historical and critical framework make it difficult for the user to engage with online museum objects in meaningful ways. This results in low levels of intellectual accessibility, which in turn, puts the whole project of digitising collections, for the purpose of increasing accessibility, into question[8].

Traditionally museums, archives and libraries are funded by governments and local authorities. However, in the aftermath of an overall move into corporate management in the 1980s, museums in particular started to expand their revenue sources by acquiring new audiences. With the emergence of computing and its fast democratisation, they found an opportunity to offer new experiences to their visitors as well as reaching new publics by implementing multimedia systems on the Internet. Using the Internet as a communication channel has been adopted by these institutions as a means to stand out of the competition. While the usual first step of creating a more or less successful website as an interface has been taken by the majority, others used Web 2.0 tools in order to develop more original and efficient communication and/or vending platforms.

With this shift towards a more experience-centered practice there exists a paradoxical dichotomy: on the one hand, the decentralisation of authority through Web 2.0 applications can be viewed as a threat to the already established culture of museum practice on the other, it can be seen

---

5   A set of metadata elements used to describe electronic resources.

6   The World Wide Web Consortium (w3c) is the main international standards organization for the World Wide Web.

7   Lena Maculan, "Museums, Web 2.0 and the illusion of access", <www.le.ac.uk/ impala/projects/museumstudies.html> (accessed July 2010).

8   *Ibid.*

as an opportunity for the museum to re-invent itself and ensure its own survival and continued relevance.

In order to have a better understanding of how Web 2.0 tools can be used, let's first have a look at some of these applications and consider their advantages and disadvantages for us. This is not a list of all the applications, but rather an overview of some of those which are most prevalent today. New applications are continually being developed and need to be examined by any institution considering taking the jump into Web 2.0 services.

1. Wikis

A wiki is a website that allows the easy creation and editing of any number of interlinked web pages via a web browser using a simplified markup language or a wysiwyg[9] text editor, the best example being Wikipedia. A wiki invites all users to edit any page or to create new pages within the wiki site. It strives to involve the visitor in an ongoing process of creation and collaboration that constantly changes the site landscape. Wikis are generally designed with the philosophy of making it easy to correct mistakes, rather than making it difficult to make them. While wikis are very open, they provide a means to verify the validity of recent additions to the body of pages.

Most wikis keep a record of changes made to the pages; often every version of the page is stored. This means that authors can revert to an older version of the page if a mistake is found or the page has been vandalized. Many implementations allow users to supply an "edit summary" when they edit a page. This is a short piece of text (usually one line) summarising the changes. It is not inserted into the article, but is stored along with that revision of the page, allowing users to explain what has been done and why.

The four basic types of users who participate in wikis are reader, author, wiki administrator and web administrator. The wiki administrator maintains wiki content and is provided additional functions pertaining to pages (e.g., page protection and deletion), and can adjust users' access rights, for instance, by blocking them from editing. The web administrator is responsible for installation and maintenance of the wiki engine and the container web server.

Wikis seem to me to be a service with very great potential for our institutions. They permit an institution to provide considerable background material for the holdings. The entries can contain illustrations and video sequences and permit content enhancement by linking to other sites with

---

[9] What you see is what you get.

supplemental information. However, before a wiki can be made public it is essential that a substantial amount of content be present as a means of encouraging participation. Likewise it is important that someone regularly review the content which is added to make certain that it conforms to guidelines which the institution needs to formulate and make accessible to users who add new content.

2. Blogs

A blog is a website, usually maintained by an individual, with regular entries of commentary, descriptions of events, or other material such as graphics or video. Entries are commonly displayed in reverse-chronological order. Viewers of a blog generally have the opportunity to comment on the content of the blog and on comments made by others, a process which may stimulate the creation of discussion forums. A blog network is a group of blogs that are connected to each other in a network and can either be a group of loosely connected blogs, or a group of blogs that are owned by the same organisation. The purpose of such a network is usually to promote the other blogs and increase the advertising revenue generated from online advertising on the blogs.

Basically a blog is an application which allows an institution to provide an environment to introduce topics for discussion.

By themselves blogs tend to focus on current reactions to current events. By incorporating this content in another format – such as a wiki – it might be viewed as an additional source for information which could be incorporated into a more stable, structurised environment for more permanent use.

3. Twitter; Text Messaging; Instant Messaging; Podcasting

Twitter[10] is a social networking and microblogging service that enables its users to send and read messages known as tweets. Tweets are text-based posts of up to 140 characters displayed on the author's profile page and delivered to the author's subscribers who are known as followers. Senders can restrict delivery to those in their circle of friends or, by default, allow open access.

Twitter can be used in a number of different ways, from advertising upcoming exhibitions – which is rather dull – to talking about behind the scenes activities of an institution.

Twitter can be regarded as a coordination and communication platform. It can be used to communicate about the content on other Web 2.0 platforms and create daily contact with the fans. It can potentially create an on-going relationship with current and potential patrons. It is an ideal

---

[10]   See <http://twitter.com>.

platform for communication at the time of an event. Institutions can use it to promote events before they happen. Communicating during the event can provide additional information about the event or about displayed objects. It is also an excellent channel to offer special discounts, discounts limited in time or special services.

Although not strictly speaking a Web 2.0 service, *text messaging* or SMS messaging is another method of communicating with known users. By inviting visitors to a website to register for text messaging, it is possible to inform them of new activities and developments in the institution.

Instant messaging (IM) is a form of real-time direct text-based communication between two or more people using personal computers or other devices, along with shared software clients. The user's text is conveyed over a network, such as the Internet. More advanced instant messaging software clients also allow enhanced modes of communication, such as live voice or video calling.

A *podcast* (or non-streamed webcast) is a series of digital media files (either audio or video) that are released episodically and often downloaded through web syndication.

The mode of delivery differentiates podcasting from other means of accessing media files over the Internet, such as direct download, or streamed webcasting. A list of all the audio or video files currently associated with a given series is maintained centrally on the distributor's server as a web feed, and the listener or viewer employs special client application software known as a podcatcher that can access this web feed, check it for updates, and download any new files in the series. This process can be automated so that new files are downloaded automatically. Files are stored locally on the user's computer or other device ready for offline use, giving simple and convenient access to episodic content.

Not only are paper-based media producing podcasts because they do not want to risk losing audiences: museums have also started offering audio- and video-based programs as feeds.

4. Facebook, Social Networks

Facebook[11] is a social networking website. Users can add friends and send them messages, and update their personal profiles to notify friends about themselves. The name stems from the colloquial name of books given to students at the start of the academic year by US university administrations to help students get to know each other better.

---

[11] See <http://www.facebook.com>.

Facebook has a number of features for interacting. They include:

- The Wall, a space on every user's profile page that allows friends to post messages for the user to see
- Pokes, which allow users to send a virtual "poke" to each other (a notification then tells a user that they have been poked)
- Photos, where users can upload albums and photos
- Status, which allows users to inform their friends of their whereabouts and actions.

Depending on privacy settings, anyone who can see a user's profile can also view that user's Wall.

One of the most popular applications on Facebook is the Photos application, where users upload albums and photos. Facebook allows users to upload an unlimited number of photos, compared with other image hosting services such as Flickr, which have limits to the number of photos that may be uploaded.

Social networks are probably the most common place that museums have started to look at the possibilities that Web 2.0 offers them. With no real cost to participate, setting up a Facebook or MySpace[12] page and collecting friends or fans is an easy place to start. But you don't need to look far to find poor examples of venues which have set up a page and then found that they do not have the time to update it properly.

One of the most interesting elements of Facebook is Facebook Apps. These are applications developed by third parties to entertain and to advertise.

The nice thing about Facebook is that you don't have to attract a huge following to virally market to a large number of people. When, for example, 150 people add a service to their Facebook profiles, this results in an exponential number of networked links to the service, since the persons attached to each profile are automatically tied in to this network.

The group and fan page tools can be used by any institution that wants to increase its brand awareness. These tools have the purpose of promoting rather than selling. By using these spaces, institutions can create a social environment in which patrons can exchange ideas, upload images and create a community around the institution. Creating a Facebook application especially tailored for an institution is another way of increasing brand awareness.

---

[12] See <http://www.myspace.com>.

5. Flickr, Images

Flickr[13] is an image- and video-hosting website. In addition to being a popular website for users to share personal photographs, the service is widely used by bloggers to host images that they embed in blogs and other social media.

Flickr offers two types of accounts: Free and Pro. Free account users may upload 100 MB of images a month and two videos. If a free user has more than 200 photos on the site, only the most recent 200 are visible in their photostream; the other uploaded photos are stored on the site and links to these images in blog posts remain active. Free users can also contribute to a maximum of 10 photo pools. If a free account is inactive for 90 consecutive days, it will be deleted.

Pro accounts allow users to upload an unlimited number of images and videos every month and receive unlimited bandwidth and storage. Photos may be placed in up to 60 group pools, and Pro account users receive ad-free browsing and have access to account statistics.

Photo submitters are supposed to provide tags for their images, which enable searchers to find images related to particular topics, such as place names or subject matter. Because of its support for tags, Flickr is a good example of the effective use of folksonomy.

Users are also able to organize their photos into "sets", or groups of photos with the same heading. Sets are more flexible than traditional folder-based methods of organising files, since a photo can belong to one set, many sets, or none at all. Sets may be grouped into "collections", and collections further grouped into higher-order collections.

With its comprehensive web-service[14] Flickr enables programmers to create applications that can execute almost any function a user on the Flickr site can perform.

Several museums and archives post images released under a "no known restrictions" license. The goal of the license is to show your hidden treasures in the world's public photography archives, and to show how your input and knowledge can help make these collections even richer.

6. Youtube, Videos

YouTube[15] is a video-sharing website where users can upload, share, and view videos. Videos uploaded by account holders are limited to

---

[13] See <http://www.flickr.com>.

[14] An application programming interface (API) is an interface that a software program implements in order to allow other software to interact with it.

[15] See <http://www.youtube.com>.

10 minutes in length and a file size of 2 GB. One of the key features is the ability of users to view videos on web pages outside the site. The YouTube interface suggests which local version should be chosen on the basis of the IP address of the user. In some cases, the message "This video is not available in your country" may appear because of copyright restrictions or inappropriate content.

The demand for online video has exploded. Over 100 million videos are watched on YouTube daily and BitTorrent, the Internet protocol which facilitates online sharing and distribution of video and audio. According to one estimate, almost half of all video online today is user-generated.

Museums can produce accessible educational videos for their educational needs, catalyse new and more formal production initiatives, and build new tools as editing, annotation or summarisation for more cost efficient video production, collaboration, and distribution worldwide. Museums can also organise new multi-institutional collaborations into a distributed educational video production network or establish an educational video commons with rich resources where use and reuse rights are identified.

7. Tagging, Delicious

Social tagging is sharing "tags" or keywords online. Users bookmark a website or an individual web page, but instead of putting the bookmark in their personal web browser, the bookmarks are saved on the web. Such an approach appeals to our type of institutions because it can fill gaps in current documentation practice. When a visitor places tags, he adds value to the institution, both for themselves and for other visitors. It enhances the personal exploration of collections and creates connections between the institution and users. Being present in such an environment should be considered an important method of making one's presentations more visible. Although an institution may actively engage in placing itself in such an environment, it is generally the users who do this. One such service for doing this is Delicious.

Delicious[16] (formerly del.icio.us) is a social bookmarking web service for storing, sharing, and discovering web bookmarks. Delicious uses a non-hierarchical classification system in which users can tag each of their bookmarks with freely chosen index terms (generating a kind of folksonomy). A combined view of everyone's bookmarks with a given tag makes it possible to view bookmarks added by other users.

Adding a social bookmarking toolbar to a website should take a web designer no more then a couple of hours, and it lets people virally

---

[16] See <http://delicious.com>.

spread the word about your latest exhibition. By joining delicious.com yourself, you can see if your venue website has been bookmarked by anyone and what comments they have made about your venue. Social bookmarks are not the only place that you'll find comments written online about your organisation: there are plenty of websites like TripAdvisor[17] where people might be talking about their experience visiting your venue.

8. Second Life, Virtual World

Second Life[18] (sl) is a virtual world. A free client program called the Viewer enables its users, called Residents, to interact with each other through avatars[19]. Residents can explore, meet other residents, socialise, participate in individual and group activities, and create and trade virtual property and services with one another, or travel throughout the world (which residents refer to as "the grid").

The advantage of such services is that virtual worlds are the only places where you can walk hand in hand with someone anywhere on earth. There are no geographical or physical barriers for a random visitor to open the door of a museum and walk in – at any time! Virtual worlds offer a 3D environment to an institution. Although at present few institutions offer their traditional services on Second Life, there is no reason why this could not be further developed.

These new tools seem to offer a full range of additional experiences to visitors. However, the main advantage of the Internet can also be its biggest weakness. While the screen as a communication interface modifies the hierarchy and the nature of relationships within the community, the loss of the aesthetic experience is difficult to evaluate.

Before we jump on the bandwagon and begin being fashionable and up-to-date we need to first answer some very important questions, whose answers may brake our initial enthusiasm.

Our use of the Web raises the same issues that we face when thinking about interpretation in our institutions. The crucial question is whether digital technology is merely being used to tell people more things, in varied ways, about what is on display and in the holdings, or whether we become more radical and use the technology to draw things out of visitors and to call on their expertise. Since there are fewer physical constraints (such as sore feet, lack of seats or restrictive opening hours) on the Web, a greater range of activity should be possible.

---

[17] See <http://www.tripadvisor.com>.

[18] See <http://secondlife.com>.

[19] An avatar is a computer user's representation of himself/herself or alter ego.

The success of Web 2.0 for our institutions depends more on being creative rather than on complex technology. And if this is the case – and there does not necessarily need to be a high technological overhead – then it should be possible to experiment in all sorts of ways to match task with content, find what works and what doesn't, and extend the range of visitor participation.

Costs

Nothing we do on the web is really free even when we use resources which have already been paid for. Content, presentation and maintenance are all part of presence and this means that staff time will be necessary to provide the content reflecting daily changes in our activities.

Just as a decision to prepare a web presence means expenditures of time and money, so does the move to Web 2.0 mean additional expenditures of time and money. This means that we need to have an initial idea of what we are willing and able to spend on this new venture, even though in the course of time this will need to undergo constant revision. We also need to be aware of our goals in doing this: are we merely doing something because it is new or fashionable as a kind of public relations project, or are we doing it to achieve something which will provide – both long- and short-term – benefits to our institution?

The time cost for Web 2.0 is not in product development but in product management, maintenance, and growth. Although it may take only a few minutes to create a blog or any of the other applications, having done this means that a commitment has been made to regularly input new content. When you start any such initiative, it is mandatory to think about and to make the necessary organisational decisions of what (and who) will maintain it over its lifespan, not just merely during the pre-release period.

I strongly suspect that much of what is presented as being a new way of interacting with users is merely giving visitors to the website a chance to express their own personal – momentary – feelings about what they see and experience on the site. The actual contributions to content are few and the use of these contributions is at best momentary – with no major influence on the content and activities of the respective institution. They are fig leaves which give the visitor to the website the feeling that they have something to say, and the institution the feeling that they are having the users be actively engaged in something – without spelling out what the visitors are actually providing for the institution.

In the past years our institutions have made some effort to be present on the Internet: almost every institution has its website where we present information about ourselves. Just how effective we are in being findable is another question. Here I would like to refer to my paper which I gave in

Vienna four years ago[20] in which I examined the findability of the websites of various SIBMAS members: the findability is relatively low – particularly when one looks at the website from a user's viewpoint. Before a move to Web 2.0 takes place, it would be advisable to consider a re-evaluation of the website to see how it can be made more effective.

A few points here:

1. Is the wording of the text on the website well-spicked with terms the user – not the head of the institution – would use when looking for content? Failure to accomplish this will result in the content not being visible and consequently not being used. This also applies to the terms used in the title of the individual pages – do they relate to the content of the page, and are the words meaningful for search engines and navigation of the website? Closely related to this is the extent to which other sites link to it – more links from external websites to the page increase the placement in search engine results.

2. How frequently are changes made to the website? If it is several years old, it may be out-of-date. Furthermore, if there are no apparent changes of the content, why should people regularly look at the site for current information?

3. Is the content interesting for non-professional users? In order for Web 2.0 to work it is imperative that people regularly visit the site and that they are encouraged to interact. If this is not done, then expenditures of time and money for Web 2.0 services will probably be wasted.

4. Are the pages visible on all devices which users may use to view the pages? Increasingly users access websites with hand-held devices. Is the website so coded that these devices can be used, or does the user become frustrated that they do not load on the chosen device?

There are nine common mistakes made with websites – not just those offering Web 2.0 services:

- There is no location listed on the home page
- They are slow loading
- They use flash pages, which have technological limitations
- The links are not obvious or there is no navigation bar
- The information provided is outdated

---

[20] See Paul S. Ulrich, "Yes, We're on the Internet, But Are Our Websites Effective? A Critical Examination of SIBMAS Members' Websites", in Ulrike Dembski and Christiane Mühlegger-Henhapel (eds.), *Performing Arts Collections on the Offensive* (proceedings of the 26th Congress of SIBMAS in Vienna, 2006), Frankfurt am Main, Peter Lang, 2007, p. 199-223.

- There are no map or navigational directions
- Bonding members to the service is not available
- There is not a collection of e-mail addresses
- Too much information is asked of the user.

Once a Web 2.0 application has been implemented, it is equally important to consider what happens with the content created. Will it remain in the form it was posted, or will something more substantial be created from it? It is at this point that most Web 2.0 applications fail to be really a part of a museum, a library or an archive. The content is at best kept together with other outgushings and nothing more is done with it. There are seldom real spinoffs from what has transpired. Why are the contents not incorporated into what is being kept and stored in the institution? Are they being made accessible for later use or do they merely remain in an unprocessed form on the website? When the latter is the case, then a major reason for using Web 2.0 technology is missing: content has not been incorporated into long-term objectives.

The purpose of libraries, museums and archives is to collect material, process it so that it can be used, and make the content available to be used. These institutions have problems getting the staff, facilities and money to achieve these goals. All complain about being under staffed and under funded. At the same time they are under pressure to have their activities visual to the public and to attract as many users as possible: the more users they have the easier it may be to get more staff, more money and better facilities.

"Library 2.0" is a loosely defined model for a modernised form of library service reflecting how services are delivered to users. The focus is on user-centered change and participation in the creation of content and community. This includes online services like the use of OPAC systems and an increased flow of information from the user back to the library.

With Library 2.0, library services are constantly updated and re-evaluated to best serve library users. It also attempts to harness the library user in the design and implementation of library services by encouraging feedback and participation. Proponents of this concept expect that the Library 2.0 model for service will ultimately replace traditional, one-directional service offerings that have characterised libraries for centuries.

Let me make a point with a few examples from libraries.

In order to make old catalog card entries electronically accessible, some libraries have scanned and OCRed[21] the cards. The problem here

---

[21] Optical character recognition, the conversion of images of text into characters.

is that the cards are not necessarily in such a condition that OCR can accurately convert them. Rather than having all the corrections done by staff, the OCRed content is placed in an interactive environment on the web and users can make corrections to the records. When a record is changed a staff member reviews the correction and authorises its correctness. The advantage here is that changes are made to records which are being used by someone who probably is familiar with the content.

In some library catalogs – in particular in the OCLC[22] WorldCat catalog[23] – users may enrich the catalog data by entering the table of contents to the record. Furthermore they can, à la Amazon, enter comments about the book. This information enriches the content the library has supplied and provides additional material for users.

Whether we like it or not, when one jumps on the Web 2.0 bandwagon, a commitment has been made to stay abreast of new developments and to incorporate them into what was begun. Time does not stand still. There will be new developments which will be fascinating; they will need to be evaluated and perhaps also incorporated into what is already being done. Likewise what once was an exciting new service will probably become obsolete – and this much quicker than we would like to think. The reason for this may be because the tools being used are no longer available or the presentation may no longer satisfy our or our user's needs and expectations. If the content of an obsolete service is still valuable[24], then there is a responsibility to create the corresponding environment where this can continue to be done. And this process will also require staff and rethinking on our part.

The use of Web 2.0 tools is a way to utilise already existing communities of web users familiar with these tools to build their own communities. In the process the institution's traditional authority as content provider is transformed to being the provider of an interactive platform for users. The virtual experience is not a replacement or substitute for a physical visit, but rather a supplement to the experience. In this virtual space, interconnectivity and social learning is a place for blogging about experiences, commenting on objects, depicting experiences through

---

[22] OCLC Online Computer Library Center, Inc. is "a nonprofit, membership, computer library service and research organization dedicated to the public purposes of furthering access to the world's information and reducing information costs", from <http://www.oclc.org/>(accessed July 2010).

[23] WorldCat is a union catalog containing the collections of 71,000 libraries in 112 countries. See <http://www.worldcat.org/>.

[24] Even if it is not current, there might be reasons why it should be preserved for archival purposes to document what we have done – and let's not forget that this is one of our main tasks and it should apply not only to what people and institutions in the performing arts leave us, but also to our own activities.

photos and videos, listening to podcasts, and connecting with other visitors via social networking sites.

There are two different types of applications which are involved in the process: those applications directly on the website/server of the institution and those having a presence on a social network server. With the former type of application the institution is totally responsible for managing the application; with the latter the institution makes use of an application which is managed by a third party. The advantage of the second type of application is that the provider already has a sizable community of people using it and hence an institution using it as a platform has fewer problems attracting visitors to its offerings.

The big question is how user-generated content will influence practice in an institution. Are these new technological tools being used as a means to bring more visitor voices into our institution, is our interest in Web 2.0 solely to keep up with technological advancements, or is there something else driving us? If building self-moderating, institution-based communicative structures is the goal, then institutions must find ways to integrate social media and its by-products into their daily practice.

The way we choose to use the Web raises the same issues we face when thinking about interpretation in our institutions. The crucial question is, are we using the new technology to merely tell people more things, in varied ways, about what we have, or, are we to be more radical and use it to draw things out of the visitor we don't know, or don't have the time and resources to prepare, and to call on their expertise. The main advantage can also be its biggest weakness. The screen as a communication interface modifies the hierarchy and the nature of relationships within the community; at the same time the aesthetic experience may be lost.

Web 3.0

Even though Web 2.0 is still very young, the next development is already emerging: Web 3.0, which is based on "intelligent" web applications using natural language processing, machine-based learning and reasoning and intelligent applications. The goal is to tailor online searching and requests specifically to users' preferences and needs. Although the intelligent web sounds similar to artificial intelligence, it's not quite the same. Web 3.0 is a further opening. By "opening" application programming interfaces, protocols, data formats, open-source software platforms and open data, it is possible to create new tools. Although openness can result in identity theft, Web 3.0 attempts to remedy this.

Conclusion

None of the Web 2.0 services mentioned work by themselves. Their use must be carefully planned and regularly re-evaluated as to their effectiveness; non-effectiveness is often a result of failing to attract the interest of potential users. When such is the case, then a re-thinking of who the potential users are and how one can best attract their attention is mandatory.

We can go as far as to question whether these projects can maintain a continued sustainability with the evolution of technology, or whether they will become ephemeral just like the technology itself. Such questions can only be answered after we have built and examined a substantial body of similar developments.

When we talk about a website user we think about a person. It is perhaps even more important for us to think about another institution as also being a "user". With some of the new Web 2.0 technologies it is conceivable that institutions reciprocally use these technologies to augment the content of the websites of other institutions. I'm not talking about merely providing links to another's website, but about interactively incorporating content from one institution into the content of another institution. In this process both institutions will mutually profit. Granted, such a procedure – which currently we only utilise in preparing exhibits – would require a re-thinking on our part. I can imagine, however, that once an institution begins to progress in this direction the rewards for everyone – institution and personal user – will be much greater than we can imagine.

Abstract

Le Web 2.0, dont on parle beaucoup dans l'utilisation de la techno-logie internet et de sa conception, a pour but de faciliter la créativité, l'échange d'informations, et, plus important encore, la collaboration entre utilisateurs. Ces concepts ont mené au développement et à l'évolution des communautés et des serveurs basés sur l'internet, tels que les réseaux sociaux, les wikis, les blogs, et les « folksonomies ».

De nombreuses possibilités existent pour la SIBMAS et ses membres concernant l'utilisation du Web 2.0 afin de développer de nouvelles façons de concevoir les choses, que ce soit dans l'innovation ou dans les valeurs sûres. Cependant, aucun service du Web 2.0 n'a mention-né le fait que des personnes travaillaient seules. Leur utilisation doit être soigneusement organisée et régulièrement réévaluée pour qu'elle soit efficace. L'inefficacité est souvent due à des manquements dans les processus destinés à attirer les utilisateurs potentiels. Lorsque c'est le cas, il est indispensable de mieux cibler les personnes qui pourraient devenir des utilisateurs potentiels, et d'imaginer la meilleure manière de susciter leur attention. Cela soulève cependant une question : ces projets vont-ils pouvoir se poursuivre selon l'évolution de la technologie, ou resteront-ils éphémères, tout comme la technologie elle-même ?

Le Portail des Arts de la Marionnette, moteur d'une nouvelle dynamique de valorisation des archives du spectacle vivant

Raphaèle FLEURY

Institut international de la Marionnette/ESNAM
(Charleville-Mézières – France)

Dans le cadre du plan national de numérisation lancé par le ministère français de la Culture et de la Communication, l'Institut international de la Marionnette a été désigné comme porteur de projet d'un Portail des Arts de la Marionnette (PAM)[1]. Ce chantier, commencé en 2009, rassemble aujourd'hui une vingtaine d'institutions françaises dont les fonds reflètent les pratiques et arts de la marionnette dans le monde, tant dans leur dimension patrimoniale que sur le plan de la création contemporaine :

- huit lieux de création, de formation, de diffusion : l'Institut international de la Marionnette (IIM)/École nationale supérieure des Arts de la Marionnette (ESNAM) ; le Festival mondial des Théâtres de Marionnettes de Charleville-Mézières ; le Théâtre de la Marionnette à Paris ; le Théâtre Jeune Public de Strasbourg (TJP)/ Centre dramatique national d'Alsace ; la compagnie Ches Panses Vertes - le Tas de Sable, lieu de compagnonnage (Amiens) ; le Vélo-Théâtre, lieu de compagnonnage (Apt) ; Odradek, lieu de compagnonnage (Quint-Fonsegrives) ; le Bouffou Théâtre à la Coque, lieu de compagnonnage (Hennebont) ;

- deux associations : l'Union internationale de la Marionnette (UNIMA) et l'Association nationale des Théâtres de Marionnettes et Arts associés (THEMAA) ;

- huit musées et monuments nationaux : le musée Gadagne de Lyon ; le musée de Picardie à Amiens ; le musée des civilisations de l'Europe et de la Méditerranée (MUCEM, ex-musée des Arts et traditions populaires) ; le musée du Quai Branly ; le musée comtois

---

[1] <www.artsdelamarionnette.eu>.

de Besançon ; le musée du Vieil-Aix à Aix-en-Provence ; le musée de l'Ardenne à Charleville-Mézières ; le Centre des monuments nationaux (pour la Maison de George Sand à Nohant) ;

– quatre bibliothèques et centres d'archives : la Bibliothèque nationale de France ; les Archives départementales de la Somme ; les bibliothèques d'Amiens-Métropole ; le Centre départemental de documentation pédagogique (CRDP) des Ardennes.

Fin 2010, le PAM doit permettre au public de consulter en ligne environ 30 000 documents numérisés : iconographie ancienne, photographies, affiches, manuscrits de répertoire, périodiques, notes de mise en scène, documents audiovisuels, articulés autour de plusieurs milliers de fiches-pivots présentant artistes, spectacles et thématiques.

Présentation du cadre général du projet

Une mission grand public

La mission première de ce portail est la démocratisation de l'accès aux collections : tous les documents numérisés dans le cadre de ce projet doivent être accessibles au grand public sur internet, en libre consultation.

À cet engagement quantitatif auprès du ministère, les partenaires du portail ont ajouté une exigence qualitative : pour mieux servir la découverte des arts de la marionnette, il faut un accompagnement pédagogique fort, un riche contenu éditorial qui implique en amont un long travail de concertation scientifique et professionnelle.

Les enjeux pour la profession

Tout d'abord, le Portail des Arts de la Marionnette constitue un outil stratégique de communication avec le public. Cette vitrine visible sur le web à l'échelle internationale (destinée à être trilingue français/ anglais/espagnol, elle sera indexée et interrogée par des moteurs plus généralistes) jouit de la crédibilité scientifique et institutionnelle que confèrent au projet la conjonction des différentes institutions partenaires et le soin particulier apporté à l'identification des sources dans tous les contenus éditoriaux du portail. La possibilité de laisser des commentaires sur les ressources, sur les actualités, ainsi que la mise en place d'un forum de discussion fait de cette vitrine une interface d'échange avec le grand public et une incitation à passer du virtuel au réel, à découvrir les œuvres dans leur contexte original en se rendant aux spectacles, aux festivals, en allant visiter musées et expositions.

De plus, en ouvrant un énorme chantier d'inventaire (inventaire des collections, des spectacles, des personnes, de la terminologie utilisée dans les différentes professions concernées par la marionnette), le PAM et sa base de données constituent d'ores et déjà un formidable outil de travail scientifique et professionnel. Il est destiné à devenir de plus en plus collaboratif, avec la mise en place d'un espace d'échange et de contribution en ligne à l'enrichissement des notices par les artistes et les chercheurs, coordonnés par un administrateur de formation scientifique.

Enfin, au-delà du web, le projet de Portail des Arts de la Marionnette permet la mise en place de réseaux thématiques ou régionaux, d'un réseau national et bientôt européen. Le pôle Picardie, par exemple, voit collaborer des professionnels du Musée, de la Bibliothèque municipale, des Archives départementales et les artistes d'un lieu de compagnonnage : les documents ainsi rassemblés permettent de donner à voir sur le PAM cinq siècles de présence de la marionnette dans cette région. Sur le plan national, ce projet est l'occasion de faire collaborer des musées dont l'objet principal n'est pas la marionnette, mais qui conservent chacun les traces d'une importante tradition locale de marionnettes. Au sein de ces réseaux, les partenaires font jouer la complémentarité des compétences : les musées et bibliothèques ont apporté leur expertise aux professionnels de la création contemporaine sur les questions de conditionnement et de conservation des documents ; inversement, les marionnettistes sont invités à fournir leurs éclairages pour la restauration (réensecrètement)[2] et la description des documents et objets conservés dans les institutions du patrimoine ; un même système d'échange entre institutions s'est mis en place sur les plans informatique et documentaire (échange de listes, d'index, de notices, conseil technique, etc.).

Pour toutes ces raisons, le Portail des Arts de la Marionnette est aujourd'hui le moteur d'une professionnalisation généralisée des différents partenaires. Il a encouragé la prise de conscience de l'importance des conditions de conservation (matérielle et dématérialisée) des documents pour les structures dont ce n'est pas la mission première : amélioration du conditionnement, classement, dépoussiérage, inventaire. Il a suscité un réflexe de collecte : pour compléter des lacunes dans des collections existantes, pour refléter l'actualité de la création. Celui-ci s'accompagne d'un réflexe d'identification des droits d'auteur et droits voisins, et de la mise en place d'un protocole de négociation des droits de diffusion pour tout nouveau document produit. Le PAM systématise enfin un réflexe de communication, pour une meilleure circulation de l'information entre les partenaires du projet.

---

[2] On appelle « ensecrètement » l'étape finale du montage d'une marionnette à fils où l'on relie le contrôle à la poupée par le moyen des fils. L'ensecret ou ensecrètement consiste à établir une suspension équilibrée à la hauteur prévue pour la manipulation, et à disposer les fils de façon à pouvoir faire exécuter à la poupée une série de mouvements choisis. *Cf.* <http://www.artsdelamarionnette.eu/app/photopro.sk/marionnettes/detail?docid=69677>.

Défis

Ce projet s'est également présenté à nous comme un défi.

Un défi technique tout d'abord, puisqu'aucun des huit premiers partenaires ne possédait en interne de services informatiques et techniques : il a fallu tout apprendre, et demander conseil.

Un défi administratif également, car nous devons établir partenariats et conventions entre des institutions de statut hétérogène : associations locales, nationales et internationales, musées dépendant de collectivités locales, grandes institutions nationales dépendant directement de l'État (avec des musées nationaux comme le Musée du Quai Branly ou le MUCEM, la Bibliothèque nationale de France) ; et l'élargissement européen se profile à l'horizon 2013, qui apportera de nouvelles problématiques.

Un défi économique aussi, puisqu'à chaque nouvelle phase éligible par le ministère, il faut trouver un financement complémentaire de 50 % du projet, auprès des collectivités locales ou du mécénat privé.

Un défi intellectuel et humain enfin, puisqu'il s'agit de faire entrer en dialogue des perceptions très différentes des arts de la marionnette : pour les uns, le cœur des arts de la marionnette réside avant tout dans l'objet à restaurer, à conserver, à exposer ; pour les autres, l'objet-marionnette n'est que l'instrument d'une pratique particulière de l'art de l'acteur ; pour d'autres enfin, la marionnette est comprise comme un phénomène social et culturel davantage qu'artistique, et réclame une approche ethnologique et anthropologique. Le portail se doit de refléter ces différentes approches afin de mieux faire comprendre au public la diversité et la richesse des arts de la marionnette, qui souffrent encore aujourd'hui de méconnaissance et d'une perception trop réductrice.

Présentation de l'outil et de son fonctionnement

Architecture générale de la solution

Sur le plan technique, ce portail se compose d'un site internet adossé à une base de données mutualisée. Celle-ci peut être alimentée par contribution directe (pour les partenaires qui ne possèdent pas de base de données), par imports (pour les partenaires disposant de bases de données sans extension en ligne) ou par moissonnage OAI (protocole d'échange de métadonnées pour ceux qui disposent d'une base de données interopérable)[3].

---

[3] Open Archives Initiative Protocol for Metadata Harvesting (OAI-PMH) : protocole informatique fondé par l'Open Archives Initiative pour échanger des métadonnées. Il permet de constituer et de mettre à jour automatiquement des entrepôts centralisés (dits « entrepôts OAI ») où les métadonnées de sources diverses peuvent être interrogées ou « moissonnées » simultanément. Il est utilisé notamment par les Archives ouvertes et les entrepôts institutionnels.

Le portail est également doté d'un entrepôt OAI ouvert, en Dublin Core simple, qui permet le moissonnage de son contenu.

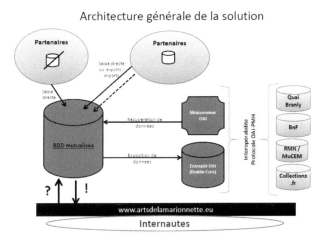

Architecture générale de la solution

Organisation de la base de données mutualisée en sous bases

La maîtrise d'ouvrage a fait le choix d'une solution mixte : logiciels libres déployés dans le cadre d'un logiciel propriétaire (Armadillo) qu'elle peut entièrement paramétrer sans avoir besoin de maîtriser la programmation informatique (système de cases à cocher).

Les partenaires du projet ont décidé d'organiser la base de données mutualisée non pas par institutions (il aurait été possible de mettre en place une sous base par partenaire) mais par type de documents et de notices.

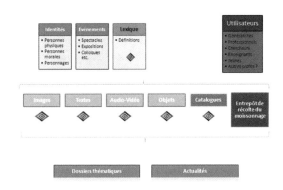

Un système de gestion des droits permet de préserver l'exclusivité de l'accès de chaque partenaire aux notices le concernant. Chaque partenaire gère ses notices et ses documents dans les bases Images, Vidéos, Textes et Objets. Tous les partenaires contribuent à l'enrichissement des bases Identités et Événements, qui sont communes à tous et permettent la consultation par rebond d'une notice à l'autre. Un administrateur coordonne l'ensemble de ces contributions et alimente les bases Lexique, Utilisateurs, Dossiers thématiques et Actualités.

Interfaces d'interrogation

Le PAM offre aux internautes trois interfaces de recherche :
- recherche simple : accessible dès la page d'accueil du portail, cette interface permet une interrogation plein texte de l'ensemble de la base de données ;
- recherche avancée combinant plusieurs critères : titre, auteur, lieu de conservation, mots-clefs, type de marionnette, type de document, date, etc. ;
- recherche thématique : afin de pouvoir guider les internautes qui découvrent pour la première fois les arts de la marionnette, on propose des chemins balisés sous forme d'arborescence de thématiques. En cliquant sur l'une des thématiques proposées, l'internaute accède à une sélection de documents ainsi qu'à une sous-liste de suggestions lui permettant d'approfondir sa recherche.

Ces trois interfaces de recherche restent accessibles en permanence pendant la consultation des documents, via un menu permettant un constant va-et-vient entre la consultation de documents et de nouvelles recherches.

Interfaces de réponse

Une fois sa requête lancée, l'internaute choisit le mode d'affichage des réponses :
- mode mosaïque (vignettes légendées) ;
- mode liste (vignettes accompagnées d'un résumé de la notice) ;
- mode notice : la sélection d'un document dans la mosaïque ou dans la liste permet d'accéder à la notice détaillée, composée de plusieurs rubriques présentées sous forme d'onglets, et au document, sur lequel il est possible de zoomer.

À tout moment de la consultation, l'internaute peut choisir de n'afficher qu'un type de média (vidéo, image fixe, texte ou objet), qu'un type de notice (notice de document, notice biographique, notice sur un événement, notice du lexique), ou de revenir à l'ensemble des réponses. Ceci est possible grâce à un système d'onglets.

Présent et avenir : chantiers ouverts

Ensembles documentaires

La mise en œuvre du Portail des Arts de la Marionnette permet progressivement de redécouvrir ou de faire émerger des fonds et des documents inexplorés, particulièrement dans les archives communales, départementales et diocésaines. Leur exploration réclame un effort particulier puisqu'il s'agit en général d'archives qui ne sont presque jamais repérées comme étant liées au spectacle vivant (archives des échevinages, de la police, état civil, factures, documents liés à la dentisterie, aux auberges), et que leur exploration nécessite bien souvent en amont un travail linguistique sur l'étymologie et sur la déclinaison du lexique de la marionnette dans les langues régionales. On ne trouvera rien en cherchant le mot « marionnettiste » dans les documents antérieurs au XIXe siècle : ce sont les expressions de « joueurs de figures artificielles », de « figures mouvantes », « agissantes » ou « dansantes », de « cabotans », de « pigmées chinoises », de « papoire » ou de « grand'goule » que l'on trouve par exemple dans les archives du chapitre de la cathédrale ou dans les suppliques adressées par les montreurs de marionnettes à l'échevinage d'Amiens au XVIIe siècle. Le repérage de ces documents est long, mais le portail a lancé une dynamique qui commence à porter ses fruits.

Par ailleurs, parallèlement au chantier de numérisation, elle donne lieu au repérage de documents déjà numérisés dont les institutions propriétaires n'avaient pas encore mis en évidence le lien avec la marionnette. Ainsi, le signalement à la Bibliothèque nationale de France d'articles de presse consacrés à des spectacles de marionnettes sans que le mot « marionnette » n'apparaisse dans le titre (il s'agit le plus souvent de comptes-rendus de spectacles du XIXe siècle) va permettre d'indexer ces documents.

Enfin, le Portail des Arts de la Marionnette permet de reconstituer dans un même espace virtuel de consultation des fonds matériellement épars. Nous avons par exemple procédé en 2010 à la prise de vue de 150 marionnettes fabriquées par Maurice et George Sand pour le petit théâtre de Nohant. Les accessoires et costumes de cette collection devraient faire l'objet d'une seconde campagne de prise de vues. Ces objets conservés et partiellement exposés dans la Maison de George Sand à Nohant dépendent du Centre des monuments nationaux, alors que tout le fonds documentaire qui s'y rapporte (correspondance, répertoire, etc.) a été donné à la Bibliothèque historique de la Ville de Paris. Nous espérons pouvoir proposer à moyen terme la consultation conjointe de ces deux ensembles.

La mobilisation des artistes dans la collecte

De la part des créateurs contemporains, le chantier de numérisation a suscité une prise de conscience du rôle qu'ils ont à jouer pour la mémoire et la meilleure compréhension de leur travail. Le portail est l'occasion de les sensibiliser à l'intérêt de conserver d'une part les traces des différentes étapes du travail (conception, fabrication, étapes de mise en scène, notation du mouvement), mais aussi les documents administratifs (contrats, factures, comptes-rendus d'assemblées générales ou de conseils d'administration).

Trop souvent détruits par les compagnies elles-mêmes, ces documents administratifs présentent un intérêt majeur pour la connaissance de certains aspects historiques, sociologiques ou politiques de la profession, mais également pour la connaissance des spectacles (pour l'identification des matériaux utilisés dans la fabrication des marionnettes par exemple). C'est ainsi que les archives administratives de la compagnie Houdart-Heuclin ont pu être sauvées *in extremis* : la compagnie, invitée à participer au PAM, a finalement décidé, en 2010, de faire don de son fonds au département des Arts du Spectacle de la Bibliothèque nationale de France, qui a pu collecter ces documents avant leur passage au broyeur. La politique actuelle du ministère de la Culture écarte ces documents du plan national de numérisation, en raison de leur caractère trop peu « grand public ». L'existence du projet permet néanmoins un travail de collecte et de conservation matérielle, qui permettra peut-être plus tard une exploitation voire une diffusion via le web pour peu qu'un accompagnement éditorial idoine permette d'en exposer l'intérêt.

Notons que malgré la lourdeur du travail que la participation au portail implique, la très grande majorité des artistes et compagnies expriment leur adhésion au projet. Pour certains, le moment est arrivé d'un regard rétrospectif sur l'œuvre, pour d'autres le portail est l'occasion de mettre en place un système de rangement. Pour tous, le Portail des Arts de la Marionnette apparaît comme un formidable outil pour prolonger l'action de sensibilisation des publics qu'ils mènent autour des spectacles, dans les écoles ou les universités.

L'aspect patrimonial du projet n'apparaît plus comme une démarche de « fossoyage » de l'art vivant – le terme avait été employé lors des premières réunions de présentation du projet –, mais comme l'occasion de remettre en perspective les pratiques contemporaines pour mieux les faire connaître et comprendre.

L'harmonisation et la normalisation des langages

La terminologie et la classification des différents types de marionnettes sont historiquement et géographiquement très labiles. Pour n'en fournir qu'un exemple, le mot « pantin » est aujourd'hui utilisé par plusieurs artistes pour désigner une « figure de taille presque humaine, parfois manipulée par plusieurs animateurs »[4] ; alors que, du XVIIIe siècle à la fin de la première moitié du XXe siècle, il s'agissait généralement d'une « petite figure de carton colorié dont on fait mouvoir les membres par le moyen d'un fil »[5].

Par ailleurs, pour la plupart des partenaires utilisant un langage normé, la marionnette n'est qu'un des « domaines » des collections conservées et du thésaurus utilisé. Appliqués à la marionnette, les termes descripteurs sont donc bien souvent lacunaires ou imprécis.

Qu'ils utilisent actuellement la liste d'autorité Rameau, les thésaurus Garnier (iconographie), Palissy (architecture et mobilier), Ethnophoto (photographie), ou qu'ils n'aient pas encore de système d'indexation, les différents partenaires du PAM ont reconnu la nécessité d'entamer un chantier de réflexion pour la création d'un thésaurus des Arts de la marionnette reflétant la diversité des techniques, leur dimension internationale (plurilinguisme), et la complexité des collections concernées (appréhension de l'objet du point de vue de sa fabrication, de sa manipulation, de sa mise en scène, etc.).

Pour la première étape du projet, en 2009, nous avons mis en place nos outils sans recourir à un mode d'indexation commun, ni normé. Ceci, en raison d'une volonté expérimentale. Fin 2011, à partir de l'outil établi par l'Institut international de la Marionnette, qui utilise la liste de vedettes-matières RAMEAU, le groupe de travail « documentaire » analysera les résultats de la première phase d'indexation en comparant le travail d'indexation spontané effectué par les partenaires n'ayant pas de langage normé aux systèmes actuellement pratiqués par d'autres partenaires. Nous croiserons cette approche avec l'examen des « nuages sémantiques » générés automatiquement (statistiquement) par notre base de données mutualisée.

Pour une phase ultérieure, nous examinons la possibilité de la mise en place d'un système d'indexation collaborative faisant intervenir les internautes, en complément d'un outil normé.

*

Le *back-office* du portail est en phase de rodage depuis fin avril 2010. En septembre 2010, une version test du moteur de recherche sera mise en ligne sur le web. Le lancement officiel du Portail des Arts de la Marionnette est annoncé pour 2011.

---

[4] *Cf.* Éric Goulouzelle de la compagnie Ches Panses Vertes, François Lazaro et Francis Marshall au Clastic Théâtre.

[5] Cf. Centre national de ressources textuelles et lexicales (C.N.R.S.) : <www.cnrtl.fr/etymologie> (consulté le 30/01/2013).

Comme en témoignent l'histoire des grandes traditions et les pratiques contemporaines, les arts de la marionnette doivent être envisagés à une échelle internationale. C'est pourquoi ce portail, partiellement bilingue pour l'instant, a vocation à s'élargir aux autres collections européennes[6].

Page d'accueil du PAM

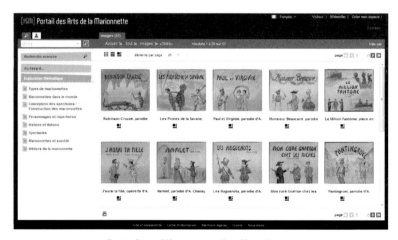

Interface d'interrogation/de réponse

---

[6]   Cet article a été écrit pour le congrès de Munich en juillet 2010, et le chantier a bien avancé depuis. Le Portail des Arts de la Marionnette est en ligne depuis septembre 2011, à l'adresse <www.artsdelamarionnette.eu>. En 2013, il compte 28 partenaires français, que rejoignent une dizaine de partenaires belges coordonnés par le Centre de la Marionnette à Tournai et Het Firmament à Mechelen. Par ailleurs, un annuaire et un agenda vont être ajoutés en 2013 afin de faire dialoguer archives et actualités des arts de la marionnette. Ce dispositif sera complété en 2014 par la mise en place d'un catalogue mutualisé des bibliothèques spécialisées dans les arts de la marionnette (MARC /FRBR),

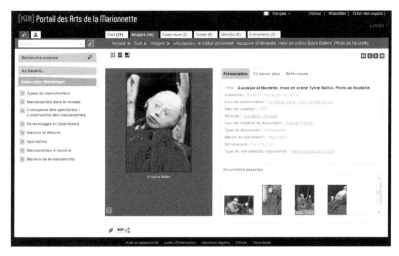

Exemple de notice

Abstract

Launched in 2009 within the framework of the National Digitisation Program for Heritage and Creation by the ministère de la Culture et de la Communication, le Portail des Arts de la Marionnette (PAM) maintains the documentation, digitisation, and editing of the project. Additionally, it also looks after information on the profession. Encouraging dialogue between heritage institutions and contemporary artists, it improves the discovery of collections and stimulates the preservation and the valuation of often abandoned collections. It also makes puppet artists and companies aware of their archives, and encourages them to think and set up methods and language which describe both the historic and contemporary realities of puppets. This is useful not only to researchers but also the general public. This project is currently expanding with international partners.

---

permettant notamment un dépouillement partagé des périodiques de plusieurs pays. Parallèlement à ces développements, le PAM a mis en place une exposition de ses notices en RDF, afin d'inscrire ses contenus dans le contexte du web sémantique. Une réflexion est menée pour placer la majorité des contenus du PAM sous licence ouverte.

Faire œuvre de mémoire

Le milieu du cirque se mobilise

Sylvie Françoise

Cirque du Soleil (Montréal – Canada)

Une rencontre professionnelle sur la conservation de la mémoire et des objets de cirque a eu lieu du 16 au 20 juin 2010 au siège social du Cirque du Soleil à Montréal (Canada). Cette rencontre faisait suite à deux autres présentations sur le même thème, dans le contexte du Projet de préservation de la Fédération mondiale de cirque, tenues en 2009 et 2010. Un panel d'experts a d'abord été accueilli à Monte-Carlo dans le cadre du 33ᵉ Festival international de cirque, puis à Budapest, à l'occasion de son 8ᵉ Festival international de cirque.

L'événement se déroulait dans l'environnement dynamique de la Cité des arts du cirque de Montréal. Notons qu'outre les installations du Cirque du Soleil, la Cité des arts du cirque accueille aussi la TOHU, salle de spectacle circulaire spécialement dédiée au cirque, les bureaux d'En Piste, l'association canadienne des arts du cirque, ainsi que l'École nationale de cirque (ENC).

Le Cirque du Soleil et En Piste ont organisé cette rencontre professionnelle en collaboration avec la Fédération mondiale de cirque. Cette dernière tenait aussi, pour la première fois de son histoire, une réunion de son conseil d'administration en dehors de l'Europe. C'est En Piste, un des membres fondateurs de la Fédération, qui en était l'hôte sur le continent américain. La rencontre se déroulait quelques semaines avant le lancement du premier Festival de cirque au Canada, *Montréal Complètement Cirque*, orchestré par la TOHU.

Intitulée « Préserver notre patrimoine : l'importance des objets de cirque », la rencontre professionnelle se démarquait des deux précédentes en souhaitant créer un forum d'échange et de discussion approfondie pour les spécialistes, collectionneurs et historiens du milieu du cirque et celui de la conservation.

Des invitations avaient été lancées à différents intervenants afin de rassembler un groupe d'une quarantaine de personnes provenant de différents pays et présentant des points de vue variés sur la mémoire de cirque. Huit panélistes et trente-cinq participants, journalistes, collectionneurs privés et représentants de compagnies de cirque ont ainsi rejoint les professionnels d'institutions vouées à la conservation pour échanger autour de quatre thèmes principaux.

- La mémoire du cirque comme patrimoine immatériel : pourquoi et pour qui doit-on le protéger ?
- Comment définir ce qui doit être préservé ?
- Comment répertorier nos collections ? Réflexion sur une terminologie universelle.
- Le développement des réseaux et des partenariats.

Chaque thème était lancé par les communications de deux panélistes abordant des points de vue différents, et était suivi d'une longue séance de discussions et d'échanges entre les panélistes et les participants. Les deux jours de discussions étaient complétés par la visite des lieux de la Cité des arts du cirque (incluant la bibliothèque de l'ENC, le centre de documentation et de recherche ainsi que la réserve des collections du Cirque du Soleil), la découverte d'expositions : Du permanent à l'éphémère : Espace de cirque, Terra Cirqua à la TOHU, Artisans du Rêve – Costume du Cirque du Soleil au Musée McCord ainsi que les prestations des artistes de cirque pour le spectacle de *Totem™* du Cirque du Soleil et les spectacles des étudiants sortants de l'ENC.

Le présent article fait le point sur les présentations lors de cette rencontre et s'attarde sur les défis et recommandations qui en ressortent.

La mémoire du cirque comme patrimoine immatériel : pourquoi et pour qui doit-on la protéger ?

Le premier panel de discussion a été lancé par Catherine Shaina, directrice du Musée des arts du cirque de Saint-Pétersbourg (Russie). Ce Musée départemental, appartenant au Cirque de Saint-Pétersbourg, offre l'accès à ses collections principalement aux artistes de cirque et chercheurs. Une salle, située dans l'entrée du cirque, permet au public de venir découvrir l'exposition permanente, une heure avant l'ouverture du spectacle.

Ses collections comprennent plus de 100 000 pièces, réparties entre la bibliothèque et les archives (manuscrits et photographies), et elles comportent des objets (œuvres, costumes et *memorabilia*), des affiches et programmes ainsi que des documents vidéo de cirques russes mais aussi internationaux.

Le lien d'appartenance entre le Musée et le Cirque fait écho à la mission première que se donne le Musée : être au service des artistes de cirque. Le Musée souhaite ainsi participer à l'essor de la culture cirque en outillant les artistes par des références historiques, des connaissances quant aux diverses pratiques, et les encourager à bonifier ses collections par des informations ou des documents. L'accueil personnalisé est donc de mise pour faire du Musée un salon de confidence, un incontournable dans la préparation et la création de nouveaux numéros. C'est le fonds de documents vidéo qui reçoit ainsi le plus de demandes de consultation et a même été classifié et documenté par type de discipline afin de faciliter la recherche. L'acquisition des documents, réalisée principalement par voie d'échange, se fait aussi en privilégiant les besoins que les artistes ont identifiés.

La deuxième présentation de ce panel a été faite par Janine Barrand, directrice de Collection, Research and Exhibition à l'Arts Centre de Melbourne (Australie) et avait pour titre : *Les carnets de cirque et autres histoires*[1]. L'Arts Centre est non seulement un lieu de diffusion mais aussi un espace de conservation et d'exposition. Le cirque y figure donc aux côtés de l'opéra, de la musique, du théâtre et de la danse. Les collections reflètent l'histoire australienne des arts de la scène et comptent plus de 40 000 pièces. Les objets collectionnés incluent les costumes et accessoires, les maquettes de décors et de costumes, les marionnettes et accessoires de scène, des photographies, des affiches et programmes ainsi que des archives, personnelles ou de compagnies.

Janine Barrand a abordé très précisément l'aspect du patrimoine immatériel tel que défini par l'UNESCO[2] afin de relever les défis que cela comportait pour une institution. Tout d'abord, le site occupé par l'Arts Centre est un ancien site forain qui, dès le XIXe siècle, a vu se succéder de nombreux cirques. L'Arts Centre a défini le patrimoine immatériel associé au cirque à partir des réflexions provenant de sa communauté circassienne. Quatre grands axes ont donc été établis : 1. les numéros et les personnalités de cirque ; 2. les sites ; 3. les structures – incluant les familles et les compagnies ; 4. les tournées. Ces axes servent de repères dans la recherche, la documentation, l'acquisition et le développement d'expositions.

---

[1] Traduction libre de l'auteure pour *Circus Diaries and Other Stories*.

[2] « On entend par "patrimoine culturel immatériel" les pratiques, représentations, expressions, connaissances et savoir-faire – ainsi que les instruments, objets, artefacts et espaces culturels qui leur sont associés – que les communautés, les groupes et, le cas échéant, les individus reconnaissent comme faisant partie de leur patrimoine culturel » Convention pour la sauvegarde du patrimoine culturel immatériel, UNESCO, Paris, 17 octobre 2003. <http://www.unesco.org/culture/ich>.

Les grands défis associés à la collecte de ce patrimoine immatériel sont : la difficulté d'établir et de conserver le contact avec une communauté itinérante de nature ; la nécessité de prendre en considération la complexité des liens généalogiques demandant beaucoup de délicatesse vu la nature très personnelle de ces relations ; la recherche face à une culture orale où les connaissances et façons de faire laissent peu de traces écrites ; et le constat d'une vision globale de l'histoire perçue comme continue par la communauté cirque et donc sans repères chronologiques. Fort d'une approche historique, visant à faire état des pratiques artistiques australiennes présentes et passées, l'Arts Centre donne la priorité à la collecte d'histoires orales[3] auprès de la communauté circassienne afin de valoriser l'apport de cette communauté, de permettre la recherche, de créer un sentiment de continuité pour le public et de soutenir le volet actuel de cet art de la scène.

Ces deux présentations soulignent le désir de définir la mémoire par et pour le milieu du cirque lui-même. L'histoire, racontée par le circassien, est primordiale, les objets et documents sont des sources d'informations qui soulignent l'histoire mais qui n'ont pas préséance sur celle-ci. Les documents ont aussi une valeur éducative importante pour le milieu lui-même afin d'inspirer la création de nouveaux numéros, d'apprendre des numéros existants (dans le cas du remplacement d'un artiste) et de contextualiser les disciplines circassiennes déjà en pratique. Il apparaît essentiel de fédérer le milieu dans lequel se situe le musée, de fortifier le lien de confiance avec les artistes (et familles d'artistes) afin qu'ils partagent leurs histoires et documents et donnent sens au contenu déjà existant. Les discussions avec les participants font particulièrement ressortir la question du patrimoine immatériel et la façon dont le cirque s'y intègre, et l'un des participants, Mathias Bizimana, chargé de programme, Culture et patrimoine mondial pour la Commission canadienne pour l'UNESCO, a accepté de prendre quelques minutes pour faire valoir la vision de patrimoine immatériel, les différentes étapes pour l'identification de ce patrimoine et le rôle des communautés liées par ces pratiques pour les faire reconnaître solidairement auprès des instances mondiales et auprès de leurs gouvernements respectifs (plusieurs pays n'ayant pas ratifié le protocole suggéré par l'UNESCO). Cette question de reconnaissance du cirque comme patrimoine immatériel est déjà à l'agenda de la Fédération mondiale de cirque et fera l'objet d'un suivi.

D'autres questions quant au rôle des collections dans l'apprentissage des métiers de cirque sont soulevées surtout pour ce qui concerne la transmission des savoirs, qui s'effectue de plus en plus par le biais des écoles et non des familles.

---

[3] *Cf.* par exemple le projet sur trois ans des Circus Diaries <http://thecircusdiaries.blogspot.com>.

Les musées et centres de documentation pourraient-ils développer des liens plus formels avec les écoles ? Quant à l'acquisition de documents, particulièrement pour les spectacles des compagnies actuelles qui n'ont pas toutes un souci de préservation, l'option du dépôt légal des programmes est soulignée comme un levier à favoriser. Ce point amène de longs échanges sur la responsabilité des compagnies à préserver leurs propres archives, la responsabilité des institutions à soutenir et outiller ces compagnies pour organiser la collecte de documents utiles, afin de les aider à les conserver, malgré l'itinérance, tout en tenant compte du refus de certains de rendre permanent l'éphémère. Pour plusieurs compagnies toutefois, la mise en valeur de la culture circassienne, par le biais de ses histoires et documents, est vue à long terme comme garante de la continuité d'une tradition de cirque et donc de son avenir. La question du don de documents par les compagnies et individus aux institutions pose aussi, pour cet auditoire international ainsi que des questions relatives au besoin de définir des politiques d'acquisition des institutions pour que les documents soient physiquement répartis selon les lieux d'accès les plus pertinents pour les communautés locales. Cela implique toutefois de créer un réseau de ces collections pour faciliter un accès plus large, mais surtout pour ne pas dupliquer des collections (particulièrement pour des objets créés en multiples exemplaires, affiches, programmes et *memorabilia*).

Comment définir ce qui doit être préservé ?

Dans la continuité des questions soulevées par le thème précédent, la deuxième séance est lancée par Janet Davis, professeur en Études américaines et en Histoire à l'Université du Texas (États-Unis). Le titre de sa présentation donne le ton : *Trouver une grand-mère, faire la dorure d'un wagon, vivre le deuil d'un père et faire l'itinéraire d'un spectacle : la collecte des histoires de cirque au sein des archives et au-delà*[4]. Si l'Université du Texas inclut des archives de spectacles au Harry Ransom Centre, ce sont plutôt les pérégrinations de Janet Davis au travers de différents fonds d'archives américains, dont notamment celui du Circus World de Baraboo, Wisconsin, qui forment le cœur de la présentation. À la question posée, une autre est ajoutée : quelles sont les histoires que nous choisissons de raconter ?

La notion de patrimoine et l'importance des archives se situent non seulement sur le plan des documents conservés mais des lieux mêmes. Les archives comme voûtes de savoir qui, par leurs choix de documents mais aussi par les connaissances de leurs archivistes ainsi que par la synergie née de la rencontre de différents chercheurs dans ces lieux,

---

[4] Traduction libre de l'auteure pour *Finding a Grandmother, Gilding a Wagon, Mourning a Father, and Routing a Show : Collecting Circus Stories in the Archives and Beyond.*

constituent un patrimoine en danger. C'est donc l'existence de ces lieux, notamment celui de Baraboo qui mérite d'être préservée. L'importance du lieu physique des archives est aussi en brèche avec le point de vue de plusieurs subventionneurs privés ou publics qui privilégient un accès dit moins coûteux par la numérisation des documents. Janet Davis considère qu'il s'agit d'un leurre pour tout chercheur, car si cela est utile dans une recherche préliminaire pour localiser les sources possibles, cela ne peut être suffisant pour alimenter une recherche. L'objet physique et le contact direct avec les gens qui s'y intéressent sont primordiaux. La préservation des lieux d'archives comme patrimoine vivant est cruciale. Dans le cas de collecte de narrations individuelles, Janet Davis s'intéresse aussi à la question du droit d'auteur et à son impact sur la non-accessibilité de sources écrites rares dans le milieu cirque, et qui laissent dormir dans des voûtes des pans d'histoires.

Pascal Jacob, historien de cirque et collectionneur privé, possède entre autre l'important Fonds Jacob-William – comprenant plus de 17 000 œuvres anciennes, modernes et contemporaines – qui est en dépôt à la TOHU et dont une partie est présentée en permanence dans l'édifice. Le fonds documentaire, constitué de plus de 5 000 pièces a, quant à lui, été confié à la bibliothèque de l'École nationale de cirque, Montréal. Ce collectionneur passionné amène un point de vue centré sur la valeur esthétique et historique d'œuvres qui par leur sujet participent à « écrire des histoires de cirque par la résonnance des objets entre eux ». Il associe sa démarche à celle d'une collection muséale (versus une collection documentaire) qui serait généraliste puisque les œuvres choisies reflètent l'inspiration provenant des arts du cirque autant dans les arts décoratifs que dans les beaux-arts, sans égard au temps ni à la provenance géographique.

Selon Pascal Jacob, collectionner se conjugue avec partager. Un partage, non seulement avec le public dans la volonté de faire connaître les arts du cirque et de faire apprécier leurs multiples reflets, mais aussi, dans un effort de transmission de connaissance, avec de nouveaux artistes. Le rapport plastique jouerait un rôle de « catalyseur de création mais aussi de compréhension des mécanismes de cirque tant dans ses architectures que dans ses structures ». Les objets occupent donc une place prépondérante dans son effort de collection, mais les livres et documents, accumulés en parallèle, servent aussi à informer et renforcer les objets choisis.

Les deux présentations soulignent la distinction, sur plusieurs plans, entre archives et collections, ce qui anime de longues discussions. Les archives, étant reliées à la vie d'un ou plusieurs individus (le collectionneur et/ou une personnalité) ou d'une compagnie, revêtent une dimension privée qui demande la mise en place d'un lien de confiance entre le propriétaire et l'institution. Son entrée dans l'inventaire d'une institution se fait d'ailleurs plutôt par le don. Cela amène des considérations délicates si l'institution ne désire pas ou n'est pas en mesure de recevoir l'ensemble du contenu. De même, l'indexation des documents peut-être orientée en fonction du donateur et non du contenu, et ce, sans lien évident pour le chercheur par la suite.

L'information peut donc se retrouver enfouie. Les collections d'objets sont, en revanche, généralement moins intimistes, les objets se vendant et s'acquérant de façon publique. Les acquisitions se font aussi dans le but d'être montrées (à quelques exceptions près) au plus grand nombre. Dans les deux cas, mention est faite du devoir de faire connaître ces fonds et objets, considérant le peu de documentation écrite sur l'histoire du cirque et l'importance qu'occupe l'image dans une discipline axée sur le corps et non sur les mots.

Comment répertorier nos collections ? Réflexion sur une terminologie universelle

La deuxième journée des rencontres a fait place à des questions plus techniques, afin de favoriser l'émergence d'actions concrètes au sortir des discussions.

Joëlle Garcia, chef du service Archives et imprimés au département des Arts du spectacle de la Bibliothèque nationale de France (BNF), présentait une communication intitulée *De Barnum à Zlatin, répertorier la diversité des collections de cirque*, qui faisait état de la réflexion actuelle de la BNF en matière de terminologie dans le domaine du cirque. Un total de 243 fonds ou collections concernant le cirque en France sont identifiés dans le *Répertoire des arts et spectacles*, mais peu sont indexés. Bien que certaines de ces collections se situent dans le département des Arts du spectacle, organisé par thème, plusieurs peuvent aussi se retrouver dans d'autres départements : Audiovisuel, Littérature et art, Estampes et photographies, Réserve des livres rares et Bibliothèque-Musée de l'Opéra. Deux types de catalogues sont utilisés à la BNF pour répertorier l'ensemble des documents : un catalogue général et un catalogue Archives et manuscrits. Ces deux outils utilisent un langage type contrôlé pour identifier les sujets (vedettes matières) qui est toutefois généraliste, puisqu'il couvre l'ensemble des contenus que l'on peut retrouver dans une bibliothèque publique.

Le département des Arts du spectacle se trouve au sein d'une large réflexion quant à l'amélioration de l'accès des collections de la BNF par une connexion des catalogues via le Web[5]. Toutefois, le département

---

[5]   Pour consulter les ressources en ligne <http://renet.bnf.fr/jsp/index.jsp>.

se heurte à la diversité de sa logique de collections, dans laquelle on peut distinguer quatre vocations : un centre d'archives avec catalogue d'archives et manuscrits ; une bibliothèque spécialisée avec catalogue de livres, périodiques, documents sonores, audiovisuels et multimédia édités ; un centre de documentation comprenant des programmes, des images et photographies, des affiches, des dossiers de presse, le tout faisant partie du catalogue général ; et un musée où sont conservés des costumes et accessoires décrits dans les fonds et collections. Bref, quatre types de collections dans presque autant de catalogues différents. Toutefois, le département est issu de l'important fonds donné par Auguste Rondel, lequel avait établi une certaine classification qui a été conservée. Au fil des ans, se sont ajoutés d'autres fonds, classifiés par les collectionneurs, des fichiers thématiques, des dossiers iconographiques, des photographies et des documents actuels[6] faisant état de nouvelles pratiques circassiennes. La diversité des sources participe à la complexité du vocabulaire associé qui, pour l'instant, existe dans les inventaires papier, faute d'avoir trouvé une logique d'inclusion dans les catalogues existants. Les fiches papier, legs des différents bibliothécaires responsables de l'indexation des documents et objets, sont toutefois des témoins privilégiés d'une logique de description ainsi qu'une source importante de détails et questionnements quant aux termes utilisés au moment de l'indexation. Il faut donc outre le fait de développer un vocabulaire révisé et une logique de catalogage unifié, trouver à conserver et rendre visible l'information compilée par ses prédécesseurs.

Faisant écho à cette vue d'ensemble des défis du catalogage, Anna-Karyna Barlati (Canada), responsable de la bibliothèque de l'École nationale de cirque à Montréal, a plongé dans le vif du sujet avec une présentation intitulée : *Le développement d'un thésaurus spécialisé : un outil documentaire à la rencontre de la recherche et de la mémoire vivante des arts du cirque*. C'est dans une approche de recherche de mots pour bien nommer les arts du cirque que l'École a décidé de créer un thésaurus, en réponse à un besoin identifié non seulement par les chercheurs, les étudiants et les bibliothécaires mais aussi par des journalistes en mal de vocabulaire pour rédiger une critique riche de sens.

Anna-Karyna Barlati souligne plusieurs enjeux parmi les caractéristiques du cirque qui ont une influence sur le développement du vocabulaire : 1° l'expression corporelle des arts du cirque est constituée de plusieurs disciplines ; 2° la recherche du spectaculaire dans la pratique des arts du cirque appelle à un renouvellement constant des disciplines et à la création de nouveaux appareils ; 3° la transmission des savoirs des arts du cirque

---

[6] Par exemple la collection des archives audiovisuelles du Centre national des arts du cirque par le biais d'un pôle associé (centre spécialisé) avec la BNF.

originalement issus d'une tradition orale évolue vers un cadre de formation académique ; 4° l'esprit de nomadisme des compagnies de cirque favorise l'ouverture à des emprunts linguistiques.

Une distinction est faite entre une valeur dite informationnelle et une valeur esthétique des documents et œuvres, afin de refléter l'angle particulier apporté par un centre spécialisé dans l'étude des documents conservés. Par exemple, un programme souvenir qui pourrait n'être indexé que sous la date, le nom de la compagnie et/ou le spectacle présenté dans une bibliothèque générale, revêt une foule de données techniques, dans les publicités, descriptions des numéros, présentation des artistes qui peuvent étayer le vocabulaire spécifique aux disciplines de cirque. L'École a choisi de construire un thésaurus, qui établit des liens entre plusieurs termes utilisés dans un milieu donné, en les classant dans une plus large structure de référents et en les définissant, plutôt qu'un dictionnaire qui fait une description de chaque terme sans opérer de lien d'équivalence ou de famille.

Ceci permet entre autres d'effectuer des recherches plus efficaces entre catalogues, par identification de nombreux termes reliés ; de garder en mémoire les termes retenus et ceux qui ont été rejetés, ce qui offre une plus grande richesse des particularités culturelles et la capacité, dans le temps, de modifier la liste selon l'acceptation ou non de nouveaux termes par le milieu. Le travail a donc été amorcé en détaillant les grandes familles de disciplines dans les arts du cirque, suivies des sous-catégories s'y rattachant, et d'exemples de référence. Le thésaurus peut être consulté en ligne[7] (en version française uniquement jusqu'ici). Dans la perspective d'élaboration des principes de réalisation d'un thésaurus commun, flexible et adaptable aux différentes langues, contextes culturels et normes documentaires, l'École souhaiterait participer au développement d'une table de concertation du milieu cirque et espère recevoir des commentaires quant au travail qu'elle a déjà amorcé et partagé publiquement via son site Web.

La question du vocabulaire suscite l'enthousiasme chez les participants, tout en mettant en relief l'ampleur de la tâche, de par la multitude des langues et des pratiques. Il est suggéré de réaliser, pour débuter, un recensement des dictionnaires et thésaurus existants ; de procéder à un état des lieux des différents centres de documentation spécialisés et de partager la liste des termes par langue. La mise sur pied d'un comité est proposée, pour coordonner la mise en commun de ces informations et surtout pour compiler les termes géographiquement ou au moins par langue. Un appel à volontaire est lancé pour débuter ce chantier. Il semble y avoir consensus sur la possibilité de commencer ce travail à

---

[7]   <http://www.ecolenationaledecirque.ca/fr/institution/catalogue-en-ligne>.

partir de ce qu'a construit l'École, en développant les équivalents anglais en premier, suivis des autres langues qui possèdent déjà un vocabulaire spécialisé (hollandais, allemand, italien et russe) et sont représentées par des participants.

Comment partager nos collections et nos connaissances ? Le développement de réseaux et de partenariats

Ce dernier panel de discussion est lancé par Antonio Giarola, directeur du Centre éducatif de documentation des arts du cirque (CEDAC) de Vérone (Italie). Il partage son expérience de mise en commun de collections privées, qui a mené à l'obtention d'un financement public pour rendre disponibles aux chercheurs et étudiants les corpus circassien de l'Italie. Plus de 10 000 pièces, estampes, affiches historiques et contemporaines ainsi que des programmes sont conservés dans ce Centre. Après un survol des contenus du Centre[8], Antonio Giarola présente les différents projets qui sont en développement et qui ont aussi en commun de mettre à profit des partenariats entre collectionneurs ou bibliothèques, pour agrandir le spectre de documents accessibles virtuellement (sans être la propriété de CEDAC), et ce, en lien avec les bases de données des bibliothèques qui possèdent les fonctionnalités de recherche avancée. La mise en commun de ressources, par échange de services, ou collaboration partagée, semble être la voie de financement possible mais se fait selon des normes quelquefois déjà établies mais d'autres fois inconnues.

Laura Van der Meer, directrice exécutive de la Fédération mondiale de cirque, conclut ces rencontres en présentant le contexte de fonctionnement de la Fédération, un organisme sans but lucratif constitué d'un regroupement d'associations professionnelles du milieu cirque et forain et parrainé par la princesse de Monaco. La Fédération, fondée en 1998 dans le but de rassembler la famille cirque, est soutenue par des groupes d'amis du cirque, et offre diverses opportunités de le célébrer. La promotion et la préservation de la culture de cirque étant au cœur de la mission de la Fédération, la mise sur pied d'un Projet de préservation de sa mémoire a été discutée très tôt par quelques membres qui s'interrogeaient sur l'ampleur des objets cirque conservés et surtout, valorisés. En réponse aux interrogations de ses membres, la Fédération a proposé de mettre sur pied un Projet de préservation qui aurait deux volets principaux : développer une liste des collections et musées existants, et favoriser la discussion avec des experts afin de comprendre les besoins liés à la conservation des collections de cirque. La Fédération a donc soutenu la

---

[8]   <http://www.cedac.eu.>

réalisation et participé à l'élaboration de rencontres thématiques sur ces sujets, à Monte-Carlo, Budapest et Montréal.

La Fédération est par ailleurs un organisme qui cherche à augmenter le nombre d'adhésions, de partenariats, ainsi que des collaborations ponctuelles autour de la promotion du cirque. Sur la base du Projet de préservation mené jusqu'à présent, la Fédération souhaite profiter de ces rencontres professionnelles pour valider le rôle qu'elle peut jouer à plus long terme et développer un plan d'action quinquennal. Ce dernier inclurait certaines initiatives lancées lors des discussions des derniers jours.

L'idée de développer un réseau dans lequel la Fédération jouerait un rôle central soulève d'intenses discussions. D'une part, les attentes sont élevées afin que la Fédération joue un rôle de coordination, de levée de fonds et de représentation auprès des institutions, d'instances gouvernementales et autres, telle l'UNESCO. De l'autre, la question de la constitution de la Fédération, comme regroupement d'associations et non d'individus pose des questions quant à sa capacité de représenter les individus présents et les différentes formes de cirque actuel. De plus, la Fédération étant une organisation jeune, il faut être réaliste et se rendre compte que ses ressources humaines et financières ne sont pas actuellement suffisantes pour prendre en charge de larges projets, et qu'elle doit continuer à s'appuyer sur des partenaires. Il est clair que le plan quinquennal qui sera présenté au Conseil d'administration devra tenir compte de ces limites, tout en positionnant bien le rôle que la Fédération peut et veut jouer en regard aussi de sa mission et de ses objectifs. Mention est toutefois faite de l'existence des réseaux d'études et d'échanges qui touchent plus largement les arts du spectacle, dont la SIBMAS, et du fait que les arts du cirque y sont malheureusement peu représentés. La Fédération est devenue membre de la SIBMAS en 2009 et compte collaborer au contenu du répertoire des collections sur le Web, lorsque ce dernier sera réactivé.

Toutefois, il appartient aussi à chaque individu de s'impliquer pour développer et fortifier de tels réseaux.

Le sommaire ou les trois grandes leçons

L'ensemble des échanges formels lors des ateliers, ou informels lors des visites et activités, a mis en relief l'énorme besoin des intervenants concernés par le cirque d'avoir des opportunités de rencontres et de discussions sur le thème des collections. L'existence d'une plateforme de communication ou d'un réseau un peu plus formel, permettant de rassembler tous ces gens de divers horizons, est certainement devenue une priorité, car elle a permis un moment de stimulation intense. Il est à souhaiter qu'un tel réseau permette de briser les silos et facilite des collaborations de recherches ou d'expositions. Sa forme reste toutefois à définir. Des étincelles ont surgi qui donneront possiblement naissance à certains projets ponctuels entre individus et collections, échanges de documents, mise en commun de contenu, découverte d'un intérêt de recherche. Les intervenants sont toutefois momentanément tous liés par leur participation à ces rencontres, ce qui forme déjà une liste de distribution potentielle, pour des communications spécifiques, qu'il ne reste qu'à activer, dans un contexte de responsabilité partagée.

Le besoin d'un projet utile et porteur pour la majorité des intervenants présents se concrétise par la mise sur pied d'un comité sur la terminologie. Il est composé de huit personnes de langues différentes, qui proposent d'agir comme représentants régionaux pour construire un vocabulaire commun à partir du thésaurus amorcé par l'ENC. Le travail de rassemblement des termes spécifiques effectué par le comité serait diffusé sur le Web. La méthode de travail et le fonctionnement devront être définis dans les semaines qui suivent. L'auteure du présent article activera ce comité.

Pour pouvoir poursuivre cet effort de mobilisation et développer une vision à moyen terme, la Fédération devra déterminer le rôle qu'elle est en mesure de jouer, le valider avec son Conseil et communiquer auprès des intervenants et de ses membres la définition actualisée et les actions concernant le Projet de préservation lancé il y a deux ans. Si une approche participative est importante entre la Fédération et tous ceux qui sont concernés par la préservation de la mémoire de cirque, la structure et les objectifs de la Fédération doivent être clairs pour tous, afin de s'assurer que l'objectif de ce projet convient à ceux qui le souhaitaient.

C'est avec la volonté de faire rayonner les arts du cirque d'aujourd'hui, en valorisant ceux d'hier et en pensant à ceux de demain que se sont conclues ces rencontres, avec en toile de fond les prouesses et l'envol des élèves sortants de l'ENC, qui entament leur vie professionnelle. C'est une vie aussi longue et fructueuse qui est souhaitée pour ce mouvement naissant, solidaire d'une mémoire du cirque au travers des formes, du temps et des frontières.

Abstract

A professional meeting on preserving circus memorabilia and objects took place from June 16 to 20, 2010 in Montreal, Canada. Cirque du Soleil and En Piste (the Canadian association of circus arts) organised this professional meeting in conjunction with the Fédération mondiale de cirque, a few weeks before the launch of Canada's first circus festival, Montréal Complètement Cirque, organised by TOHU.

Titled Preserving our Memory: The Importance of Circus Artifacts, the meeting aimed to create a forum for exchange and in-depth discussion with specialists, collectors and historians working in the fields of circus and circus preservation. Eight panellists and 35 participants, journalists, private collectors and circus company representatives got together with professionals from institutions dedicated to preserving circus memories to discuss four main topics:

- Circus memory as an intangible heritage : why should we protect it and who are we protecting it for?
- How to identify what needs to be preserved?
- How to index our collections? Reflections on a universal terminology.
- Developing networks and partnerships.

These exchanges have brought to light the real need for those involved with the circus to have opportunities for meetings and discussions on the subject of collections. A communication platform or a slightly more formal network that would bring together people from various fields has become a priority given the intense discussion and debate of these few days. Hopefully, such a network will break down barriers and promote research and exhibition collaborations. At this point, neither the final form of such a platform nor the institution/person that would coordinate it, were established.

However, a joint project took shape with the setting up of a terminology committee who would work based on the thesaurus initiated by the enc. Furthermore, the potential leading role of the Fédération should be determined and approved by its board as well as communicated to members together with actions concerning their Preservation Project started two years ago. It is with strong hopes of enhancing the memory of circus in its various forms – over time and across borders – that this meeting ended.

A. P. Tchekhov et le ballet

Mises en scène et interprétations

Tatiana Egorova

Musée National du Théâtre A. A. Bakhrouchine
(Moscou – Russie)

Le présent exposé propose une réflexion sur l'une des thématiques les plus intéressantes du théâtre de Tchekhov aujourd'hui – celle de l'adaptation de la dramaturgie et de la prose tchekhoviennes à la danse. Le rapport du ballet aux sujets et aux images créés par Tchekhov, et les particularités de leur mise en œuvre dans l'art chorégraphique, méritent de faire un jour l'objet d'une recherche approfondie et d'un exposé spécifique.

L'éminent metteur en scène Peter Stein disait de Tchekhov qu'il était, à l'égal des auteurs de l'Antiquité ou de Shakespeare, l'un des piliers du théâtre contemporain. Dans les pages de la *Süddeutsche Zeitung* du 15 juillet 2004, année du centième anniversaire de la mort de Tchekhov, Stein écrit :

> Tchekhov est l'auteur qui a marqué l'histoire du théâtre européen du XXᵉ siècle. Il a popularisé la tragédie grecque, fondement du théâtre européen, en lui conférant un caractère contemporain. Ses écrits traitent du désespoir, du caractère insoutenable de l'existence humaine, de cela que nous ne voyons le jour que pour mourir, et que la vie est dépourvue de sens. C'est pourquoi, chez Tchekhov, les gens souffrent en permanence, dans la parfaite conscience de l'absurdité de la vie… De fait, une vie dépourvue de sens est intolérable. Le plus important, c'est d'endurer cette altérité paradoxale.[1]

Un tel contraste entre cette absurdité imaginée, prévisible, évidente, et le nombre incalculable d'émotions offertes par l'existence, émotions susceptibles de se révéler à chaque instant d'une vie quotidienne

---

[1] D'après T. K. Chakh-Azizova, « Le Tchekhov allemand », dans P*roscaenium. Questions au sujet du théâtre*, n° 1-2. Moscou, 2008, p. 148.

ordinaire, parfois ressenties ou, plus rarement, pleinement conscientes, crée également de manière paradoxale « … quelque chose qui donne un sens à l'existence humaine »[2]. La dramaturgie de Tchekhov, dans sa substance, fut perçue de cette manière au tournant des XX et XXIe siècles, au travers du destin objectif et impitoyable des personnages, dans les contacts qu'ils nouent, les conflits qu'ils endurent au quotidien. Il en va de même pour ce qui est du caractère « non fortuit » de l'existence et de sa continuité. Cette distanciation de l'auteur n'a rien à voir avec de l'indifférence. S'il devait apparaître une forme quelconque de « chaleur »[3], il s'agirait, d'après Vladimir Koliazine, d'une combinaison unique « de romantisme, de poésie et de pragmatisme »[4] ouvrant la voie à une multitude d'interprétations, qui contribuent aussi à ce que cette dramaturgie se réclame de différentes formes d'art scénique[5].

Quelques-unes des réalisations les plus intéressantes des œuvres de Tchekhov au tournant des XXe et XXIe siècles ont été produites dans le domaine chorégraphique.

Il est difficile de dire avec certitude quel rapport Tchekhov entretenait avec la danse.

On sait que les Tchekhov se distinguaient par leurs talents pour la musique et les arts[6]. Le chant et la musique étaient les passe-temps favoris

---

[2]   *Ibid.*

[3]   Comparons avec Alexeï Souvorine : « Tout ce qu'il faisait, il le faisait de manière étrangement simple… Il semble que cet homme ait vécu sans se poser de questions, n'aspirant à rien, vivant parce qu'il était né, mais tout ce qui lui était proche, ce qui trouvait grâce à son âme, obtenait de lui une sorte d'attention bienveillante. » A. S. Souvorine, *Le Tchekhov humain. Voyage vers Tchekhov*. Moscou, 1996, p. 430-431.

[4]   V. Koliazin sur les mises en scène contemporaines allemandes de Tchekhov, dans Proscaenium : Questions sur le théâtre… *op. cit.*, p. 159.

[5]   Par ailleurs, la découverte d'un contraste aussi paradoxal n'est probablement pas propre à l'époque du post-modernisme, contraste qui s'attachait et savait réunir l'irréunissable dans un tout indissoluble. Il y a plus de cent ans, Alexeï Souvorine s'étonnait de l'ambiguïté du caractère et du talent de Tchekhov, qu'il croyait appartenir à une autre époque, voire plutôt à aucune époque du tout : « En lui, l'on trouvait à la fois un poète et un homme doté d'un bon sens appréciable… Alors que la maladie ne s'était pas manifestée chez lui, il se distinguait par une joie de vivre sans pareilles et par une soif de vie dont il aimait jouir… Apparaissait un homme dans tout le charme que lui conférait son esprit, sa sincérité et son indépendance. En Tchekhov, il y avait quelque chose de neuf, d'indépendant, comme si cela provenait d'une tout autre existence, d'un autre univers : sans sentimentalité, ni grandes phrases. Parfois même cela paraissait être de la cruauté, mais cependant une cruauté juste et ferme. » A. S. Souvorine, *Le Tchekhov humain, op. cit.*, p. 430-431.

[6]   Le frère d'Anton Tchekhov Nikolay, décédé jeune (1858-1889), était un peintre et dessinateur-caricaturiste de talent dont la sœur Marie (1863-1957) prenait des leçons de dessin et de peinture chez le grand paysagiste russe Isaac Ilytch Lévitan qui appréciait ses travaux.

de Tchekhov et de ses hôtes dans la maison de Mélikhovo, où musiciens et interprètes, professionnels et amateurs talentueux, étaient toujours accueillis avec plaisir et même avec certains égards[7]. Anton Pavlovitch lui-même avait une bonne oreille musicale : ce n'est pas un hasard si la prose de Tchekhov, de par son « caractère mélodieux » était si juste et pure, et ce n'est pas un hasard non plus si, par exemple, *La Légende valaque* de Gaetano Braga, si souvent exécutée dans la demeure de Mélikhovo par Lydia Stakhievna (Lika) Mizinova, est devenue le leitmotiv, le « chant du destin », l'incontournable force agissante de la nouvelle de Tchekhov *Le Moine noir*.

Parmi les proches connaissances de Tchekhov figuraient Piotr Ilitch Tchaïkovski – qui éprouvait pour l'écrivain une réelle sympathie –, Sergueï Rachmaninov et Fédor Ivanovitch Chaliapine, qui, d'après les mémoires de I. A. Bounine, avait été « charmé » par Tchekhov, à la fois par l'homme et par l'écrivain[8]. Il n'y a toutefois pas de danseuse professionnelle ni dans son entourage proche, ni dans sa famille, ni parmi ses héroïnes. Il ne faut pas considérer comme le témoignage d'une sérieuse passion pour le ballet la remarque quelque peu malicieuse de sa lettre du 7 décembre 1889 adressée au célèbre éditeur pétersbourgeois et critique de théâtre Alexeï Sergueïevitch Souvorine, faisant allusion à l'actrice du Petit théâtre de Moscou, Glafira Panova, ex-ballerine au Grand théâtre :

> Lorsque j'étais en 2e année je m'étais amouraché d'une ballerine et je fréquentais les ballets. J'ai ensuite connu des actrices qui étaient passées du ballet au théâtre dramatique. Hier, … je suis allé rendre visite à l'une des dites actrices. Le ballet, désormais, elle le méprise et le regarde de haut, mais malgré tout, elle ne parvient pas à se défaire de ses mouvements de ballerine.[9]

On peut supposer que le manque de considération de Tchekhov à l'égard de cette forme d'art était dû en partie à la condition du ballet académique impérial de l'époque, où une virtuosité dans la maîtrise de la technique chorégraphique et une scénographie proche de la perfection s'accompagnaient de personnages conventionnels et d'une « immuabilité » des poses et des mouvements.

Il se passa presque vingt années avant l'apparition des Saisons Russes de Serge de Diaghilev, qui ont marqué le ballet et démontré la capacité de la danse classique à fusionner avec la musique, en un tout stylistique et harmonieux, pour devenir un moyen d'expression des émotions les plus subtiles et des désirs les plus ardents. Néanmoins,

---

[7]   You. A. Bytchkov, *Le Meilleur des hommes*, Moscou, Helios ARV, 1994, p. 45, 48.

[8]   *Ibid.*, p. 312.

[9]   *Ibid.*, p. 157.

le recours du ballet contemporain au théâtre de Tchekhov apparaît aujourd'hui comme tout à fait naturel aussi bien pour les chorégraphes que pour les danseurs et les spectateurs. Les spectacles de ballet tirés des pièces de Tchekhov et des thèmes de ses nouvelles ont pris une place prépondérante et, si l'on se réfère aux meilleurs exemples du genre, ils font partie intégrante de la tradition classique littéraire et artistique basée sur son œuvre.

Comment expliquer l'intérêt que le spectacle de ballet porte à Tchekhov ?

L'une des principales raisons semble être l'« universalité vis-à-vis du genre humain » que présente l'œuvre de Tchekhov, au sujet duquel Léon Tolstoï déclara en 1904 : « Tchekhov est un artiste incomparable. Un artiste de la vie. Et ce qui fait la valeur de son œuvre c'est qu'il est compris et accepté non seulement par les Russes mais par l'humanité entière »[10]. Mais la capacité d'être intelligible à tout être humain, de « communiquer sans paroles » est aussi propre à la danse. L'authenticité de la psychologie des personnages des pièces de Tchekhov leur conférait une vie scénique et une destinée propre et tout à fait légitimes ; la barrière invisible qui sépare la scène du monde réel, si l'on y adjoint une exécution artistique de haut vol, devient quasi inexistante. Les meilleurs metteurs en scène et acteurs des œuvres de Tchekhov ont été poussés à rechercher une authenticité non seulement des mots, mais aussi de l'intonation et du geste, une « authenticité non verbale » dont l'auteur lui-même avait pris conscience. « Il faut rendre les souffrances comme elles s'expriment dans la vie, c'est-à-dire non avec des gestes des mains et des pieds, mais avec une simple intonation, un regard. Pas de gestes, mais de la grâce » écrivait-il à Olga L. Knipper[11].

Partant de ce postulat, il ne manquait sans doute pas grand-chose pour que l'on prenne conscience qu'il est possible d'exprimer les émotions authentiques de Tchekhov à travers l'art de la danse, prise de conscience qui s'est faite également dans le monde des grands chorégraphes de la fin du XXᵉ siècle. « Le 1ᵉʳ janvier 1996, j'ai vu *La Mouette* au théâtre berlinois Schaubühne », se rappelle John Neumeier qui a mis cette pièce en scène à Hambourg en 2002 et qui cinq ans plus tard l'a restituée sur la scène du Théâtre Musical de Moscou K. S. Stanislavski et V. I. Nemirovitch-Dantchenko.

Ma conception du ballet basé sur l'œuvre de Tchekhov s'est transformée puisque dans cette pièce l'on ne traite pas des rapports entre les gens issus

---

[10]   Interview de Léon Tolstoï dans le journal Rus, n° 212, 15 juillet 1904. Cité d'après : You. A. Bytchkov, *Le Meilleur des* hommes, *op. cit.*, p. 190.

[11]   Anton Tchekhov, *Lettre à Olga Knipper*, du 2 janvier 1900, citée dans Sophie Laffitte, *Tchekhov par lui-même*, Paris, Seuil « Écrivains de toujours », 1966, p. 101.

d'un groupe défini, mais plutôt d'une chose, en quelque sorte, universelle. J'y ai vu un thème qui peut être transposé dans la danse.[12]

Ceci dit, cette transposition de la tradition de Tchekhov à la scène du ballet n'impliquait pas l'abandon de la trame thématique et les spécificités psychologiques propres à l'auteur. Neumeier déclare :

> En tant que chorégraphe, je travaille souvent sur la littérature. Et je suis de plus en plus convaincu que le texte, qui sert de base à mon ballet, est bien plus important pour moi que pour les futurs spectateurs… Je tiens à visualiser l'histoire, le texte, la pièce… Je ne veux pas interpréter *La Mouette* comme quelqu'un qui se contenterait de restituer le texte sur la scène. Pour mon ballet, j'imagine des situations qui expriment quelque chose qui soit similaire au texte.[13]

Une prémisse importante pour la mise en œuvre et l'évolution de la chorégraphie des œuvres de Tchekhov se trouve dans les propriétés musicales de sa littérature et de la plastique photographique qu'il a créée. D'une manière générale, Tchekhov se caractérise par une musicalité du discours que souligne V. I. Nemirovitch-Dantchenko : « Basses graves et abondance des instruments métalliques, douces intonations passant à une sorte de léger chant »[14]. Il se peut que cette musicalité innée ait justement été liée au caractère polyphonique des thèmes de *La Mouette*. Selon Maïa Mikhaïlovna Plissetskaïa :

> Cette pièce est de bout en bout un mystère. […] Je crois que c'est l'unique pièce de théâtre russe dans la conception de laquelle les metteurs en scène successifs se sont débrouillés pour faire de chaque personnage (et ils sont treize) à tour de rôle la figure principale de leur « relecture hardie et novatrice ».[15]

Dans la mise en scène de M. M. Plissetskaïa sur une musique de R. K. Chtchedrine, dont la première a eu lieu au théâtre Bolchoï de Moscou le 27 mai 1980, chacun des personnages « suit sa ligne, raconte son sort sans joie »[16]. Ces interprétations au caractère plastique et mélodieux se rejoignent parfois, pour créer une harmonie, mais elles apparaissent le plus souvent comme un contrepoint, reflétant le sentiment de perte intérieure des protagonistes qui sont « tous amoureux. Mais chacun d'un

---

[12] *La Mouette* de Neumeier. Récit du chorégraphe. Programme du spectacle. Théâtre musical Stanislavski et Némirovitch-Dantchenko. Moscou, 2007, p. 15.

[13] *Ibid.*, p. 15-16.

[14] Cité d'après You. A. Bytchkov, *Le Meilleur des hommes, op. cit.*, p. 167.

[15] Maïa Plissetskaïa, *Moi, Maïa Plissetskaïa...* Paris, Gallimard, 1995, p. 397. « Auparavant, l'on reprochait à la grande littérature de ne pas avoir de propriétés plastiques… J'ai été offensée pour la grande littérature » a dit M. M. Plissétskaïa le soir de la réception au Musée National de Théâtre Bakhrouchine à Moscou, le 8 avril 2010.

[16] Maïa Plissetskaïa, *Moi, Maïa Plissetskaïa..., op. cit.*, p. 401.

amour sans retour »[17]. « Ils sont à un pas les uns des autres et pourtant dissociés, tragiquement seuls »[18], pratiquement accoutumés à ne pas trouver d'écho dans le cœur de l'être cher. Cependant, dans un contexte où se mêlent « ces destins malheureux » l'on perçoit distinctement le leitmotiv de l'amour et de la passion créatrice et, à l'origine, les espoirs enflammés de Nina Zaretchnaïa et de Constantin Treplev.

L'intensité des émotions de ces héros les distingue des autres protagonistes qui ont perdu la foi, qui sont renfermés sur eux-mêmes, sans espoir, et dont la transposition, dans l'interprétation de Maïa Plisseeskaïa, a fait appel à un procédé artistique singulier : les personnages qui entourent Nina et Kostia se déplacent avec lenteur, comme dans un film au ralenti ; tout en les suivant, les personnages principaux ont un rythme de mouvement qui paraît impétueux et plein de force intérieure.

Les changements de cadence, de rythme, d'esthétique et de tissu musical de la chorégraphie sont le principal procédé de transcription de la psychologie des personnages dans le spectacle *La Mouette* de John Neumeier.

La « plastique brisée » de Nina Zaretchnaïa, dans le ballet d'avant-garde *L'âme de la mouette* créé pour elle par Constantin Treplev (sur une musique d'Evelyn Glennie), s'oppose à la régularité, la rondeur, la justesse du mouvement d'Arcadina – selon la conception de la chorégraphe, danseuse classique, célèbre vedette des théâtres impériaux (au premier acte, elle danse sur la musique de P. I. Tchaïkovski).

Notons que les interprétations différentes de la gestuelle, chez Plissetskaïa et chez Neumeier, aboutissent parfois à des styles semblables et tout aussi profondément « tchékhoviens ». Ainsi, dans la mise en scène de Plissetskaïa, la Macha sans caractère, indolente, détruite par la non-réciprocité, est étonnamment proche de la Macha de Neumeier, tendue et agitée, figée dans son malheur, et dépourvue de sa douce souplesse de jeune fille : dans les deux cas, nous assistons à un tragique oubli de soi dans le quotidien, à un refus de l'espoir et à une fuite du spirituel.

Une telle correspondance des contenus, à travers des voies différentes, montre qu'un spectacle chorégraphique inspiré par la pièce peut être proche de celle-ci en « traitant des rapports entre les mondes intérieurs et extérieurs »[19], très proche de l'esprit tchekhovien dans son « fondement littéraire ».

La troisième condition *sine qua non* de la recréation d'un esprit authentiquement tchékhovien dans un spectacle chorégraphique est le perfectionnement et la diversification des techniques de la danse :

---

[17] *Id.*

[18] *Ibid.*, p. 400.

[19] *La mouette* de Neumeier. Récit du chorégraphe, *op. cit.*, p. 18.

un nouveau langage de la danse est apparu dans la seconde moitié du XXᵉ siècle, fondé sur la maîtrise des acquis de l'école classique tout en étant capable de s'approprier et d'adapter les éléments empruntés à d'autres arts plastiques, et en particulier la danse-théâtre. Cette capacité, sans être une fin en soi, est justifiée et nécessaire à la transmission de la pensée du chorégraphe. Elle engendre une authenticité sémantique et psychologique. Une synthèse justifiée et légitime entre la danse et la danse-théâtre a été dévoilée au public dans le ballet tiré de la nouvelle de Tchekhov *La Dame au petit chien*, mis en scène par Maïa Plissetskaïa sur la musique de R. K. Chtchedrine et présenté pour la première fois sur la scène du théâtre Bolchoï le 20 novembre 1985.

« Comme j'ai rêvé – du délire – de traduire par la danse les nuances illimitées de Tchekhov, l'ambiance inimitable du récit, le ton, la poésie, le non-dit, la mélancolie, le mystère et la simplicité de sa musique »[20], écrivait Maya Plissetskaïa.

Des moyens d'expression essentiels ont concouru à permettre de trouver un écho dans l'œuvre de Marc Chagall, chez qui les personnages amoureux sont constamment renfermés dans leur propre monde, sont détachés de la foule et semblent planer sur elle. La danseuse se souvient :

[…] *La Dame* n'occupait que deux danseurs : moi-même (Anna Serguéievna) et Boris Efimov (Gourov). Les autres participants étaient des figurants d'opéra.

[…] le ballet répondait à une structure précise, toute l'action portant sur cinq grands pas de deux. […] Le reste n'était qu'un fond, un accompagnement, des éclairs de conscience. Le public en promenade à Yalta, c'était la figuration. Anna Serguéievna et son loulou sur la jetée de la mer Noire, une doublure, une figurante. Le veilleur de nuit qui épie les deux héros, un figurant. Les tableaux de l'hiver à Moscou, encore la figuration. La foule aux multiples visages aussi, ces bourgeois, leurs concitoyens qu'ils ne remarquent même pas.[21]

Ainsi, dans les spectacles les plus aboutis basés sur l'œuvre de Tchekhov, le chorégraphe mettant Tchekhov en scène et l'artiste, dansant son personnage, sont sans doute des virtuoses, mais des virtuoses réfléchis, qui sauront mettre en œuvre tous les moyens et formes d'expression plastique à leur disposition afin de pénétrer l'essence et l'atmosphère du drame tchekhovien, afin de réaliser « la transposition de Tchekhov dans le langage de la danse ». C'est là que prend tout son sens le concept de John Neumeier de l'artiste qui « danse/parle » au spectateur[22].

---

[20] Maïa Plissetskaïa, *Moi, Maïa Plissetskaïa…*, *op. cit.*, p. 404.
[21] *Ibid.*, p. 403.
[22] *La Mouette* de Neumeier. Récit du chorégraphe, *op. cit.*, p. 16, 18.

Abstract

Anton Chekhov in reflection of the Ballet.

The subject of this presentation is the adaptation of Chekhov's dramaturgy, one of the most interesting aspects of his work, to ballet. The focus is put here on the brilliant way Chekhov highlights how meaningless and absurd life is while bringing a major paradox into light: a meaningless life can give a meaning to life.

Many art forms can fit in Chekhov's theater. The author embraced a passion for music and singing.

However, it is difficult to know whether Chekhov was passionate about ballet, because at that time, ballets and their characters were only picturing the life of the elite, which was of little interest to Chekhov.

It took almost twenty years to see the Diaghilev's Russian Seasons adapted into ballet. It is at that very moment that dancing, associated to classical music, was finally considered as a way to express emotions.

Nowadays, three principles are needed to make a good adaptation of Chekhov's plays happen. The music must be perfectly adapted to Chekhov literature. The changes of rhythm, choreography, aestheticism and harmony are another characteristic that must be present. And the last and essential characteristic needed is an extreme diversity and a strive for perfection in the use of dancing techniques.

So all in all, Chekhov's plays are recreated by virtuosos, who are able to use all the expression forms and all the possible means to make it happen.

The Don Juan Archiv Wien

A Private Research Institute for Opera and Theatre History[1]

Matthias J. PERNERSTORFER

Don Juan Archiv (Vienna – Austria)

Don Juan is an important figure in cultural and theatre history, which since its origins in Spain in the early 17th century has become increasingly widespread in Europe and since the late 18th century also continues to be disseminated overseas. The traces of this theatrical triumphal procession are numerous and are being systematically catalogued and documented by the Don Juan Archiv Wien[2]. A particular focus is Da Ponte and Mozart's *Don Giovanni* (world premiere in Prague, 1787): its genesis, premiere, performances involving its authors, and its reception.

Hans Ernst Weidinger, who since the 1970s has dedicated himself to the history of Don Juan materials from its origins until the end of the 18th century, founded the archive in the Don Juan anniversary year 1987 and presented a part of his research in 2002 in the form of a sixteen-volume dissertation titled *Il Dissoluto Punito. Untersuchungen zur äußeren und inneren Entstehungsgeschichte von Lorenzo da Pontes und Wolfgang Amadeus Mozarts Don Giovanni*[3].

In order to make the fruits of these collecting and research activities accessible to other researchers, the until then private archive was opened to the public in 2007 as a research centre for theatre and cultural history with an archive and research library under the name *Don Juan Archiv Wien*. The

---

[1] I would like to take the opportunity here to thank the editor of this volume for giving me the opportunity to publish a revised article on the same topic as that presented at the SIBMAS conference in Munich, as it would no longer make sense to report about the "current" state of projects at the Don Juan Archiv in 2010. Furthermore, in the past couple of years the focus has shifted in some respects and several projects have since been completed.

[2] See <www.donjuanarchiv.at>.

[3] Hans Ernst Weidinger, *Il Dissoluto Punito. Untersuchungen zur äußeren und inneren Entstehungsgeschichte von Lorenzo da Pontes und Wolfgang Amadeus Mozarts Don Giovanni*, 16 Vols., dissertation, University of Vienna, 2002.

archive was first situated in the first municipal district (Goethegasse 1) and since May 2012 has been officially housed in new premises – including a new centre for digitisation – in the eighth district (Trautsongasse 6/6).

At present, the continuously growing collection comprises ca. 20,000 libretti and printed dramas as well as approximately 10,000 playbills and programmes: original, microfilm and digitised copies. In addition, it contains around 30,000 volumes of editions and secondary literature. Of particular interest is an individual collection of almost 3,000 printed theatre texts, ranging in date from the middle of the 18th century to the 1930s (known as the Komplex Mauerbach, acquired in 1996), which will be discussed in more detail below.

The Don Juan Archiv is a member of several international organisations, such as SIBMAS and IAML[4], and collaborates with archives, libraries, museums, research institutions and businesses – particularly in Vienna, Salzburg, Prague, Florence and Rome – both generally and on specific projects. The archive fosters academic and artistic exchanges on both a regional and international level through numerous events – Don Juan Days, conferences, workshops, dialogue meetings and notably the series of symposia *Ottoman Empire and European Theatre*, which has been held since 2008. In addition, the Don Juan Archiv has presented its research in the consolidated form of publications, which are generally brought out by the in-house publisher HOLLITZER Wissenschaftsverlag[5].

Three specific fields of activity at the Don Juan Archiv will be presented below in order to highlight the spectrum of its projects: firstly, the cataloguing, digitisation and research into the collection of plays in the Komplex Mauerbach; secondly, a discussion of possibilities to evaluate the large bibliographic works by Claudio Sartori and Reinhart Meyer; lastly, I will conclude with research into repertoire and the "playbill initiative" that stemmed from this.

1. The So-called Komplex Mauerbach:
A Collection of Plays

On 29 and 30 October 1996 the so-called Mauerbach Benefit Sale was held at Christie's auction house. Objects that had been stored for decades in the Carthusian monastery at Mauerbach and deemed impossible to restitute – including a collection of almost 3,000 volumes of theatre literature, prints and (a mere few) manuscripts dating from the middle of the 18th century to the 1930s whose provenance was unknown – were brought to auction.

---

[4]   The International Association of Music Libraries, Archives and Documentation Centres, <www.iaml.info>.

[5]   See <www.hollitzer.at>.

H. E. Weidinger acquired the Komplex Mauerbach (the name given to the collection by him) and donated it to the Don Juan Archiv for cataloguing and research purposes after its foundation in the year 2007. As Brigitte Dalinger's research project has shown, the collection of plays was once in the possession of the actor and theatre historian Otto Rub. It was purchased in 1943 by National Socialist authorities for the planned Führerbibliothek in Linz and was shortly afterwards stored in the salt mine Altaussee in order to protect it from air raids. From there, it passed through various stations under the supervision of American authorities until it arrived in the Carthusian monastery at Mauerbach in 1969. As it was legally acquired from Otto Rub, it is now also clear why there was no claim for a restitution of the whole collection – why several volumes, however, were restituted raises new questions.

Alongside research conducted by the Don Juan Archiv into the provenance of the collection, a priority was to catalogue and appropriately store the books. Our first step was to check and expand the auction inventory and in 2008 digitisation of the front matter, necessary for bibliographic identification, was begun[6]. During this time, the books were stored in new acid-free boxes in order to meet the necessary requirements for preserving a historical collection of this kind.

In order to make the Komplex Mauerbach accessible online, we developed parallel to this process a digital library which should be more than simply a bibliographic reference system: rather it should offer the possibility of viewing the digital copies. It was important to us not only to make the searching and reading of individual plays possible online, but also to allow one to form an impression of the collection as a whole. The visualisation allows for a quantitative analysis of the entire collection and enables one to compare the covers (of volumes and title pages) in order to show which items belong together, and should therefore not be restricted to providing a good viewer. The software NAINUWA developed by Treventus Mechatronics, even in its earliest stages of development, showed potential for such a visualisation of data and convenient access to the scans (fast and progressive zooming, etc.). Therefore, a presentation of the Komplex Mauerbach was developed in conjunction with Treventus between August 2009 and November 2012.

---

[6] Various colleagues, who I would like to thank here, worked on the project Komplex Mauerbach: Gabriele C. Pfeiffer (project management, 2007-2008), Matthias J. Pernerstorfer (project management, since 2008), Christoph Taumberger and Jennifer Plank (digitisation, 2008-2010), Brigitte Dalinger (historical research, since 2009), Margot J. Pernerstorfer (inventory and digital library, 2008-2011), Nora Gumpenberger (inventory and digital library, since 2011), Alison J. Dunlop (digital library and research – and translation of this paper, since 2011), Andreas Hanzl (relational database, since 2012), and Andrea Gruber (library system, since 2013).

In order to meet the abovementioned requirements, the digital library for the Komplex Mauerbach offers two viewing modes:

- According to individual works: <http://www.nainuwa.com/at-djarch-kmb/>

- According to volumes: <http://www.nainuwa.com/at-djarch-kmb/volumes/>

The viewing of individual works is suited to bibliographic interest as it is possible to identify individual titles and to examine the front matter. Additionally, it is possible to conduct quantitative analysis, for example, according to year and place of publication.

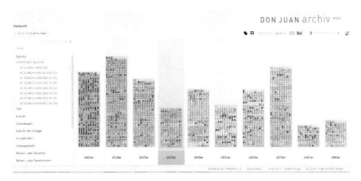

Figure 1. Dated Plays in the Komplex Mauerbach from the 19ᵗʰ century.

If one's priority is to research the history of the collection, the viewing of volumes is recommended as, for example, it enables a comparison of bindings. In many cases, one can find older shelf marks or ex libris marks, which are of interest for historical research and will be listed in their entirety in the printed catalogue (currently under preparation).

Figure 2. KMB 1144, Karl Julius: Blau und Gelb, oder: *Ein Wiener Stuben-mädchen* (Wien, 1861), annotated print with various signatures.

2. Bibliographic Cataloguing of Historical Theatre Materials

Not least, the digital library of Komplex Mauerbach should improve the ability to find it online; in the future it will also be integrated into Europeana[7], the virtual library of the European Union for cultural heritage. The request to have the plays found in the collection included in Reinhart Meyer's *Bibliographia Dramatica et Dramaticorum*[8] has already been accepted. There has been cooperation between the bibliographer and the archive since a project on the Pálffy theatre library, which is housed at the Institut für Theater-, Film- und Medienwissenschaft at the University of Vienna, was conducted in 2007[9], and last year it led to the publication of his *Schriften zur Theater- und Kulturgeschichte des 18. Jahrhunderts*[10]. This 900-page book also contains a review of Claudio Sartori's standard work, *I libretti italiani a stampa dalle origini al 1800*[11], published in the 1990s, in which Meyer underlines the cultural and historical significance of this great biographical achievement. Bibliographies are considerably more than mere reference system: depending on the conception, they can broaden or disguise our view of historical reality. In this context reading of the article "Wie hinderlich Wissen sein kann, oder: Über die Dialektik von Irrtum und fortschreitender Erkenntnis. Überlegungen zu den Arbeiten an der *Bibliographia Dramatica et Dramaticorum*"[12] is recommended.

And bibliographies want to be read. In 1996, H. E. Weidinger acquired the publishing rights to develop Sartori's *Catalogo Analitico* into a database[13], and in his abovementioned dissertation on *Don Giovanni*, he

---

[7] See <www.europeana.eu>.

[8] Reinhart Meyer, *Bibliographia Dramatica et Dramaticorum. Kommentierte Bibliographie der im ehemaligen deutschen Reichsgebiet gedruckten und gespielten Dramen des 18. Jahrhunderts nebst deren Übersetzungen und Bearbeitungen und ihrer Rezeption bis in die Gegenwart*, 1. Abteilung: *Werkausgaben, Sammlungen, Reihen*, Vols. 1-3, Tübingen, Niemeyer, 1986; 2. Abteilung: *Einzelausgaben*. Tübingen, Niemeyer, 1993f.

[9] Matthias J. Pernerstorfer, «Die Theater-Bibliothek Pálffy», in Birgit Peter and Martina Payr (eds.), «*Wissenschaft nach der Mode*»? *Die Gründung des Zentralinstituts für Theaterwissenschaft an der Universität Wien 1943*, Vienna, Lit Verlag, 2008, p. 124-134.

[10] Reinhart Meyer, *Schriften zur Theater- und Kulturgeschichte des 18. Jahrhunderts*, Matthias J. Pernerstorfer (ed.), Vienna, Hollitzer Wissenschaftsverlag, 2012 (Summa Summarum 1).

[11] Claudio Sartori, *I libretti italiani a stampa dalle origini al 1800. Catalogo analitico con 16 indici*, 7 Vols., Cuneo, Bertola & Locatelli Editori, 1990-1994.

[12] Reinhart Meyer, *Schriften* (No. 2), p. 485-506.

[13] This database is housed at the Don Juan Archiv.

analysed it in exemplary fashion in two different respects. On the one hand, the mentioning of biographies or singers (for example, those who participated in the Prague premiere of *Don Giovanni*) in libretti allow one to reconstruct various aspects of performances – the same is true for librettists, composers, choreographers and all others who took part in performances of operas and ballets and are named in Sartori's *Catalogo Analitico*. On the other hand, repertoire of Italian operas, as well as Latin and Italian oratorios, can be reconstructed for various places (towns, castles, monasteries and churches). Although such detailed analyses depend on the reliability and completeness of Sartori's data, this does not change the fact that this is the only means of obtaining a broader overview.

3. Research on Repertoire and the Playbill Initiative

Neither Sartori's *Catalogo Analitico* nor Meyer's *Bibliographia Dramatica* (which is currently being digitised by the Don Juan Archiv) contain information about all known performances: although they serve as a starting point for research on repertoire, it is imperative to incorporate other primary sources and secondary literature.

A systematic compilation of research on opera and theatre repertoire has not yet been undertaken. For example, concerning Viennese repertoire in the 18th century, although there is a series of works about opera at the imperial court and individual theatres, and another series about sources that are important for research on the repertoire, it is not possible at present to call up the daily programme, say for 29 October 1787, at the touch of a button. In order to change this situation, the Don Juan Archiv is dedicated to collecting, digitising, verifying, and where possible elaborating on already published programmes and creating a means of presenting the material online.

In order to link research data with digitised sources, the Don Juan Archiv relies on cooperation with other archives, libraries and museums. In 2010, to make a virtue of necessity, a "playbill initiative" involving several Viennese institutes, in particular the Wienbibliothek im Rathaus and the Österreichisches Theatermuseum, was established. Various meetings (Forschungsgespräche) have taken place, as well as an international conference on this subject on 28 and 29 June 2011, at which employees of archives, libraries, museums, and universities as well as students presented their findings[14]. In October 2012, the expanded conference proceedings for this event were published under the title *Theater – Zettel – Sammlungen.*

---

[14] A report about the conference by Jana-Katharina Mende appeared in *Nestroyana* 31 (2011), No. 3-4, p. 200-203, and in *AKMB-News* 17 (2011), p. 50-53.

Erschließung, Digitalisierung, Forschung[15]. Because of the positive response to this, we decided to continue this work and publish a second volume dedicated to this topic.

The activities of the Don Juan Archiv are, as can be seen in this brief overview, diverse – this diversity is determined by the figure of Don Juan and its history, which forces one to think outside the box, as well as by the historical genesis of the archive itself. In conjunction with research on Don Juan, individual collections such as Komplex Mauerbach, or specific themes such as *Ottoman Empire and European Theatre*, we undertake large-scale projects. In other areas, the Don Juan Archiv serves as a kind of initiator and is always open to interesting collaborations.

Abstract

Don Juan est une figure phare de l'histoire de la culture et du théâtre. Depuis ses origines, en Espagne au xviie siècle, son mythe n'a cessé de s'étendre à travers toute l'Europe et, depuis la fin du xviiie siècle, à travers le monde. Les traces de cette triomphale procession théâtrale sont nombreuses et sont systématiquement cataloguées et documentés par la Don Juan Archiv Wien.

Hans Ernst Weidinger, qui, depuis les années 1970, a consacré sa vie à la recherche sur l'histoire de Don Juan, de ses origines jusqu'à la fin du xviiie siècle, a fondé les archives en 1987, date anniversaire de la création de l'opéra de Mozart à Prague (1787).

Hans Ernst Weidinger a par ailleurs présenté une partie de son travail en 2002, sous la forme d'un essai comportant seize volumes. Actuellement, la collection, en constante expansion, comprend environ 20 000 livrets et pièces écrites ainsi qu'approximativement 10 000 affiches et programmes : des originaux, des microfilms et des copies numérisées. De plus, elle contient 30 000 volumes d'éditions et notamment de littérature secondaire. La collection de près de 3 000 textes théâtraux en version papier, s'étendant du milieu du xviiie siècle jusqu'aux années 1930, connue sous le nom de *Komplex Mauerbach*, acquise en 1996, est d'un grand intérêt.

Afin d'étendre cette collection et de rendre les recherches accessibles aux autres chercheurs, les archives, qui étaient encore privées il y a peu, ont été ouvertes au public en 2007 en tant que centre de recherche dans le domaine de l'histoire de la culture et du théâtre. La bibliothèque, qui rassemble ces archives et ces recherches, porte le nom de Don Juan Archiv Wien.

---

[15] Matthias J. Pernerstorfer (ed.), *Theater – Zettel – Sammlungen. Erschließung, Digitalisierung, Forschung*, Vienna, Hollitzer Wissenschaftsverlag, 2012 (Bibliographica 1).

Trois domaines spécifiques d'activités de la Don Juan Archiv sont présentés dans ce papier, dans le but de mettre en exergue l'étendue du projet : tout d'abord, dans la collection de pièces au sein du Komplex Mauerbach, le catalogage, la numérisation et la recherche ; ensuite, la discussion des nombreuses possibilités d'évaluation des importants travaux bibliographiques réalisés par Claudio Sartori et Reinhart Meyer ; enfin, des recherches dans le répertoire et la collection d'affiches qui en découle.

Les maquettes de décor au théâtre

De l'outil de travail à la valorisation d'un patrimoine

Jan Van Goethem & Sybille Wallemacq

Théâtre Royal de la Monnaie (Bruxelles – Belgique)

Introduction

Durant la saison 2009-2010, nous avons entamé un projet de description, restauration et conservation des maquettes de décor au Théâtre Royal de la Monnaie. Pour commencer, il nous a paru souhaitable de profiter de l'expérience en la matière de différentes maisons d'opéras, théâtres et autres institutions : un réseau de contacts que nous avons pu mettre à profit grâce à nos collègues de la SIBMAS (Société internationale des bibliothèques, et musées des arts du spectacle).

Dans le cadre de notre collecte d'informations, nous avons réalisé un questionnaire-type qui a été envoyé aux institutions suivantes : the Royal Opera House à Londres, the Royal Swedish Opera, la Comédie-Française, la Bibliothèque nationale de France – Cellule de restauration des documents graphiques et maquettes, le Centre canadien d'Architecture, le Victoria & Albert Museum – Theatre and Performance, le Theaterinstituut Nederland, le Grand-Théâtre de Genève, le Centre de Documentació i Museu de les Arts Escèniques, le Harry Ransom Center – University of Texas et la Columbia University Libraries – New York.

A. Les résultats de l'enquête

Les questions portaient sur les points suivants : la conservation des maquettes et des éléments, la construction des boîtes et les matériaux utilisés, les modalités en cas de transport de la maquette, l'éclairage, la solution « idéale » et enfin, les erreurs à éviter absolument. Pour une meilleure compréhension, nous avons demandé à nos interlocuteurs de joindre des visuels, dans la mesure du possible.

Le texte qui suit constitue donc une synthèse de l'enquête, présentée par institution, le compte rendu des précieuses informations que nous avons pu récolter. Nous livrons également un aperçu de notre visite à Paris au sein de la Cellule de restauration des documents graphiques et maquettes la Bibliothèque nationale de France et à la Comédie-Française. Enfin, nous décrivons la méthode adoptée à La Monnaie.

Theaterinstituut Nederland – Amsterdam

Pour la construction des boîtes, utilisation de différentes sortes de bois, du contreplaqué à l'aggloméré, et du plexiglas (polyméthacrylate de méthyle) pour les vitrines (plexiglas sur socle de bois). Une grande partie des maquettes sont conservées dans des coffres de présentation – également utilisés pour le transport. Dans ce cas, les maquettes sont protégées par du bois, du plexiglas et du papier de soie afin d'amortir les chocs éventuels. Concernant l'éclairage, parfois, réutilisation de l'éclairage d'origine (lampe à incandescence ou LED) ou, en cas de nouvel éclairage (pour une exposition), préférence pour une solution avec de la fibre optique. Jusqu'à récemment, la méthode expliquée ci-dessus était utilisée mais des répercussions négatives sur la longévité des maquettes (grandes différences entre les variétés de bois utilisés) et des risques de préjudice mécanique lors du transport ont été relevés (coffres trop lourds). En conséquence, un autre système est développé en collaboration avec des restaurateurs.

The Royal Opera House – London

One box for an entire production or one box for each act. Larger part of the models such as back drops or floors will be stored separately in « model room folders » (large folders containing technical drawings and some art work for the set). The model room keeps all the models disassembled in pieces and flat in large boxes and they are transferred to the archives in this state. Only a few models are assembled for exhibition purposes. The model room takes photographs of the assembled model sets as part of their work. They try out lighting effects and the positioning of props. They photograph objects that they loan out for exhibitions : front – ¾ view – a side and a side view.

The Royal Swedish Opera – Stockholm

Most of the models have been taken apart and are now stored in acid-free paper and carboard or wooden boxes specifically made for the model by the set department.

**Figure 1. Exemples de conservation des maquettes au
Royal Swedish Opera.**

Centre de Documentació i Museu de les Arts Escèniques – Barcelona

Les maquettes sont, à 90 %, des aquarelles sur papier marouflé sur du contreplaqué. Les différents rideaux sont fixés à la base. Le tout est conservé dans des boîtes sur mesure ARCHIVART en carton PH neutre. Ces dernières comportent une ouverture et une poignée (ruban de coton blanc) sur un des côtés latéraux comportant une pochette (APLI, auto-adhésive 55 x 102 mm), dans laquelle est insérée une fiche avec photo et titre. Les maquettes sont rangées dans une zone qui leur est propre sur des étagères. (Mesures moyennes de maquettes : 1 m de largeur x 0,6 m de profondeur). Les boîtes de transport sont en bois sur mesure, plus robustes et sécurisées avec des protections intérieures en matériaux de conservation.

Figure 2. Exemples de boîtes de conservation réalisées sur mesure au Centre de Documentació i Museu de les Arts Escéniques.

Figure 3. Les maquettes rangées sur des étagères dans une zone spécifique.

Le Centre canadien d'Architecture – Montréal

Construction de boîtes sur mesure pour les très grandes maquettes et parfois pour celles de plus petites dimensions. Cependant, le plus souvent, pour ces dernières, réaménagement des boîtes préfabriquées en ajoutant de la mousse, boîtes préfabriquées en ajoutant de la mousse, des diviseurs ou compartiments en carton ou autre matériau. Ils sont sans acide sauf pour les maquettes qui sont construites totalement en carton acide. Quelques très grandes maquettes en bois sont entreposées directement dans leur caisse de transport également en bois. Les boîtes de conservation sont placées à l'intérieur des caisses en bois pour le transport. Le type d'éclairage dépend de l'exposition : lampe à incandescence à filaments de tungstène, LED ou lumière fluorescente filtrée contre les UV. Le taux de lumière visible dépend des matériaux de construction des maquettes. S'ils sont très sensibles à la lumière, alors le taux de luminosité est limité à 50 lux. Pour éviter les « coups de chaleur », construction de vitrines où la lumière paraît venir de l'intérieur alors qu'elle est située dans un compartiment latéral ventilé.

The Victoria & Albert Museum – Theatre and Performance – London

A designed box based on two pieces of Correx crossed at right angles. Four or five rivets were used to join the 2 box-pieces and so created a strong base from which the rest of the box rose. All corners of the board were rounded. The sheets were cut to create small flaps on the sides ; they provided a more efficient closure and helped maintain the box's shape. However, instead of being tucked within the box, they were left on the outside preventing possible abrasion against the models contained within, and for general ease during closure. The boxes were not designed to be stacked. Long strips of polyester webbing with Velcro® (strong and allows quick and easy fastening and refastening) sewn onto their ends should be laced through the walls of the box to wrap around and close it. A Melinex sleeve was riveted onto the front flap to allow for an A4 size sheet bearing the object's photograph and relevant information. It was hoped this would reduce unnecessary opening of the box. As with every design, improvements could be made : the webbing around the box would be used inappropriately as a handle resulting in the Velcro separating, the box provides good closure, but is not totally sealed. It's beneficial in terms of preventing an enclosed environment, but it does mean that the object is not completely protected against pest attack, pervasive dust or fluctuating relative humidity.

Le Grand-Théâtre de Genève – Genève

Les maquettes ont été restaurées, reconstituées puis démontées pour être conditionnées dans des cartons où toutes les pièces sont regroupées ensemble.

Harry Ransom Center, University of Texas – Austin

The boxes are usually 60 pt acid-free lignin-free paperboard. Lately tried to phase out the use of PVA and use methyl cellulose or starch paste (problematic with larger boxes). There is use of string ties, rivets and

TOP PIECE OF BOX

TOP	SIDE	BOTTOM	SIDE	TOP
½ MODEL LENGTH	MODEL HEIGHT	MODEL LENGTH	MODEL HEIGHT	½ MODEL LENGTH

(MODEL WIDTH — vertical label on Bottom panel)

LENGTH OF TOP PIECE = 2 x MODEL LENGTH + 2 x MODEL HEIGHT + 4 x CREASE
= 2 MODEL LENGTH + 2 MODEL HEIGHT + 4(10 mm)
= 2 MODEL LENGTH + 2 MODEL HEIGHT + 40 mm

WIDTH OF TOP PIECE = MODEL WIDTH

CUT FOR WEBBING	∿
CREASE	--------
RIVET HOLE	o

BASE PIECE OF BOX

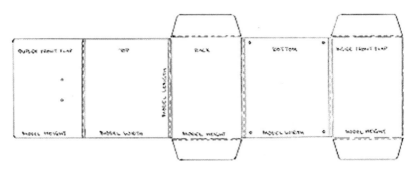

OUTSIDE FRONT FLAP	TOP	BACK	BOTTOM	INSIDE FRONT FLAP
MODEL HEIGHT	MODEL WIDTH	MODEL HEIGHT	MODEL WIDTH	MODEL HEIGHT

(MODEL LENGTH — vertical label on Back panel)

LENGTH OF BASE PIECE = 3 x MODEL HEIGHT + 2 x MODEL WIDTH + 4 x CREASES + 5 x BOARD THICKNESS
= 3 MODEL HEIGHT + 2 MODEL WIDTH + 4(10mm) + 5(5mm)
= 3 MODEL HEIGHT + 2 MODEL WIDTH + 65 mm

WIDTH OF BASE PIECE = MODEL LENGTH

SIDE FLAP OF BASE PIECE = ¼ MODEL WIDTH + 1 x CREASE + 1 x BOARD THICKNESS
= ¼ MODEL WIDTH + 1(10mm) + 1(5mm)
= ¼ MODEL WIDTH + 15 mm

BOARD THICKNESS	
CREASE	--------
RIVET HOLE	o

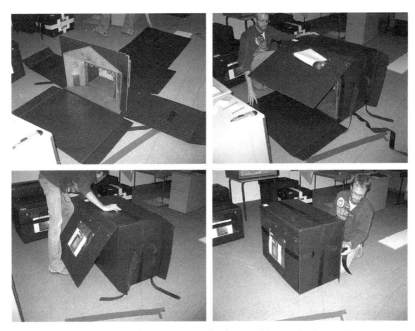

**Figure 4. Les boîtes sont constituées au départ de deux pièces
de CORREX, cf. plans ci-dessus.**

polypropylene plastic washers for closing systems (also as in standard
phase boxes). Also use of blue acid-free corrugated board for boxes,
but worry that insects can infest the corrugations. One model was
simply covered with polyethylene sheeting (keeps the dust off) and
one with a fine lightweight polyester lining fabric (good temporary fix).
Most of the boxes have photographic images of the set model affixed
to the outside of the box. Several models arrived in their own wooden
crate and remain in these. Paperboard boxes are made sturdy enough
for transportation within the building. For transport offsite: sturdy
wooden or other hard-wall container with ethafoam constructions
inside to keep the model in place. Loose pieces would be wrapped
individually. About lighting: The great majority of gallery lamps are
90 watt, 130 volts, PAR 38, floods. Some spots are used, all are ceiling
mounted on tracks. A few of their larger exhibit cases have internal
lighting. The storage area is lit with T8 fluorescent lamps covered with
UV filtering sleeves.

Figure 5. Pour *Scare Box* (James Newton, 1986), les parois latérales sont devenues amovibles afin de pouvoir faire glisser la maquette délicatement.

Figure 6. Pour *Iphigenia in Aulis* (Norman Bel Geddes, 1935) un panneau supérieur et un autre, frontal et mobile ont été fabriqués.

The Columbia University Libraries – New York

Cleaned and repaired pieces are stored into acid-free boxes with trays which are held in place by soft pieces of plastic cut to fit.

B. Visites à Paris

Visites à La Comédie-Française (Agathe Sanjuan, conservateur-archiviste et Hernan Penuela, responsable du Bureau d'études) et à la

Bibliothèque nationale de France, Cellule de restauration des documents graphiques et maquettes (Lucile Dessennes, restauratrice).

La Comédie-Française

Au théâtre, chaque maquette reçoit une boîte de conservation réalisée par le bureau d'études ou les ateliers. Il y a environ cinq maquettes par saison. La boîte est en triplex, peinte en noir à l'intérieur et à l'extérieur, avec une ouverture totale du devant et une ouverture aux 2/3 du dessus en polycarbonate 3 mm anti-feu. Le tout est isolé avec du tape 3 м de 5 cm de largeur. Le cadre de scène est également reproduit pour chaque maquette, par souci d'homogénéité.

Figure 7. L'éclairage des maquettes est de type zénithal d'où l'utilité de l'ouverture supérieure.

Figure 8. Le ruban adhésif noir isole la maquette.

 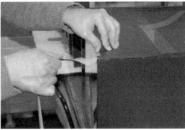

Figure 9. Les boîtes en triplex peint et les panneaux frontal et supérieur en polycarbonate anti-feu.

Chaque maquette se voit figée sur l'acte le plus représentatif préalablement choisi. Les éléments sont collés par une colle néoprène et les éléments inutilisés sont rangés dans une boîte d'archivage fournie par les Archives. Chaque boîte peut contenir les éléments de plusieurs maquettes.

Figure 10. Les éléments non utilisés sont conservés à part.

Les boîtes de conservation sont empilées sur des supports à roulettes ou placées sur des étagères dans les locaux du bureau d'études. Chaque boîte reçoit un numéro d'identification.

Figure 11. Les maquettes présentées sur des étagères ou empilées sur des supports à roulettes.

L'éclairage des maquettes est de type zénithal, d'où la nécessité de l'ouverture en polycarbonate. Il est mis en place uniquement lors de l'exposition des maquettes dans la boutique de La Comédie-Française. C'est l'une de maquettes des productions de la saison qui est choisie en fonction de l'alternance des représentations.

Lorsqu'il est nécessaire de transporter une maquette, on se sert d'une boîte en bois dans laquelle est placée la boîte de conservation. Le tout est protégé avec du papier bulle, de la mousse ou autre afin d'éviter les chocs. Des autocollants UP et FRAGILE sont placés sur la boîte de transport. Un formulaire de demande de prêt et une feuille de recommandation pour le transport existent afin d'assurer le bon déroulement des opérations.

La Bibliothèque nationale de France

À la BNF, au sein de la cellule de restauration des documents graphiques et maquettes, il existe des boîtes d'exposition et des boîtes de conditionnement/transport. Ces boîtes sont réalisées par l'atelier de conditionnement.

Les boîtes d'exposition sont en carton neutre, peintes à l'extérieur à l'acrylique noire et à l'intérieur avec du vernis acrylique. Elles comportent une ouverture frontale en plexiglas ou en PETG (polyéthylène téréphtalate) pour une identification visuelle aisée.

Figure 12. Le sol de la maquette rigidifié et les compartiments sous le socle pour le rangement des éléments.

Les éléments de la maquette sont collés sur le sol, original ou non, avec un papier japonais intermédiaire et de la colle d'amidon. Le papier japonais permet un démontage aisé car il se dédouble par laminage dès que l'on tente de décoller les éléments du sol. Le sol est rigidifié par un carton non original, monté avec des bandes de papier japonais. Le socle est ainsi glissé dans la boîte. En dessous du socle se trouvent des compartiments dans lesquels peuvent être rangés les éléments inutilisés.

Lorsque l'une des dimensions de la maquette dépasse 70 cm, on passe à une boîte en bois multiplex (en contreplaqué) pour la boîte d'exposition. Les différents panneaux sont assemblés mécaniquement par des quarts, ou des charnières « pianos ». On procède comme pour les boîtes d'exposition en carton : l'extérieur est peint en noir et l'intérieur est recouvert de vernis acrylique.

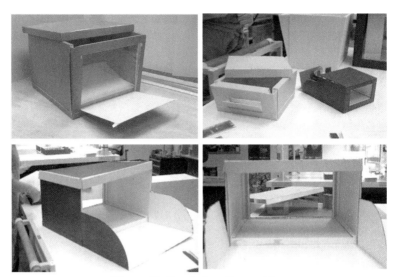

Figure 13. Les boîtes d'exposition.

Il existe également des boîtes de transport/conditionnement réalisées en carton neutre. Elles sont alors renforcées par du carton nid d'abeille ou du carton mousse neutre et présentent une fenêtre frontale refermable pour une identification et une surveillance aisées de la maquette.

Il faut éviter absolument d'asphyxier les maquettes avec des matériaux trop « étouffants » de type polypropylène, il faut les laisser respirer. C'est pour cela que le carton semble une réponse adaptée : renforcé par la mousse, il joue non seulement un rôle de « tampon » hygrométrique mais préserve aussi les maquettes des chocs auxquels elles sont très sensibles.

Résultat : une méthode adaptée au Théâtre Royal de la Monnaie

Trouver une solution pour les maquettes de décors dans un théâtre fut un exercice d'équilibrisme. À l'origine, une maquette n'est qu'un simple document de travail à l'échelle, un brouillon en 3D pour le décor lui-même où le scénographe traduit la vision que le metteur en scène a de la pièce. Ce que le département technique d'un théâtre regarde comme un outil de travail devient un objet rare dans le patrimoine de ce dernier.

En premier lieu, il a fallu résoudre la question de la responsabilité de chaque département mais également proposer des solutions budgétaires. À La Monnaie, il a été décidé que tous les frais de conservation des anciennes maquettes (44, datant de 1992 à 2010) relèveraient de la responsabilité du service des archives. Tous les frais pour les maquettes à venir, environ cinq par saison, incombent au budget du département technique.

La phase préliminaire exigeait de déterminer une échelle sur laquelle toutes les maquettes à venir devraient être construites. Le Bureau d'études a alors élaboré une « boîte de construction » en carton mousse à l'échelle 1/25. Cette dernière est envoyée au décorateur de chaque production et est devenue un outil obligatoire à utiliser lors de la présentation du projet de scénographie.

Figure 14. Le premier prototype de la boîte de construction.

Lorsque le décorateur vient présenter sa maquette au théâtre, on fait appel à un spécialiste en photographie muséale afin qu'il immortalise chaque changement de décor en une vue frontale.

Les archives en profitent pour faire une première description de la maquette et l'encode dans C.a.r.m.e.n., notre base de données.

Aussi longtemps que la production est en préparation, la maquette est conservée au bureau d'études. À partir du moment où le décor est construit sur scène, la maquette est envoyée dans une boîte de conservation au service des archives ou, dans le cadre d'une coproduction, à l'extérieur dans sa boîte de construction.

La boîte de conservation est une boîte sur mesure en triplex, basée sur le modèle de la Comédie-Française avec des solutions non asphyxiantes

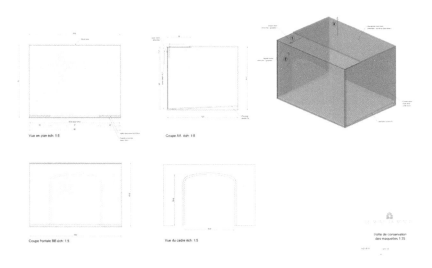

Figure 15. Plan du prototype de la boîte de conservation.

et réversibilité aux impératifs de conservation de la BNF. Les panneaux sont peints d'un même nombre de couches à l'extérieur et à l'intérieur, afin d'éviter les tensions entre les différents pans, avec une peinture acrylique noire (FRESCOLIGHT-LASCAUX). La boîte présente une ouverture frontale et une autre sur la moitié de la face supérieure en polycarbonate anti-feu d'une épaisseur de 3 mm.

Les boîtes de conservation sont réalisées en interne par les ateliers. Dans la boîte, la maquette est présentée figée sur un acte préalablement choisi en fonction de sa pertinence esthétique ou historique. Les éléments sont fixés avec une colle réversible (LINECO).

Les autres éléments sont conservés, emballés tout d'abord individuellement, puis regroupés par acte, dans du papier de soie non acide, et placés dans une boîte standard en carton PH neutre, pourvue de compartiments.

Toutes les maquettes reçoivent alors une description définitive, encodée dans la base de données C.a.r.m.e.n.

En cas de demande de prêt, la maquette sera expédiée dans une boîte de transport, dont un modèle a été commandé à la Bibliothèque nationale de France, cellule de restauration des documents graphiques et maquettes.

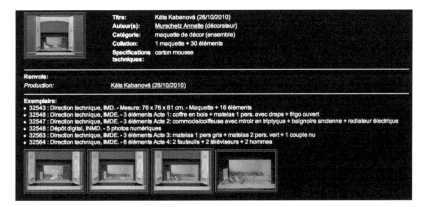

Figure 16. Exemple de présentation dans C.a.r.m.e.n.

Abstract

A theatre's set model is, at its origin, a simple working document – a three-dimensional scale draft of the actual stage set where the designer translates the director's vision of the play.

What the theatre's technical department sees as something functional can also be looked at – once neatly displayed and backlit – as an object of beauty, sophistication and creativity… a work of art !

This paper presents a step-by-step approach to the preservation, display and cataloguing of set models. It will comment on discussions with stakeholders, the benefits of international enquiries and visits, and the actual method chosen by the Royal Opera House La Monnaie.

Hamlet. Europe. Transfer (H.E.T.)

Topic Outline and Organisational Structure of the Exhibition Project "Hamlet"

Winrich Meiszies

Theatre Museum (Düsseldorf – Germany)

Topic Outline

Aims and Ideas

Theatre is created in the minds of the spectators. As an ephemeral art it fades quickly from the memory and is therefore in need of special protection as a form of our cultural heritage. Centres for theatre documentation and research preserve the artistic heritage of a playhouse, keep alive its artistic highlights and thus have a share in creating national identities.

Such efforts for the community are to be shown in a project dealing with the topic of "Hamlet" and the historical and national implications of the drama. The aim is to draw up a project of documentation and information consisting of a touring exhibition, preparatory research programmes and theatre performances.

The "Hamlet" exhibition will collect objects and information representatives of a common identity of culturally active nations, and aims at demonstrating and comparing differences as well. Accordingly, it is an excellent means to further mutual understanding.

An approach through comparison supports co-operation between archives, museums, research departments and performing artists, and in that way underlines their extraordinary share in the cultural life of the individual community.

The procedure promotes an exchange of experts, and it helps to set up standards for methods and techniques of presentation and communication.

Museums and collections concerned with the performing arts will be obliged to review and categorise their relevant holdings, and so permanently secure part of their stock.

The exhibition with its accompanying programmes forms the more tangible part of a comprehensive inter-cultural dialogue.

Planning and shaping the exhibition will form a considerable part of the project and keep up a dialogue between experts and institutions, and will eventually help to set up common professional standards.

Theatre museums, collections and document centres, as well as departments of literature, language, and decorative arts, will join in a network with the aim of enquiring into, documenting and spreading information on the reception-history of Shakespeare's "Hamlet" in their respective countries, from the moment the play was first taken notice of, up to its later performing history and public echo.

Participating countries should be Germany, Denmark, United Kingdom, Poland, Italy, France, and Spain.

Significance

No other play or character is identified with the theatre as clearly as Shakespeare's "Hamlet". Its stage history reflects national theatrical and cultural traditions as well as world history. Almost everybody knows the famous line, and is able to picture Hamlet holding Yorick's skull. With the creation of Hamlet, Shakespeare gave expression to the problem of the individual confronted with the world outside.

"Hamlet" is one of the dramatic characters all great actors in the world dream of. The history of the Prince of Denmark is part of the permanent repertoire of world theatre. New adaptations and film versions testify to the unbroken power of Shakespeare's drama.

There is evidence of an "Ur-Hamlet" as far back as 1589. Shakespeare wrote his tragedy about 1600. But it is doubtful to which sources Shakespeare owed his "Hamlet". It may be assured that the work was inspired by various predecessors. First performances are recorded for London in 1602 and for Oxford and Cambridge in 1603.

Many actors aspire to play the part of Hamlet as the crowning achievement of their career. Also a number of eminent actresses felt drawn to the part, among them the French actress Sarah Bernhardt, as well as Asta Nielson, the Danish film star of the silent era, and quite recently, Frances de la Tour in a British production and Angelika Winkler in a German production.

If the significance of the "Hamlet" substance is to be understood it is most important to study and show clearly what a hold it has over our everyday language and images.

Activities

Conferences

Meetings will be held at regular intervals when specimen contributions will be presented to show the stage that the activities have so far reached, and to outline the eventual scope of the project. A planning committee of active partners will regulate organizational steps and work out a schedule for further activities.

Decisions on methods of documentation, educational programmes, architecture and technical aspects of the exhibition, as well as funding and advertising, will have to be taken in common agreement by all groups concerned.

Website

Material results will first be made available to all participants on a website. A special Internet platform will be run by young university graduates as a project of "Kulturwirtschaft" (cultural economics). It will inform participants of the state of the exhibition project as well as advertise it to an interested public.

Documentation

Decisions must be taken concerning the nature of the exhibits – as to how they should be presented, registered, explored, secured – and how the material might be enriched by further data and information on the subject of "Hamlet". Preparatory talks will enliven routine work at the participating institutions, and further an exchange of opinions beyond the project under discussion.

Networks

Theatre museums and collections in charge of the relevant material will join in a network. By an exchange of expert knowledge and experiences they will work together to open up ways for comparative studies of theatrical, cultural, and linguistic developments. University scholars will be approached for papers on the special fields of the theatre, literature and language. University students and young scholars will be offered a considerable share in these research projects.

Results of the respective individual, national, and bi- or multi-national partnership projects (each of them supported by various sponsors) will be included in the general project. Exchange visits of scholars, document experts, designers and translators to their fellow institutes in other countries will strengthen co-operation.

Public Relations

The exhibition envisaged will give a survey of the performing traditions and reception-histories of Shakespeare's "Hamlet" in the European countries from the beginning.

The show marks the provisional end to the "Hamlet Transfer" project.

During the preparatory stages of the exhibition project, seminars and workshops focussing on particular aspects will sustain the interest of professional scholars as well as attract an interested public.

The above-mentioned exchange of participants will not only promote co-operation but also provide the opportunity for a continual flow of information on various professional and geographical levels.

European Gains

The exhibition lays bare the more tangible roots of this European myth. Drawing from their own resources, theatre museums and collections from all over Europe unite in documenting and reshaping the part of "Hamlet" as an outstanding stage character, a figure with which a large number of the educated middle-class public readily identifies.

Any social and cultural specifics of the countries involved are reflected in their reception of the play. Once established the exhibition will be touring the principal cities of the countries participating or interested, and in that way may help to create a common identity.

Visitors to the touring exhibition will not only learn more about staging traditions in their own country but will also broaden their minds by comparing them with different traditions in other countries. The project will be accompanied by an international programme of theatre performances, as well as seminars and workshops for scholars, theatre experts and enthusiasts, offering sufficient opportunity for exchange and comparison as a further means of creating a common national and international consciousness.

Lasting Effects

Once established, the guiding principles of research, documentation, and educational offers may become the basis of permanent co-operation and communication between the institutes concerned. The principles can be adapted to further projects, and are open to other participants.

Organisation and Structure of the Project

General Management of the Exhibition Project

The entire project will be managed by the *Theatre Museum of Düsseldorf*, which will (for the time being) also be responsible for the German part of the enterprise.

The Theatre Museum of Düsseldorf will also take charge of the application for EU financial support (cultural funds).

In co-ordinating the project the Theatre Museum of Düsseldorf will be assisted by the Instytut Teatralny of Warsaw.

Organising Committee

The organising committee co-ordinates all activities between the countries participating. It is recruited from representatives of the local institutions responsible for the arrangement of the exhibition in their own country. They speak for all groups and individual contributors in their country, and co-ordinate national activities.

Arrangement and Integration of National Results within the Scope of the Entire Enterprise

Each country will name one organising institution to present the results of local research and studies to their fellow participants in Europe, and will constantly keep in touch with the institution in charge of the entire project. It will also take charge of co-funding the enterprise as far as their own country is concerned.

Early theatrical history, varieties of stagecraft, and ways of public response will be regarded differently from one European country to the next. Consequently it becomes absolutely necessary to work out the social and political implications of the presentation. This is the point where the European dimension of the comparative approach becomes most evident.

Organisation and Structure of Activities in the Course of the Preparatory Stages of the Exhibition

Until now a communication network covering institutions of research and documentation has not yet been established on a European level. It requires interdisciplinary contacts and co-operation between institutions which operate on different organizational lines. Students and young scholars, document experts and others will work together with experienced practicians in preparing and running the exhibition.

With planning and realization of all these measures, the goal is a project where co-operation will function Europe-wide.

During the preparatory stages of the exhibition, activities will take the form of separate units corresponding with each other and with the general concept of the exhibition.

These units can be initiated and realised by any partner in the project, but they will have to be submitted to, discussed by, and finally accepted by the organising committee. The outcome of activities in the individual sections will form a part of the final presentation of project results in the exhibition and/or will find its place in the accompanying media.

These units will be considered as separate projects as far as funding is concerned, and contributors will have to present their own conception and financial planning, both of which will have to be approved by the organising committee. Co-operation between the individual partners of the entire project will be regulated on the basis of a partnership contract for the whole.

Individual units can be devised by students, young scholars, theatre experts, and actors. Work at the units can for a limited period also be taken on by outside organisations and institutions that may be able to assist the project by expert knowledge in their special fields.

Work at several units in the course of the preparatory period and later on the exhibition itself will provide opportunity for inter-cultural dialogue between members of the different European countries.

This prospect for dialogue is particularly strong in units that will be presented in the accompanying programmes at different places.

Internet Platform

Presentation of the project on the Internet serves a triple purpose: it is a means of communication between the participants, it advertises current activities, and it lends weight to the exhibition. The Internet entry will be edited in Germany, with all participants providing their contributions. Essential parts will be rendered in the language of the country currently showing the exhibition.

Necessary Contractual Agreements

In each participating country the institutions in charge sign as official partners in the project. At the outset of the common enterprise they will found a Commission chaired by the Theatre Museum of Düsseldorf. Terms of co-operation within the exhibition project will have to be settled by legal contracts.

This procedure has the advantage that agreements will be the same and binding for all during the entire run of the project, including the touring period of the exhibition.

EU funds can only be applied for if all contracts have been legally bound.

Abstract

Le fait de suivre Hamlet à travers l'Europe nous a ramenés aux racines du théâtre des différentes nations. Des comédiens anglais arrivent sur le continent au XVIe siècle par les Pays-Bas, traversent l'Allemagne et l'Autriche, bifurquent vers le Danemark et la Pologne et laissent des traces de leur passage dans les cultures nationales.

La préparation d'une exposition sur le thème de Hamlet offrirait aux bibliothèques, collections et musées des arts de spectacle une occasion de collaboration durable. La coopération entre archives, musées, départements de recherche et artistes implique un rapprochement. Simultanément, cette coopération souligne l'importance du théâtre dans chacune des communautés.

Le processus de préparation de l'exposition favorise l'échange d'experts et permet de trouver un consensus sur les méthodes et techniques de présentation et de communication.

Musées et collections de théâtre peuvent en outre profiter de cette expérience pour uniformiser et catégoriser les éléments les plus pertinents de leurs fonds et les répertorier en amont du projet.

L'exposition et ses mesures d'accompagnement constituent donc la partie matérielle d'un dialogue interculturel intense.

World Scenography Book Project

Peter McKɪɴɴoɴ

York University (Canada)

World Scenography[1] is a new book series that will document and contextualise significant contemporary theatrical design worldwide since 1975. There has been no comprehensive documentation of global scenography since the four-volume series *Stage Design throughout the World*, by Belgian professor René Hainaux, covered the period 1935-1975. This new three-volume series, to be published both in print and online, will cover the periods of 1975-1990, 1990-2005, and 2005-2015 respectively. The first volume will be published at the usɪᴛᴛ Conference in Long Beach, California in March 2012; Volume Two at the World Stage Design 2013; and Volume Three at the Prague Quadrennial 2015. It is anticipated that following the publication of these three volumes, oɪsᴛᴀᴛ will continue to publish another volume every ten years. The book series is an official project of oɪsᴛᴀᴛ, the International Organization of Scenographers, Theatre Architects and Technicians. The international editorial team for *World Scenography* will be led by co-editors Peter McKinnon (Canada) and Eric Fielding (usᴀ).

Like all performance-based art, stage design (whether scenery, costumes, lighting or sound) is ephemeral. If it is not recorded, it disappears. The scenery will go to the landfill or elements of it will be broken down for reuse. The costumes will usually go to storage. The light and sound will never have had a tangible existence. And if the designs are not contextualised through scholarship, their meanings will become obscure. A stage design's meaning can be understood better through increased understanding of the culture or society, time, and place in which the design was conceived and presented. The aim of the writing accompanying the images in the books is to focus on placing the stage art in the context of time and place, vis-à-vis the political, social, economic and artistic events and movements of the time.

---

[1]   See <http://www.yorku.ca/wrldscen/project.html> (consulted in February 2013).

These three books fill a significant gap in the study of international stage design and provide a foundation for future documentation of scenography. As noted above, this kind of research, on a worldwide basis, has not been undertaken and published in any form since 1975. While some works have been published on stage design and designers during the past thirty-odd years, it was not until 2005, when the catalogue documenting the World Stage Design exhibition in that year was published, that an international record of contemporary scenography was undertaken. The stage designs contained in that publication were not juried. The catalogue contained no scholarly text, and is out of print. The publication of the *World Scenography* will mark the resumption of publishing a scholarly record of contemporary stage design.

Since 1975, there have been no means to study and compare contemporary scenography on a worldwide scale, other than by attending the Prague Quadrennial Exhibition of Scenography. Even if one has the opportunity to attend the PQ, the ability to make international comparisons has limits: the first is that the PQ tends to encompass only the four years leading up to it; and the national exhibits each tend to have a different focus, so cross-national comparisons are often difficult to make. *World Scenography* is a survey of significant stage design work around the world and across time since 1975. And, most importantly, such a survey needs thorough contextualisation. The research thus aims to be thorough, if not exhaustive. An encyclopaedia of contemporary stage design is a dream that unfortunately would be too monumental (even if enticing for the editors), given the reality of available time and resources. The editors aim to facilitate the comparative assessments of stage designs from a plurality of perspectives, rather than provide definitive statements of either specific designs, periods of designs, or social contexts for these designs.

The reason for such a large part of the books being photographic is that the editors believe very strongly that the reader needs to be able to see the images with clarity and detail, which requires that the photographs be large format. The contextualizing text and photographic evidence have been organized straight through the books chronologically, with no political or national divisions. In the modern age, it is relatively commonplace for audience members and designers to travel widely and quickly, so it is not unreasonable to have designs in theatres that are continents apart be on adjacent pages of the books. Individual designers, shows, playwrights, composers, choreographers, directors and producing companies are cross-referenced in the index.

The choice of art to be included has been based on a matrix of cultural importance, quality, impact (seen both contemporaneously and historically) and/or importance in the development of either the individual artist or the society/culture/organisation in which it was created. For example, Michael Levine's designs of the Canadian Opera Company's production of *Erwartung* and *Blue Beard's Castle* were seminal in both Mr Levine's artistic development, and in the Canadian Opera Company's repositioning of its audience demographic in Toronto, and its artistic repositioning in the opera world at the Edinburgh International Festival. Each editor has amassed a long list for possible inclusion, from which the editorial board made selections. We have sought designs that have proven to be influential in the world of stage design and production; designs that made a difference. We are much less interested in exemplary and typical designs, notwithstanding their inherent value.

We also have chosen to have a mix of renderings, sketches and photographs of models, in addition to production shots. It is our contention that the original artwork of the designer is just as informative as the finished product on the stage; frequently, the sketches, renderings and models are actually more informative. These original artworks are also more available in colour than many production photographs from the period covered in Volume I.

Abstract

World Scenography est une nouvelle collection qui se propose de documenter et de remettre en contexte l'essentiel de la scénographie théâtrale contemporaine dans le monde, à partir de 1975. Depuis la série de quatre volumes réalisés par le professeur René Hainaux, *Stage Design throughout the World/Le Décor de théâtre dans le monde*, qui couvrait la période 1935-1975, il n'y a pas eu de documentation complète de la scénographie dans son ensemble.

La nouvelle série de trois volumes sera imprimée et publiée en ligne et elle couvrira respectivement les périodes de 1975 à 1990, de 1990 à 2005 et de 2005 à 2015.

Le premier volume sera publié par l'USITT Conference à Long Beach, Californie en mars 2012, le deuxième en 2013 pour la World Stage Design et le troisième à l'occasion de la Quadriennale de Prague en 2015.

Après les trois premiers tomes, l'OISTAT (Organisation internationale des scénographes, techniciens et architectes de théâtre) prévoit la publication d'un nouveau volume tous les dix ans.

Cette collection est un projet officiel de l'OISTAT.

L'équipe éditoriale internationale pour la *World Scenography* est dirigée par les coéditeurs Peter McKinnon (Canada) et Eric Fielding (États-Unis).

ANNEXES

Assemblée générale

Munich, 30 juillet 2010

Claire Hudson, présidente, donne lecture de l'ordre du jour envoyé aux membres, et propose une modification : l'inversion des points 6 (rapport des commissions) et 8 (élections), afin que le décompte des votes puisse se faire après le point 5 (rapport du secrétaire des membres).

Un membre de l'assemblée relève une erreur dans l'ordre du jour : l'assemblée se tient durant la xxviiie édition du congrès et non la xxixe tel que mentionné dans la convocation. La secrétaire générale présente ses excuses.

Les comptes-rendus de l'Assemblée générale de Glasgow sont acceptés.

Il est demandé d'ajouter la date au titre du procès-verbal. Le procès-verbal publié dans les actes du congrès de Glasgow est accepté à l'unanimité.

Rapport de la présidente (Claire Hudson)

Au cours des deux dernières années, nous avons poursuivi notre œuvre dans plusieurs domaines. L'excellent travail accompli par l'équipe de rédaction sous la direction de Nicole Leclercq a mené à une autre publication de qualité, celle des actes du congrès de Glasgow en 2008. Nous sommes d'ailleurs parvenus à recueillir des fonds suffisants pour couvrir tous les frais de publication de cet ouvrage. Je suis convaincue que vous êtes aussi satisfaits que moi du magnifique volume produit par Nicole, Jan Van Goethem, Kristy Davis, Mathias Auclair, Sylvie François et Helen Adair. J'en profite pour vous annoncer que l'organisateur du congrès, Alan Jones, a remporté un prix du conseil municipal de Glasgow pour sa contribution à la promotion de la ville à l'échelle internationale.

De mon côté, je publie toujours le *Bulletin de la présidente*, que j'ai lancé à mon entrée en poste en 2004 pour entretenir les liens avec nos membres et faire la promotion de nos activités. S'y est ajoutée récemment l'*Infolettre*, publiée par Désirée Neumann sous la direction de Jan Van Goethem à Bruxelles.

Nous travaillons par ailleurs au développement de notre site Internet. D'ici la fin de l'année, quand nous entamerons la première phase de remplacement du site, de grands changements devraient avoir eu lieu. Nous remercions vivement Jan, Guy et Sylvie pour cette entreprise.

Nos projets de réseautage avec d'autres organismes internationaux se poursuivent. Cette semaine, notre congrès nous a fourni d'excellentes occasions de rencontrer des membres de la FIRT. Je souhaite de tout cœur que les membres de la SIBMAS tirent profit des possibilités de partenariats avec le secteur académique.

Notre partenariat avec PERSPECTIV, l'Association des théâtres historiques d'Europe, donne lieu à une demande conjointe de financement à l'Union européenne, pour réaliser une exposition itinérante traitant de l'influence du théâtre sur le développement de la culture européenne. Nous soumettrons une version révisée de notre proposition en septembre et, si la demande est acceptée, les partenaires de la SIBMAS collaboreront avec PERSPECTIV pour préparer cette exposition qui se déroulera dans des institutions partenaires et pourra s'enrichir d'objets de provenance locale.

Nous savons par ailleurs que l'OISTAT mène l'ambitieux projet de poursuivre le travail de René Hainaux sur le décor de théâtre dans le monde[1]. Plusieurs de nos membres participent aux trois volumes dont le premier devrait paraître l'année prochaine, et qui couvrent la période de 1976 à nos jours.

Au congrès, nous avons eu le plaisir de faire la connaissance de Kenneth Schlesinger, président de la TLA (Theatre Library Association), qui collabore maintenant étroitement avec nous, particulièrement dans le cadre des négociations autour de l'organisation du congrès conjoint de la TLA et de la SIBMAS à Austin en 2012.

Au cours des deux dernières années – et j'ajouterais : des six années de ma présidence –, de nombreux membres ont grandement œuvré à faire avancer notre organisme. L'un d'entre eux a joué un rôle capital dans l'amélioration de l'administration et de la santé financière de la SIBMAS. Grâce à lui, nous avons pu planifier nos activités de manière stratégique et investir dans des initiatives nécessaires. Le prochain comité exécutif bénéficiera d'une très bonne situation financière qui lui permettra de mettre en œuvre les projets que nous avons mis au point. Bien entendu, il s'agit de nul autre que Jan Van Goethem, qui quitte le poste de trésorier et de secrétaire des associés qu'il occupe depuis huit ans. Il nous manquera beaucoup lors des réunions du comité et, au nom de tous, je tenais à écrire ces quelques mots à son sujet, pour attester de ses réalisations et manifester notre reconnaissance à son égard.

---

[1] René Hainaux (ed.), *Le décor de théâtre dans le monde depuis 1935*, Bruxelles, Elsevier, 1956 ; René Hainaux (ed.), *Le décor de théâtre dans le monde depuis 1950*, Bruxelles, Meddens, 1964 ; René Hainaux (ed.), *Le décor de théâtre dans le monde depuis 1960*, Bruxelles, Meddens, 1973 ; René Hainaux, avec la collaboration de Nicole Leclercq, *Spectacles 70-75 dans le monde : Nouvelles mises en scène, nouveaux décors, nouveaux auteurs...*, Bruxelles, Meddens, 1975.

Enfin, j'aimerais remercier Claudia Blank et l'équipe du Musée du théâtre de Munich pour tous les efforts et le soin mis à organiser cette agréable semaine de communications et d'événements. Grâce à elles, nous avons pu bénéficier d'une ambiance parfaite pour le réseautage et l'échange. Au nom de tous, merci. Nous témoignons notre reconnaissance à Claudia non seulement pour la mise au point du programme de la semaine, mais pour le travail remarquable réalisé au sein de la SIBMAS, tant à titre de membre du comité exécutif que de présidente. Je crois que ses états de service, qui s'étendent sur plus de quatorze ans, ne connaissent pas d'équivalent dans notre organisme.

En guise de conclusion, j'aimerais ajouter que mes six années de présidence ont été très plaisantes et sources de nombreux défis. Je suis heureuse d'avoir occupé un poste qui m'a permis de rencontrer nos membres et de bénéficier de leur expérience. Je souhaite beaucoup de succès au nouveau président et longue vie à la SIBMAS !

Rapport de la secrétaire générale (Sylvie François)

Sylvie François remercie brièvement les membres du Conseil pour leur collaboration au cours de son premier mandat, et se réjouit de débuter un deuxième mandat, maintenant en pleine connaissance des tâches liées à sa fonction.

Rapport du trésorier (Jan Van Goethem)

Le trésorier communique un résumé de l'état du budget durant son mandat (2004-2010). Après quelques difficultés concernant les revenus (principalement issus des cotisations des membres) les entrées se sont stabilisées et d'autres sources de revenus (principalement la levée de fonds associée aux actes des congrès) se sont ajoutées. La SIBMAS se trouve à la tête de la somme totale de 17 000 euros, disponibles pour de nouveaux projets.

Rapport du secrétaire des membres (Jan Van Goethem)

Le secrétaire des membres fait le point sur le travail entrepris durant les dernières six années afin de mettre à jour la base de données (et notamment, de supprimer les membres individuels et institutionnels restés inactifs). Une lettre-type a été rédigée et envoyée à tous les membres n'ayant pas acquitté leurs cotisations afin de s'assurer de leur désir de garder un lien actif avec la SIBMAS. En 2004, l'institution comptait 157 membres inscrits ; en 2010, il y en a au total 180 dont 10 membres honoraires. Ces membres sont géographiquement répartis comme suit : 85 % en Europe, 9 % en Amérique, 3 % en Océanie, 3 % en Asie.

Élection des membres du Comité exécutif et du Conseil

Ulrike Dembski et Helena Hantakova, qui ne sont pas candidates, sont nommées responsable des élections. Un total de 23 bulletins de vote pour les institutions et de 10 bulletins de vote pour les individus sont valides et ont été dépouillés. Des absentions ont été notées :

– deux pour les postes au Conseil et une pour un poste au Comité exécutif, dans les bulletins de vote des individus,

– sept pour les postes au Conseil et une pour le poste de président, dans les bulletins de vote des institutions.

Ont été élus à l'unanimité :

Président : Winrich Meiszies (D)

Première vice-présidente : Helen Adair (USA)

Deuxième vice-présidente : Nicole Leclercq (B)

Secrétaire générale : Sylvie François (CAN)

Trésorière : Véronique Meunier (F)

Membres du Comité exécutif : Mathias Auclair (F), Guy Baxter (UK), Susan Cole (USA), Kristy Davis (UK)

Membres du Conseil : Janine Barrand (AUS), Nena Couch (USA), Tatiana Egorova (RUS), Knud Arne Jürgensen (DK), Christina Mühlegger-Henhapel (AT), Ramona Riedzwenski (UK), Anne Zendali (CH).

Rapports des commissions

Commission des expositions (Claudia Blank)

La réunion de la commission des expositions a été entièrement consacrée aux deux projets d'expositions internationales dans lesquels sont impliqués plusieurs membres de la SIBMAS de divers pays : « Hamlet » et « Les théâtres historiques d'Europe ».

Si, en session plénière, Winrich Meiszies a rendu compte du projet « Hamlet » dans sa globalité[2], il a donné à la commission un compte rendu des problèmes et réussites spécifiques liés à son travail.

En voici un bref aperçu : suivre la trace d'Hamlet à travers l'Europe nous mène aux racines du théâtre des différentes nations. Les acteurs anglais ont accosté sur le continent au XVIe siècle via les Pays-Bas, ont sillonné l'Allemagne et l'Autriche, se sont dirigés vers le Danemark et la Pologne et ont laissé leurs traces dans ces cultures nationales.

Cette exposition commune autour d'Hamlet donnera aux bibliothèques, musées et collections d'arts du spectacle la possibilité d'élaborer une

---

[2] *Cf.* p. 349-355.

coopération durable. Une approche comparative dans le travail favorise la collaboration entre les archives, les musées, les départements de recherches et les artistes de spectacles vivants. En ce sens, elle met en exergue leur extraordinaire contribution à la vie culturelle de chaque communauté.

La procédure encourage les échanges d'experts et aide à établir des normes pour les méthodes et les techniques de présentation et de communication.

Les collections et musées consacrés aux arts du spectacle seront tenus d'examiner et de classifier leurs pièces pertinentes et, en conséquence, de sécuriser définitivement certaines de leurs collections.

L'exposition et ses programmes d'accompagnement formeront la partie la plus tangible d'un dialogue de compréhension interculturelle.

La planification et la mise en forme de l'exposition constitueront une part considérable du projet et maintiendront le dialogue entre les experts et les institutions.

Carsten Jung, de PERSPECTIV, a ensuite rendu compte du projet « Historische Theater erzählen die Geschichte Europas ».

Sept musées de théâtre de sept pays collaborent à la création commune d'une nouvelle exposition itinérante sous le titre provisoire de « L'Histoire de l'Europe racontée par ses théâtres ».

Ces sept musées sont : Victoria & Albert Museum Performing Arts Collection (Royaume-Uni) ; Theatre Museum in the Court Theatre (Danemark) ; Theatre Museum at the Teatr Wielki (Pologne) ; German Theatre Museum (Allemagne) ; Austrian Theatre Museum (Autriche) ; Slovenian Theatre Museum (Slovénie) ; National Theatre Museum (Espagne). Le projet est organisé par PERSPECTIV – Association des théâtres historiques d'Europe.

La nouvelle exposition présentera le développement des bâtiments de théâtre des origines à nos jours, en expliquant comment certains d'entre eux sont devenus des modèles pour le théâtre partout en Europe. Elle mettra par ailleurs en évidence les différences et alternatives régionales et montrera comment des changements de société s'expriment, à chaque période, dans l'évolution de ces bâtiments.

Au cours d'une série de rencontres, les musées définiront les grandes lignes de l'exposition et dresseront une première liste parmi les pièces appartenant leurs collections. Par la suite, d'autres collections théâtrales européennes seront invitées à proposer des objets complémentaires. La même proposition sera faite aux théâtres historiques sur la route européenne du théâtre.

Une deuxième série de réunions débouchera sur un choix définitif et sur la présentation de l'exposition. Cette présentation sera flexible, pour s'adapter à chaque lieu ; sa dimension aussi sera flexible, constituée d'une exposition de base avec quelques objets originaux seulement, et d'une exposition complète avec de nombreux objets originaux. Ceci permettra à chacun des musées qui accueilleront l'exposition d'ajouter sa propre section pour mettre en lumière certains points importants d'intérêt national.

L'exposition sera tout d'abord présentée dans les musées partenaires. L'exposition initiale deviendra ensuite disponible pour tous les musées, théâtres et villes d'Europe qui souhaiteraient l'accueillir dans les années à venir.

Tout ceci constitue le plan initial. Tout ce dont le projet a besoin pour démarrer est le soutien financier de l'Union européenne. Une demande de subventions au Programme culturel de l'Union européenne est actuellement en préparation et nous espérons commencer le travail au printemps 2011[3].

En conclusion à la réunion de la commission, une discussion a porté sur l'analyse des différentes voies d'accès pour les deux responsables de projets : d'une part, en tant qu'étape initiale, une plus forte concentration sur le contenu (Hamlet) et, d'autre part, une approche organisationnelle comme point de départ. La SIBMAS forme des vœux pour la réussite des deux projets d'exposition. Il sera intéressant, lors de sa prochaine réunion, que la commission des expositions en apprenne davantage sur les avancées de ces deux projets.

Commission du site Internet (Guy Baxter)

Guy Baxter fait le point sur les changements apportés à l'administration du site internet depuis le congrès de 2008, notamment sur la création de l'infolettre et sur les discussions entourant la nouvelle structure de site proposée par le comité exécutif de la SIBMAS.

Jan Van Goethem présente le projet de modification du site internet aux membres de la commission qui émettent des commentaires et des suggestions pertinentes. On établit la marche à suivre pour accéder au site-pilote est établie et les participants sont invités à faire d'autres commentaires. Guy Baxter remercie Jan des efforts surhumains qu'il a déployés pour faire avancer le projet.

On discute ensuite des priorités concernant la présence en ligne de la SIBMAS : utilisation d'images interactives, ajout d'information sur le site pour expliquer comment et pourquoi s'abonner à l'infolettre, intégration

---

[3] Information complémentaire à l'occasion de la publication des actes du Congrès de la SIBMAS : l'Union européenne a décidé d'injecter des fonds pour la période 2012-2017. Le travail a débuté en septembre 2012 et l'exposition s'ouvrira à Varsovie, début 2015.

de la technologie RSS, et ajout d'en-têtes pour l'accès des membres institutionnels au site. On discute longuement de la possibilité d'offrir une section réservée aux membres. Le potentiel des applications Web 2.0 est évoqué.

Guy Baxter remercie les membres pour leurs nombreuses suggestions pertinentes, leur apport et leurs propositions d'aide. Il confirme qu'il s'informera auprès des présidents des autres comités de leurs besoins respectifs.

Commission de catalogage (Kristy Davis)

Participants : Kristy Davis (présidente), Susan Cole, Stephan Dörschel, Helena Hantakova, Véronique Meunier, Margaret Schild, Louise Stephens.

Kristy Davis, présidente de séance, remercie les membres présents. Elle donne un aperçu et fait une mise à jour des réunions précédentes qui se sont déroulées à Vienne (2006) et à Glasgow (2008). La création de la page Web de la commission sur le site de la SIBMAS concernant les moyens de catalogages internationaux, les normes de contrôle bibliographiques et l'ajout de descriptions brèves de chacun. Une discussion porte sur la poursuite des actions concernant la page Web. Il est décidé de laisser la page telle quelle pour le moment et de demander au webmaster d'ajouter dans une section de l'infolettre des « Nouvelles du Catalogage » dans lesquelles les membres de la commission pourraient soumettre des informations ou des liens internet portant sur les normes internationales. Les réponses seront reconsidérées et il sera ensuite décidé de la manière de procéder lors de la prochaine rencontre de la commission à Austin en 2012. Le nouveau site internet devrait être opérationnel à ce moment-là et certaines des idées émises pourraient y trouver leur place. Il est aussi proposé de demander au webmaster une mise en évidence des informations sur la commission telles que le catalogage et les références bibliographiques.

Les congrès SIBMAS 2012 et 2014

Helen Adair présente le thème du congrès de 2012 : « Repenser les collections pour aller à la rencontre des publics de proximité » (Engaging Communities, Reimagining Collections). Ce thème cherche à explorer les multiples relations des collections avec leurs donateurs, leurs utilisateurs et le public en général, en mettant à l'avant-plan et en racontant l'histoire des arts du spectacle. Helen Adair dresse le portrait de l'institution hôte, le Harry Ransom Centre à l'Université du Texas à Austin ainsi que de la vie culturelle de cette ville. Kenneth Schleslinger, président de la Theatre Library Association (TLA), est présenté à l'assemblée : le congrès de 2012 sera organisé conjointement avec cette association. Kenneth Schleslinger donne un aperçu de la TLA et de ses membres, qui sont principalement des étudiants, archivistes, chercheurs et conservateurs américains unis par la pratique des arts de la scène. 2012 sera une année anniversaire pour TLA, qui se réjouit de célébrer ses vingt ans en joignant ses intérêts à ceux de la SIBMAS. La TLA a publié plusieurs ouvrages sur la documentation des maquettes de costumes et prépare un autre volume sur la documentation des maquettes scénographiques. Le congrès se déroulera début ou mi-juin ; la date sera confirmée sous peu. Cela marquera la deuxième collaboration de la SIBMAS et de la TLA, la première ayant eu lieu en 1985.

Pour la tenue du congrès de 2014, deux institutions soumettent une proposition mais elles nécessitent une confirmation de la part de leurs directions. Claire Hudson rappelle qu'elle se tient à la disposition de toute institution susceptible d'accueillir le futur congrès pour répondre à toute question utile.

Questions diverses

Claire Hudson remercie Claudia Blank pour l'organisation de cette conférence ainsi que pour ses quatorze ans de présence active au sein de la SIBMAS. À l'occasion de son retrait du Comité exécutif, Claire Hudson lui offre au nom du conseil un cadeau. Claudia Blank remercie tous les participants au congrès et souligne à son équipe du Musée allemand du Théâtre sa profonde appréciation de leur implication qui a rendu possible la tenue de cet événement.

Claire Hudson invite le nouveau président à prononcer quelques mots. Winrich Meiszies déclare qu'il a été surpris et honoré qu'on lui demande de présenter sa candidature à la présidence. Il résume sa vision du travail à venir par deux questions adressées aux participants : « Êtes-vous fiers d'être membres de la SIBMAS et l'exprimez-vous ? Être membre de la SIBMAS modifie-t-il votre vie quotidienne ? »

Winrich Meiszies remercie Claire Hudson et Jan Van Goethem pour leur travail assidu et, pour marquer leur départ du conseil exécutif, leur offre un cadeau aussi éphémère que le théâtre…

La séance est levée à 10 h 25.

General Assembly

Munich, July 30th, 2010

Claire Hudson, President, reads the agenda sent to the members and makes some modifications to point 6 (Reports form Commissions) and 8 (Elections), so the voting can be done after point 5 (Membership Secretary Report), leaving enough time for the election committee to count the votes during the following points.

A note is made of an error on the Agenda: this General Assembly is held in the xxviiith issue of the Conference and not xxixth as written in the Agenda. Apologies are given by the General Secretary.

Acceptance of the minutes of the General Assembly in Glasgow 2008.

A note is made requesting to add the year following the titles of the Minutes. The minutes that have been published in the Proceeding of Glasgow are accepted with unanimity.

Report by the President (Claire Hudson)

The last two years have seen a continuation of our work in a number of areas. The excellent efforts made by the editorial team under the leadership of Nicole Leclercq has resulted in yet another successful publication – this time the proceedings from our 2008 conference in Glasgow. We were successful in raising sufficient sponsorship to cover all the costs of publishing these proceedings. I hope that you are as happy as I am with the handsome volume which Nicole, Jan Van Goethem, Kristy Davis, Mathias Auclair, Sylvie Francois and Helen Adair have produced. On the subject of the Glasgow Conference, I can report that the organiser, Alan Jones, won an award from the City Council for his contribution to the promotion of the Glasgow internationally.

My *President's Newsletter* which I began when I was elected in 2004 has continued, as a means of keeping in touch with our membership and promoting our activities. This has been recently joined by the *eNewsletter* which has been produced by Désirée Neumann and published under the direction of Jan Van Goethem in Brussels.

Work on developing our website has been going on behind the scenes, and you can expect some major changes before the end of this year, as a first phase of replacing the existing site is implemented. In this case, we have Jan, Guy and Sylvie to thank for driving this forward.

Our networking projects with other international organisations are continuing. This week's conference has provided some really valuable opportunities to meet members of IFTR and I hope very much that SIBMAS members can exploit the opportunities which exist for partnership projects with the academic sector.

Our partnership with PERSPECTIV, the association for historic theatres in Europe, is moving forwards through a joint funding application to the EU to create a touring exhibition about the relationship of theatre to the development of European culture. A revised proposal will be submitted in September, and if successful, SIBMAS partners will be working with Perspective to create an exhibition which will tour to partners' institutions and allow for the addition of locally sourced exhibits.

OISTAT too, as we've heard, is working on an ambitious project to continue the work of René Hainaux[1] on world stage design. Several of our members are contributing to the three volumes planned to be published from next year, covering the period from 1976 onwards.

At this conference we have been delighted to make the acquaintance of Kenneth Schlesinger, the Chair of TLA (Theatre Library Association) which has also become an important associate for us, especially through negotiations for the joint TLA/SIBMAS conference planned for Austin in 2012.

Throughout the last two years, many people have contributed greatly to the work of our organisation, and also over the six years of my presidency. One especially has had a major impact on improving the operation of SIBMAS and the financial health of our organisation. This has allowed us to plan more strategically and also to invest in initiatives where necessary. The next Executive Committee will inherit a very positive bank balance which will allow the plans we have been developing to be implemented. That person of course is Jan Van Goethem, who is standing down as Treasurer and Membership Secretary after eight years. He will be sorely missed from the committee table, and on behalf of us all I wanted to make this small presentation to him and put down on record in my report an acknowledgement of his achievements and of our gratitude.

Finally, I would like to extend my thanks to Claudia Blank and her team at the German Theatre Museum in Munich for their hard work and care in planning a really enjoyable and interesting week of papers and events.

---

[1]   René Hainaux (ed.), *Stage Design throughout the World*, Bruxelles, Elsevier, 1956; René Hainaux (ed.), *Stage Design throughout the World since 1950*, Bruxelles, Meddens, 1964; René Hainaux (ed.), *Stage Design throughout the World since 1960*, Bruxelles, Meddens, 1973; René Hainaux, avec la collaboration de Nicole Leclercq, *Spectacles 70-75 dans le monde: Nouvelles mises en scène, nouveaux décors, nouveaux auteurs...*, Bruxelles, Meddens, 1975.

They have provided an ambience which has encouraged good networking and the exchange of information and ideas. Thank you on behalf of us all. This token of our gratitude is not only for Claudia's efforts to create this week's programm, it is also in recognition of her outstanding work on behalf of SIBMAS, as a member of the ExCom and as President. I think her record of service to our organisation, extending over fourteen years, is probably unsurpassable.

And finally, I would like to add that my six years as president has been very enjoyable as well as challenging. I have really appreciated the opportunities which it has given me to meet members and learn from their experiences. I wish every success to the new president and to the continuing growth and wellbeing of SIBMAS.

Report by the Secretary General (Sylvie François)

Sylvie François thanks the Board for their collaboration in her first tenure and looks forward to another term now that knowledge of the function has been gathered.

Report by the Treasurer (Jan Van Goethem)

Jan Van Goethem gives an overview of the state of the budget during his tenure (2004-2010). After some difficulties in the income (mainly generated by members fees), the revenue has stabilised and some other sources of revenues (mainly funding for proceedings) were added. SIBMAS has a total of 17,000 euros available budget for new projects.

Report from the Membership Secretary (Jan Van Goethem)

The membership secretary reflects on the work undertake in the last six years to clear the membership database of all individual and institutions with no active status. A letter has been formatted and is sent to all members who have not paid their subscription to verify whether they are still interested to be active members or not. In 2004 there were 157 members registered, in 2010 there is a total of 180 members including the 10 honorary members. Members are distributed as follow: 85% Europe, 9% America, 3% Oceania, 3% Asia.

Election of new Executive Committee and Council members

Voting officials are designated: Ulrike Dembski and Helena Hantáková who are not running for positions at ExCom. A total of 23 ballots for institutions and 10 ballots for individuals were valid and were counted. Abstencia were noted:

- two votes on Council members and one for ExCom member on the individual ballots
- seven votes for Council members and one for President on the institutional ballots.

The following persons were elected unanimously:

President: Winrich Meiszies (D)
First Vice-President: Helen Adair (USA)
Second Vice-President: Nicole Leclercq (B)
General Secretary: Sylvie François (CAN)
Treasurer: Véronique Meunier (F)

Excom Members: Mathias Auclair (F), Guy Baxter (UK), Susan Cole (USA), Kristy Davis (UK)

Council Members: Janine Barrand (AUS), Nena Couch (USA), Tatiana Egorova (RUS), Knud Arne Jürgensen (DK), Christina Mühlegger-Henhapel (AT), Ramona Riedzwenski (UK), Anne Zendali (CH)

Reports from the Commissions

Exhibition Commission (Claudia Blank)

The SIBMAS Munich's Exhibition Commission meeting focused on the two international exhibition projects in which several SIBMAS members from various countries were involved: "Hamlet" and "Europe's Historic Theatres".

While Winrich Meiszies reported more generally on his "Hamlet" project during the plenary session[2], he gave a more specific account of the successes and problems relating to his work. He noted that:

Tracing Hamlet through Europe will lead us to the roots of the theatre of different nations. English players entered the continent in the 16th century via the Netherlands, roamed Germany and Austria, headed to Denmark and Poland and left their traces in the national cultures.

Working on a common *Hamlet*-themed exhibition will give libraries, collections and museums of performing arts the opportunity for a lasting cooperation. An approach through comparison supports co-operation between archives, museums, research departments and performing artists, and in that way underlines their extraordinary share in the cultural life of the individual community.

---

[2]   p. 349-355.

The procedure promotes an exchange of experts and it helps to set up standards for methods and techniques of presentation and communication. Museums and collections concerned with the performing arts will be obliged to review and categorise their relevant and so permanently secure part of their stock.

The exhibition with its accompanying programmes forms the more tangible part of a comprehensive inter-cultural dialogue. Planning and shaping the exhibition will form a considerable part of the project and keep up a dialogue between experts and institutions.

Afterwards, Carsten Jung from PERSPECTIV reported on his exhibition project, "Historic theatres tell the History of Europe (Historische Theater erzählen die Geschichte Europas)".

Seven theatre museums from seven countries are cooperating to jointly create a new travelling exhibition under the working title: "The history of Europe – told by its theatres".

The seven theatre museums are: Victoria & Albert Museum Performing Arts Collection (United Kingdom); Theatre Museum in the Court Theatre (Denmark); Theatre Museum at the Teatr Wielki (Poland); German Theatre Museum (Germany); Austrian Theatre Museum (Austria); Slovenian Theatre Museum (Slovenia); National Theatre Museum (Spain). The project is organized by PERSPECTIV – Association of Historic Theatres in Europe.

The new exhibition shall feature the development of the theatre building till today, explaining how a certain building type became the model for theatres everywhere in Europe. It will also highlight the regional differences and alternatives and show how a changing society expresses its changing point of view in these buildings in each period.

In a series of meetings the museums will develop the outline of the exhibition and draw up a first list of exhibits from their collections. Subsequently other theatre collections in Europe will be asked to suggest additional exhibits from their collections, and the same opportunity will be given to the historic theatres on the European Route of Historic Theatre.

A second series of meetings will result in the final choice and the design of the exhibition. It will be a flexible design that fits into every venue; it will also be flexible in size, consisting of a core exhibition with just a few original exhibits, and the full-fledged exhibition with many original items; it will also allow a museum that shows the exhibition to add one section itself to highlight some important points of national interest.

The exhibition will first be shown in the partner museums. After that, the core exhibition will be available to all museums, theatres and cities in Europe that would like to show it in the years to come.

This is the plan. All we need to start is the financial support of the EU. An application for funding by the Culture Programme of the European Union is presently being prepared, hoping that the work can begin in spring 2011[3].

In the short concluding discussion there was an analysis of the different access routes of the two project planners. One route, and as an initial stage, was to have access focusing more on content (i.e. *Hamlet*), and the other, having the organisational approach as a starting point.

SIBMAS wishes both exhibition projects every success. It will be interesting to learn more about the progress of the two projects at the next meeting of the Exhibition Commission.

Web Commission (Guy Baxter)

Guy Baxter provided an update on changes to the website administration since the 2008 Conference, including the development of the e-newsletter and the discussions of a new website structure by the SIBMAS ExCom.

Jan van Goethem introduced a proposed redesign of the site, and there were several very useful comments and suggestions from the Commission. Details of how to access the test site were distributed and further comments were encouraged. Guy Baxter thanked Jan for his supreme efforts in moving the project forward.

There followed some further discussion of priorities for the online presence of SIBMAS: suggestions included the dynamic use of images, more information on the site about how and why to subscribe to the e-newsletter, the addition of RSS technology, and the addition of subject headings to institutional members' entries on the site. There was also a long discussion of issues surrounding the potential restriction of some content in a "members only" section. The potential of Web 2.0 applications was also raised.

Guy Baxter thanked the Commission for the many useful suggestions, contributions, and offers of help, and he confirmed that he would be in discussion with the Chairs of the other Commissions regarding their needs.

Cataloguing Commission (Kristy Davis)

Attendants: Kristy Davis (Chair), Susan Cole, Stephan Dörschel, Helena Hantáková, Véronique Meunier, Margret Schild, Louise Stephens.

---

[3] Additional information for the proceedings of the SIBMAS conference: subsequently, the European Union decided to fund the project in the period 2012-2017. Work started in September 2012, and the exhibition will open in Warsaw in early 2015.

Kristy Davis, Chair, thanked the SIBMAS members who attended the commission and then gave an overview and update on the previous meetings in Vienna (2006) and Glasgow (2008) highlighting the creation of the Commission's webpage on the SIBMAS site for resources for international cataloguing and bibliographic control standards and the subsequent thought to add brief descriptions to each. A discussion followed on how to proceed with the webpage for the future. It was decided to leave the page alone for the moment, but to ask the SIBMAS webmaster to add in a 'Cataloguing News' section to the e-newsletter in which Commission members could submit information or requests for more international links to standards to be added to the Commission's resource page. Then, at the Commission's meeting in Austin in 2012, we would review the response and then decide how to proceed. It was hoped that the new website would be operational by then so that some of our other ideas may be accommodated at that time. It was also proposed that we ask the SIBMAS webmaster to make the Cataloguing and Bibliographic Commission Resource page, which also has information about the Commission itself, more visible on the new site.

SIBMAS **conferences 2012 and 2014**

Helen Adair presents the conference theme: "Engaging Communities, Reimagining Collections". This theme aims to explore the main relations between collections and their users, donors, and the general public in putting forward and telling the performance history. Helen Adairs gives an overview of the host venue, the Harry Ransom Centre at the University of Texas in Austin as well as the lively cultural scene of Austin. Kenneth Keslinger, the president of Theatre Library Association (TLA) is introduced, as this conference will be jointly organised with TLA. Kenneth Keslinger presents TLA and its membership mainly American students, librarians, archivists, scholars, and curators brought together by the practice of performing arts. 2012 will be the 20th anniversary of TLA, a great way to celebrate by joining interests with SIBMAS. TLA has published documents on the documentation of costume designs and is preparing another one on the documentation on set designs.

The conference will be held early to mid-June, date to be confirmed soon. This will mark the second collaboration of SIBMAS and TLA, the first one happened in 1985.

Regarding the 2014 Conference, two propositions have been put forward but need to be confirmed by the administrations. Claire Hudson reiterates that for any institutions interested in hosting a future conference, they should not hesitate to ask her any question.

Other Business

Claire Hudson thanks Claudia Blank for organising the conference as well as on her 14 years involvement with SIBMAS, as she is standing down from the ExCom and presents a gift from the ExCom. Claudia Blank thanks all present for their participation and gives her deep appreciation to her team at the German Theatre Museum who have made this possible.

Claire Hudson invites the new president to give a few words. Winrich Meiszies confides that he was surprised but honoured to be asked to run for president. He formulates his vision of the work to come by two questions to the participants: Are you proud of being a SIBMAS member and do you show it? Does being a SIBMAS member changes your daily life?

Winrich Meiszies offers thanks to Claire Hudson as well as Jan Van Goethem for their hard work as they are both standing down and offers a gift, as vanishing as theatre...

Meeting is adjourned at 10:25am.

Annexes

Situation of the treasury of SIBMAS
from the 1. January 2008 till the 31. December 2008

Income:	EUR	Expenses:	EUR
Bank Paris Saldo 1. January 2008	12.738,90	Bank costs 2008	94,60
Cash 1. January 2008	616,91	Website	-
		Bulletin FIRT/SIBMAS	1.677,39
Membership fees		Leaflet	-
at the 31. December 2008	5.473,19	Postal costs 2008	740,34
Other receivings	570,00		
		Proceedings	1.995,98
		Other depenses	400,72
		Approved travel expenses	603,54
		Balance at 31. December 2008	13.886,43
	19.399,00		**19.399,00**

Composition of assets at the 31. December 2008

	EUR
Bank Paris Saldo 31. December 2008	12.924,24
Cash 31. December 2008	962.19
Balance at 31. December 2008	13.886,43

The treasurer:

Jan Van Goethem

Situation of the treasury of SIBMAS

from the 1. January 2009 till the 31. December 2009

Income:	EUR	Expenses:	EUR
Bank Paris Saldo 1. January 2009	12.924,24	Bank costs 2009	67,00
Cash 1. January 2009	962,19	Website	-
		Bulletin FIRT/SIBMAS	1.219,22
Membership fees		Leaflet	-
at the 31. December 2009	5.350,79	Postal costs 2009	608,03
Other receivings	235,33		
		Printing costs	-
		Other depenses	-
		Approved travel expenses	-
		Balance at 31. December 2009	17.578,30
	19.472,55		**19.472,55**

Composition of assets at the 31. December 2009

Bank Paris Saldo 31. December 2009	17.104,14
Cash 31. December 2009	474,16
Balance at 31. December 2009	17.578,30

The treasurer:

Jan Van Goethem

Budget SIBMAS

	Accounts 2004	Accounts 2005	Accounts 2006	Accounts 2007	Accounts 2008	Accounts 2009	Accounts 2010	Budget 2010 München 25/07/2010	Budget 2011 München 25/07/2010
Income									
Balance at 1st January	6.344,85	6.816,21	8.804,86	12.961,81	13.355,81	13.886,43	17.578,30	17.578,30	15.000,00
Membership fees	5.788,15	5.547,18	7.724,68	3.450,00	5.473,19	5.350,79	5.681,39	5.500,00	5.500,00
Other credits	0,00	927,88	0,00	0,00	570,00	235,33	0,00	2.650,00	0,00
Total	*12.133,00*	*13.291,27*	*16.529,54*	*16.411,81*	*19.399,00*	*19.472,55*	*23.259,69*	*25.728,30*	*20.500,00*
Expenses									
Bank charges	38,00	143,75	206,45	87,45	94,60	67,00	39,00	75,00	75,00
Bulletin / Newsletter	3.117,49	0,00	1.825,27	1.873,70	1.677,39	1.219,22	470,00	1.500,00	1.500,00
Website + directory	0,00	0,00	72,99	42,68	0,00	0,00	936,27	5.000,00	5.000,00
Printing costs	2.000,00	1.781,37	0,00	0,00	1.995,98	0,00	2.754,68	2.900,00	0,00
Postal costs	0,00	330,60	278,20	404,18	740,34	608,03	1.026,49	850,00	500,00
Approved travel expenses	0,00	2.200,29	970,72	588,00	603,54	0,00	0,00	500,00	500,00
Other expenses	161,30	30,40	214,10	59,99	400,72	0,00	380,57	500,00	500,00
Total	*5.316,79*	*4.486,41*	*3.567,73*	*3.056,00*	*5.512,57*	*1.894,25*	*5.607,01*	*11.325,00*	*8.075,00*
Totals									
Income	12.133,00	13.291,27	16.529,54	16.411,81	19.399,00	19.472,55	23.259,69	25.728,30	20.500,00
Expenses	5.316,79	4.486,41	3.567,73	3.056,00	5.512,57	1.894,25	5.607,01	11.325,00	8.075,00
Balance at 31st December	**6.816,21**	**8.804,86**	**12.961,81**	**13.355,81**	**13.886,43**	**17.578,30**	**17.652,68**	**14.403,30**	**12.425,00**

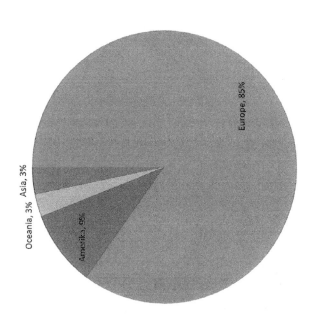

Sibmas Members World

Europe, 85%

Amerika, 9%

Oceania, 3%   Asia, 3%

Europe
Amerika
Oceania
Asia

Liste des participants/
List of Participants

Allemagne/Germany

BLANK, Claudia   Deutsches Theatermuseum (München)

DÖRSCHEL, Stephan   Archiv der Akademie der Künste (Berlin)

JUNG, Carsten   Perspectiv, Association of Historic Theatres in Europe (Berlin)

KERSTING-MEULEMAN, Ann   Universitätsbibl. J. Ch. Senckenberg (Frankfurt a.M.)

MEISZIES, Winrich   Theatermuseum der Landeshauptstadt (Düsseldorf)

SCHILD, Margret   Theatermuseum der Landeshauptstadt (Düsseldorf)

ULRICH, Paul S.   (Berlin)

Australie/Australia

STONE, Richard   National Library of Australia, Performing Arts (Hughes)

Autriche/Austria

DEMBSKI, Ulrike   Österreichisches Theatermuseum (Wien)

MÜHLEGGER, Christiane   Österreichisches Theatermuseum (Wien)

PERNERSTORFER, Matthias J.   Don Juan Archiv (Wien)

TRABITSCH, Thomas   Österreichisches Theatermuseum (Wien)

Belgique/Belgium

LECLERCQ, Nicole   Archives & Musée de la Littérature (Bruxelles)

RADERMECKER, Vincent   Archives & Musée de la Littérature (Bruxelles)

VAN GOETHEM, Jan   La Monnaie/De Munt (Bruxelles)

Canada

FRANÇOIS, Sylvie   Cirque du Soleil (Montréal)

MCKINNON, Peter   Dept. of Theatre, York University (Toronto)

Corée du Sud/South Korea

AE, Kang Choon — Dongguk University (Séoul)

SHIN, Sun-Hi — Seoul Institute of the Arts (Séoul)

Danemark/Denmark

JACOBSEN, Kenneth — University of Copenhagen (Copenhagen)

JÜRGENSEN, Knud Arne — Drama Collection, Royal Library (Copenhagen)

Espagne/Spain

SAUMELL, Mercè — Institut del Teatre (Barcelona)

Estonie/Estonia

VOITKA, Annely — Estonian Theatre and Music (Tallinn)

États-Unis/United States

ADAIR, Helen — Harry Ransom Center, University of Texas (Austin)

COLE, Susan — ConstellationCenter (Cambridge)

SCHLESINGER, Kenneth — Lehman College, Leonard Lief Library (New York)

France

AUCLAIR, Mathias — Bibliothèque-Musée de l'Opéra (Paris)

FLEURY, Raphaèle — Institut international de la Marionnette (Charleville-Mézières)

MEUNIER, Véronique — Bibliothèque nationale de France (Paris)

OBLIGI, Cécile — Bibliothèque nationale de France (Paris)

SANJUAN, Agathe — Bibliothèque-Musée de la Comédie-Française (Paris)

Japon/Japan

UEDA, Yoko — The Tsubouchi Memorial Theatre Museum, Waseda University (Tokyo)

YAGI, Masako — Université Gakushuin, École doctorale d'étude des représentations culturelles du corps (Tokyo)

Pays-Bas/The Netherlands

VAN KEULEN, Hans — Theater Instituut Nederland (Amsterdam)

Pologne/Poland

ADAMIECKA, Ada — Theatre Institute (Warsaw)
BUCHWALD, Dorota — Theatre Institute (Warsaw)
KOWALSKA, Agnieszka — The Historical Museum of the City of Krakow, Dept. History of the Theatre (Krakow)

République Tchèque/Czech Republic

HANTÁKOVÁ, Helena — Divadelní ústav – Theatre Institute (Praha)
HONSOVÁ, Petra — Théâtre Činoherní klub (Praha)
PINKEROVÁ, Helena — Municipal Library of Prague (Praha)
ŠŤASTNÁ, Denisa — Divadelní ústav – Theatre Institute (Praha)
VALTROVÁ, Marie — Municipal Library of Prague (Praha)

Royaume-Uni/United Kingdom

BAXTER, Guy — University of Reading (Reading)
CLEARY, Stephen — The British Library, Drama and Literature – Sound Archive (London)
DAVIS, Kristy — Mander and Mitchenson Theatre Collection (London)
HUDSON, Claire — V&A Museum, dept. of Theatre and Performance (London)
JONES, Alan — Royal Scottish Academy of Music and Drama (Glasgow)
PRITCHARD, Jane — V&A Museum, Dance, Theatre & Performance Coll. (London)
RIEDZEWSKI, Ramona — V&A Museum, dept. of Theatre and Performance (London)
STEPHENS, Louise — Playwrights' Studio Scotland, University of St. Andrews (Edinburgh)

Russie/Russia

EGOROVA, Tatiana — The State central Theatrical Museum A.A. Bakhrushin (Moscou)
GAMULA, Irina — The State central Theatrical Museum A.A. Bakhrushin (Moscou)
IVANOVA, Galina — Bibliothèque nationale théâtrale (Saint-Pétersbourg)

KATKOVSKAYA, Yulia   The Russian State Art Library (Moscou)
RODIONOV, Dmitry   The State central Theatrical Museum A.A. Bakhrushin (Moscou)

Slovénie/Slovenia
SLIVNIK, Francka   Slovenski Gledaliski in Filmski Muzei (Ljubljana)

Suède/Sweden
IGGANDER, Helena   Kungliga Operan AB (Stockholm)
LEWENHAUPT, Inga   (Stockholm)

Suisse/Switzerland
ZENDALI, Anne   Grand Théâtre de Genève (Genève)

Notices biographiques/
Biographical Notes

Adamiecka-Sitek Agata, PhD from the University of Silesia, Katowice, is the custodian at the Theatre Institute in Warsaw, Poland. She graduated from a cultural studies programme. In 2003, she was awarded the Kosciuszko Foundation scholarship and was a visiting scholar at Stony Brook University (USA). She has published in major Polish theatre journals and in 2004 she published her first book on *Theatre and Text. Mise-en-scene in Postmodern Performance.* (in Polish) At the Theatre Institute, she is responsible for two long-term academic programmes and publications. She has established two editorial series: *The Other Stage* dedicated to gender and queer issues in Polish theatre and *New Histories* concentrated on methodology of theatre historical writing. She was a member of the editorial board of the first edition of the Jerzy Grotowski *Collected texts* – first comprehensive edition of his textual heritage (Grotowski Institute, Theatre Institute, Krytyka Polityczna, Warsaw 2012).

Auclair Mathias, archiviste paléographe, diplômé d'études approfondies en histoire (Université de Paris I – Panthéon-Sorbonne) et conservateur en chef à la Bibliothèque-musée de l'Opéra (Bibliothèque nationale de France). Commissaire et membre du conseil scientifique de plusieurs expositions, il est l'auteur de nombreux articles sur les collections de la Bibliothèque-musée de l'Opéra, sur l'histoire de l'Opéra de Paris, sur les relations entre la danse et les arts ainsi que sur la scénographie aux XIXe et XXe siècles.

Blank Claudia, studies of Theatre Research, German Literature and History of Art. Since 1983, working in "Deutsches Theatermuseum" in Munich, responsible for the collection of photographs. 1993-2002 Vice-Director of "Deutsches Theatermuseum". Numerous exhibitions and catalogues, for example: Theaterfotografie, 1989; Theatergöttinnen. Inszenierte Weiblichkeit. Clara Ziegler, Sarah Bernhardt, Eleonora Duse, 1994; (Together with Brygida Ochaim) Varieté-Tänzerinnen um 1900. Vom Sinnenrausch zur Tanzmoderne, 1998. From 2000 to 2004, president of SIBMAS.

Buchwald Dorota, Director of the Documentation Division at the Theatre Institute (Warsaw, Poland). She graduated from the Theatre Academy in Warsaw in 1985. In addition to having extensive experience as journalist and documentation specialist, she edits the major Polish

389

theatre journal *Dialog*. Her recent interests include the application of new IT technologies in documenting and popularising theatre history. She was the Polish coordinator for the international project *Theatre Architecture of Central Europe*, editor of many books about Polish theatre, recently: *30 x Warsaw Theatre Meetings* (*30 x Warszawskie Spotkania Teatralne*), Hanna Trzeciak *Ekonomika teatru* (Theatre Economy), Frederic Martel *Theater, Sur le déclin du théâtre en Amérique et comment il peut résister en France, Zabawa w teatr* (*Playing with theatre*) ed. Ewa Dąbek-Derda, Dorota Buchwald, Jerzy Juk Kowarski.

Cleary Stephen has been Curator of Drama and Literature at the British Library Sound Archive since 2003. The department collects and makes accessible documentary recordings of literary readings, drama and other non-musical performance in Britain, together with recordings of ancillary material such as interviews and discussions.

Cole Susan has been the sole librarian/archivist at ConstellationCenter since June 2005. Before this, she was the Project Transcriber for the John Adams Library Digitization Project at the Boston Public Library. She gained a Bachelor of Arts in Classical Languages at Randolph-Macon Woman's College and a Master of Library Science at the Graduate School of Library and Information Science, Simmons College.

Egorova Tatiana, diplômée de l'Université d'État de Moscou M.V. Lomonossov en 1984. Docteur en Histoire, spécialisée dans l'histoire culturelle de l'Europe médiévale, elle a enseigné l'histoire européenne et l'histoire de la culture à la Haute École de Langues de Moscou. En 2002, elle a commencé à travailler au Musée d'état des beaux-arts Pouchkine et, à partir de 2006, au Musée central du théâtre d'état de Bakhrushin, en tant que directrice du Département des relations internationales. Depuis 1911, elle travaille au Département de la politique d'information et des relations internationales du ministère de la Culture de la Fédération de Russie.

Fleury Raphaèle, chef de projet du Portail des Arts de la Marionnette de 2009 à 2011, elle est aujourd'hui responsable du pôle Recherche et Documentation de l'Institut international de la Marionnette (IIM/ ESNAM, Charleville-Mézières, France), dont elle coordonne les activités patrimoniales, scientifiques et éditoriales. Le Portail des Arts de la Marionnette prend place au sein de ces activités, dont l'IIM est désormais porteur pour l'ensemble des partenaires. Docteur de l'Université de Paris-Sorbonne en Littérature et civilisation françaises, elle est l'auteur de plusieurs publications sur le théâtre de Paul Claudel et sur les marionnettes, parmi lesquelles : *La marionnette traditionnelle* (2010) et *Paul Claudel et les spectacles populaires, le paradoxe du pantin* (2012). Elle a été élue conseillère de l'Union Internationale de la Marionnette (2012, Chengdu,

Chine) pour laquelle elle est responsable de la stratégie numérique. En octobre 2012, elle a été élue conseillère auprès du Comex de la SIBMAS.

François Sylvie, directrice de l'action culturelle au Cirque du Soleil à Montréal, elle gère les programmes de soutien au milieu artistique, d'accès aux arts pour la communauté et d'intégration des arts dans la vie des employés. Ses responsabilités incluent aussi la conservation, le développement et la mise en valeur des collections de l'entreprise tant celle des œuvres d'art contemporain, que la collection patrimoniale des costumes et accessoires. Titulaire d'un diplôme d'études supérieures en conservation-restauration du Textile Conservation Centre, Courtauld Institute of Art (Londres), elle possède aussi un baccalauréat en Beaux-Arts de l'Université Concordia (Montréal). Sylvie François est impliquée dans diverses associations faisant la promotion du patrimoine et est secrétaire générale de la SIBMAS. Elle a récemment été commissaire de « Artisans du rêve – Costumes du Cirque du Soleil », une exposition présentée au Musée d'art contemporain de Baie-Saint-Paul, au Québec, dans le cadre du 25ᵉ anniversaire du Cirque du Soleil.

Gamula Irina, conservatrice en chef du Musée d'État de Théâtre A. A. Bakhrushin à Moscou, commissaire de nombreuses expositions, notamment à l'étranger, elle prend une part active dans les conférences sur l'histoire du ballet et l'émigration des ballets russes. Ses articles sont publiés dans des périodiques et des anthologies russes. La société Les amis du Ballet Bolchoï a été créée au Musée en 2001, avec son concours. Elle dirige une partie des réunions de cette société.

Honsová Petra is graduated in Theatre Studies from the Arts Faculty of the Charles University in Prague. She is now studying on the doctoral programme Scenology – scenic creation and theory of scenic creation at the *Theatre* Faculty of the Academy of Performing Arts in Prague. She is a member of Society of Scenology. She publishes in the journal DISK and translates from German. She has been working for the theatre Činoherní klub (Drama Club) since 1994 and is the co-author of the book *Činoherní klub 1965-2005*. She is also on the editorial team of the regular publicity brochure Činoherní čtení and works in the archive of the theatre (which is a member of the national centre of SIBMAS).

Hudson Claire is Head of Collections Management at the Theatre Museum in London, where she has worked since 1987. Her role is to co-ordinate the intellectual control of the museum's very diverse collections of objects, archives and library materials, and to provide public access services relating to them. She has been involved with SIBMAS throughout her period at the Theatre Museum, and has served on the Executive Committee since 1996, taking on the role of Secretary General between 2000 and 2002.

Ivanova Galina est conservateur-archiviste à la Bibliothèque nationale théâtrale de Saint-Pétersbourg depuis 1992. Bibliothécaire diplômée de l'Université de la Culture de Saint-Pétersbourg, elle exerce depuis 2011 la fonction de conservateur en chef du Département des acquisitions, du catalogage et de l'indexation des fonds de la bibliothèque.

Katkovskaya Yulia studied the History of Art at Lomonosov Moscow State University. She is the Cataloguing Department Librarian of the Russian State Art Library and takes part in professional conferences on terminology databases in libraries.

Kersting-Meuleman Ann, Dr, studied musicology, Romance languages and theology. Since 1991 she has been Director and expert adviser at the Department of Music, Theatre and Film at the University Library Johann Christian Senckenberg at Frankfurt/Main.

Kowalska Agnieszka, PhD in Polish theatre, is the senior assistant in the Department of History of the Theatre at the Historical Museum of the City of Krakow. Since 2008 she has been the project manager and curator of the new permanent exhibition at The History of the Theatre Department in Krakow where she is writing a scenario for the exhibition and doing scientific research concerning reconstruction of performance, theatrical objects and exhibits. She also participated in a scientific grant programme on the project *Description of Theatre Iconography in Photography Collections from the Jagiellonian's Library and Artistic Archive of The Julius Slowacki's Theatre (2007-2010)*.

McKinnon Peter, Professor of Design and Management in the Department of Theatre at York University. He has a BA in English from the University of Victoria and an MFA in Directing, History and Design from the University of Texas in Austin. He worked as a Lighting Designer on some 450 shows, principally for dance and opera. He taught for six years at the Banff School of Fine Arts. He edited new *Theatre Words*, a dictionary of theatre terminology in some twenty-eight languages. In 2005, he wrote *Designer Shorts, a Brief Look at Contemporary Canadian Scenographers and Their Work*, and in 2007 he edited *One show, One Audience, One Single Space* by Jean-Guy Lecat. He is a past President of Associated Designers of Canada and has been on the Executive Committee of the International Organisation of Scenographers, Theatre Architects and Technicians for fourteen years. He was the founding General Manager of Summer at the Roxy in Owen Sound, Front Porch Productions, and Rare Gem Productions. He has recently started producing shows, both off-and on-Broadway and in Edinburgh.

Meiszies Winrich, Dr of Philosophy, studied Theatre, Film and Television History, German Language and Literature and Philosophy at the University of Cologne before commencing work as a Research

Assistant at the Theatermuseum of the City of Düsseldorf in 1980. He became deputy director of the Theatermusuem in 1985, and later, lecturer at the Heinrich-Heine-University, Düsseldorf. He has been a member of the board of SIBMAS Germany, secretary of the Friends of the Theatermusuem of the City of Düsseldorf, deputy director and director of the Filminstitute of the City of Düsseldorf, director in charge of the same institute, director on charge of the Theatermuseum of the City of Düsseldorf and, since 2000, head of this museum. Since 2007, he has been a member of the council of the Association of Museums on the Rhine and since 2008, member of the Executive Committee of SIBMAS. He has published on the subjects of theatre on the 18th and early 20th century, on actors in exile, on theatre museums and has been involved with exhibitions since 1991.

Mühlegger-Henhapel Christiane, Dr, studied Comparative Literature and French language and literature at the University of Innsbruck. Since 1999 she has been custodian in the Austrian Theatre Museum/Collection of Autographs and Legacies, where she is responsible for the collection of autographs. She has completed several exhibitions and publications e.g. Johann Nestroy, Oskar Werner, Hans Moser.

Obligi Cécile est conservatrice au département des Arts du spectacle à la Bibliothèque nationale de France depuis 2006. D'abord responsable de la conservation, elle est en 2010 en charge du traitement de fonds d'archives de la deuxième moitié du xxe siècle, ainsi que des dossiers de numérisation du département.

Pernerstorfer Matthias Johannes, Dr, studied Theatre, film and media studies in Vienna and Munich; his diploma thesis was about the character of the parasite in Ancient Greek Comedy (2001). He received a grant from the Austrian Academy of Sciences for a dissertation published in 2009: *Menanders Kolax. Ein Beitrag zu Rekonstruktion und Interpretation der Komödie* (2009). He has been a member of the Don Juan Archiv Wien since 2007, working on several projects about the popular theatre in Vienna in the 18th and 19th Century, including editions of texts of the so called Wiener Volkstheater; he has also worked on project about archives, libraries, museums and theatre institutions in Central Europe and projects involving cataloguing and digitalising of theatre collections: Komplex Mauerbach and Theater-Bibliothek Pálffy.

Pritchard Jane, co-curator of the exhibition, Diaghilev and the Golden Age of the Ballets Russes 1909-1929, for the Victoria and Albert Museum in 2010. Since 2006, is appointed Curator of Dance for the Theatre & Performance Collections, V&A. Previously, she was Archivist for Rambert Dance Company and English National Ballet. She created the Contemporary Dance Trust Archive (now part of the

T&P Collections at the V&A) and remains an archive consultant for a number of dance organisations. She has curated seasons of dance films for the BFI Southbank, London, and for the British Council in Japan, the Philippines and South Korea as well as serving as Film Curator for the Rudolf Nureyev Foundation. She lectures on dance and has contributed to numerous journals, magazines, books, dictionaries and catalogues including the *Oxford Dictionary of National Biography*, *The Annual Register*, *Ballet News*, *Dance Chronicle*, *Dance Research*, *The Dancing Times* and *Dance Now*. Her most recent book is *Anna Pavlova Twentieth-Century Ballerina*.

Radermecker Vincent est diplômé de l'Institut des Arts de Diffusion (section théâtre) et de la Faculté de Philosophie et Lettres de l'Université catholique de Louvain-la-Neuve (département histoire). Il a travaillé comme comédien sous la direction d'Otomar Krejča et de Gérard Lefur. Un temps spécialiste de l'histoire économique et sociale en région bruxelloise, il est actuellement archiviste et scientifique aux Archives et Musée de la Littérature (Bruxelles) où il est notamment en charge de l'édition critique de l'œuvre complète de Jean Louvet.

Rodionov Dmitry V., General Director of the A.°A.°Bakhrushin State Central Theatre Museum in Moscow, Russia. He studied at the State Institute of the Theatre Arts named after A. Lunacharsky (theatre researcher), the Finance Academy under the Government of the Russian Federation (economist), he has worked on administrative positions at Moscow theatres (the Stanislavsky and Nemirovich-Danchenko Moscow Academic Music Theatre, the Novaya Opera Theatre, and the Bolshoi Theatre). He is a current associate professor of the Russian Academy of the Theatre Arts, and the chief editor of the *Stage* magazine.

Sanjuan Agathe, archiviste-paléographe, elle est actuellement conservatrice-archiviste de la Comédie-Française après avoir travaillé au département des Arts du spectacle de la Bibliothèque nationale de France. Elle a récemment été commissaire de deux expositions : L'Art du costume à la Comédie-Française (Moulins, CNCS, 2011) et La Comédie-Française s'expose au Petit Palais (Musée des Beaux-Arts de la Ville de Paris, 2011-2012).

Schild Margret, graduated in Documentarianship (1986), has been the Head of the Libraries of the Theatre Museum and the Film Museum Düsseldorf since 1993. In 1995, she was a founding member of the Arbeitsgemeinschaft der Kunst- und Museumsbibliotheken (AKMB) [The Working Group of Art and Museum Libraries] and a member of the board of the AKMB from 2004-2008. Since 1995, she has been a member of the editorial board of the journal *AKMB-News*.

Štastná Denisa was graduated at the FF UP in Olomouc, Theory and History of the Drama Art in 2003. Since 2006 she has been working as a Stage design collection curator at the Theatre Institute in Prague. She became a head of the Collections and Archive Department in 2009. She was a curator of the several stage design exhibitions (in 2009, Prolomit prostor; in 2008, Proměny; from 2006 to 2009, exhibitions of several Czech scenographers).

Stone Richard was a senior librarian in the National Library of Australia for many years and is now retired. He is the author of many conference papers and articles on ephemera, performing arts resources and Australian theatre history. He is actively involved with a national organisation dedicated to collecting and preserving Australia's performing arts resources, the Performing Arts Heritage Network (previously known as PASIG) and continues volunteer work organising theatre collections housed in various heritage institutions.

Trabitsch Thomas, PhD in theatre-history and the history of art from the University of Vienna and the University of Kansas, is the director of the Austrian Theatremuseum since 2002. From 1983 to 1985, he was the dramaturge at the Städtische Bühnen Regensburg; and from 1985 to 1996 he was at the concert bureau of the Musikalische Jugend (Musical Youth) in Austria. He then worked for many years at the Kunsthistorisches Museum in Vienna. He has contributed to numerous exhibitions and publications on Marcel Prawy, Max Reinhardt, Bertold Brecht, Arthur Schnitzler, Fritz Grünbaum, on the Cabaret Fledermaus, the Ballets Russes and Gustav Mahler among others.

Ueda Yoko, PhD in philology in 2009 (thesis on the works of the Polish-Russian writer Sigizmund Krzhizhanovsky), is an adjunct researcher at The Tsubouchi Memorial Theatre Museum in Waseda University (Tokyo). From April 2008 to March 2011 she worked there as research associate. She is also a Russian-Japanese interpreter and translator. Her area of study is the Russian theatre and the Japan-Russian cultural exchange through theatre arts. In 2012 she published the first Japanese selection of his novels entitled *In the Pupil: Selected works* (2012, in collaboration with Shunichiro Akikusa). She is an author of articles: "Representation and Visualisation in Sigizmund Krzhizhanovsky's Novel *In the Pupil*" (*Slavic Studies*, No. 55, 2008); "Medea, a Stranger. Interview with Yury Lyubimov" (*Theatre Culture*, No. 7, 2005); "Theatrical Incarnation of Kafka's Novel, *The Metamorphosis* directed by Valery Fokin" (*Engekijin*, No. 9, 2002). As an interpreter, she has worked with several international theatre projects.

Ulrich Paul S. is a retired librarian, formerly at the Zentral- und Landesbibliothek in Berlin (10 years head of computer systems, 14 years reference librarian). He has been active in SIBMAS since 1988 (1988-2009, editor of SIBMAS International Directory of Performing Arts Collections). He is president of the Gesellschaft für Theatergeschichte; treasurer of and publication editor for Thalia Germanica. He has published extensively on German-language theatre in 19th century and on reference topics. His major publications are *Biographical Index for Theatre, Dance and Music* (1996, also bi-lingual as CD-ROM) and *Das Jahr 1848. Kultur in Berlin im Spiegel der Vossischen Zeitung* (2010, with Lothar Schirmer).

Valtrová Marie, Master of Science in theatre and film studies from the Faculty of Arts, Charles University in Prague, is a theatre historian, publicist and scenarist. She has been the head of the Theatre and Film Department of the Municipal Library of Prague since 1997.

Van Goethem Jan, Archivist and Head of Collections of the Théâtre Royal de la Monnaie (Brussel). He holds Masters Degrees in both Art History (Musicology) and Information Sciences. He is the author of several articles on Flemish music and on the digitisation of archives.

van Keulen Hans, has had a career in museums ever since completing his law studies – first at the Jewish Historical Museum in Amsterdam, then at the Nieuwe Kerk and later at the Film Museum. He became director/ conservator at the Dutch Resistance Museum in Gouda in 1990, and in 1998 was appointed head of presentation at the University Museum in Utrecht. Here he was responsible for exhibitions, education and public relations and marketing. The job he took in 2002 at the Theatre Instituut Nederland gave him the chance to combine his interests in both theatre and museums. As head of Collection and Documentation, he has been responsible for the extensive theatre museum collections as well as for bibliotheca-collections. During the past few years he has also overseen the running of the exhibitions, marketing and media centre. He has been studying Art History (part-time) since 2004. He got his bachelor's degree in 2010. Since 2006 he has been chairman of the collections workgroup of the Dutch Museum Association.

Wallemacq Sybille, assistante de rédaction et rédactrice pour le mensuel francophone belge *L'Éventail*. Elle est diplômée d'un master en Histoire de l'Art, orientation art contemporain. Durant son parcours, elle a notamment collaboré avec Jan Van Goethem (La Monnaie) à la conservation des maquettes décor en 3D.